ANTI-DISCRIMINATION LAW IN BRITAIN

GW00702803

AUSTRALIA
LBC Information Services
Sydney

CANADA and USA
Carswell
Toronto, Ontario

NEW ZEALAND
Brooker's
Auckland

SINGAPORE and MALAYSIA
Thomson Information (S.E. Asia)
Singapore

ANTI-DISCRIMINATION LAW IN BRITAIN

COLIN BOURN B.Sc. (Econ.)
Practising Barrister,
Director of the International Centre for Management,
Law and Industrial Relations,
University of Leicester

JOHN WHITMORE B.A., B.C.L.
Practising Barrister,
formerly Legal Director, Commission for Racial Equality

THIRD EDITION

LONDON
SWEET & MAXWELL
1996

First Edition (published as
Discrimination and Equal Pay) 1989
Second Edition (published as
Race and Sex Discrimination) 1993
Second Impression 1994
Third Edition 1996

Published in 1996 by
Sweet & Maxwell Limited of
100 Avenue Road, London, NW3 3PF

Computerset by Wyvern Typesetting Limited, Bristol
and printed and bound in Great Britain
by Hartnolls Ltd, Bodmin

A CIP catalogue record for this book is available
from the British Library

ISBN 0 421 564 202

PREFACE

In addition to the usual plethora of new case-law, in this edition we introduce the Disability Discrimination Act 1995.

It has not been easy to decide how best to deal with the new Act. It shares much common ground with the existing discrimination legislation. But there is considerable novelty also. In the end we opted to have one chapter dedicated to an overview of the whole of the new disability law, and dealing with both its employment and non-employment aspects. It may be that in future editions we shall aim for greater integration of the subject. For now, however, our thinking is that many readers will have some familiarity with race and sex discrimination law and want to graft on an overall perspective of the new law. For their convenience that perspective is available in one chapter without either the detail of statutory provisions where they are similar to existing provisions under the sex or race legislation, or the encumbrance of existing case law. These matters can be pursued and perused in other chapters to which readers are directed and where there are also references to the Disability Discrimination Act. At the same time we do not think our chosen approach will present any real difficulties to a reader coming new to discrimination law, and may indeed add something of an historical perspective.

No time ever seems to be ideal for a new edition, since legal changes keep coming thick and fast, and in the end other considerations such as the start of a new academic year become important to a publisher. The book started life primarily as a practitioners' guide (and still has that emphasis), but there is a growing interest in the study of discrimination law in universities and a fair number of copies of the previous edition were bought by students. Hence the appearance this time of the book in paperback.

We were in fact slightly late in getting our text to the publishers, but were instantly forgiven because it meant the pages were not scattered to the winds by the South Quay Plaza bomb blast. We were amazed and grateful that Sweet & Maxwell were back in business at an alternative location such a short time afterwards, and ready to deal calmly (and firmly!) with us.

The law is stated as at the end of August 1996.

Colin Bourn
John Whitmore
Leicester

ACKNOWLEDGMENTS

The publishers would like to record their grateful thanks to the following for permission to reprint extracts from their publications as indicated.

Eclipse Group Limited (*Industrial Relations Law Reports*): Commission for Racial Equality v. Dutton [1989] I.R.L.R. 8; King v. The Great Britain–China Centre [1991] I.R.L.R. 513; J.H. Walker v. Hussain [1996] I.R.L.R. 11.

The Incorporated Council of Law Reporting for England & Wales (*Appeal Cases* and *Industrial Cases Reports*): Mandla v. Dowell Lee [1983] 2 A.C. 548; Eaton Ltd v. Nuttall [1977] I.C.R. 272.

CONTENTS

9. Strategic Enforcement Powers

10. Public Aspects of Discrimination Law

TABLE OF CASES

TABLE OF STATUTES

TABLE OF STATUTORY INSTRUMENTS

TABLE OF CODES OF PRACTICE

TABLE OF TREATIES
AND CONVENTIONS

TABLE OF E.C. LEGISLATION

Directives

Recommendations and Proposals

1 THE LEGAL FRAMEWORK OF EQUALITY LAW

Introduction

Race relations and disability discrimination legislation in Great Britain con-   **1-01**
sists of only one layer: the Race Relations Act 1976 (RRA), as amended and
the Disability Discrimination Act 1995. Sex discrimination legislation consists of two layers: a Community layer and a subordinate national layer.
Legally, Community law is supreme, but it makes more chronological and
political sense to begin by describing the origins of the national law and then
to turn to examine how, and by what processes, national law has been modified by Community law.

In the United Kingdom there is also the separate and more rigorous regime   **1-02**
which attempts to ensure the fair participation of the two religious communities in Northern Ireland, but it is beyond the scope of this book to do more
than compare and contrast that regime with the law on race, sex and disability
discrimination at appropriate points. There are, however, several developments in the Fair Employment (Northern Ireland) Act 1989 which merit initial attention, by way of contrast to what follows with regard to the British
legislation.

Comparison between Great Britain and Northern Ireland

The Fair Employment (Northern Ireland) Act 1989

The Fair Employment (Northern Ireland) Act deals with religious and polit-   **1-03**
ical discrimination and strengthens the 1976 legislation in force in the Province. It was in part a response to the threat of sanctions by United States
corporations operating under the MacBride principles and to the Anglo-Irish
agreement. It is useful to quote directly from the Government document "The
Act at a Glance" as to the aims of the legislation:

- "Active practice of fair employment by employers;
- Close and continuous audit of that practice by new and stronger
  enforcement agencies;
- Use of affirmative actions, and goals and timetables, to remedy
  under-representation;

- Use of criminal penalties, and economic sanctions, to ensure good employment practices''.

1-04   In overall terms the main importance of the legislation for equal opportunities is that apart from dealing with discrimination in a more forceful way, with a special tribunal empowered to award compensation of up to £30,000, it gives substance to the whole idea of equal opportunities.

1-05   The main features of the legislation are:

- Compulsory registration of all public employers and private employers with a workforce of more than ten employees (sections 22–26);
- Compulsory monitoring of the workforces of all registered employers and the monitoring of applications for employment to all public employers and private employers of 250 or more (sections 27–30);
- Compulsory reviews of recruitment, training and promotion practices to determine if fair participation in the concern is provided for the members of the two religious communities (section 31), with audit by the Fair Employment Commission under sections 32–35;
- Mandatory affirmative action, and goals and timetables, as directed by the Commission under sections 36–37.

"Fair participation in the concern"

1-06   The concept of "fair participation in the concern" is not defined in the Act but McCrudden suggests that it will be achieved when under-representation has been eliminated.[1] Whilst the Act speaks of fair participation in the concern, McCrudden argues that regard should be had to the overall position of Catholics and Protestants, at least until a broad balance is achieved. If attention is focused only on the balance within any one concern, whilst Catholics might gain where they are under-represented, they may lose where they are over-represented, resulting in less rapid progress towards an end of under-representation at large.

1-07   As the Commission for Racial Equality say in their *Second Review of the Race Relations Act 1976*:

"The whole thrust of the Northern Ireland legislation moves away from the narrow notion of eliminating discrimination to the idea of a 'more effective practice of equality of opportunity in employment', with the ultimate aim of 'fair participation' by the two communities.''

The Commission also observe:

"No doubt the politics of the situation, the level of violence between the two communities, could be used to justify legislating earlier for Northern

---

[1] C. McCrudden, "Affirmative Action and Fair Participation: Interpreting the Fair Employment Act 1989", *Industrial Law Journal*, Vol. 21, 3, p. 186.

Ireland. They cannot, however, be long-term arguments against treating equal opportunities equally seriously in Britain.''

Contract compliance

The Northern Ireland legislation uses not only criminal penalties but also the economic sanctions of loss of grants and contracts to punish bad practice. A useful albeit very basic system of contract compliance has been introduced.   **1-08**

In Britain by contrast, no attempt has ever been made to monitor compliance with equal opportunity clauses in Government contracts. Indeed, the Commission for Racial Equality once backed off from a formal investigation into this matter, rather than endanger approval of its Code of Practice in Employment. There has been a retreat from allowing local authorities to carry out contract compliance in their contracts. After the 1988 Local Government Act it was stopped altogether for sex equality and allowed only in a very restricted form for racial equality. It is a sad fact that a previous Chair of the British Equal Opportunities Commission told one of the authors that she did ''not believe in contract compliance''. Happily this is not the presently prevailing view. We set out in chapter 10 a brief account of contract compliance in the United States under Executive Order 11246.   **1-09**

The obligation placed upon employers to draw up and implement plans to deal with inequality is also a measure that can be taken with regard to equal pay, as is demonstrated by pay equity legislation in Ontario where employers are under a duty to give notice of a pro-active pay equity plan, rather than simply awaiting the receipt of equal value complaints from employees.   **1-10**

The nature of anti-discrimination legislation in Britain

The anti-discrimination legislation which has been passed both in the Community and in Britain is essentially complaints based. This contrasts sharply with the Northern Ireland scheme for religious discrimination. The Northern Irish scheme is pro-active and requires employers to plan and monitor the composition of their workforces, under the general supervision of the Fair Employment Commission to ensure the fair participation of the two religious communities. The Commission for Racial Equality (CRE) has called for compulsory monitoring with regard to race in its recent review of the Race Relations Act, but this proposal has been rejected by the Government.   **1-11**

The British and Northern Irish legislation each strikes a different balance between a conception of anti-discrimination law as an individual right not to be the subject of discriminatory decisions and the use of the law as a tool to remedy social and economic disadvantage. The level of violence and social unrest in Northern Ireland has dictated a concerted attempt to eradicate the long term disadvantages suffered by the Catholic community, utilising economic, administrative and investigatory powers, in addition to litigation by individuals. Yet the Fair Employment (Northern Ireland) Act defines equality   **1-12** of opportunity as existing where a person has the same opportunity to be considered for and hold employment on the same terms as any other person, "due allowance being made for any material difference in their suitability" (section 20(2)). Although equality of opportunity is not impugned by anything lawfully done in the pursuance of affirmative action (section 20(3)), it is nonetheless subject to the merit principle set out in section 20(2). Hepple, in a critical comment on the Report of the Standing Advisory Committee on Human Rights,[2] which formed the basis of the legislation, makes the point that an excessive concern with merit at the point of selection may detract from the realisation that even where candidates are more or less equal, elements of prior disadvantage or discrimination may contribute to the poor showing of candidates from certain groups. "Merit" in this sense is a socially produced good; only the exceptional person is able to transcend the conditions of his or her upbringing and social experience.[3]

Real or formal equality

1.13 In Britain the sex and race discrimination laws are primarily concerned with ensuring formal equality for individuals, less emphasis being placed on the eradication of social disadvantage. Indeed, the only elements of affirmative action which are permitted relate to training rather than to employment opportunities. Equality is thus seen as neutrality, a symmetrical application of the law which ignores the structural and social conditions which form each individual. It has frequently been asserted that anti-discrimination law incorporates a white and/or male norm by which applicants are to be judged. Fredman, reviewing European discrimination law from a feminist standpoint, observes that anti-discrimination law has often seen:

> "Equality as neutrality. It assumes that equality is an end in itself, rather than a mechanism for correcting disadvantage, and in doing so, it makes it impossible for the anti-discrimination principle to make real inroads into the disadvantaged position of women."[4]

Formal symmetrical equality law can be more sensitive to signs of reverse discrimination which run counter to currently accepted thinking, than it is to detecting commonly accepted practices which put women or minorities at a disadvantage. For example, an absence of "career breaks" may do long term damage to the careers of many women but will not necessarily be perceived

---

[2] *Religious and Political Discrimination and Equality of Opportunity in Northern Ireland*, Standing Advisory Commission on Human Rights, Cmnd. 237 (1987) commented on by Hepple, *Oxford Journal of Legal Studies*, Vols. 10, 3, Autumn 1990, pp. 408–421.

[3] Thus the influence of family patterns on womens' work participation is demonstrated in data from the 1989 Labour Force Survey, *Employment Gazette* 1990, pp. 619–643. See also "Ethnic Origins and the Labour Market", *Employment Gazette*, 1991, pp. 59–72 for factual data and Simon Field, "The Changing Nature of Racial Disadvantage". *New Community* in XIV 1/2, pp. 118–122 for a summary of the way in which racial factors operate in the labour market.

[4] S. Fredman, "European Community Sex Discrimination Law: a Critique" in *Industrial Law Journal*, Vols. 21, 2, pp. 119–134. See also Nicola Lacey, "From individual to Group" (Hepple and Szyszczak eds, *Discrimination: the Limits of the Law*, Mansell, 1992), pp. 99–124. Fenwick & Hervey, "Sex Equality in the Single Market; New Directions for the E.C.J.", C.M.L. Rev. 32, 443–470 (1995).

as a problem because such a practice does not run counter to a formal conception of equality based on typical male career patterns. Under the legislation in force on the mainland of Britain, there is no obligation to engage in monitoring or to review employment practices with a view to ensuring fair participation. A primary concern with real, rather than formal, equality would at least require, as the CRE have urged, that monitoring be made obligatory and contract compliance be more widely permitted in the public sector. These, together with a more effective framework for the exercise of the strategic investigatory powers of the Commissions, would provide the bases for a pro-active policy and complement the present emphasis of the law on formal individual equality.

It is notable that the Disability Discrimination Act 1995 provides only for the protection of disabled people *vis-à-vis* the able-bodied. An able-bodied person who feels that he has been treated adversely in comparison with a disabled person has no right to bring a complaint. It is therefore possible to engage in forms of positive action which favour the integration of the disabled into the world of work, or into society in general, including giving preference to otherwise suitably qualified disabled persons in selection decisions, without any risk of legal action from the able-bodied based on the concept of "reverse discrimination".

The British legislation draws upon American experience, but is framed to take into account the differences which exist between the two legal systems. The main avenues for legal action under the British Acts in the U.K. are the industrial tribunals and county courts, in which cases are brought at the behest of individual complainants. As Community discrimination law derived from Article 119 only concerns employment matters, cases which draw upon Community rights will normally be taken in the industrial tribunals, although Community discrimination law has been the basis of a number of judicial review cases in the High Court. Legal aid is not available in the industrial tribunals, although suitable cases can be assisted by the CRE or EOC.[5] Assistance by one of the two Commissions can help to overcome the difficulties faced by an inexperienced litigant, especially one who would in other matters look to the Legal Aid Fund. The National Disability Council formed under the 1995 Disability Discrimination Act has no power to fund individual applications to courts or tribunals. Not only must the initiative come from individual litigants, but the remedies which can be awarded by the tribunals are also limited to the case in hand and are not of general application to others in similar circumstances. The difficulties faced by individual complainants in employment cases have been well documented in a survey undertaken by the EOC, which showed that even successful complainants found the experience difficult and stressful, the short term rewards limited, and in the longer term often experienced a deterioration in the relationship with their employer and even, on occasion, with fellow workers.[6] The survey showed that employers who suffered an adverse decision in an industrial tribunal did not necessarily modify the practice upon which the complaint had been founded, to the bene-

1-14

---

[5] Consideration was given to extending legal aid to tribunals, but no firm proposals have emerged. The Employment Rights (Dispute Resolution) Bill 1996 proposes that industrial tribunals be known as "employment tribunals".

[6] Alice M. Leonard, *Pyrrhic Victories; Winning Sex Discrimination and Equal Pay Cases in the Industrial Tribunals*, HMSO (1987).

fit of other workers. Complainants were shown to be very dependent on receiving skilled advice and representation, because discrimination law is a specialised field which constitutes only a small part of the workload of industrial tribunals.[7]

Representative and class actions

1-15   Although there is no equivalent to the American class action, the Industrial Tribunal Rules of Procedure[8] do allow for a representative action to be brought. Strictly, Rule 17(3) provides for the selection only of industrial tribunal representative respondents, but the Court of Appeal in *Ashmore v. British Coal Co*[9] held that where a dozen sample cases had been selected to be heard from a total of 1,500 similarly situated applicants whose cases had been stayed, it was an abuse of process to attempt to re-open the issues in the absence of fresh evidence. Thus, provided there is some agreement, a group of applicants may concentrate their resources, or the resources of their trade union, on a few sample cases, the other complainants following the decision in those cases.

1-16   The collective aspect of discrimination is reflected in the role given to the CRE and the EOC. As well as having powers to assist individual claimants, the two Commissions can take up more widespread issues by the process of a formal investigation. These can be either of a general exploratory kind or, where there is a suspicion that discriminatory actions have taken place, against a named respondent. The use of these powers has been limited by the procedural complexities which have accrued round them, although the CRE recommends that these limitations should be repealed.[10] The Commissions also have an educational role, which has resulted in the issuing of Codes of Practice and other guidance documents under the two Acts. The purpose of the Codes is to assist in the reduction of discrimination and the promotion of equality of opportunity in employment between men and women or between racial groups. The Codes do not impose legal obligations, but are admissible and may be taken into account in any proceedings under the Acts.[11] Both Commissions have been active in commissioning research and disseminating advice about equality issues. The National Disability Council has no powers of formal investigation, which has given rise to widespread criticism of the 1995 Act.

---

[7] These difficulties illustrate the point made by Lustgarten in ''Racial Equality and the Limits of the Law'', M.L.R., Vol. 49 No. 1, p. 68 that essentially protective legislation, *i.e.* employment protection statutes generally and others of like kind, are relatively ineffective in promoting social change unless widely used by well supported litigants, such as has been the case with unfair dismissal. In that case many employers have improved their disciplinary practices and introduced a more professional approach, (even if there is little effective change in the extent of managerial discretion) but there are far more unfair dismissal than equal opportunity claims.

[8] The Industrial Tribunal (Constitution and Rules of Procedure) Regulations 1993 (S.I. 1993 No. 2687).

[9] [1990] I.R.L.R. 283, C.A. and *British Coal Corporation v. Smith*, EAT 29/91.

[10] *Second Review of the Race Relations Act*, Consultative Paper, (CRE, 1991).

[11] Sex Discrimination Act 1975, s.56A (10) & Race Relations Act 1976, s.47 (10).

The national legislative framework

In considering the legislative framework of equality law it is more helpful **1-17**
and historically correct to take a chronological view of its development,
examining first equal pay, then sex discrimination and race relations law and
finally disability discrimination.

Equal pay legislation

The movement for equal pay in Britain can be traced back as far as the 1888 **1-18**
Trades Union Congress (TUC), at which the first resolution in favour of this
proposal was carried.[12] From that date until the call for legislation in the
1963 TUC, forty more resolutions in favour of equal pay were passed, whilst
three Royal Commissions[13] and three Government Committees[14] looked into
the question. As early as 1916, the Atkin Committee considered the question
of equal pay in the course of its deliberations, distinguishing between situations where one sex or the other was excluded from taking up an employment, situations where both were employed but where there was a clear distinction between men's and women's work, and situations where both men
and women were employed and where there was a sphere of common duties.
It was only in this third situation that the Committee felt that equal pay was
appropriate, by which was meant "equal pay in proportion to efficient
output." Beatrice Webb, in a dissenting note, preferred the approach of a
national minimum wage, combined with paying the rate for the job. She
accepted that if, as has often been supposed, women were less effective as
workers than men, there would be some re-allocation of work between the
sexes, but she did not think that such an approach would lead to increased
unemployment amongst women.

The Asquith Commission

A similar division of views occurred in the Asquith Commission, which **1-19**
reported in 1946. The Commission accepted the principle of equal pay in the
public services, although they were not in favour of the principle being
applied in the private sector. The majority of the Commission felt that
existing differentials reflected, albeit not perfectly, differences in efficiency
and that a move towards equal pay would be likely to lead to increased
female unemployment. The minority took a broader view of the notion of

---

[12] See M. Snell, P. Glucklich and M. Povall, ''Equal Pay and Equal Opportunities'', *Research
Paper No. 20* in Department of Employment (1981) and W. E. Creighton, ''Working Women
and the Law'', Mansell (1979) for general accounts of the history of equal pay and equal
opportunities.
[13] Royal Commission on Civil Service Pay (McDonnel Commission) Cd. 7338 (1912–16), Royal
Commission on the Civil Service (Tomlin Commission) Cmd. 3909 (1929–31), Royal Commission on Equal Pay (Asquith Commission) Cmd. 6937 (1944–46).
[14] The Women's Employment Committee, Cd. 9239 (1918), Report of the War Cabinet Committee on the Employment of Women in Industry (Atkin Committee) Cmd. 135, (1919) Anderson
Committee on the Pay etc. of State Servants, Cmnd. 1923.

equal pay and argued in a note of dissent for the acceptance of the principle of paying the rate for the job, irrespective of the sex of the worker. The Report of the Commission was accepted by the post-war Labour Government, but its implementation was delayed, because other reforms were felt to have a greater priority when only limited resources were available. In the following years there was political pressure in favour of the adoption of equal pay in the public services, which finally resulted in an agreement in 1955 that the Whitley Council would introduce equal pay in the non-industrial civil service in seven equal instalments, a process which was duly completed in 1961. The Government took the view that as a minority employer in the industrial grades it must respect the "fair relativity" principle.

1-20   The movement towards equal pay lost some of its political impetus with the granting of equal pay to non-industrial civil servants, who had been amongst its best organised advocates. But in 1961 there was a change in view by the TUC who called for the Government to ratify International Labour Organis-ation Convention 100, which called for the recognition of the principle of equal pay for work of equal value. The 1962 TUC recognised that this might mean the need for legislation, instead of relying on voluntary methods of reaching agreement with employers through collective bargaining, which hitherto had been its policy. "Voluntaryism" and abstention from statutory regulation of labour relations, had been the hallmark of British industrial relations for many years, although it has to be said that the unions had not been very effective in pressing employers on this issue.[15] In 1964 the Labour Government came to power, committed to legislate on equal pay and in 1970 the Equal Pay Bill was introduced. The Equal Pay Act came into force at the end of 1975, giving employers and trade unions five years to prepare for its implementation. By this time the Sex Discrimination Act had reached the statute book, with its complementary emphasis on equal opportunities. Prior to 1975 women working full-time were earning 63 per cent of male full-time earnings, although by 1980 this figure had reached 72 per cent. The differen-tial in earnings between women and men changed little until 1987, when an upward trend became perceptible, with the figure for 1990 being 77 per cent,[16] rising to 80 per cent for 1994.

The Equal Pay Act 1970

1-21   The Equal Pay Act 1970 (EqPA) was initially effective because it applied collective solutions to a collective problem. The wages of 50 per cent of the

---

[15] Writing as long ago as 1920 Barbara Drake said: "Men trade unionists are accused of sex privilege and prejudice . . . A belief in the divine right of every man to his job is not peculiar to kings and capitalists, and men in organised trades are not disposed to share these advantages with a host of women competitors." Barbara Drake, *Women in Trade Unions*, 1920 reprinted in *Waged Work: A Reader* (Virago, 1987). See also the account of contemporary practice in *Women and Trade Unions*, Nicola Charles, in *Waged Work* (*supra*). Davies makes the point that the Department of Employment was concerned that an "equal value" based statute would have upset settled patterns of collective bargaining. P. L. Davies, "EEC Legislation, U.K. Legislation and Industrial Relations", in *Women, Employment & European Equality Law* (C. McCrudden, ed.) (Eclipse, 1988), p. 28.

[16] Source EOC: *Women and Men in Britain* (HMSO, 1995).

workforce are determined directly or indirectly by collective bargaining. Section 3 of the Equal Pay Act 1970 conferred on the Central Arbitration Committee (CAC) a power to amend collective agreements which contained terms which applied only to women and not to men. Prior to that date it had been common practice in many sectors of industry for there to be a skilled rate, an unskilled rate and a women's rate which was often less than the rate for unskilled men. In such circumstances the EqPA, s.3 gave the CAC power to amend any such non-inclusive terms, cutting out lower women's rates. At the very least the women's rate had to be brought up to the rate for unskilled men. Many employers went further than this in harmonising the pay of men and women, perhaps because the CAC took a very liberal view of its powers under section 3 to harmonise the rates of men and women, not simply eliminating the separate women's rate. Other employers simply clothed previous discriminatory practices in uni-sex language, so that although there would be no formal bar to men being in a certain grade, in practice it would contain only women. In such circumstances the CAC looked behind the formal equality of men and women and encouraged the employer to create new grades. This practice of reviewing pay structures was brought to an end in 1979 by the decision of the Divisional Court in *R. v. CAC, ex p. Hy-Mac*[17] that the CAC had no jurisdiction to hear such claims except where the employer's pay policy or collective agreement "does not on the face of it contain any provision applying specifically to men or to women". The result was a sudden collapse in applications to the CAC and an effective end to any collective jurisdiction in matters of equal pay.

Ironically the remaining equal pay jurisdiction of the CAC was removed as a result of enforcement proceedings brought against the U.K. Government in 1982.[18] The E.C. Commission contended that the U.K. had not fully implemented the Equal Treatment Directive (76/207) in that it had not taken action to declare void or amend discriminatory terms in collective agreements, rules of undertakings or professional bodies. The Government responded by repealing section 3 of the 1970 Act and providing in the Sex Discrimination Act 1986 that any discriminatory provisions in collective agreements or the rules of undertakings which, if incorporated into the contracts of individuals, would be contrary to the statutory equality clause implied by the EqPA, s.1(1), were void. The result is that there is now no means of seeking the amendment of discriminatory terms in collective agreements or employers' pay structures, except the unrealistic provision that affected individuals may seek redress in the County Courts under the Sex Discrimination Act 1975 s.77. This major gap in current equality legislation was the subject of adverse comment by the EOC[19], which proposes that the power to review collective agreements should again be vested in the industrial tribunals or a similar "industrially literate body". The proposals put forward by the EOC in its 1990 review of sex equality law were largely rejected by the Government in 1993.

1-22

However, the Trade Union Reform and Employment Rights Act 1993 inserted new sections 4A-C in the Sex Discrimination Act 1986, in order to provide a limited right to present a complaint to an industrial tribunal. The

---

[17] [1979] I.R.L.R. 461.
[18] *E.C. Commission v. U.K.* [1982] I.C.R. 578.
[19] *Equal Pay for Men and Women; Strengthening the Acts*, (EOC, 1990).

purpose of such a complaint is to declare void unlawfully discriminatory provisions in collective agreements, employers' rules and the rules of trade unions, employers associations, professional or qualifying bodies. Industrial tribunals have not, however, been given power to amend such agreements or rules, but only to declare them void by virtue of section 77 of the Sex Discrimination Act 1975. This amendment gives effect to Articles 3–5 of the Equal Treatment Directive (76/207) and is discussed further in chapter 5 on discrimination in employment.

The Sex Discrimination Act

1-23   The history of the Sex Discrimination Act is much shorter than that of the Equal Pay Act. It owes its origins to the changing climate of opinion about the position of women in society which came about during the 1960s and more particularly during the early 1970s. This changed climate of opinion was both caused by, and reflected in, concurrent social changes, such as women's increased participation in the labour market during the period of labour shortage created by the prolonged post-war boom, the fall in the birth rate which began in the middle sixties, (itself perhaps associated with more reliable contraception and more easily available abortion), the increased rate of marital breakdown and the rise in the number of one-parent families. These developments all contributed to a changed perception of gender roles, whilst at the same time being evidence of the existence of that perception. The development of a popular feminist ideology can be traced from that era. The passage into law of the American Civil Rights Act 1964, encompassing prohibitions on both racial and sex discrimination, further stimulated interest in legislation on equal opportunities in Britain. The Labour Party set up a study group which reported in 1972, the same year in which the TUC reversed its previous policy and concluded that legislation was necessary and desirable in order to achieve equal opportunities. Two Private Member's Bills on this issue were referred to a Parliamentary Select Committee, which heard a wide range of evidence, including testimony from officials of the U.S. Equal Employment Opportunity Commission and concluded in favour of legislation on sex discrimination. The Conservative Government published a consultative document and was in the process of preparing legislation at the time of its defeat in the 1974 election. The incoming Labour Government published a White Paper, Equality for Women in 1974, and went on to introduce the legislation which became the Sex Discrimination Act 1975. The Sex Discrimination Act 1975 has been amended by the Sex Discrimination Act 1986, which arose primarily from the need to harmonise conditions as between the public and private sectors, following the *Marshall* case on retirement ages. Whilst the Sex Discrimination Act 1975 (SDA 1975) was conceived only shortly before the E.C. Equal Treatment Directive, which covers substantially the same ground, it owes little to the Directive and was not conceived as implementing legislation.[20] The existence of the SDA was, how-

---

[20] P.L. Davies, "European Equality Legislation, U.K. Legislative Policy and Industrial Relations" in *Women, Employment and European Equality Law* (C. McCrudden, ed.) (Eclipse, 1987), pp. 23–51.

ever, the substantial reason why no specific implementing legislation was considered necessary to fulfil Britain's obligations under the Directive.

The aim of the SDA 1975 was to increase women's access to employment opportunities at all levels. The continuing earnings differential between men and women can, however, be put down to three main factors, namely: **1-24**

    (i) The effects of horizontal and vertical occupational segregation;
    (ii) The under-valuing of the skills entailed in occupations usually dominated by women;
    (iii) The lower level of human capital, in the form of training and experience, which women on average possess.[21]

Hakim,[22] in a review of the effects of occupational segregation, concludes that occupational segregation has diminished in the 1980s, with the decline in male full time work proceeding apace, whilst the proportion of women working full-time has risen from 33.9 per cent in 1986 to 38.7 per cent in 1990. The rise in women working full-time has been accompanied by a rising level of work commitment, with more women in top jobs, leading Hakim to conclude that the earnings gap will continue to narrow in the 1990s. This is predicted to come about as women demand a more equitable return on their increased investment in work and their career, with the re-evaluation of traditionally under-valued female skills, especially in areas of labour shortage. Hakim tends to discount the significance of the rise in females working part-time, arguing that the outlook and expectations of workers are shaped by their main activity, which for part-timers is less likely to be work. Perhaps it is more likely that the experiences of women working in the "core" of the employment market will increasingly diverge from that of those working at the "periphery".

The Race Relations Act

The Race Relations Act 1976 takes its form from the Sex Discrimination Act; the two are substantially equivalent, except that in the one case discrimination on grounds of gender is being dealt with, whereas in the other it is discrimination on racial grounds which is proscribed. The Race Relations Act 1976 is, however, the successor to the Race Relations Acts of 1965 and 1968 and incorporates many of the lessons learned from that legislation, lessons which were also incorporated into the drafting of the Sex Discrimination Act. **1-25**

---

[21] See Shirley Dex, *The Sexual Division of Work* (Wheatsheaf, 1985), and in particular chap. 5, for a review of the economic theories as to why women and men are paid differently. For a more recent review see Jill Rubery, *The Economics of Equal Value* (EOC, 1992).

[22] Catherine Hakim, "Explaining Trends in Occupational Segregation; the Measurement, Causes and Consequences of the Sexual Division of Labour" in *European Sociological Review*, 8,2 (September 1992), pp. 127–144.

Background to the legislation

The origins of legislation to combat racial discrimination lie in the post-war wave of immigration from the Caribbean and the Indian sub-continent. The prolonged post-war shortage of labour created a range of vacancies which employers found hard to fill from amongst the indigenous population, but which immigrants were willing to undertake. It was not until the end of the decade that serious questions came to be asked about the policy of unrestricted immigration from the Commonwealth. The result was the Commonwealth Immigrants Act 1962, followed in 1968 by a further Act,[23] the effect of which was to limit the immigration of non-dependent heads of households to 8,500 a year.

1-26   Part of the response to the problems which were perceived to be associated with immigration was the adoption of a policy of integration; indeed the two were explicitly linked by Roy Hattersley in defending the 1965 White Paper: "Without integration, limitation is inexcusable; without limitation, integration is impossible."[24] The result was the Race Relations Act 1965, which prohibited discrimination in places of public resort, such as hotels, restaurants, entertainment and public transport. There was clear evidence[25] that discrimination in other vital aspects of life remained substantial, and in 1968 a further Race Relations Act was introduced. The need to do something serious and effective about race relations was underlined by the Watts riots which took place that year in Los Angeles and subsequently in many other American cities. Under the 1968 Act, the Race Relations Board was asked to investigate complaints of discrimination across a wider field, including housing and employment, and if conciliation was ineffective, to initiate civil proceedings. Complainants only had access to the courts via the Race Relations Board, whereas the Board had no independent power to undertake investigation of racialist practices, but could only follow up complaints.

1-27   Racial discrimination has persisted in Britain despite the presence on the statute book of first the 1968 Act and then the 1976 Act. Further Political and Economic Planning (PEP) (now PSI) surveys in 1973–4[26] and in 1983–4[27] show a substantial level of discrimination in employment, which remained largely unchanged in the decade between the two surveys. Between 1984 and 1985, PSI used controlled tests and found one-third of employers discriminated against Black and Asian applicants. The survey measured direct discrimination only, and the researchers estimated that nationwide there were tens of thousands of these acts of racial discrimination in recruitment each year.[28] The latest analysis by the P.S.I.[28a] shows Britain's ethnic minorities diverging, with faster educational progress being achieved by some groups than others. A higher proportion of young people of Indian, African or Chinese origins

---

[23] Commonwealth Immigrants Act 1968.
[24] Quoted by Cashmore and Troyna, *Introduction to Race Relations*, (Routledge & Kegan Paul, 1983), p. 53.
[25] W. W. Daniel, *Racial Discrimination in England* (PEP, 1968).
[26] David Smith, *Racial Disadvantage in Britain* (PEP 1977).
[27] Colin Brown, *Black and White in Britain* (Gower, 1985).
[28] Colin Brown and Pat Gay, *Racial Discrimination: 17 years after the Act* (P.S.I., 1986).
[28a] *Britain's Ethnic Minorities*, Trevor Jones, P.S.I., 1993.

in the 16–24 age group had achieved ''A'' level or better qualifications than white people. By 1988–90 a similar proportion of these groups were in managerial or professional positions as white people, though the precise occupational profile differed.

1992 Review of the Act

There has been criticism of the effectiveness of an Act which endeavours to remedy essentially social and collective phenomena by means of individual actions.[29] The CRE has faced great difficulties in pursuing strategic investigations[30] intended to highlight the existence of what has been termed ''institutional racism''.[31] A second review of the Race Relations Act, published by the CRE in 1992,[32] advocates the removal of the limitations placed upon its powers to conduct formal investigations by the *Prestige* case. The Review also advocates extending legal aid to race cases heard in the industrial tribunals. The existing Code of Practice and advocates ethnic monitoring and the adoption of positive action programmes, but these recommendations lack legal force. The Review advocates that such practices should enjoy a statutory basis and that the Government should use its economic strength to support these policy objectives. However, the Government was not sympathetic to these proposals and has not adopted them. It is instructive to note that many of these reforms have already been realised in the Fair Employment (Northern Ireland) Act 1989 with respect to religious discrimination in the Province. The difference may be that the provision of equal opportunities with respect to the religious divide in Northern Ireland may be perceived as having a greater political salience, than do the forms of discrimination more commonly present on the mainland.

1-28

Disability discrimination

The Disability Discrimination Act 1995 was the end result of a popular campaign for improved rights for the disabled. The Disabled Persons (Employment) Acts 1944 and 1958 provided a legislative framework for the treatment of disabled persons with regard to employment which had come under increasing criticism, as being ineffective and inadequate to serve the interests of the disabled. The 1944 Act set up a register of disabled persons. It was a criminal offence for any employer of 20 or more not to give employment to disabled persons up to a quota of 3 per cent. However, many disabled persons saw registration as a stigma and declined to do so, with the result that the quotas were not effective to protect them. In 1990 a Department of Employment Consultation Paper proposed the replacement of the quota

1-29

---

[29] See Laurence Lustgarten, *Racial Equality and the Limits of the Law*, above.
[30] See paragraphs 9–36 *et seq.* for a discussion of the conduct of the investigative powers of the CRE & EOC.
[31] See for instance the Scarman Report (1981), Cmnd. 8427, p. 11.
[32] *Second Review of the Race Relations Act 1976*, (CRE, 1992).

system by 'supply side' measures, such as improved training, but the Government retreated from repeal of the quota system in the face of grass roots opposition. The aspirations of those who favoured anti-discrimination legislation for the disabled were raised by the 1990 Americans With Disabilities Act. The Civil Rights (Disabled Persons) Bill, modelled on the American legislation, was first introduced in the 1991/92 Parliamentary session but failed to make progress. It was re-introduced in 1993/94 where it failed due to a plethora of what were alleged to be Government inspired amendments introduced on the floor of the House. It was estimated by the Government that the Bill would have cost £17 billion to implement over a five year period plus an ongoing cost of £1 billion per annum. These estimates were strongly challenged by disabled persons organisations. The embarrassment surrounding the affair led the Government to introduce a Consultation Paper, which gave rise to the Disability Discrimination Act 1995.

Whilst the Civil Rights (Disabled Persons) Bill would have extended the concepts of direct and indirect discrimination utilised in the sex and race legislation into the disability field, the 1995 Act provides two new definitions of discrimination, namely, unjustifiable direct discrimination for a reason related to a person's disability and discrimination arising from the respondent's failure to make adjustments to arrangements or premises. The possibility of justifying direct discrimination in the Disability Discrimination Act is premised on the ground that, whilst the sex or race of an individual is irrelevant to, say, employment decisions, disabled persons are not an homogeneous group and the precise nature of a person's disability may be relevant to a given decision. Indirect discrimination is omitted from the Disability Discrimination Act even though many ordinary arrangements and practices, such as steps or rigidly fixed working hours, could put disabled people at a disadvantage. However, an employer who fails in the duty to make reasonable adjustments to accommodate a person's disability which puts that person at a substantial disadvantage, will be covered by the second head of discrimination in the 1995 Act. This qualified duty to make reasonable adjustments to the physical features of the premises occupied by the employer or to any arrangements for determining who will be selected for employment, promoted or trained, etc., in principle covers much of the ground occupied by indirect discrimination in the race and sex legislation. However, it is only a duty to take such steps as are reasonable, having regard to their cost, practicability and likely effectiveness. However, if a disabled person is, say, rejected for a reason which relates to his or her disability, then that rejection cannot be justified if the employer has failed in a duty to make reasonable adjustments which would have obviated that person's disadvantage.

The Community framework of equality law

The supremacy of Community law

1-30   In the case of conflict between rights established under Community law and those arising under national law, according to the judgement of the ECJ in *Costa v. Enel* it is Community law which must prevail. This doctrine of the supremacy of Community law arose from the contention that "the EEC Treaty has created its own legal system which, on the entry into force of the

Treaty, became an integral part of the legal systems of the Member States and which their courts are bound to apply.''
This situation:

> "makes it impossible for the States, as a corollary, to accord precedence to a unilateral and subsequent measure over a legal system accepted by them on the basis of reciprocity ... The obligations undertaken under the Treaty establishing the Community would not be unconditional, but merely contingent, if they could be called into question by subsequent legislative acts.''[33]

In *Simmenthal*[34] the ECJ declared that ''direct applicability ... means that rules of Community law must be fully and uniformly applied in all the Member States from the date of their entry into force'' by the national courts, *i.e.* the date from which they are to be implemented. The ECJ went on to hold, in a ruling which foreshadowed *Factortame*[35] by 10 years, that:

> "A national court which is called upon, within the limits of its jurisdiction, to apply provisions of Community law is under a duty to give full effect to those provisions, if necessary refusing of its own motion to apply any conflicting provisions of national legislation, even if adopted subsequently, and it is not necessary for the court to await a prior setting aside of such provisions by legislative or constitutional means.''

No case may be brought in respect of matters, the material facts of which arose before the date by which implementation was to have occurred (*Suffritti v. Instituto Nazionale Della Previdenza Sociale (INPS)*).[36]

The European Communities Act

The principle of the supremacy of Community law is a principle of Community law which could be expected to cause difficulties for the national courts of the Member States, especially where the requirements of Community law appear to run counter to the fundamental provisions of national constitutions.[37] In Britain the matter is dealt with by the provisions of the European Communities Act 1972, s.2(1) of which provides as follows: **1-31**

> "All such rights, powers, liabilities, obligations and restrictions from time to time created by or arising by or under the Treaties, and all such remedies and procedures from time to time provided for by or under the Treaties, as in accordance with the Treaties are without further enactment to be given legal effect or used in the United Kingdom, shall be

[33] Case 6/64 [1964] E.C.R. 585 at 593–594.
[34] Case 106/77, *Amministrazione delle Finanze dello Stato v. Simmenthal SPA* [1978] E.C.R. 629.
[35] Case C-213/89, *R. v. Secretary of State for Transport, ex p. Factortame et al*: [1990] E.C.R. 1–2433; 1 A.C. 603, H.L. (procedure), [1991] E.C.R. 1–3905, [1992] Q.B. 680 (substance).
[36] Cases C-140/91, C-141/91 & C-278/91 [1993] I.R.L.R. 289.
[37] See Jean-Victor Louis, ''The Community Legal Order'' (E.C., 1990), pp. 139–149, for a discussion of the reception of this doctrine into the law of the member states generally.

recognised and available in law, and be enforced, and allowed accordingly.''

In *Coomes (Holdings) Ltd v. Shields*[38] and in *McCarthys Ltd v. Smith*[39] the Court of Appeal accepted the supremacy of Community law. As Docksey and Fitzpatrick[40] observe, British lawyers only really became aware of the significance of the supremacy of Community law with the *Factortame*[41] case, which had the effect of granting an interim injunction against the Crown and of disapplying a later British statute.

1-32   The obligation to disapply domestic law was accepted in *R. v. Secretary of State ex p. EOC*,[42] in which judicial review was sought of the longer periods of service needed by part-timers to qualify in respect of redundancy and unfair dismissal rights. It was successfully argued that these requirements were indirectly discriminatory contrary to Article 119 and the Equal Treatment Directive. The Lords held that, following *Factortame*, it was possible to grant a declaration that the provisions of the Employment Protection (Consolidation) Act (EP(C)A) 1978 were incompatible with Community law, even though a prerogative order would not apply. Thus a declaration can be sought determining the compatibility of primary legislation with Community law, which in this case has led to an amendment of section 64 of the EP(C)A 1978.

In *Biggs v. Somerset County Council*,[43] following the *EOC* case a teacher sought to bring an action for unfair dismissal in respect of her dismissal in 1976, at a time when she had insufficient service to bring her claim under the EP(C)A 1978, s. 64. It was argued that there is a so-called ''free-standing right'' to bring an action relying directly on Article 119 or one of the relevant directives, where no claim is available under domestic law. ''Free-standing'' rights to rely directly on Article 119 were accepted by the EAT in a series of cases,[44] but according to Mummery J. the position is correctly to be under-

[38] [1978] I.R.L.R. 263.

[39] Case 129/79 [1979] 3 C.M.L.R. 44; [1980] E.C.R. 1275; [1980] I.R.L.R. 209.

[40] C. Docksey and B. Fitzpatrick, "The Duty of National Courts to Interpret Provisions of National Law in accordance with Community Law" in *Industrial Law Journal*, 20,2, pp. 113–120 at p. 115.

[41] Case 213/89, *R. v. Secretary of State for Transport, ex p. Factortame*: [1990] 3 W.L.R. 818 (ECJ and HL). In that case regulations made under the Merchant Shipping Act 1988 limited the right to fish under the British quota to fishing vessels registered in Britain and owned by British nationals or in the case of companies with more than 75 per cent of the shares held by British nationals. This had a disastrous effect on certain Spanish owned vessels which had registered in Britain to take advantage of the British quota, and was arguably contrary to the relevant directly effective Article of the Treaty. The applicants sought interim relief in the form of an injunction against the Crown to disapply the Regulations whilst an Article 177 reference was made to the ECJ on their substantive rights. The question of the seeking of such an interim injunction was referred to the ECJ which held that a rule of national law prohibiting such an injunction must be set aside, thus having the effect of disapplying a later enacted statute contrary to directly effective rights. In *Factortame (No. 3)* the UK government has been held liable to compensate the Spanish fishing companies for their losses arising from the unlawful provisions of the Member Shipping Act.

[42] [1994] I.R.L.R. 176, HL.

[43] [1995] I.R.L.R. 452 at 458, approved Court of Appeal, *The Independent*, February 1, 1996.

[44] *Secretary of State for Scotland v. Hannah* [1991] I.R.L.R. 187, EAT; *McKechnie v. UBM Building Supplies (Southern) Ltd* [1991] I.R.L.R. 283, EAT; *Livingstone v. Hepworth Refractories plc* [1992] I.R.L.R. 63, EAT; *Rankin v. British Coal Corporation* [1993] I.R.L.R., EAT and *Methihill Bowling Club v. Hunter* [1995] I.R.L.R. 232, EAT. This view perhaps owes its origins to the observations of Lord Denning in *Coomes (Holdings) v. Shields* that

stood[45] as one in which "the application of Community law may have the effect of displacing provisions in domestic law statutes which preclude a remedy claimed by the applicant." He held that "an industrial tribunal is bound to apply and enforce relevant Community law, and disapply an offending provision of UK domestic law, in order to give effect to its obligation to safeguard enforceable community rights."

It is worth observing at this point, however, that it is for the domestic legal system to determine the procedural conditions governing actions to ensure the protection of Community rights, so long as these are not less favourable than those relating to similar domestic actions and do not make it impossible in practice to exercise Community rights.[46] The application of national time limits is dealt with at paragraphs 1–43 and 6–40.

Equal pay under Article 119

The Equal Pay Act 1970 enacted a right to equal pay under domestic law   1-33
which has been engulfed and expanded by rights arising from Article 119 EEC, which provides that men and women should receive equal pay for equal work. Article 119 forms part of the original social provisions contained in Articles 117–120 of the Treaty of Rome. The founders of the Community were concerned with realising the political aim of European integration via economic means. So-called functional integration would "spill over" into the closer political integration which was clearly not accessible directly. Whilst this integration was to be achieved primarily by the creation of a common market, the broader aims of the Community can be seen reflected in Article 2 of the Treaty (as amended by the Single European Act 1986) which looks forward to "a continuous and balanced expansion, an increase in stability, an accelerated raising of the standard of living and closer relations between the States" via the creation of a Common Market. Whilst social aims have always formed part of the aims of the Community, the harmonisation of working conditions was also dictated by the need to ensure a level playing field for competitors within the common market. Although the Spaak Report of 1956 took the view that the harmonisation of social and working conditions would follow the integration of the Market, as labour and capital flowed to whatever region provided the most favourable terms, this view did not entirely prevail amongst those who drafted the Treaty. The social provisions contained in Title III represent in part the need (as expressed in Article 117) to promote "improved working conditions and an improved standard of living for workers" and also a response to the fears that French industry

"Suppose that the Parliament of the United Kingdom were to pass a statute inconsistent with Article 119: as, for instance, if the Equal Pay Act gave the right to equal pay only to married women. I should have thought that a married woman could bring an action in the High Court to enforce the right to equal pay given to her by Article 119. I may add that I should have thought that she could bring a claim before the Industrial Tribunal also."

[45] *Amies v. Inner London Education Authority* [1977] I.C.R. 308; *Snoxell and Davies v. Vauxhall Motors Ltd* [1977] I.R.L.R. 123; *Biggs v. Somerset County Council* [1995] I.R.L.R. 452.
[46] Case 33/76, Rewe: [1976] E.C.R. 1989 and Case C-208/90, *Emmot v. Ministry of Social Welfare*: [1991] I.R.L.R. 387.

would be undermined without some harmonisation of working conditions. In particular, France had already introduced equal pay in 1957 and generally enjoyed longer holidays than other countries in the Community. The dual nature of Article 119 was clearly expressed by the ECJ in the second *Defrenne*[47] case.

> "Article 119 pursues a double aim. First in the light of the different stages of development of social legislation in the Member States, the aim of Article 119 is to avoid a situation in which undertakings established in states which have actually implemented the principle of equal pay suffer a competitive disadvantage in intra-Community competition as compared with undertakings established in States which have not yet eliminated discrimination against women workers as regards pay. Secondly, this provision forms part of the social objectives of the community, which is not merely an economic union, but is at the same time intended, by common action, to ensure social progress and seek the constant improvement of the living and working conditions of their peoples, as is emphasised by the Preamble to the Treaty . . . This double aim which is at once economic and social, shows that the principle of equal pay forms part of the foundations of the Community."

1-34   Article 119 can be distinguished from the other social provisions of Title VIII by the directness of its expression, which has enabled it to give rise to directly enforceable rights for individuals. The other provisions in the social chapter are more programmatic, setting out broad aims to harmonise, co-ordinate and improve working conditions, including health and safety, but not giving rise to specific rights without further legislation. Once the right to equal pay was held to be directly applicable within the Member States in the second *Defrenne* case, and was elevated to the status of a fundamental right by the third *Defrenne* case, the way was open for the evolution of an autonomous jurisprudence of Community sex equality law. Little substantive progress had taken place towards equal pay in the early years of the Community, a fact attested to by the the the Sullerot Report of 1972. Even prior to the renewed concerns about unemployment which followed the rise in oil prices and economic dislocation associated with the Arab-Israeli conflict of 1973, the Community had embarked upon its first Social Action Programme in January 1974. One result was the Equal Pay Directive 75/117, introduced under Article 100 as a measure directly affecting the functioning of the Common Market. This Directive, intended to expedite the achievement of equal pay, first made reference to equal pay for work of equal value in Community legislation. The British legislation of equal pay and discrimination owed little to this development, having been inspired largely by internal political pressures.[48] Indeed the general view was that the Equal Pay Act 1970 went further than Article 119 with its reference only to equal pay for equal work. Subsequently British law on equal pay has been much influenced by Article 119 and the Equal Pay Directive, as discussed in the chapter on equal pay.

---

[47] Cast 43/75, *Defrenne v. Sabena*: [1976] E.C.R. 455; [1976] 2 C.M.L.R. 98.
[48] P.L. Davies, "EEC Legislation, UK Legislative Policy and Industrial Relations", in *Women, Employment and European Equality Law* (C.McCrudden ed. Eclipse Publications, 1987), p. 26.

The Equal Treatment Directive

Shortly after the Sex Discrimination Act was passed into law, the E.C.   **1-35**
adopted the Equal Treatment Directive 76/207 under Article 235.[49] This Directive arose from the 1974 Social Action Programme, which had as one of
its objectives:

> "achieving equality between men and women as regards access to
> employment and vocational training and promotion and as regards
> working conditions, including pay."

The purpose of the Equal Treatment Directive is to put into effect the principle of equal treatment for men and women as regards access to employment, working conditions and social security. Article 2(1) of the Directive
provides that the principle of equal treatment means that there "shall be no
discrimination whatsoever on grounds of sex directly or indirectly by reference in particular to marital or family status." The principle of equal treatment can be excluded from application to situations where "the sex of the
worker constitutes a determining factor" under Article 2(2), and under Article 2(3) where special provision is made for the protection of women, particularly as regards pregnancy and maternity and under Article 2(4) when
positive action measures are taken to remove existing inequalities which
affect women's opportunities. Article 3 applies these requirements to selection and promotion decisions, Article 4 provides similarly for vocational
guidance and training, whilst Article 5 covers discriminatory dismissals and
Article 7 victimisation. Article 6 provides that Member States must enact a
right to a remedy by judicial process. Article 9 requires States to inform the
Commission about measures taken to implement the Directive, which the
U.K. Government considered were not necessary in view of the prior existence of the Sex Discrimination Act 1975. The Directive is broad and comprehensive in its treatment of discrimination in employment, but does not apply
to non-employment situations. Decisions made under the Directive, such as
the *Marshall*[50] case on retirement age, have had a profound effect upon
domestic law.

[handwritten margin note: Marshall case decided. Ind. citizens cannot have claims brought against firm on the strength of a Directive until the legislature of their state has introduced the necessary domestic legislation]

Four other Directives also relate to sex discrimination. The Sex Discrimina-   **1-36**
tion (Social Security) Directive 79/7 covers matters of state social security,
whilst the Sex Discrimination (Occupational Social Security) Directive 86/
378 (originally implemented in the U.K. by the Social Security Act 1989)
covers occupational pensions, although following the *Barber*[51] case the coverage of that Directive has been greatly circumscribed and is now covered by
the Pensions Act 1995. The Sex Discrimination (Self-employed) Directive
86/631 covers the position of self-employed women, in particular in agricul-

---

[49] Article 235 allows for action to be taken by the Community to achive one of its objectives
where the Treaty has not otherwise provided the necessary powers. Unanimity is required in
the Council of Ministers for such measures.
[50] [1986] I.R.L.R. 140, ECJ.
[51] *Barber v. Guardian Royal Exchange Assurance* [1990] I.R.L.R. 240, ECJ. An amended Directive has been proposed and is discussed in chapter 6.

ture and family businesses, a problem which perhaps bulks larger in some Community countries than in the U.K. Directive 92/85 provides for the protection of the health and safety of pregnant and breast feeding women.

The direct effect of Community law

1-37   The supremacy of Community law is essential to the very idea of the European Community; if the States could opt out of aspects of the Community legal order not to their liking there would be little left of the Community except pious hopes and aspirations.[52] Community instruments which give rise to rights which need no further legislative enactment in the Member States are usually described as being of ''direct application''. For example, Regulations which need no further enactment are necessarily directly applicable. All Community instruments which may be invoked directly before their national courts, are said to be of ''direct effect'', even though, like directives, they are required to be implemented by the Member States. Such a legislative instrument can only be said to be of direct effect until it is fully and properly implemented; after that it is necessary to rely on the national law. The use of these two terms has not always been wholly consistent, either by the courts or by commentators.

The direct effect of Treaty provisions

1-38   In *Van Gend en Loos*[53] a case concerning the application of Article 12 restricting the right of States to introduce import duties, the ECJ held that:

> ''the Community constitutes a new legal order of international law for the benefit of which states have limited their sovereign rights, albeit within limited fields, and the subjects of which comprise not only Member States but also their nationals. Independently of the legislation of Member States, Community law therefore not only imposes obligations on individuals but is also intended to confer on them rights which become part of their legal heritage. These rights arise not only where they are expressly granted by the Treaty but also by reason of obligations which the Treaty imposes in a clearly defined way upon individuals as well as upon Member States and the institutions of the Community.''

The ECJ went on to define the characteristics of Community law which may

---

[52] *Amministtrazionne delle Finanze dello Stato v. Simmenthal* [1978] E.C.R. 629, ECJ. The ECJ held at ground 18 ''(A)ny ... legislative measures which encroach upon the field within which the Community exercises its legislative power or which are otherwise incompatible with the provisions of Community law ... would amount to a corresponding denial of the effectiveness of obligations undertaken unconditionally and irrevocably by Member States pursuant to the Treaty and would thus imperil the very foundations of the Community.'' See also Case 6/64 *Costa v. ENEL* ie see also Case 6/64, *Costa v. ENEL*: [1964], etc [1964] E.C.R. 585; *Factortame v. Secretary for State for Transport* [1989] 2 All E.R. 692.

[53] [1963] E.C.R. 1.

have direct effect by reference to Article 12, holding that it was "ideally adapted to produce direct effects" because it was a:

> "clear and unconditional prohibition which is not a negative but a posit-
> ive prohibition", which was "not qualified by any reservations on the
> part of states, which would make its implications conditional upon a
> positive legislative measure enacted under national law."

Treaty provisions can have direct effect not only as between an individual and the State, so-called vertical direct effect, but also as between individuals, so-called horizontal direct effect. Article 119 was held to be of direct vertical and horizontal effect in the *Defrenne (No.2)*, in that:

> "since Article 119 is mandatory in nature, the prohibition on discrimina-
> tion between men and women applies not only to the actions of public
> authorities, but also extends to all agreements which are intended to
> regulate paid labour collectively, as well as to contracts between
> individuals."[54]

In *Defrenne (No.2)* the direct effect of Article 119 was limited to

> "direct and overt discrimination which may be identified solely with
> the aid of the criteria based on equal work and equal pay," as opposed
> to "indirect and disguised discrimination which can only be identified
> by more explicit implementing provisions of a Community or national
> character"[55]

The ECJ went on to hold that:

> "Among the forms of direct discrimination which may be identified
> solely by reference to the criteria laid down by Article 119 must be
> included in particular those which have their origin in legislative provi-
> sions or in collective labour agreements and which may be detected on
> the basis of a purely legal analysis of the situation."

Whilst this decision can be seen as delimiting the scope of direct effect to that which is clear and unconditional,[56] in its earlier case law, as regards both nationality[57] and, more hesitantly, gender equality,[58] the Court had accepted a concept of indirect discrimination in the sense of the adverse impact of facially neutral criteria. Advocate General Warner pointed up this confusion in *Jenkins*,[59] a case concerned with the question as to whether it was discrim-

---

[54] *Defrenne v. Sabena (No. 2)*, Case 43/75 [1976] E.C.R. 455; [1976] 2 C.M.L.R. 98, at ground 39.

[55] *Ibid.*, ground 18.

[56] T.C. Hartley, *The Foundations of European Community Law* (2nd ed., Clarendon Press, 1988), p.189.

[57] Case 152/73, *Sotgiu v. Deutsche Bundespost*: [1974] E.C.R. 153.

[58] *Sabbatini*, n.47 and *Airola*, n. 49 *supra*. See Prechal and Burrows, *Gender Discrimination Law of the European Community* (Dartmouth, 1990), pp. 8–19 for further discussion of this issue.

[59] Case 96/80, *Jenkins v. Kingsgate (Clothing Productions) Co*: [1981] E.C.R. 911; 2 C.M.L.R. 24.

inatory to pay part-time workers less than full-time workers, but the Court did not resolve the matter in its judgement, referring to the need to test whether the differential ''is or is not in reality discrimination based on sex.'' It was not until the *Bilka-Kaufhaus*[60] case that the ECJ unambiguously set out a formulation of indirect sex discrimination akin to the British statutory use of the term indirect discrimination and the American usage of adverse impact discrimination. It remains true, however, that Community law will not be of direct effect where it is programmatic in the way which is manifested by Article 117, or inoperative without more detailed implementing legislation.

The direct effect of directives

1-39   Whilst Regulations are, by virtue of the second paragraph of Article 189, expressly provided to be binding in their entirety and directly applicable in the Member States, the third paragraph of Article 189 provides only that:

> ''A directive shall be binding, as to the result to be achieved, upon each Member State to which it is addressed, but shall leave to the national authorities the choice of form and method.''

In the labour field, with the exception of the Regulations governing free movement, harmonisation has been achieved by directive. In *Van Duyn v. Home Office*, a case concerning a challenge to the right of the Home Office to refuse entry into Britain by a Dutch member of the Church of Scientology, an action which was alleged to be contrary to the provisions of the relevant directive on free movement, the ECJ held that.[61]

> ''If, however, by virtue of the provisions of Article 189 regulations are directly applicable and, consequently, may by their very nature have direct effects, it does not follow from this that other categories of acts can never have similar effects. It would be incompatible with the binding nature attributed to a directive by Article 189 to exclude, in principle, the possibility that the obligation which it imposes may be invoked by those concerned.''

This proposition was justified by holding that the *effet utile* or ''useful effect'' of the directive:

> ''would be weakened if individuals were prevented from relying on it before their national courts and if the latter were prevented from taking it into consideration as an element of Community law''

provided, of course, that the provision in question is sufficiently clear and precise to give rise to direct effect and does not leave a significant measure of discretion to the Member States. The question arises therefore as to the position when a State has failed to implement a directive or implemented it

---

[60] Case 170/84, [1986] E.C.R. 1607; [1986] 2 C.M.L.R. 701.
[61] Case 41/74, [1974] E.C.R. 1337 at 1348.

incompletely or incorrectly. In *Ratti*,[62] the ECJ held that a Member State which has not implemented a directive may not rely on its own failure to perform its obligations. This proposition is fundamental to the ruling in *Marshall*[63] that directives are only effective against the Member States and may not be relied on as against an individual. However, the ECJ in *Marshall* held that only the State could be liable in this context, because the basis of any such action is the default of the State. This estoppel-like principle applies whether the State was acting as a public authority or only as an employer. Thus the Equal Treatment Directive was held to be only of direct *vertical* effect, *i.e.* only in respect of "organs of the State".[64]

In *Facinin Dori v. Recreb Sr*[65] the ECJ confirmed that the direct effect of directives does not impose obligations which can be relied upon as against an individual, whether a natural or legal person, but only against the state or state entities.

Boundaries of "the state"

As might be expected, having thus narrowed the scope of the direct effect   **1.40**
of directives, the ECJ adopted a wide view of the boundaries of the State. In *Foster v. British Gas plc*[66] six employees were compulsorily retired at the age of 60 just prior to the enactment of the Sex Discrimination Act 1986. They sought to rely on Article 5(1) of the Equal Treatment Directive, contending that the pre-privatisation British Gas Corporation was an emanation of the State. The issue of direct effect was referred to the ECJ by the House of Lords. The Court held that where a public body, acting as such or as an employer, has been made responsible under some form of statutory authority for providing a public service under the control of the State and has been granted special powers for that purpose, it is included in any event among the bodies against which the provisions of a Directive capable of direct effect may be relied upon. Thus the direct effect of directives is confined to actions brought against organs of the State, although the boundaries of the State have been widely drawn and could include a wide variety of formally autonomous

---

[62] Case 148/78, *Ratti*: [1979] E.C.R. 1629; Case 102/79, *Commission v. Belgium*: [1980] E.C.R. 1473; Case 158/80, *Rewe*: [1981] E.C.R. 1805 and Case 8/81, *Becker*: [1982] E.C.R. 53 where at para. 24 the ECJ holds that a Member State "which has not adopted the implementing measures required by the directive within the prescribed period may not plead as against individuals, its own failure to perform the obligations which the directive entails."

[63] Case 152/84, *Marshall v. Southampton and South West Hants Area Health Authority*: [1986] E.C.R. 723.

[64] Even though the matter was not strictly in point the Advocate General's opinion in *Marshall (No. 2)* supports reconsideration of the limitation of the concept of direct effects to organs of the State for three reasons. Firstly that the concept of direct effect already covers public bodies which cannot realistically be described as responsible for the default of the State in failing to implement the relevant directive, secondly that the obligation to interpret national law in conformity with directives gives rise to problems of the delimination of judicial powers and thirdly that individuals in defaulting States are still disadvantaged in comparison with individuals in States which have fully implemented the relevant directive, notwithstanding the possibility of *Francovitch* type actions.

[65] Case C-91/92 [1995] All E.R.(E.C.) 1.

[66] [1990] I.R.L.R. 353, ECJ. On its return from the ECJ the Lords ([1991] I.R.L.R. 268, HL) held that according to the tests set out by the ECJ the pre-privatisation British Gas Corporation was providing a public service under the control of the State under special powers contained in the Gas Act 1972.

public bodies. The ECJ went on to hold that the preliminary question of whether Community measures may be relied on against certain classes of persons necessarily involves the interpretation of the Treaty and is a matter for the ECJ, whereas the national courts may decide if proceedings before them fall within one of the categories so defined.

The question remains as to where the U.K. courts will draw the boundaries of the State, a question of increasing importance in view of established Government policy to reduce the scope of the State. For example, in *Doughty V. Rolls Royce Ltd*[67] the Court of Appeal held that Rolls Royce was not an emanation of the State whilst it was in public ownership because, whilst it was under the control of the State, it was not providing a public service, nor was it reliant on special powers granted by the State in the same sense as the nationalised British Gas Corporation. By contrast, the High Court in *Griffin v. South West Water Services Ltd*[68] held that a privatised water company was providing a service under the control of the state by virtue of special statutory powers and was therefore an emanation of the state, under the tests set out in *Foster*. The precise extent of the State, and therefore of the direct effect of directives, remains uncertain and a gap remains in which non-directly effective Community law finds no direct expression in the national system unless it has been fully and correctly implemented.

1-41 Whilst in the *Marshall* case the ECJ held that the Equal Treatment Directive was of direct effect, the position of the Equal Pay Directive is different, in that there has been no decision in terms that it is of direct effect. Rather the position is that in *Jenkins* the ECJ held that Article 1 of the Equal Pay Directive (which introduces the concept of equal pay for work of equal value):

> "is principally designed to facilitate the practical application of the principle of equal pay outlined in Art. 119 of the Treaty in no way alters the content or scope of that principle as defined in the Treaty."[69]

It would seem to follow that Article 1 of the Equal Pay Directive is directly effective in the Member States, in the same way as is Article 119, but it is arguable that as the implementation of the concept of equal value relies upon the complex machinery of the Equal Pay (Amendment) Regulations, that it is not directly applicable. This dilemma arises from the observation that whilst the ECJ has held that Article 1 of the Equal Pay Directive[70] does not extend or alter Article 119, the concept of equal value is not one which is necessarily implicit in the wording of Article 119.

Yet in so far as an issue may be decided by a purely legal analysis of direct and overt discrimination as indicated in *Defrenne (No. 2)*, Article 119 is directly effective both vertically and horizontally and there is no necessity to rely on the Equal Pay Directive.

---

[67] [1992] I.R.L.R. 126, C.A.

[68] [1995] I.R.L.R. 15, H.L.

[69] But in *Worringham* [1981] I.C.R. 558 A.G. VerLoren Van Themaat was of the opinion that the extension of the term "equal work" in Article 119 by Article 1 of the Directive was more a clarification than an extension of that term, relying on dicta in paras. 20 and 54 of *Defrenne (No. 2)*.

[70] Case 129/79 *McCarthys Ltd v. Smith* [1980] 2 C.M.L.R. 205, [1980] E.C.R. 1275 [1981] 1 Q.B. 180, ECJ at point 10; Case 157/86, *Murphy v. Bord Telecom Eirann* [1988] 1 C.M.L.R. 879 at point 13.

The effect of recommendations

In *Grimaldi v. Fonds des Maladies Professionelles*[71] the ECJ held that whilst   **1-42**
Article 189(5) provides that recommendations have no binding force and do
not in themselves confer rights on individuals upon which they may rely
before national courts, such recommendations cannot be considered as lacking in legal effect.[72] The ECJ goes on to hold that:

> "National courts are bound to take Recommendations into consideration
> in order to decide disputes submitted to them, in particular where they
> clarify the interpretation of national provisions adopted in order to
> implement them or where they are designed to supplement Community
> measures."

Such "soft law" measures can be utilised as an aid to the interpretation of
relevant law, as with the Code of Practice on the Dignity of Men and Women
at Work, which has been cited by U.K. tribunals in sexual harassment cases.

Time limits in Community law claims

The principle of effectiveness embodied in Article 5 of the Treaty implies   **1-43**
that it is for the national courts to give effect to Community law rights,
subject to the normal procedural rules of each legal system. Furthermore the
Court in *Rewe-Zentralefinanz and Rewe-Zentral AG v. Landwirtschaftskammer für das Saarland*[73] held that though Community law must be exercised in accordance with national procedural rules and time limits, unless
such conditions render impossible the exercise of Community law rights,
"this is not the case where reasonable periods of limitation are fixed."[73] In
Rewe the applicant had paid customs duties which were subsequently held
by the ECJ to be in breach of Community law, but by the time the applicant
companies were able to seek reimbursement they were out of time for making
such a claim under German national law. It was in a second reference on
those strong facts in which the applicant companies could not have known
of their rights until the relevant limitation period had passed, that the ECJ
set out its proposition as to the application of national time limits. The general
rule was restated in the sex discrimination context by the ECJ in *Emmot v.
Ministry of Social Welfare and the Attorney General*[74] that the national courts
must:

> "in the absence of Community rules on the subject, apply national pro-

---

[71] [1990] I.R.L.R. 400.
[72] See Jean-Victor Louis, "The Community Legal Order", EC, 1990 for a general view of the
effects of the various Community legislative instruments and the note by E. Szyszcak in
Industrial Law Journal, 20, 2, pp. 156–158.
[73] Case 33/76, *Rewe-Zentralefinanz and Rewe-Zentral AG v. Landwirtschaftskammer fur das
Saarland*: [1976] E.C.R. 1989, [1977] 1 C.M.L.R. 533: Case 45/76 *Comet BV v. Pruktschap
voor Siergewassen* [1976] E.C.R.: 2043, [1977] 1 C.M.L.R. 533.
[74] Case C-2-208/90, [1991] I.R.L.R. 387.

cedural rules and time limits provided that such conditions are not less favourable than those relating to similar actions of a domestic nature nor framed so as to render virtually impossible the exercise of rights conferred by domestic law''.

1-44   In the *Emmot* case, however, the ECJ went on to hold that time does not begin to run under national time limits until a directive has been fully and effectively transposed into national law. Only then will individuals be able to ascertain the full extent of their rights and rely on them in the national courts. Consequently, as a State may not benefit from its own default, it may not rely on national time limits in an action brought against it by an individual so long as the directive in question has not been properly transposed in to national law.[75] The principle in *Emmot* that time limits do not run until the relevant directive has been correctly transposed was relied upon by the EAT in *Cannon v. Barnsley Metropolitan Council*[76] in relation to a claim arising under the Equal Treatment Directive 76/207. The application of the rule in *Emmot* was, however, rejected as being inapplicable to appeals to the EAT in *Setiya v. East Yorkshire Health Authority.*[77]

1-45   Yet national rules of law limiting the retroactive effect of claims are not contrary to E.C. law and do not fall within the rule in *Emmot* that time limits do not apply in respect of an inadequately implemented directive until that directive has been properly transposed. In *Steenhorst-Neerings v. Bestuur van de Bedrijfsvereniging voor Detailhandel, Ambachten en Huisvrouwen*[78] the ECJ held that a national rule limiting the retrospective effect of a claim for an incapacity benefit to one year satisfied the test that the conditions under which the claim is made are not less favourable than those relating to similar domestic claims, nor such as to render the exercise of community law rights virtually impossible. *Emmot* was distinguished because the present rule did not affect the right to rely upon a directive in bringing a claim, but merely limited the extent of that claim in the interests of sound administration and the financial balance of the scheme.

Even though the Lords had declared the threshold for bringing an unfair dismissal claim to be contrary to the Equal Treatment Directive in *R. v. Secretary of State, ex p. EOC*, the Court of Appeal held in *Biggs v. Somerset County Council*[79] that this did not affect the application of the normal three month time limit for unfair dismissal. The Court of Appeal reasoned that decisions of the European Court of Justice are declaratory of the law as it has been since its inception and that it was therefore ''reasonably practicable'' for someone to have argued that the time limit was discriminatory at any time since 1973. The complainant's mistake was one of law, not fact. The claims for retrospective entry into a pension scheme following the *Vroege* and

---

[75] Note that the claims for retrospective entry into a pension scheme in *Preston v. Wolverhampton Healthcare NHS Trust* [1996] I.R.L.R. 484, EAT were held to have arisen under Article 119, rather than under any of the equality directives.
[76] [1992] I.R.L.R. 474.
[77] [1995] I.R.L.R. 348.
[78] Case C-338/91, [1993] E.C.R. 1–1574, [1994] I.R.L.R. 244, ECJ and see Case C-410/92, *Johnson v. Chief Adjudication Officer (No. 2)*: [1995] I.R.L.R. 157 to similar effect. The application of the two year limit in s.2(5) of the Equal Pay Act has been referred to the ECJ in *Leveg v. TH Jennings (Harlow Pools) Ltd* [1996] I.R.L.R. 499.
[79] *The Independent*, February 2, 1996, C.A.

Fisscher (see paragraph 6–40, note 92) cases, arising in *Preston v. Wolver-hampton Healthcare NHS Trust*[80] were found to fall outside the national time limit of six months. This limit did not render the exercise of Community rights virtually impossible, the EAT concluded, because the position was said by the ECJ in *Fisscher* to have been clear since the 1986 decision in *Bilka Kaufhaus* (see paragraph 6–40).

An applicant who seeks to re-open an issue heard and dismissed under **1-46** domestic law on the basis, say, that the working hours threshold is not in accord with Community law, faces a further difficulty in that the matter may be *res judicata*. The Court of Appeal in *Barber v. Staffordshire County Council*[81] held that where an application for unfair dismissal by a part-time worker was withdrawn and formally dismissed by an industrial tribunal, but without a reasoned decision, there was nothing to preclude the application of the principles of cause of action or issue estoppel.

The indirect or interpretative effect of Community law

In the *Von Colson* case the ECJ held that: **1-47**

"in applying national law and in particular a national law introduced to implement Directive 76/207, national courts are required to interpret their national law in the light of the wording and purposes of the directive in order to achieve the results referred to in article 189(3)",

suggesting that any national law covering the same ground should be construed in conformity with Community law. Reliance on this principle is not limited to cases against the State or emanations of the State.

The ECJ acknowledged in *Kolpinghuis Nijmegen*[82] that by interpreting national law in conformity with Community law, national courts run the risk of offending against the principles of legal certainty and legitimate expectations, particularly in criminal cases. Nonetheless, the principle of *indirect effect* was developed in *Marleasing SA v. la Commercial International de Alimentacion SA* to encompass all relevant domestic legislation irrespective of whether it was passed before or after the particular Community instrument or whether or not it was passed in order to implement Community obligations. In *Marleasing* the ECJ held that though:

"a Directive cannot, in itself, impose obligations on the rights of an individual and, consequently, the prescriptions of a directive cannot be invoked as such against such a person" nonetheless "in applying the national law the national court called upon to interpret it is obliged to

---

[80] [1996] I.R.L.R. 484, EAT.
[81] The Independent, February 2, 1996, C.A., *cf. Methihill Bowling Club v. Hunter* [1995] I.R.L.R. 232, EAT.
[82] Case 80/86 [1987] E.C.R. 3969; [1989] 2 C.M.L.R. 18, although as that case concerned a possible extension of criminal liability, it could be rationalised as concerning more the non-retroactivity of penal legislation.

do so wherever possible in the light of the text and of the (purpose) of the Directive''.[83]

In *Pickstone v. Freemans*[84] the House of Lords looked at the way in which the draft of the Equal Pay Amendment Regulations 1983 were presented to Parliament by the relevant Minister.[85] Even the need to imply words into a section of the Regulations, which Lord Oliver admitted was on its face unambiguous, did not prevent a purposive construction because it was plain that Parliament could not possibly have intended a failure to implement Community obligations fully and correctly. A similar approach marked the decision of the Lords in the transfer of undertakings case of *Litster v. Forth Dry Dock and Engineering Co.*,[86] where a strongly purposive construction of the regulations was adopted, even though they were not of direct effect.

The binding nature of directly effective Community rights under section 2(1) of the European Community Act is reinforced in section 2(4), which provides that ''any enactment passed or to be passed . . . shall be construed and have effect subject to the foregoing provisions of this section . . .''. As a matter of U.K. law it follows from the wording of section 2(4) that the U.K. courts are only obliged to interpret national law in conformity with Community law where that law is of direct effect, *i.e.* that referred to in section 2(1) as being ''without further enactment to be given legal effect''. The logic of the section can be seen at work in *Duke v. GEC Reliance* (a case brought by an employee of a private employer on facts similar to those found in *Foster v. British Gas*) in which the House of Lords rejected the contention that the Sex Discrimination Act 1975 should be construed so as to conform to the provisions of the subsequent Equal Treatment Directive. Templeman L.J., giving the judgment of the court, held that:

> ''Of course a British court will always be willing and anxious to conclude that United Kingdom law is consistent with Community law. Where an act is passed for the purpose of giving effect to an obligation imposed by a directive or other instrument a British court will seldom encounter difficulty in concluding that the language of the Act is effective for the intended purpose. But the construction of a British Act of Parliament is a matter of judgement to be determined by the British courts and to be derived from the language of the legislation considered in the light of the circumstances prevailing at the date of enactment . . . Section 2(4) of the European Communities Act 1972 does not in my opinion enable or constrain a British court to distort the meaning of a British statute in order to enforce against an individual a Community Directive which has no direct effect between individuals. Section 2(4) applies and only applies where Community provisions are directly applicable.''[87]

---

[83] Case 106/89 at paras. 6 and 8.
[84] [1987] I.R.L.R. 218, C.A.; [1988] I.R.L.R. 356, H.L.
[85] Alan Clark admits in his diaries that he was, however, drunk at the time!
[86] [1989] I.R.L.R. 161, H.L.
[87] [1988] I.R.L.R. 118 at 123 and *Finnegan v. Clowney Youth Training Programme* [1990] 2 A.C. 407, a case concerning the Sex Discrimination (Northern Ireland) Order 1976 (S.I. 1976 No. 1042), which was adopted after the Equal Treatment Directive but which was intended to implement the terms of the Sex Discrimination Act 1975 in Northern Ireland, rather than the Directive.

The consequences of the principle of indirect effect can best be seen in *Webb v. EMO (Air Cargo) Ltd.*[88] In *Webb* the Lords held that though dismissal of a pregnant woman on grounds of her pregnancy can be discriminatory, in this case the complainant was dismissed because she would be absent at the same time that the person she was replacing would also be on maternity leave. The relevant circumstance in which a comparison fell to be made with the treatment of a hypothetical man was prospective absence from work; the reasons for that absence were not relevant to the comparison. On that basis her treatment was held to be comparable to that which a similarly placed man with an arthritic hip might have received. As, following *Marshall (No. 1)*, directives are not of direct effect as between private individuals, the Lords held that it would distort the meaning of the Sex Discrimination Act to interpret it so as to give effect to the ECJ decision in *Dekker* that a pregnancy related dismissal was necessarily contrary to Article 2(1) of the Equal Treatment Directive. Subsequently, the ECJ held that it was impermissible to compare absence arising from pregnancy with the putative absence of a man who would be off sick for a comparable period, because pregnancy is a condition unique to women and not in any way comparable with a pathological condition or with unavailability for work on non-medical grounds. On the return of *Webb* to the Lords, Lord Keith of Kinkel, giving the judgement of the House, reconciled their earlier ruling with that of the ECJ by holding that the fact that pregnancy was the reason for the employee's absence was a circumstance relevant to her case, which could not be present in the case of a hypothetical man, thus enabling the unique nature of pregnancy to be recognised by this interpretation of s.5(3). By contrast the limits of the principle are exposed in *Marshall (No. 2)* in which the ECJ held that the statutory limit on compensation claims under the Sex Discrimination Act were contrary to the Equal Treatment Directive, but in such a stark case it was only possible to reconcile the domestic with the Community provisions by legislative means.

Damages claims against the state

In *Francovich and Boniface v. Republic of Italy*[89] the ECJ held that Community law lays down that a Member State is liable to make good damage to individuals caused by a breach of Community law for which it is responsible. *Francovich* arose from the failure of Italy to implement the Insolvency Directive, with the result that workers affected by insolvencies in Italy did not enjoy the rights which they were intended to enjoy under Community law. Although the failure to implement the Directive was established in enforcement proceedings brought by the Commission, the ECJ held that the rights in question, though intended to benefit persons such as the plaintiff in the action, were not of direct effect. Nonetheless, Member States could be liable for such a breach of Community law provided that three conditions were met, namely, that the result required by the Directive includes the conferring of rights for the benefit of individuals, the content of these rights may be

1-48

[88] [1993] I.R.L.R. 27; [1994] I.R.L.R. 482, ECJ; [1995] I.R.L.R. 645, H.L.
[89] Cases 6/90 & 9/90 [1992] IRLR 84, ECJ.

determined by reference to the Directive and that a causal link exists between breach of the obligation of the state and the damage suffered by the individual. It was unclear from the decision in *Francovich* whether the State had to be "at fault" for liability to arise and whether liability could arise from legislative, as opposed to executive acts. Thus *Francovich* left unresolved the question as to whether the incomplete or inaccurate implementation of a directive could give rise to liability.

These and other questions concerning the conditions under which non-contractual state liability could arise were considered in *Brasserie du Pecheur v. Federal Republic of Germany* and *R. v. Secretary of State for Transport ex p. Factortame (No. 3)*[90] *Francovich* had concerned a right which was not directly effective, though intended to benefit individuals such as the plaintiffs, but in *Factortame (No. 3)* the Court of Justice extended this liability to provisions which are directly effective. Liability can arise from legislative acts, even where the legislature has a wide discretion in implementing Community policy, provided "the breach is sufficiently serious and there is a direct causal link between the breach and the damage sustained by the individuals." Liability for loss or damage cannot be made conditional upon fault (whether intentional or negligent) going beyond that of a sufficiently serious breach of Community law, such as would be the case where the Member State con cerned manifestly and gravely disregarded the limits on its own discretion.[91] A breach of Community law may be established from a preliminary ruling of the Court of Justice or by virtue of the settled case law of the Court.

Whilst non-contractual liability for damage may be subject to normal domestic rules on liability, these must not be such as to make reparation impossible or excessively difficult to obtain. In *Factortame (No. 3)* the Court held that to subject such a claim to the normal rules governing liability for misfeasance in public office would render it excessively difficult to obtain reparation. It follows that breach of statutory duty, and not only misfeasance in public office, could be an appropriate cause of action in English law.

Yet in assessing the loss or damage for which reparation may be sought "the national court may enquire whether the injured person showed reasonable diligence in order to avoid the loss or damage or to limit its extent and whether, in particular, he availed himself in time of all the legal remedies available to him." (point 84). Thus where a person seeks compensation for a failure of the U.K. Government to implement Community law correctly, or otherwise to act in conformity with it, the issue will arise as to whether that person has taken appropriate and timely legal action to protect his or her legal interests.[92–96]

---

[90] Joined Cases C 468 48/93 (5/3/96) [1996] I.R.L.R. 267 *Brasserie du Pecheur* was concerned with the maintenance of German beer purity and labelling laws contrary to Article 30, whilst *Factortame* concerned the imposition of nationality restrictions as regards the ownership of fishing vessels registered in Britian and fishing under the British fishing quota, contrary to Article 52. In each case economic loss was caused to traders whose business was thereby disrupted and the plaintiffs sought to recover such losses from the Member States in question.

[91] Factors which might be taken into account in considering whether there has been a sufficiently serious breach include (at point 56) "the clarity and precision of the rule breached, the measure of discretion left by that rule to national or community authorities, whether the infringement and the damage caused was intentional or voluntary, whether any error of law was excusable or inexcusable, the fact that the position taken by a Community institution may have contributed to the omission, and the adoption or retention of national measures or practices contrary to Community law."

[92–96] See paragraphs 1–43 to 1–46.

Liability for inaccurate, incomplete or faulty implementation of directives could arise,[97] provided that the necessary procedural conditions are met. Yet time would not run for an application in the industrial tribunal until the time that the defect in quesiton was remedied by Parliament, following the decision of the ECJ in *Emmot v. Ministry of Social Welfare*.[98] An industrial tribunal would have had the power to disapply any offending provision of domestic law following *Factortame (No. 2)*. According to the decision in *Factortame (No 3)* any failure to take action in time in the industrial tribunal would prejudice a claim in respect of state liability for damage under *Francovich*. Thus whilst there is a broad definition of the liability of the State for damage in *Francovich*, as amplified in *Factortame (No. 3)*, procedural difficulties springing from the application of national time limits following *Emmot* and *Biggs v. Somerset County Council*, may make it difficult to realise this right in the employment sphere.[99]

Equality as a fundamental right

Community law has recognised the elimination of discrimination based on sex as a fundamental right. The ECJ in the third *Defrenne* case sets forth the fundamental nature of the principle of equality in Community law and its place in the Community legal order:

> "The Court has repeatedly stated that respect for fundamental personal human rights is one of the general principles of Community law, the observance of which it has a duty to ensure. There can be no doubt that the elimination of discrimination based on sex forms part of those fundamental rights."[1]

1-49

The case-law of the European Communities contains many references to the general principles of Community law, but what is their significance?[2] The source of authority for such propositions lies in general principles common to the law of the Member States especially where there are embodied in the European Convention of Human Rights to which all Member States of the

1-50

---

[97] Except where the interpretation of the directive in question which was adopted by the Member State was reasonably capable of bearing that meaning and not contrary to the case law of the Court of Justice (*R. v. H.M. Treasury, ex p. B.T.*, Case C 392/93, [1996] I.R.L.R. 300).

[98] Case C-208/90, [1991] 3 C.M.L.R. 894.

[99] Yet it is reported (E.O.R. 64) that H.M. Government recently settled a claim for damages for £34,000 from the applicant in *Porter v. Cannon Hygiene* [1993] I.R.L.R. 329, N.I.C.A. whose original claim against her private sector employer under the Equal Treatment Directive was dismissed.

[1] Case 149/77, *Defrenne v. Sabena* [1978] E.C.R. 1365 at 1378.

[2] For a general discussion of the origin and scope of general principles in Community law see, T.C. Hartley, *The Foundations of European Community Law*, (Clarendon Press, 2nd ed., Oxford), pp. 129–153, Jean-Victor Louis, *The Community Legal Order*, (E.C. Commission, 1990). For a discussion of the application of selected principles to substantive law see A. Arnull, *General Principles of Community Law* (Leicester University Press, 1990) and for a specific treatment of the right to equality see Sacha Prechal and Noreen Burrows, *Gender Discrimination Law of the European Community*, (Dartmouth, 1990), pp. 1–23 and Evelyn Ellis, *European Sex Equality Law* (OUP, 1991), pp. 117–134.

Community are signatories. In the *Internationale Handelgesellschaft*[3] case the ECJ held that:

> "(t)he protection of such rights, whilst inspired by the constitutional traditions common to the Member States, must be ensured within the framework of the structure and objectives of the Community".

The case arose from the contention that a requirement of Community law was contrary to the fundamental rights guaranteed by the German constitution, to which all German national law was subject. To avoid a conflict with the German constitutional court, in which the doctrine of the supremacy of Community law might be tested, the ECJ deferred to the German constitutional position, but neatly placed this constraint as falling within the confines of Community law. Further steps were taken down this road in *Nold v. Commission*[4] when the ECJ held that:

> "it cannot uphold measures which are incompatible with fundamental rights recognised and protected by the constitutions of (the Member) States."

In that case, international treaties signed by the Member States for the protection of human rights[5] were also recognised as a source of such general principles. These have included the European Convention on Human Rights,[6] the European Social Charter[7] and I.L.O. Conventions No. 100[8] and 111.[9]

E.C. "general principle of equality"

1-51   The elimination of discrimination based on sex, as noted above, has been held by the ECJ in the third *Defrenne* case to form part of the corpus of fundamental human rights to be observed by Community law. The ECJ has, however, elucidated a "general principle of equality which is one of the fundamental principles of Community law. This principle requires that similar situations shall not be treated differently unless differentiation is objectively justified."[10] As Millet observes[11]:

> "Being a general principle, it is applicable in all fields and may be used not only as a guide to interpreting legislation but also to fill lacunae in

---

[3] [1970] E.C.R. 1125.
[4] [1974] E.C.R. 491.
[5] At p. 507, para. 13.
[6] Case 36/75, *Rutili*: [1975] E.C.R. 1219.
[7] Case 149/77, *Defrenne v. Sabena* [1978] C.M.L.R. 312 (ground 28), Case 24/86, *Blaizot and the University of Liege v. Belgium*: [1989] 1 C.M.L.R.57.
[8] See A.G. VerLoren Van Thematt in Case 61/81 *E.C. Commission v. U.K.* [1982] C.M.L.R. 284 at 292.
[9] Case 149/77, *Defrenne v. Sabena* [1978] C.M.L.R. 312 (ground 28).
[10] *Ruckdeschel* [1977] E.C.R. 1753, para. 7, *Moullins Pont-a-Mousson* [1977] E.C.R. 1795, paras. 16–17. *Finanzamt Köln-Alstadt v. Schumacher* [1995] All E.R. (E.C.) 319, "Discrimination can only arise through the application of different rules to comparable situations or the application of the same rule to different situations."
[11] *Sex Equality: The Influence of Community Law in Great Britain*, pp. 219–246.

legislation or even override legislative provisions which are contrary to it.''

The general principle of non-discrimination on grounds of sex can be seen operating in cases brought seeking review of decisions made under the regulations governing the employment of Community staff.[12] Even though Advocate General Roemer rejected the notion of such a higher principle in Community law in *Sabbattini v. European Parliament*,[13] the Court itself held that the Staff Regulation which made expatriation allowances payable only to the head of a married household created an arbitrary difference between male and female officials and should be declared inapplicable under Article 18.[14] In that case, a female official had married and lost her allowance because she did not become the head of the household under the Regulations. A similar result was obtained in *Airola v. E.C. Commission*,[15] where a female official working in Italy married an Italian citizen, losing her right to an expatriation allowance because, under Italian law, she necessarily took her husband's nationality. It is perhaps notable that both these early decisions incorporate a notion of indirect discrimination, in that neither rested upon explicit differences in treatment between men and women. In *Razzouk and Beydoun v. E.C. Commission*,[16] a case heard after *Defrenne (No. 3)*, the Court held that:

> ''in relations between the Community institutions on the one hand and their employees or those claiming under them on the other, the requirements arising from this principle (of equal treatment of the sexes) are by no means limited to those flowing from Article 119 of the Treaty or the Community directives issued in this field.''

The Court went on to hold that the Commission's decisions applying the Regulations, to the effect that widowers should not enjoy the same rights to survivors' benefits as widows, were contrary to a fundamental right and inapplicable in so far as they treated surviving spouses differently according to their sex.

The other type of action in which the general principles can have play is that **1-52** of questions of interpretation submitted to the European Court of Justice by the national courts under Article 177. Thus, in reviewing the derogations which are permitted from the principle of equality on grounds of public safety, the ECJ in *Johnston v. RUC*[17] held that such derogations could only be allowed in so far as they are appropriate and necessary, *i.e.* they must conform also to the principle of proportionality and must be reconciled with

---

[12] Being a closed group, Community staff fall within the scope of judicial review actions by natural or legal persons under either Articles 173 or 184.

[13] Cases 20/71 & 32/71[1972] C.M.L.R. 945; [1972] E.C.R. 345.

[14] Again *locus standi* is restricted to those to whom the decision is addressed, where it is based upon an illegal regulation.

[15] Case 21/74, [1975] E.C.R. 221. In *Van den Broeck*, [1975] E.C.R. 235 such a case was rejected because the acquisition of the spouse's nationality was not mandatory under national law.

[16] Cases 75/82 & 117/82: [19840] 3 C.M.L.R. 470.

[17] Case 222/84, *Johnston v. RUC*: [1986] E.C.R. 1651; [1986] 3 C.M.L.R. 240; [1986] I.R.L.R. 263.

the principle of equal treatment. Equally, in the *Marshall*[18] case on retirement ages the ECJ held that "in view of the fundamental importance of the principle of equality" the exclusion of social security matters such as retirement age contained in Directive 79/7 "must be interpreted strictly."

1-53   There are no independent rights based upon the general principles, but rather as Millet suggests above, the general principles can be used as guides to interpret legislation, to fill in gaps or to override contrary provisions. The general principle of non-discrimination, as with all the principles of Community law, needs a positive law on which to operate. For example, in the third *Defrenne* case, the Belgian court was seeking an answer to the question whether the enforced retirement of air hostesses at 40 constituted discrimination contrary to Article 119 or to "a principle of Community law". The case was brought prior to the adoption of the Equal Treatment Directive, and for this reason the ECJ responded that at the time of the events then before the courts the Community had not assumed responsibility:

> "for supervising and guaranteeing the observance of the principle of equality between men and women in working conditions other than remuneration."

For this reason Docksey[19] argues that the right to non-discrimination on grounds of race or religion remains inchoate. Rights to non-discrimination on grounds of nationality under Article 7 and to free movement under Article 48 relate only to nationals of Member States and do not affect the position of third country nationals, nor do they have any direct impact upon the position of members of ethnic minorities who possess Community nationality. Whilst the Charter of Fundamental Social Rights of Workers makes reference to the need for comparable treatment of non-nationals, no proposals are made with reference to racial discrimination. The Declaration on Racism and Xenophobia adopted in 1986 led to the Evrigenis Committee of Inquiry, which recommended the preparation of a draft directive on race discrimination. However, the Resolution on Racism and Xenophobia adopted by the Council and representatives of the Member States in 1990 placed primary responsibility for action with the Member States. There are, nonetheless, both economic and social arguments for a Community wide race discrimination law. The CRE has argued, by analogy with the position under Article 119, that a Member State which adopts race discrimination legislation may put itself at a competitive disadvantage, thus causing a distortion of competition within the common market. This would provide grounds for Community measures to avoid such distortion to be introduced under Articles 100, 100A or 235. Moreover, Article 8, as revised by the Maastricht Treaty, provides for Community citizenship. If ethnic minority citizens are truly to enjoy full Community citizenship, it can be argued that there is a need for harmonisation of race discrimination laws across the Community. In a communication at the beginning of 1996 on racism, xenophobia and anti-semitism the European Commission sets out its aim of introducing legislation inspired by Article 14 of the European Convention on Human Rights, which states that the rights

---

[18] Case 152/84 [1986] 1 C.M.L.R. 688; [1986] E.C.R. 723; [1986] I.R.L.R. 140.
[19] C. Docksey, "The Principle of Equality as a Fundamental Right under Community Law" in *Industrial Law Journal*, 20, 4, pp. 258–280. at p. 261.

and freedoms provided for in the Convention "shall be enjoyed without discrimination on any ground". Further, the Commission is to propose an appropriate Treaty amendment to the 1996 Inter-governmental Conference to give a legislative base for measures to do with racism. The emphasis on subsidiarity and labour market flexibility which has developed since Maastricht makes it hard to forecast how these issues will develop, but given the political will there could be a legal basis for a Community race discrimination law.[20]

The basis of the Social Dimension

At the Madrid Summit in June 1989, the Member States declared that: **1-54**

> "... in the course of the construction of the single European market, social aspects should be given the same importance as the economic aspects and should accordingly be developed in a balanced fashion."

Yet prior to the Maastricht protocol there was no clear mandate for social programmes within the Community with the result that social measures need to be brought within an appropriate Treaty base, *i.e.* directed towards an improvement in health and safety under Article 118A or justified as necessary to the establishment and functioning of the common market under Article 100 or Article 100A because they reduce distortions of competition. The   **1-55** problem is that directives which, as Hepple argues,[21] *predominantly* concern the rights and interests of employed persons still require unanimity in the Council of Ministers and have to be voted under Article 100, so that they could be blocked by the U.K. or any other hostile government. The U.K. government has taken the view that the Working Time Directive, introduced by qualified majority voting under Article 118A, is not in reality a health and safety measure but should have been introduced under procedures which require unanimity in the Council, because the Directive bears on the rights and interests of employed persons. At the time of writing, the opinion of the Advocate-General is that the Directive is a valid health and safety measure.

Charter of the Fundamental Social Rights of Workers

It is well known that the Charter of the Fundamental Social Rights of   **1-56** Workers and subsequently the Social Protocol of the Maastricht Treaty, were agreed by 11 of the then 12 Member States of the Community, but not by the U.K. The Charter has no legal status as a legislative instrument, but is

---

[20] See Ian Forbes & Geoffrey Mead, "Measure for Measure; a Comparative Analysis of Measures to Combat Racial Discrimination in the Member States of the European Community," department of Employment Research Series, No. 1 1992; Erika Szyszczak "Race Discrimination: The Limits of Market Equality" in *Discrimination; the Limits of the law*, Hepple and Szyszczak eds. (Mansell, 1992), and the *Report of the European Parliament on Racism and Xenophobia*, rapporteur Glyn Ford, AS-195/90. See also the Joint Declaration in 1995 of the Social Partners on the Prevention of Racial Discrimination and Xenophobia and the Promotion of Equal Treatment at the Workplace.

[21] Bob Hepple, "The Implementation of the Community Charter of Fundamental Social Rights" in *Modern Law Review*, 53, September 1990.

more in the nature of a solemn declaratin of the direction of policy intended by the signatories. Opposition to the Charter by the U.K. government was in part based on the policy of deregulation of the labour market, but the British tradition is one of freedom of contract and the abstention of the State from all but an auxiliary role in labour relations. Where regulation has been traditional in Britain, as with genuine health and safety measures, there has been little principled objection to the proposals contained in the Charter. The tradition of statutory regulation of health and safety matters stretching back to 1833 makes this aspect of the Charter look more natural and acceptable to British eyes. Likewise, there has been little objection to the principle of developing Community equality law and indeed it is widely accepted that Britain is ahead in Europe with respect to specific legislation on race.[22] As Wedderburn observes, the principle of equal pay contained in Article 119 and "the Directives on equal pay pay and equal treatment have never had to prove their legitimacy as corrections to distortions of competition".[23]

The Social Protocol Agreement

1-57   At Maastricht, the other 11 wished to make progress towards the implementation of the proposals contained in the Social Charter, although Britain remained adamantly opposed to any extension of Community competence in the employment sphere. In the event, the other 11 signed a Protocol to the Treaty of European Union to which is appended an agreement which allows the other 14 Member States access to the Community Institutions in making progress towards realising the principles contained in the Social Charter, with which the new Member States of Austria, Sweden and Finland concurred. The result is that if Britain disagrees with proposals brought forward with respect to subjects which require unanimity under the pre-Maastricht rules, the other 14 are not precluded from going ahead with those proposals, as with the Directive on Parental Leave. What the protocol does not do is reduce or in any way alter the *acquis communitaire, i.e.* it does not put the clock back or undermine existing provisions such as the equality directives.

1-58   The Social Protocol contains both a new substantive agenda for a social Europe and new legislative processes based upon the concept of social dialogue.[24] The new Articles 1 and 2 provide a basis for more detailed Community measures to support and complement the activities of the Member States in improving living and working conditions, facilitating entry into work and increasing equality between men and women. The new Article 6 which concerns the same matters as Article 119, gives a clearer legal basis for equal opportunities programmes. Articles 2 to 4 contain a new legislative procedure giving an established place to the social partner and involving them in any decision making.

---

[22] *Second Review of the Race Relations Act* (CRE, 1992).
[23] W. Wedderburn *University Dublin Law Journal*, 20, I.
[24] See Manfred Weiss "The Significance of Maastricht for European Community Social Policy" in *International Journal of Comparative Labour Law and Industrial Relations*, Spring 1992, pp. 3–14, and Barry Fitzpatrick "Community Social Law after Maastricht" in *Industrial Law Journal*, 21, 3, pp. 199–213.

The future of Community equality law

The European Commission produced a Medium Term Social Action Pro-   **1-59**
gramme 1995–1997 in April 1995, under which it has developed a fourth
equal opportunities action plan. The plan has been adopted by the Council,
but the original budget of 60 million ECUs has been cut to 30 million. The
equal opportunities plan envisages efforts to integrate equal opportunities into
the mainstream of Community policy and the promotion of a better gender
balance in decision making. A draft code of practice on equal pay has been
produced.

The plan contains specific proposals for legislation on the reconciliation
of work and family life and on the burden of proof in sex discrimination
cases. Due to opposition from the U.K., draft directives on these topics failed
in the Council as regards the whole Community. The result has been that
the Commission has had to resort to the Social Protocol and Agreement as
a vehicle for promoting legislation to which the present U.K. administration
remains adamantly opposed. One result of this approach has been the conclusion of a framework agreement on parental leave under the procedures established at Maastricht. This framework agreement has gone forward to the
Council for a ''decision'' under Article 4(2) of the Agreement. The Commission proposes a directive which will give effect to the Agreement on Parental
Leave which has been concluded by the social partners, but the proposed
directive will not apply to the U.K., unless a changed U.K. Government
decides to sign up to the Agreement itself. Consultations are proceeding
under the Agreement for legislation on the burden of proof in sex discrimination cases.

The only equality legislation which is likely to go through the Council in
the foreseeable future and have effect in the U.K. is the draft revised directive
on occupational social security. This incorporates the effects of the *Barber*
decision on pensions and is discussed in chapter 6.

Proposed legislation on 'atypical workers', most of whom are women,
failed in the Council due to U.K. opposition. Only the Directive on health
and safety requirements for part-time workers passed into law. Existing case
law reveals that any discrepancy in conditions for part-timers is likely to be
found to be indirectly discriminatory against women. Better protection of
part-time and temporary workers, with conditions of employment comparable
to full-timers, could be of great benefit to women and indeed to minorities.
However, it can be argued that the greater labour market flexibility available
to employers with respect to part-timers has led to the expansion of part-time
employment opportunities which have largely been taken by women. It is
for this reason that the U.K. government opposed Community wide regulation
of part-time work, with the result that consultations have now begun with
the social partners under the Social Policy Protocol and Agreement for legislation which would introduce minimum standards as regards the other members of the Community.

2 SEX AND RACE DISCRIMINATION

What is discrimination?

2-01   If one were to describe another person as discriminating, that would be generally understood as a compliment. The inference would be that such a person has the capacity to choose, to distinguish between one option and another on the basis of a fine appreciation of the situation. Yet if one were to describe another person's conduct as discriminatory, that would normally be understood as a condemnatory or disapproving statement. What is the distinction between these two commonly understood usages of different parts of the same verb?

The essence of the matter is that those who are guilty of such discrimination have failed to distinguish between their fellow human beings as individuals. They have reacted to a whole group on the basis of the generally assumed characteristics of that group, without troubling to treat each individual on his or her merits according to the criteria which are truly relevant to the situation in hand. Such actions often spring from generalised assumptions about the characteristics of particular groups as in *Hurley* v. *Mustoe*[1] in which the employer acted on the assumption that all married women with small children were unreliable. The import of the case is not that employers must recruit women irrespective of whether or not they are reliable, but that the employer should have been prepared to assess all candidates on the grounds of their own potential reliability (amongst all their characteristics) and to choose accordingly. Reliability is relevant, whereas sex and motherhood as such are not. There was a failure to distinguish between the individuals who apply for a job (*i.e.* to discriminate in the first sense) according to criteria which are relevant to the choice which has to be made. The purpose of a job selection procedure is to select the best man or woman for the job. If choices are being made according to criteria which are not relevant to that purpose, the result must be that in practice the best person is not being selected for the job.

Discrimination

2-02   The purpose of Part 1 of the Sex Discrimination and Race Relations Acts is to describe two basic types of discrimination-known as direct and indirect discrimination, but not so referred to in the legislation-which can form the basis for individual actions. In addition there is also discrimination by way

---

[1] [1981] I.C.R. 490.

of victimisation. Part 2 of the statutes go on to set out the forms of discrimination in employment rendered unlawful by the legislation, whereas Part 3 proscribes various forms of discrimination outside of employment. Note, however, that a claim for "race discrimination" or "sex discrimination" incorporates a claim for direct or indirect discrimination according to the Employment Appeal Tribunal (hereafter EAT) in *Quarcoopome v. Sock Shop Holdings*.[2]

The scope of direct discrimination

Discrimination entails treatment of a person on one of the prescribed grounds (here race and sex, but also disability[3] and religion in Northern Ireland), which has an adverse impact on him or her by comparison with the treatment afforded to persons not of the group in question.[4]

Direct discrimination is defined in section 1(1)(a) of the Sex Discrimination Act 1975 (SDA):

> "A person discriminates against a woman in any circumstances relevant to the purposes of any provision of this Act if
>
> (a) on the ground of her sex he treats her less favourably than he treats or would treat a man."

Direct discrimination against married people is defined in similar terms in section 3(1)(a) as occurring where:

> "on the ground of his or her marital status he treats that person less favourably than he treats or would treat an unmarried person of the same sex."[5]

In the Race Relations Act 1976 (RRA) direct discrimination is defined in similar terms in section (1)(a) as occurring where:

> "on racial grounds he treats or would treat that other less favourably than he treats or would treat other persons."

It is noteworthy that the Equal Pay Act 1970, whilst requiring that an "equality clause" shall be implied into all contracts of employment, does not rely on the term "discrimination" at all. The concept of discrimination is, however, implicit in the Equal Pay Act, for if there is an inequality of pay between comparable groups of workers which cannot be accounted for in some other way, the Act offers a remedy, impliedly because the difference in pay must be attributable to discrimination.[6]

As regards sex discrimination only, Community law proscribes discrimina-

---

[2] [1995] I.R.L.R. 353.
[3] See chapter 3.
[4] See Evelyn Ellis, "The Definition of Discrimination in European Sex Equality Law," (1994) 19 in *European Law Review* 563–579 for further discussion of this issue.
[5] Note that the protection on grounds of marital status applies only to protect married as against single persons and not vice versa. Neither does this provision apply to cases brought under Part 3 of the SDA 1975.
[6] Note in *Ratcliffe v. North Yorks. C.C.* [1995] I.R.L.R. 439, that Lord Slynn held that the Equal Pay Act does not distinguish between direct and indirect discrimination.

tion on grounds of sex, both as regards equal pay, and equal treatment in employment and social security. In view of the principle of the supremacy of Community law,[7] where there is a conflict between the provisions of Community law and those of domestic law, Community law will normally prevail.

Sex discrimination is dealt with in Article 119 and within a number of directives, principally the Equal Pay Directive 75/117 and the Equal Treatment Directive 76/207.[8]

Article 119 introduces the "principle of equal pay" into Community law and provides as follows.

"Each Member State shall ... ensure and subsequently maintain the application of the principle that men and women should receive equal pay for equal work.

For the purposes of this Article "pay" means the ordinary basic or minimum wage or salary and any other such consideration, whether in cash or in kind, which the worker receives directly or indirectly, in respect of his employment from his employer.

Equal pay *without discrimination* based on sex means:

(a) that pay for the same work at piece rates shall be calculated on the basis of the same unit of measurement;
(b) that pay for work at time rates shall be the same for the same job."

Thus Article 119 refers to "equal pay without discrimination based on sex" but does not define discrimination. Similarly Article 1 of the Equal Pay Directive, in elaborating the definition of "equal pay" refers to "the elimination of discrimination on grounds of sex" but does not offer a definition of the key term itself.

The Equal Treatment Directive provides in Article 1 that:

"1. The purpose of this Directive is to put into effect in the Member States the principle of equal treatment for men and women as regards access to employment, including promotion, and to vocational training and as regards working conditions and, on the conditions referred to in paragraph 2, social security. The principle is hereinafter referred to as 'the principle of equal treatment'."

Article 2(1) goes on to provide that:

"For the purposes of the following provisions, the principle of equal treatment means that there shall be *no discrimination whatsoever on grounds of sex* either directly or indirectly by reference in particular to family or marital status." (emphasis added)

Article 3(1) provides that there shall be no discrimination whatsoever on grounds of sex in the conditions, including selection criteria, for access to all jobs or posts, whatever the sector or branch of activity, and to all levels of the occupational hierarchy" whilst Article 5(1) applies the principle of

---

[7] See paragraphs 1–30 to 1–32.
[8] See paragraphs 1–37 to 1–42 for a discussion of the status of the various Community law legislative measures.

equal treatment to working conditions, including the conditions governing dismissal . . . without discrimination on grounds of sex.''

Neither the Equal Pay Directive nor the Equal Treatment Directive define discrimination as such but simply refer to it, relying on the established case law of the ECJ as regards a concept which is central to much of Community law.[9] This has left the ECJ much more free than are the British courts when interpreting domestic equality legislation.

It is worth noting that as regards discrimination on grounds of marital status, British law protects only the married as against the single person, whereas the Equal Treatment Directive proscribes all discrimination on grounds of marital or family status, *i.e.* it protects both the single and the married person and would also seem to encompass such matters as divorce. As ''family status'' is distinguished from ''marital status'', arguably it encompasses a wider range of matters not directly related to marriage, such as maternity and motherhood.

The scope of the Equal Treatment Directive may also be wider than that of the domestic legislation, in that it may encompass transsexuality. In *P v. S and Cornwall County Council*[9a] a man was taken on in a managerial role in an educational setting. A year later he informed his employer that he intended to have a sex change operation. Soon afterwards she was dismissed. An industrial tribunal dismissed the employer's argument that her dismissal was on grounds of redundancy but was unable to find that the case fell within the Sex Discrimination Act which requires that a woman be treated less favourably than a man or vice versa. The Tribunal nonetheless referred to the European Court of Justice the question as to whether detrimental action taken on grounds of transsexuality was ''discrimination on grounds of sex'' contrary to Article 2(1) of the Equal Treatment Directive. Advocate General Tresauro has put forward the opinion that such discrimination does fall within the ambit of the Equal Treatment Directive, arguing that it is a fundamental value of modern legal traditions in the advanced countries that a person's sex is irrelevant to the rules regulating relations in society. Although the Advocate General acknowledged that the Court would be taking a ''courageous'' decision if it were to follow his lead, the Court of Justice held that ''Article 5(1) of the Equal Treatment Directive precludes dismissal of a transsexual for a reason related to his gender reassignment.'' The Court argued that discrimination arising from gender reassignment ''is based, essentially if not exclusively, on the sex of the person concerned'', in that ''he or she is treated unfavourably by comparison with persons of the sex to which he or she was deemed to belong before undergoing gender reassignment. To tolerate such discrimination would be tantamount, as regards such a person, to a failure to respect the dignity and freedom to which he or she is entitled and which the Court has a duty to respect.''

The emphasis which the Court placed on the protection of the dignity and freedom of the individual concerned, is linked to the emphasis which the Court places in this judgment, at points 17–18, on the principle of equal treatment for men and women, ''as an expression, in the relevant field, of the principle of equality, which is one of the fundamental principles of Community law.'' Not only is the argument linked to equality as a fundamental

---

[9] See paragraph 1–49 *et seq.* for discussion of the concepts of equality and discrimination in E.C. law and for a discussion of the status of ''principles'' in E.C. law.

[9a] C13/94; [1996] I.R.L.R. 347, ECJ.

principle of Community law, but also at point 19 to equality as "one of the fundamental human rights whose observance the Court has a duty to ensure." This broad argument, linking the treatment of transsexuals to questions of dignity and freedom and sex equality as a human right, suggests that the European Court of Justice would take a sympathetic view of any cases referred to it on grounds of sexual orientation. Should the Court of Justice adopt the view that questions of sexual orientation fall within the scope of the Equal Treatment Directive, there would be a clear distinction between that approach and that adopted by the U.K. courts under the Sex Discrimination Act.[9b]

In *R. v. Ministry of Defence ex p. Smith and Grady*[10] both male and female former members of the army and navy sought judicial review of the Armed Services "blanket" policy of dismissing homosexuals. The Court of Appeal, though seemingly sympathetic to the need for a review of the policy and alive to its effects upon the human rights of those affected, nonetheless formed the view that those who drafted the Equal Treatment Directive 20 years ago had only gender in mind and not sexual orientation.

The Disability Discrimination Act 1995 (DDA) wording on causation is rather different. The prohibited ground is stated in section 5(1)(a) as "for a reason which relates to the disabled person's disability." See chapter 3 on this point. It seems to us that the provision is capable of being construed very widely, particularly in view of the fact that it is possible to justify disability discrimination.

The elements of direct discrimination

"Treatment" on grounds of race or sex

2-03   It is the ground of the alleged discriminator's action which is important in cases of direct discrimination. It is unnecessary to show that the discriminator intended or wanted to discriminate if the effect of his actions is that women (or members of other racial groups) are treated less favourably by reason of their sex (or race). Thus in *R. v. Birmingham City Council ex p. EOC*[11] the Council inherited a situation where more grammar school places were provided for boys than girls, and all that it was necessary to prove to establish direct discrimination was that girls were thereby placed at a disadvantage, rather than that the Council intended to place girls at a disadvantage. Lord Goff of Chieveley put the matter as:

> "There is discrimination under the statute if there is less favourable treatment on grounds of sex, in other words if the relevant girl or girls would have received the same treatment as the boys but for their sex. The intention or motive of the defendant to discriminate, though it may be relevant so far as remedies are concerned . . . is not a necessary

---

[9b] The decision of the EAT in *Smith v. Gardner Merchant Ltd* [1996] I.R.L.R. 342 that harassment of a gay man on grounds of his sexual preferences fell outside the protection of the SDA or the Directive, must be questionable after *P v. S and Cornwall County Council.*

[10] [1996] I.R.L.R. 100, C.A.

[11] [1988] I.R.L.R. 430, C.A., [1989] I.R.L.R. 172, H.L.

condition of liability: it is perfectly possible to envisage cases where the defendant had no such motive, and yet did in fact discriminate on grounds of sex ... In the present case, whatever may have been the intention or motive of the Council, nevertheless it is because of their sex that the girls in question receive less favourable treatment than the boys and are the subject of discrimination under the Act of 1975.''

The "but for" test

Thus the *Birmingham City Council* decision disposes completely of the notion that it is necessary to have an intention to discriminate for an act to constitute direct discrimination. It is the ground of the respondent's action which is important; intentions or motives are irrelevant. A married couple, Mr and Mrs James, both aged 61 went swimming at their local pool, where the wife was permitted to swim free as a pensioner but the husband was charged 75p. Mr James' claim that he had been subjected to discrimination was dismissed in the County Court. His appeal was refused in the Court of Appeal, but allowed in the House of Lords. In *James v. Eastleigh Borough Council* [1990] Lord Goff held that[12]   **2-04**

"cases of direct discrimination under s.1(1)(a) can be considered by asking the simple question: would the complainant have received the same treatment from the defendant but for his or her sex? This simple test possesses the double virtue that, on the one hand, it embraces both the case where the treatment derives from the application of a gender based criterion and the case where it derives from the selection of the complainant because of his or her sex; and on the other hand it avoids, in most cases at least, complicated questions related to concepts such as intention, motive, reason or purpose, and the danger of confusion arising from the misuse of those elusive terms.''

Lord Goff identifies the requisite intention under section 1(1)(a) as simply an intention to perform the relevant act of less favourable treatment. Whether or not the treatment is less favourable in the relevant sense, *i.e.* on grounds of sex or race, may derive from the application of gender-or race-based criteria to the complainant, or from selection of the complainant because of his or her sex or race. On this reasoning the statutory pensionable age, being fixed at 60 for women and 65 for men, is itself a criterion which directly discriminates between men and women, and it follows that any differential treatment based upon it must equally involve discrimination on grounds of sex. Likewise, the ECJ in *Barber v. Guardian Royal Exchange Assurance Group*[13] held that: **2-05**

"it is contrary to Article 119 to impose an age condition which differs according to sex in respect of pensions ... even if the difference ... is based on the one provided for by the national statutory scheme.''

It is evident from the treatment of discrimination cases which are based upon the fact that the applicant is pregnant that the ECJ has adopted a test which is the functional equivalent of the "but for" test, although the Court has   **2-06**

---

[12] [1990] I.R.L.R. 288 at 295, para. 39.
[13] Case 262/88, [1990] I.R.L.R. 240, ECJ.

declined to spell out the precise basis of its reasoning. In *Dekker v. Stichting Vormigscentrum Voor Jonge Volwassen (VJV-Centrum) Plus*[14] the ECJ held that

> "As an employment can only be refused because of pregnancy to a woman, such a refusal is direct discrimination on grounds of sex."

This reasoning has been applied both to pregnancy itself and to the financial and/or administrative consequences of pregnancy, as where the employer is mainly concerned about the cost or difficulty of providing a replacement for the worker in question. In *Webb v. EMO (Air Cargo) Ltd*,[15] a woman recruited primarily as a maternity leave replacement found herself to be pregnant and due to give birth at much the same time as the woman whom she was replacing. As the Lords took the view that it was the complainants prospective absence from work which was the cause of her dismissal, rather than her pregnancy *per se*, they held that it was appropriate to compare her treatment with that of a hypothetical man who needed comparable time off, say, for an arthritic hip. The ECJ held that it was impermissible to compare absence arising from pregnancy of a woman on an indefinite contract[16] with the putative absence of a man who would be off sick for a comparable period and stated that:

> "(T)here can be no question of comparing the situation of a woman who finds herself incapable, by reason of pregnancy discovered very shortly after the conclusion of her employment contract, of performing the task for which she was recruited with that of a man similarly incapable for medical or other reasons . . ."

In this sense "but for" the fact of her pregnancy the complainant should not have been dismissed, whatever the other precise circumstances of her situation or the pressures upon her employer. Note, however, that in *Gillespie and others v. Northern Health and Social Services Board*,[17] in which a woman away on maternity leave claimed that she should receive normal pay, the Advocate General excluded the application of Article 119 and the Equal Pay Directive. He first restated the general proposition which encapsulates the concept of discrimination in Community law, *i.e.* "Discrimination can consist only in the application of different rules to comparable situations or else in the application of the same rule in different situations."[18] Relying on the passage in *Webb* quoted above, he concluded that it would be judicially incorrect to compare a woman away from work on maternity leave with a

---

[14] Case 177/88, [1991] I.R.L.R. 27 at para. 12, *Handels-Og Kontorfunktion aernes Forbund I Danmark (acting for Hertz) v. Dansk Arbedjdsgiverforening (acting for Aldi Marked K/S)* Case 179/88, [1991] I.R.L.R. 31, *Habermann-Beltermann v. Arbeiterwohlfahrt, Bezirksverband* Case C-421/92, [1994] I.R.L.R. 364; *Webb v. EMO Air Cargo (UK) Ltd* Case C-32/93, [1994] I.R.L.R. 482.

[15] Above.

[16] And see *Habermann-Beltermann v. Arbeiterwohlfahrt Begirksverband* C-421/92, [1994] I.R.L.R. 364.

[17] Case C-342/93.

[18] Recently retated by the Court in *Schumaker* Case C-279/93. The Advocate General further held that the provisions of the Equal Treatment Directive which allow for the protection of women in respect of pregnancy were permissive and left the capacity to settle such matters within the discretion of the Member States.

man working normally, because this would not constitute a comparison between a man and a woman under similar circumstances. The Court of Justice adopted a similar analysis, concluding that a woman away on maternity leave is in a position which "is not comparable with either that of a man or with that of a woman actually at work."

The principles of causation in sex discrimination cases were reviewed by Mummery J. in the EAT in *O'Neil v. Governors of St. Thomas More RC Upper School*, a case in which a Catholic teacher of religious education and personal relationships became pregnant by a Catholic priest who visited the school where she worked. After the matter entered the public domain the teacher was dismissed. The industrial tribunal held that the reason for her dismissal was not pregnancy *per se* but the fact that the applicant's position as a teacher of religious education and personal relationships in a Catholic school had become untenable. The EAT held that the tribunal were mistaken in considering the motives of the governors, rather than considering whether the dismissal was on the ground of sex, when all the other factors, such as paternity of the child and her position in the school, were causally related to the applicant's pregnancy, a condition which is unique to women. Pregnancy was the effective and predominant cause of the dismissal.

The "but for" test does not, however, dispense with the need for the decision in question to have been taken "on grounds of sex (or race)". A simple juxtaposition of a woman and a man who have received different treatment, or of two persons of different racial groups who have been treated differently, is insufficient. Thus, in *Bullock v. Alice Ottley School*[19] grounds and maintenance staff were allowed to retire at 65, but the common retirement age for administrative and domestic staff was 60. The EAT held that such differential retirement ages were contrary to the dictum of the House of Lords in *James*, but such a comparison of domestic and grounds staff does not establish that "but for" her sex a female domestic would have been treated any differently to a male in similar circumstances. It is submitted that, properly understood, the case illustrates the fact that the "but for" test still leaves a niche for indirect discrimination, in that direct discrimination must still occur on the grounds of sex or race or by the application of a race or gender based criterion. As the Court of Appeal emphasised, the comparison must be one of like with like and:

2-07

> "there is nothing in section 5(3) which prevents an employer having a variety of different retiring ages for different jobs, provided that in the system which he uses there is no direct or indirect discrimination based on gender. In a case of alleged direct discrimination the question is: would a man in the same job have been treated differently?"[20]

Similarly in *Barclays Bank Ltd v. Kapur (No. 2)*[21] the Court of Appeal held that East African Asians whose service in East Africa was not credited for

---

[19] [1991] I.R.L.R. 324.
[20] [1992] I.R.L.R. 564, C.A. *per* Neill L.J. at 568. The Court of Appeal also held that whilst such a requirement was undoubtedly indirectly discriminatory, it was justifiable due to the difficulties experienced in recruiting and retaining grounds and maintenance staffs.
[21] [1995] I.R.L.R. 87, C.A.

pensions purposes when they transferred to the U.K., were not treated unfavourably on racial grands, because they had already received compensation for their service in Kenya.

2-08   It is not necessary that the the sole reason why the complainant experienced discriminatory treatment shall be a racial or gender factor so long as it is an effective cause, according to the Court of Appeal in *Owen & Briggs v. James*,[21] a case in which a coloured applicant was turned down for a job when race was established as being at least an important part of the employer's reasons, even though not the sole reason. Where there are mixed motives for the doing of an act, one of which may be discriminatory, it is highly desirable that there be an assessment of the causative importance of that factor, according to Knox J. in the victimisation case of *Nagarajan v. Agnew*. He held that "If the industrial tribunal finds that the unlawful motive or motives were of sufficient weight in the decision making to be treated as a cause, not the sole cause but as a cause, of the act thus motivated, there will be unlawful discrimination. An important factor in the decision is clearly well within that principle."[21a] In *Seide v. Gillette Industries Ltd*[22] a Jewish workman was transferred away from an anti-semitic colleague and, when he sought to involve a new workmate in his former dispute, was transferred again so that he could be placed under more active management supervision. The EAT held that:

> "notwithstanding that the appellant might not have been transferred had he not been Jewish ... It does not seem to us to be sufficient merely to consider whether the fact that the person is a member of a particular racial group ... is any part of the background. ... (T)he question which has to be asked is whether the activating cause of what happens is that the employer has treated a person less favourably than others on racial grounds."[23]

At first sight this approach seems at variance with the "but for" test, although it would be possible to reconcile it with that test by reasoning that the complainant was moved because he attempted to involve a workmate in a personal dispute. In those circumstances a hypothetical comparison could be made between his situation and that of any other employee who attempted to involve a workmate in, say, a marital dispute, thus removing from the ambit of comparison the issue of race. In other words, it would not be true to say that "but for" his Jewishness the applicant would have been treated less favourably, if the comparison is made with a person who attempted to involve a colleague in some previous non-racial fracas, although this decision is now highly questionable.[24]

2-09   Even if the motives and intentions of the alleged discriminator are benign they do not overcome the discriminatory effect of his actions. It is certainly highly questionable, notwithstanding the decision in *Seide* above, to move the

[21] [1995] I.R.L.R. 87, C.A.
[21a] [1994] I.R.L.R. 61 at 65.
[22] [1982] I.R.L.R. 564.
[23] [1980] I.R.L.R. 427, EAT.
[24] See also *Barclays Bank plc v. Kapur* [1995] I.R.L.R. 87, C.A. at 91.

victim of discrimination or harassment in order to avoid further difficulties or industrial unrest.[25] In *Din v. Carrington Viyella*,[26] a Pakistani employee was not re-engaged on returning from a prolonged trip to his homeland. Just prior to his departure there had been some trouble between the applicant and his foreman which had not been resolved. The Industrial Tribunal found that the reason for not re-engaging the applicant was the employer's desire to avoid a repetition of the industrial unrest to which the previous incident had given rise. The EAT held that to seek to resolve actual or potential unrest by removing an employee against whom racial discrimination has been shown may itself be a discriminatory act, even if the employer acts from good motives. The EAT remitted the case to a freshly constituted tribunal to consider whether the potential industrial unrest, which was the proximate cause of the employer's action, was due to previous racial discrimination by a fellow employee for which the employer was responsible under section 32. Likewise, in *R. v. CRE ex p. Westminster City Council*[27] the employer moved a black dustman who had been the subject of discrimination by fellow employees, but such an action, though taken to avoid industrial action, was held to constitute less favourable treatment on racial grounds.

In *Greig v. Community Industry*[28] a YTS trainee was not allowed to start on   **2-10**
her course because, following the withdrawal of another girl, she would have been the only female member of a group which was to be engaged upon various building tasks. In those circumstances the employer felt that the one remaining girl might be the subject of unwelcome attentions from some of her fellow course members, but such an action was nonetheless held to be unlawful. Thus it is the reason for discriminatory acts and not intentions and motives which are important. If the discriminator performs an act on grounds of sex or race, his intentions or motives are irrelevant. The House of Lords makes clear in the *Birmingham* case that customer preference, saving money or avoiding controversy are not defences.

The comparison to be made

Any comparison made between persons of different genders, marital status   **2-11**
or racial group must be such that the relevant circumstances in the one case are the same, or not materially different, in the other.[29] Even though the need to compare like with like, to ensure that the relevant circumstances are the same in one case as the other, has been described as fairly obvious,[30] it has nonetheless given rise to not inconsiderable difficulties, especially in ensuring that the circumstances are gender-or race-neutral. For example, in *James v. Eastleigh Borough Council*[31] the Court of Appeal compared the treatment of persons of pensionable age and concluded that there was no direct discrimination between them. This decision was criticised by the majority in the Lords

---

[25] And in cases of sexual harrassment, incompatible with the E.C. Code of Conduct on the Protection of the Dignity of Men and Women at Work.
[26] [1982] I.C.R. 256.
[27] [1985] I.C.R. 827, C.A.; affirming [1984] I.C.R. 770, EAT.
[28] [1979] I.C.R. 356.
[29] SDA 1975, s.5(3) and RRA 1976, s.3(4).
[30] *Bain v. Bowles* [1991] I.R.L.R. 356, C.A.
[31] [1990] I.R.L.R. 288; [1989] I.R.L.R. 318, C.A.

on the ground that in comparing persons of pensionable age, the comparison itself was gender-based, so that the Court of Appeal was not comparing like with like. The true comparison was between men and women age 61, between whom the application of a gender based criterion, *i.e.* pensionable age, caused a discriminatory differentiation in their treatment. The matter was put clearly by Browne-Wilkinson J. (as he then was) in *Showboat Centre v. Owens*[32]:

> "Although one has to compare like with like, in judging whether there has been discrimination you have to compare the treatment actually meted out with the treatment which would have been afforded to a man having all the same characteristics as the complainant except his race or his attitude to race. Only by excluding matters of race can you discover whether the differential treatment was on racial grounds."

2-12   The decision of the Court of Appeal in *Dhatt v. McDonalds Hamburgers Ltd*[33] is more problematic. In *Dhatt* a young man of Indian nationality who had entered the U.K. as a child with indefinite permission to stay, and who did not therefore need a work permit, applied for a job with McDonalds. The application form included the following question "If you are not a British citizen or from the EEC, do you have a permit to work in Britain? Yes/No. If yes, please provide evidence." Ultimately he was dismissed by an assistant manager who did not appreciate that the stamp in the applicant's passport "Given leave to enter the U.K. for an indefinite period" indicated that he was not subject to any restrictions as to his seeking work. The appellant claimed that comparison should be made between two young men otherwise qualified for the post, one of whom was a British or EEC national whilst the other was not. Any difference in treatment was contended to be on grounds of nationality. The Court of Appeal took the view that the appropriate comparison was not that between U.K. or EEC nationals and others, because that would not be to compare like with like; U.K. and EEC nationals do not need work permits, as other nationals normally do. The correct comparison was held to be between persons of different nationalities, each of which needed a work permit. This approach places the admittedly racially tainted factor of needing a work permit outside the ambit of comparison on the ground that it is a distinction sanctioned by Parliament in the context of immigration rules. *James* was distinguished on the ground that the adoption of pensionable age by the local authority was a voluntary act, whereas in this context even though there is no express obligation on employers to ensure that employees comply with immigration law and are free to work, there is a general obligation on employers to ensure that employees who work in their businesses are free to do so.[34] The Court of Appeal appears to have approached this question by the circuitous route of adapting the scope of comparison, perhaps because RRA, s.41, which governs conflicts between the RRA and other statutory rules, seems not to have been cited.

2-13   In *Bain v. Bowles*,[35] the proprietors of "The Lady" refused to place an

---

[32] [1984] I.R.L.R. 7, EAT.
[33] [1991] I.R.L.R. 130, I.C.R. 238, C.A.
[34] This decision has been heavily criticised by Ross in I.L.J., 20, 3, pp. 208–214, both on the ground that it takes nationality into the ground of comparison and because it ignores the operation of RRA, s.41.
[35] [1991] I.R.L.R. 356.

advertisement for a housekeeper from a single gentleman living in Tuscany in their magazine. It was the policy of the magazine not to place such advertisements for positions abroad unless there was a woman resident in the household concerned, as it was considered from experience that women who answered such advertisements might otherwise find themselves in a vulnerable position. The defendant magazine proprietors sought to argue that in any comparison to be made as to whether a like advertisement would have been accepted from a woman, the putative fate of those who might respond to the advertisement was one of the relevant circumstances. The Court of Appeal held, however, that the only relevant circumstances were those which concerned the placing of the advertisement and not subsequent events which might or might not occur, for if the motives of the defendants were to be encompassed the result would be inconsistent with *James v. Eastleigh Borough Council.*

The "but for" test gave rise to difficulties for the Court of Appeal in *Shomer*   **2-14**
v. B. & R. Residential Lettings Ltd,[36] in which a negotiator for a residential lettings company became pregnant and, having agreed that her employment would terminate in approximately three months time, went on holiday for two weeks. Good negotiators were, it was agreed, in short supply, so Mrs Shomer was a valued employee. Just prior to her leaving for her holiday, the firm engaged a chauffeur to drive clients to appointments and as no other car was immediately available, the managing director of the firm ordered Mrs Shomer to return her company car whilst she was away on holiday. In the event she left it parked at Gatwick whilst she was away, but returned to find a notice of dismissal posted by hand through her letter box. In alleging that her dismissal was the result of her pregnancy, the appellant pointed to the fact that a replacement had been engaged to start when she left and, once the managing director had ascertained that the replacement could start within the next two weeks, her dismissal for alleged misconduct was contrived. Her claim was supported by a majority of the Industrial Tribunal members, who based themselves on *Hayes v. Malleable Castings* but concluded that a sick or disabled man who would have had to leave in three months time would not have been dismissed. The EAT held that this decision was perverse, but the Court of Appeal preferred to base themselves on the view that the Industrial Tribunal had ignored the necessity for the comparable sick man to have committed some misconduct, or alternatively that the decision was perverse in that there was no evidence to suggest that a sick man who had committed some comparable act of misconduct would not have been dismissed. It is clear that the application of the "but for" test does not eliminate all difficulties and great care is needed to determine the appropriate ground of comparison.

"Less favourable treatment"

Direct discrimination occurs where a person is less favourably treated by   **2-15**
virtue of their sex or on racial grounds.[37] Less favourable treatment is gener-

---

[36] [19921] I.R.L.R. 317.
[37] Where the issue concerns a condition which is unique to women (pregnancy) it is difficult to make comparison with treatment which would be afforded to men; see paragraph 2–28 below.

ally associated with a narrowing of opportunities, a deprivation of choice which is experienced as a detriment. In *Jeremiah v. MoD*[38] Brightman L.J. put the matter as follows:

"I do not say that the mere deprivation of choice for one sex, or some differentiation in their treatment, is necessarily unlawful discrimination. The deprivation of choice, or differentiation, must be associated with a detriment. It is possible to imagine a case where one sex has a choice but the other does not, yet there is nevertheless no detriment to the latter sex and therefore no unlawful discrimination."

2-16 Likewise in *R. v. Birmingham City Council, ex p. EOC*, the House of Lords held that the loss of a chance of something reasonably considered to be of value, *i.e.* the diminished possibility of a grammar school place, constituted less favourable treatment. It was not necessary for the EOC "to show that the selective system was 'better' than non-selective education. It was enough that, by denying the girls the same opportunity as the boys, the council was depriving them of a choice, which (as the facts showed) was valued by them, or at least by their parents, and which (even though others may take a different view) was a choice obviously valued, on reasonable grounds, by many others."[39]

2-17 Under the Race Relations Act, s.1(1)(2) it is declared that to segregate a person from other persons on racial grounds is to treat him less favourably than they are treated. In *PEL Ltd v. Modgill*[40] the EAT held that if there is evidence of a policy to segregate, or of the fact of segregation arising from an employer's act, there may be a breach of section 1(1)(2) but where, as in this case, a shop had been staffed entirely with Asian workers who had recommended their friends and relatives for employment, a failure to recruit non-Asian workers did not constitute less favourable treatment.[41]

Stereotyped assumptions
2-18 It is characteristic of discriminatory behaviour to treat all the members of a group as possessing some ascribed characteristic and then to act on the basis of that characteristic. For example, in *Alexander v. Home Office*,[42] a West Indian prisoner whose request to work in the kitchens was refused, was described in his induction report as showing "the anti-authoritarian arrogance that seems to be common in most coloured inmates." It was found that this had the effect of not treating him as an individual but as an example of a damaging racial stereotype. Similarly, in *Hurley v. Mustoe*,[43] women with children were considered as a group to be unreliable. Likewise it may be thought that husbands are likely to be the breadwinners in a family[44] or that

---

[38] [1979] I.R.L.R. 436, C.A. 440.
[39] *Supra* at [?].
[40] [1980] I.R.L.R. 142, EAT.
[41] It should be noted, however, that the complaints in this case arose from the segregated workers themselves. Had the complaint arisen from a rejected applicant for a job, the employer may have been held to be liable for less favourable treatment, which would not have been based upon the s.1(1)(2) definition of segregation.
[42] [1988] I.R.L.R. 190, C.A.
[43] Note 1 above.
[44] *Coleman v. Skyrail Oceanic* [1981] I.R.L.R. 398, C.A.

wives are more likely to follow the careers of their husbands than vice versa.[45] These are all examples of less favourable treatment based upon generalised examples about the characteristics of one sex or the other, in which the employer failed to investigate the true position of the individual in question. That is not to say that characteristics which may be generally ascribed to one sex or to a racial group may not be relevant to, say, an applicant's suitability for a job or for promotion. What is important is that the decision should be based upon the degree to which the particular individual possesses that characteristic, rather than upon an assumption.[46]

Less favourable treatment on racial grounds

Where section 1 of the Race Relations Act deals with direct discrimination,   **2-19** it refers to "racial grounds," and where it deals with indirect discrimination refers to "racial group." These expressions are defined by section 3 of the Act, though in practice those definitions have become overlaid by case law. "Racial grounds" means on the grounds of colour, race, nationality, ethnic or national origins.

The act complained of has to be taken on racial grounds under the Race Relations Act, s.1(1)(a). These words can encompass any actions based upon race, whether or not it is the race of the person who is affected by the action. Thus a white employee who was dismissed when he refused to obey an order to exclude young blacks from an amusement arcade in *Showboat Entertainments Centre v. Owens*[47] was held to have been discriminated against on racial grounds.[48] By contrast, under the Sex Discrimination Act, s.1(1)(a), the discrimination has to be based upon her sex, *i.e.* the sex of the person bringing the complaint, so that a situation analogous to that in *Owens* but based on questions of gender (or marital status under section 3) would not be encompassed by the legislation. Likewise, the Disability Discrimination Act prohibits discrimination only for a reason which relates to the disabled person's disability, under s.5(2).

"National origin"

"Nationality" was added as a ground in the 1976 Act because of the earlier House of Lords decision in *Ealing London Borough Council v. Race Relations Board*[49], to the effect that "national origins" meant race as opposed to nationality, (so that discrimination against a Polish national was not under that earlier legislation unlawful). Despite the changed definition the Ealing decision continues to cause problems. It was followed by the Court of Appeal in *Tejani v. Superintendent Registrar for the District of Peterborough*[50] which concerned a British national born abroad. He was required to produce his passport before marriage, as were all persons coming from abroad. National origin was held to have a racial connotation and mean more than merely

---

[45] *Horsey v. Dyfed County Council* [1982] I.C.R. 755.
[46] See also *Perera v. Civil Service Commission & Department of Customs & Excise* 1983 I.R.L.R. 166, C.A. on the question of proficiency in English and see *Coyne v. Export Credits Guarantee Department* [1981] I.R.L.R. 51, and equal pay case turning upon similar issues.
[47] [1984] 1 W.L.R. 384.
[48] See also *Zarczynska v. Levy*, I.C.R. 184, [1978] I.R.L.R. 532, EAT.
[49] [1972] A.C. 342.
[50] [1986] I.R.L.R. 502.

coming from abroad, so Mr Tejani's claim of discrimination failed. (The Tejani decision stands as a general warning to all litigants in race cases: the point on which the Court of Appeal decided the case was not one on which the parties to the appeal had chosen to argue it, but suggested by the Court itself.)

2-20 The 1976 Act does not say that the colour, race, nationality, ethnic or national origins need be that of the applicant or plaintiff. Accordingly racial discrimination can involve treating a person less favourably because of another's colour, etc. In *Zarczynska v. Levy*[51] the EAT held that it was unlawful discrimination where the applicant was dismissed for serving a black customer contrary to her employer's instructions. There was a similar decision in *Showboat Entertainment Centre Ltd v. Owens*.[52] Thus the legislation does not limit the racial grounds to the position of the applicant. But the same protection appears not to exist under the SDA as that legislation is differently worded in this respect.

Racial group
2-21 The Act says: "'racial group' means a group of persons defined by reference to colour, race, nationality, ethnic or national origins." The section goes on to say that: "The fact that a group comprises two or more distinct racial groups does not prevent it from constituting a particular racial group for the purpose of this Act."

Whereas the word "race" has some connotation of common stock, the House of Lords in *Mandla v. Dowell Lee*[53] construed the meaning of "ethnic" relatively widely in a broad, cultural historic sense. Lord Fraser of Tullybelton approved a passage from the judgement of Richardson J. in the New Zealand Court of Appeal in *King-Ansell v. Police*[54]:

> "a group is identifiable in terms of its ethnic origins if it is a segment of the population distinguished from others by a sufficient combination of shared customs, beliefs, traditions and characteristics derived from a common or presumed common past, even if not drawn from what in biological terms is a common racial stock. It is that combination which gives them an historically determined social identity in their own eyes and in the eyes of those outside the group. They have a distinct social identity based not simply on group cohesion and solidarity but also on their belief as to their historical antecedents."

In that case it had been held that Jews in New Zealand formed a group with common ethnic origins for the purposes of a statute under which the appellant had been convicted:

> "that with intent to excite ill-will against a group of persons in New Zealand, namely, Jews on the ground of their ethnic origins, did publish written matter, namely a pamphlet which was insulting and likely to excite ill-will against the said group of persons."

---

[51] [1978] I.R.L.R. 532.
[52] [1984] I.R.L.R. 7, EAT.
[53] [1983] 2 A.C. 548.
[54] [1979] 2 N.Z.L.R. 531, at 543.

Jews were held by the New Zealand Court to be a racial group in the sense of an ethnic grouping applying Richardson J.'s criteria even though the evidence before the magistrate had been that: "there is no biological means of establishing that Jewish people are a race and that members of the Jewish People have diverse racial origins." The court also went on to say that: "The Magistrate was satisfied that Jewishness was much more than a matter of religion only."[55]

Does an ethnic group exist?

The national origins of the immigrant population of Great Britain may for many of them from day to day become less important than their religious groupings. Whilst Sikhs were held to be an ethnic group, the Birmingham Industrial Tribunal in *Tariq v. Young*[56] held that Muslims are not a racial but simply a religious group. The industrial tribunal in *Crown Suppliers v. Dawkins*, after hearing expert evidence accepted that Rastafarians were an ethnic group, but the EAT concluded that they were not, a view sustained in the Court of Appeal.[57]

2-22

Mandla v. Dowell Lee[58] is the leading case on the criteria to be applied in establishing whether an ethnic group exists. The House of Lords decided that Sikhs were a distinct ethnic group. The case was followed by the Court of Appeal in *CRE v. Dutton*[59] who decided that Gipsies were an ethnic group. In *Mandla* at 562 Lord Fraser set out the position as follows:

> "For a group to constitute an ethnic group in the sense of the Act of 1976, it must, in my opinion, regard itself, and be regarded by others, as a distinct community by virtue of certain characteristics. Some of these characteristics are essential; others are not essential but one or more of them will commonly be found and will help to distinguish the group from the surrounding community. The conditions which appear to me to be essential are these: (1) a long shared history, of which the group is conscious as distinguishing it from other groups, and the memory of which it keeps alive; (2) a cultural tradition of its own, including family and social customs and manners, often but not necessarily associated with religious observance. In addition to these two essential characteristics the following characteristics are, in my opinion, relevant; (3) either a common geographical origin, or descent from a number of common ancestors; (4) a common language, not necessarily peculiar to the group; (5) a common literature peculiar to the group; (6) a common religion different from that of neighbouring groups or from the general community surrounding it; (7) being a minority or being an oppressed or dominant group within a larger community, for example (say, the inhabitants of England shortly after the Norman conquest and their conquerors might both be ethnic groups.) A group defined by reference to enough of these characteristics would be capable of including converts, for example, persons who marry into the group, and of exclud-

---

[55] See also *Seide v. Gillette Industries Ltd*, above on the position of Jews.
[56] Case 247738/88, EOR Discrimination Case Law Digest No. 2.
[57] *The Crown Suppliers (PSA) v. Dawkins*, [1991] I.R.L.R. 327, EAT. *Dawkins v. Department of the Environment, sub nom Crown Suppliers PSA* [1993] I.R.L.R. 284, C.A.
[58] See above, n. 53.
[59] [1989] I.R.L.R. 8, C.A.

ing apostates. Provided a person who joins the group feels himself or herself to be a member of it, and is accepted by other members, then he is, for the purposes of the Act, a member. That appears to be consistent with the words at the end of section 3(1): 'reference to a person's racial group refers to any racial group into which he falls.' In my opinion, it is possible for a person to fall into a particular racial group either by birth or adherence, and it makes no difference, so far as the Act of 1976 is concerned, by which route he finds his way into the group.''

In fact it was largely conceded that Sikhs met the wider definition of ethnic group, so Lord Fraser merely summarised the evidence on this point. He said:[60]

"They were originally a religious community founded about the end of the 15th Century in the Punjab by Guru Nanak, who was born in 1469. But the community is no longer purely religious in character. Their present position is summarised sufficiently for present purposes in the opinion of the learned judge in the County Court in the following passage: 'The evidence in my judgement shows that Sikhs are a distinctive and self-conscious community. They have a history going back to the 15th Century. They have a written language which a small proportion of Sikhs can read but which can be read by a much higher proportion of Sikhs than of Hindus. They were at one time politically supreme in the Punjab'.''

2-23   In *CRE v. Dutton*[61] Nicholls L.J. summarised the state of the evidence on this issue as follows:

"On the evidence it is clear that such Gipsies are a minority, with a long-shared history and a common geographical origin. They are a people who originated in northern India. They migrated thence to Europe through Persia in medieval times. They have certain, albeit limited, customs of their own, regarding cooking and the manner of washing. They have a distinctive, traditional style of dressing, with heavy jewellery worn by the women, (although this dress is not worn all the time). They also furnish their caravans in a distinctive manner. They have a language or dialect, known as 'pogadi chib,' spoken by English Gipsies (Romany chals) and Welsh Gipsies (kale) which consists of up to one fifth of Romany words in place of English words. They do not have a common literature of their own, but they have a repertoire of folktales and music passed on from one generation to the next. No doubt, after all the centuries which have passed since the first Gipsies left the Punjab, Gipsies are no longer derived from what, in biological terms, is a common racial stock, but that of itself does not prevent them from being a racial group as widely defined in the Act.I come now to the part of the case which has caused me most difficulty. Gipsies prefer to be called 'travellers' as they think the term is less derogatory. This might suggest a wish to lose their separate distinctive identity so far as the general public is concerned. Half or more of them now live in houses like most other people.

[60] At p. 565.
[61] *Supra*, n. 59.

Have Gipsies now lost their separate, group identity, so that they are no longer a community recognisable by ethnic origins within the meaning of the Act? The judge held that they had. This is a finding of fact. Nevertheless, with respect to the judge, I do not think that there was before him any evidence justifying his conclusion that Gipsies have been absorbed into a larger group, if by that he meant that substantially all Gipsies have been so absorbed. The fact that some have been so absorbed and are indistinguishable from any ordinary member of the public, is not sufficient in itself to establish loss of what Richardson J.[62] referred to as an historically determined social identity in own eyes and in the eyes of those outside the group. There was some evidence to the contrary from Mr Mercer, upon whose testimony the judge expressed no adverse comment "we know who are members of our community" and that "we know we are different." In my view the evidence was sufficient to establish that, despite their long presence in England, Gipsies have not merged wholly in the population, as have the Saxons and the Danes, and altogether lost their separate identity. They, or many of them, have retained in separateness, a self-awareness of still being Gipsies."

Following the *Mandla* criteria it has been held by the EAT that language is only one of a number of factors in deciding upon the existence or otherwise of an ethnic group and not decisive in itself. Accordingly, it was not possible to divide up the Welsh people into two ethnic groups comprising those who do and those who do not speak Welsh, at least on the basis of the language criteria.[63]   **2-24**

As section 3 of the 1976 Act recognises, a person will in fact belong to several racial groups for the purposes of the Act at the same time, and the relevant group will depend on the circumstances of the case.

Less favourable treatment "On grounds of her sex"

The Sex Discrimination Act 1975, s.1(1)(a) provides that discrimination occurs "if, on the ground of her sex he treats her less favourably than he treats or would treat a man." Most of the problems with this definition occur either where there is no direct comparison to be made between men and women or where the circumstances of men and women are likely to be materially different, whether for biological or socially constructed reasons.   **2-25**

Special concern for women

A comparable issue arises where the employer acts out of concern for the welfare of one sex, perhaps giving special consideration to the needs of women. In *Peake v. Automotive Products Ltd*[64] the employer allowed the women to leave work five minutes before the men, in order that they should   **2-26**

---

[62] See *King-Ansell* case at p.543.
[63] *Gwynedd County Council v. Jones* [1986] I.C.R. 833.
[64] [1977] I.C.R. 968.

not be jostled in the rush for the buses.[65] One of the able-bodied men complained that the rule was discriminatory. The Court of Appeal rejected the application on two grounds, firstly, that the rule was formulated on grounds of safety, chivalry and good administrative practice and secondly, that the wrong complained of was such as trivial nature that it came within the reach of the doctrine *de minimis non curat lex*.[66]

2-27   In the subsequent case of *Jeremiah v MOD*[67] Lord Denning M.R. held that the only sound ground for his judgement in the Peake case was the *de minimis* rule, *i.e.* that differentiation in the interests of chivalry, safety and good administrative practice was not an adequate justification for an otherwise discriminatory practice.[68] In *Jeremiah* men were from time to time required to work in the colour bursting shop of an ordnance factory, which was dusty and dirty work. No such requirement was made of women. It was not a sufficient justification of this rule that it was introduced out of deference to the wishes of women workers. Nor did 4p an hour obnoxious money compensate for any detrimental aspects of the work, for it is contrary to the Sex Discrimination Act, s.77 or the Race Relations Act, s.72 to attempt to contract out of the provisions of anti-discrimination law.

Pregnancy

2-28   The treatment of pregnancy is but the most obvious example of the fact that in making the central test of discrimination law a comparison with a similarly situated man, whether real or hypothetical, no allowance is made for the way in which either sex, or the social construction of gender, make women distinct from men. How far though does the law genuinely accommodate pregnancy and motherhood and make appropriate allowance for them? Section 1(1)(a) of the 1975 Act calls for a woman to have been treated less favourably than a man would have been treated, but what is to happen when the woman is pregnant, or suffering from any other condition which is unique to women.[69] Since it is absurd to postulate a pregnant man, what approach is to be adopted? In *Turley v. Allders Department Store*[70] the majority of the EAT held that a dismissal on grounds of pregnancy could not be discriminatory as there is no masculine counterpart to pregnancy. The minority held that as pregnancy is a medical condition, the appropriate comparison is with a man

---

[65] By chance one of the authors was formerly employed at the firm in question and can personally vouch for the likelihood of being trampled in the rush to leave work at the end of the day. The rule covered all women and disabled men. cf. *Hayes v. Malleable Working Men's Club* (see above).

[66] Literally "the law does not deal with trifles."

[67] See above.

[68] cf. *Page v. Freighthire (Tank Haulage) Ltd* [1981] I.C.R. 229 in which it was held that the only exceptions to the requirement not to discriminate are those prescribed in the Acts, so that only the breach of a statutory safety requirement could justify otherwise discriminatory working practices. The Employment Act 1989 has further narrowed this exception to those safety procedures which deal with a reproductive or foetal risk (see para. 2–93).

[69] In the I.T. case of *Reynolds v. Mitsubishi Trust and Banking Corporation* Case No. 14003/91, DCLD 13 dismissal on grounds that the employee was to have a hystorectomy was held to be directly discriminatory.

[70] [1980] I.C.R. 66.

suffering from some other medical condition, as, for example, a man who
needs a hernia operation, who will require comparable time off. In the subsequent case of *Hayes v. Malleable Working Men's Club and Institute*[71] the
EAT declined to follow the majority in *Turley*, preferring to compare a pregnant woman to a sick man and concluding that the applicant's treatment was
less favourable than that which would have been accorded to a man.

Even though the EAT was endeavouring to be sympathetic to the woman   **2-29**
and to recognise the problem associated with pregnancy, the comparison with
a sick man has unfortunate connotations. Pregnancy is unique to women and
a "normal" part of the lives of the great majority of women. It is not in any
sense pathological, and therefore the comparison with a sick or disabled man
is arguably inappropriate. An illness which necessitated as much time off as
is normal for maternity leave would be relatively serious and not something
which the majority of men would ever experience during their working lives.
Thus, in assimilating the experience of pregnant women to that of the long
term sick or disabled man, no recognition is given to the "normality" of
pregnancy and the fact that it is a usual facet of life for younger women.
This difficulty has been expressed as the using of a "male norm" on which
to build the concept of equality,[72] which fails to recognise the fact that the
possibility of pregnancy is intrinsic to the female condition. Some employers,
mainly in the banking and finance sectors which rely heavily on the services
of women, have instituted a recognised pattern of "career breaks". These
schemes attempt to reconcile the needs of motherhood and career and tend
to "normalise" maternity but this practice is the exception rather than the
rule.

In judging what constitutes less favourable treatment on grounds of sex or   **2-30**
marriage, section 5(3) of the Sex Discrimination Act requires that the comparison must be such that "the relevant circumstances in the one case are the
same, or not materially different, in the other", whilst the Race Relations
Act, s.3(4) requires the same to be true when comparisons are made on racial
grounds. But what constitutes less favourable treatment when the behaviour
in question has no counterpart in the other sex, such as is the case with
pregnancy? At first sight it might seem uncontroversial to apply the "but
for" test in *James v. Eastleigh Borough Council* to pregnancy cases by concluding that "but for" the fact that she is female a woman could not be
dismissed or refused employment on grounds of pregnancy. *Webb v. EMO
Air Cargo*[73] concerned a woman taken on as a maternity leave replacement
who turned out to be pregnant and expecting her child quite soon after the
woman whom she was replacing. Consequently Mrs Webb was dismissed.
The Court of Appeal could not accept her argument that since only a woman
can be pregnant, a woman dismissed for any reason related to her pregnancy
would not have been dismissed but for her sex. The notion of an inherent
comparison with a man was rejected, on the ground that "it does not, of

---

[71] [1985] I.C.R. 703.
[72] Sandra Fredman, "European Community Discrimination Law: A Critique" *Industrial Law
Journal*, 21, 2, pp. 119–134 and the references given therein.
[73] (No.2) [1995] I.R.L.R. 645, H.L.; (No.1) [1994] I.R.L.R. 482, ECJ; [1993] I.R.L.R. 27, H.L.;
[1992] I.R.L.R. 116 C.A.; [1990] I.R.L.R. 124, EAT.

itself, provide any comparisons with the reasons why a man might be dismissed from the same employment.''

2-31   The House of Lords based themselves firmly on the view that Ms Webb was dismissed because of her projected absence at the time when her services would be needed and not directly on her grounds of her pregnancy. The Lords recognised, however, that a dismissal or failure to employ which was based on pregnancy would constitute the application of a gender based criterion which would be directly discriminatory.

Pregnancy in Community Law

2-32   In the *Dekker*[74] case, the complainant was a pregnant woman who was selected as the most suitable candidate for the post of training instructor in a youth centre run by the employers. The Board of the Centre refused to endorse her appointment because she was already pregnant, as she had told the selection committee at her interview, with the result that the employers would have been unable to reclaim the cost of a temporary replacement during her maternity leave from their insurers. Although there had been no male candidates for the post, Mrs Dekker claimed that her refusal of employment was discriminatory. The case was referred to the ECJ by the Dutch courts under Article 177 to ascertain whether the employer was in breach of the Equal Treatment Directive. The ECJ concluded:

> "As employment can only be refused because of pregnancy to women, such a refusal is direct discrimination on grounds of sex. A refusal to employ because of the financial consequences of absence connected with pregnancy must be deemed to be based principally on the fact of the pregnancy. Such discrimination cannot be justified by the financial detriment in the case of a pregnant woman suffered by the employer during her maternity leave.''

The implication of this proposition is that direct discrimination cannot be justified under Community law, in that such justification cannot be established even if "the employer is more or less compelled not to recruit pregnant women." The ECJ also held that it is not relevant that there were no male candidates for the position.

2-33   The Court in *Dekker*[75] was also required to consider if it was relevant whether the employer was at fault in committing the discriminatory act. The Court concluded that fault was not a necessary component of liability for a discriminatory act, on the basis that exceptions to the principle of equal treatment are stipulated in Article 2(2)–(4) and that these do not include a provision for the respondent to be shown to be at fault. In this the ECJ took a view consistent with the "but for" test in *James v. Eastleigh Borough Council* i.e. that it is the effect of the action and not the intention of the discriminator which is important.

2-34   Neither did the ECJ consider that a discriminatory act which is caught by

---

[74] Case 177/88, *Dekker* v. *Stichting Vormingscentrum voor Jonge Volwassen (VJV-Centrum)*: [1991] I.R.L.R. 27 at para. 12.
[75] See above.

the Equal Treatment Directive could be justified by restrictions on liability contained in the national legal system. In *Dekker* the problem arose for the employer because of the interrelation between the requirements of the Directive and the application of the national law concerned with the financing of sick pay. The ECJ was nonetheless clear that "no account can be taken of grounds of justification provided for under national law."[76] This robust rejection of the possibility of justifying direct discrimination[77] is in line with the absence of any such provision in U.K. law.

In the *Hertz*[78] case, decided on the same day as *Dekker*, a woman had considerable time off as a result of an illness originating in pregnancy and was eventually dismissed on grounds of her non-attendance. The ECJ held that whilst it would be contrary to the terms of the Equal Treatment Directive to dismiss a woman because of her pregnancy, the question of illnesses which have their origins in pregnancy is not directly dealt with. Article 2(3), however, allows Member States to create specific rights for the protection of women, particularly as regards pregnancy and maternity, and in the view of the ECJ it "follows that during the maternity leave from which she benefits under national law, a woman is protected from dismissal because of her absence".[79] Thus there arises a period of special protection for pregnant women from the inception of pregnancy to the completion of maternity leave, which is now defined in sections $ 33–38A of the Employment Protection (Consolidation) Act 1978 as lasting some 14 weeks. This provision implements the provisions of the Pregnancy Directive 92/85.

2-35

The ECJ in *Webb* held that:

2-36

> "there can be no question of comparing the situation of a woman who finds herself incapable, by reason of pregnancy discovered very shortly after the conclusion of the employment contract, of performing the task for which she was recruited with that of a man similarly incapable for medical or other reasons. (P)regnancy is not in any way comparable with a pathological condition, and even less so with unavailability for work on non-medical grounds, both of which are situations that may justify the dismissal of a woman without discriminating on grounds of sex."[80]

However, the ECJ left an avenue of escape open to employers in *Webb*-type circumstances by limiting the application of the above principle to situ-

---

[76] At para 26. This conclusion can also be seen as an expression of the principle of the supremacy of Community law.

[77] See also *Roberts v. Birds Eye Walls Ltd* at n 6.46 in the context of equal pay.

[78] Case 179/88, *Handels-og Kontorfunktionaernes Forbund I Danmark (acting for Hertz) v. Dansk Arbejdgiverforening (acting for Aldi Marked K/S)*: [1991] I.R.L.R. 31.

[79] In *Brown v. Rentokil Ltd* [1995] I.R.L.R. 21 the Court of Session extended the effect of *Hertz* so as to exclude illness arising from pregnancy "unless a provision giving protection applies under the employers national law". As the applicant lacked the service necessary for qualification for unfair dismissal protection at that time and dismissal was as a result of illness not pregnancy *per se*, the Court of Session dismissed the appeal. Yet *Hertz* clearly is dealing with issues outside pregnancy and maternity leave whilst Mrs Brown was still inside her period of maternity leave when dismissed.

[80] Points 24 and 25.

ations where a woman has been recruited for an indefinite period,[81] rather than for a limited term simply to cover the maternity leave. However, outside of such special circumstances, the protection of pregnant women does not depend upon their ability to perform the tasks for which they were recruited, according to the ECJ, which places its ruling in the context of the protections subsequently afforded to pregnant women by Directive 92/85.[82] The Pregnancy Directive prohibits the dismissal of workers during pregnancy and maternity leave, save in exceptional circumstances not connected with their condition, and the decision in *Webb* can be seen to be interpreting the Equal Treatment Directive in such a way as to accord with that approach.

Webb represents a strong case of the principle that because pregnancy is a condition unique to women, any dismissal or other detrimental act must be discriminatory. In this sense it is not a question of comparing the treatment of even a hypothetical man in such a situation, but what Ellis regretfully terms as identifying "nasty treatment" on grounds of sex.[83]

On the return of *Webb* to the House of Lords,[84] Lord Keith of Kinkel, giving the judgement of the House, reconciled their earlier ruling with that of the ECJ by holding that the fact that pregnancy was the reason for the employee's absence was a circumstance relevant to her case, which could not be present in the case of a hypothetical man. Lord Keith followed the distinction made by the ECJ between the case of a woman engaged for an indefinite period and one engaged for a fixed period, during the whole of which she would be unavailable by reason of pregnancy, when the fact of her pregnancy might not be considered as a relevant circumstance in any dismissal or non-engagement.

However, employers should be wary of thinking that this aspect of the House of Lords decision in *Webb* provides an obvious escape route from their obligations towards pregnant employees. The EAT emphasised in *Caruana v. Manchester Airport plc* that it is only where an employee will be unavailable for work during the whole of the period of a fixed term contract that the exception posited by Lord Keigh could apply. In *Caruana* a woman was engaged under a series of fixed term contracts as an independent subcontractor providing archival services to the respondent. After she gave notice of her intention to take maternity leave, she was told that her contract would not be renewed on the expiry of the current term. Baxter J. in the EAT held that such were not the circumstances contemplated by Lord Keith, and that to exclude such a woman from the protection of the rule in *Webb* would be "a positive encouragement to employers to impose a series of short term contracts to avoid the impact of discrimination law, rather than offer a continuous and stable employment. Neither the ECJ nor the House of Lords did or would support such an approach." Neither could Baxter J. find any material in the ECJ's ruling on which to ground any exceptions to the rule in *Webb*.[84a]

---

[81] C-421/92, *Habermann–Beltermann v. Arbeiterwohlfahrt Bezirksverband Ndb/OpfeV*: [1994] 364, ECJ in which it was held to be discriminatory to terminate the contract of a pregnant woman night attendant by reason of a German national provision limiting night work for pregnant women, where that woman was engaged under an indefinite contract.

[82] Council Directive 92/85 on the introduction of measures to encourage improvements in the health and safety of pregnant workers and workers who have given birth and are breastfeeding.

[83] See above.

[84] *Webb v. EMO (Air Cargo) Ltd (No. 2)* [1995] I.R.L.R. 645.

[84a] [1996] I.R.L.R. 378.

In *Gillespie and others v. Northern Health and Social Services Board*[85] the applicant argued on the basis of *Dekker* that it was discriminatory not to pay full pay to a woman away from work on maternity leave, in that treatment arising from the fact of pregnancy was *per se* discriminatory. The Court held that women away on maternity leave are in a special position which is not comparable either with that of a man or with that of a woman actually at work. *Gillespie* arguably tends to reduce the scope of *per se* discriminatory actions based upon pregnancy, confining them to issues such as dismissal or other detrimental actions based on pregnancy. Claims to gain a benefit by comparison with other workers may fall within the ambit of the decision in *Gillespie*.

2-37

The facts in *Gillespie* took place before the entry into force of the Pregnancy Directive 92/85, which provides for a maternity allowance no lower than statutory sick pay. Nonetheless, the Court held that such a woman should not receive a maternity allowance so low as to undermine the purpose of maternity leave, namely, the protection of women before and after giving birth. She must also receive the benefits of any pay rise awarded whilst she is away from work, because, as she is still connected to her employer by a contract of employment, to deny her such an increase would be to ''discriminate against her in her capacity as a worker, since, had she not been pregnant, she would have received the pay rise.'' (point 22).

Whilst in general a comparative approach to discrimination seems to us to be the appropriate one, pregnancy and maternity are clearly exceptions where the relevant condition is inherent to women. Indeed it is notable that the Pregnancy Directive 92/85 is essentially an employment protection measure based on general social policy, rather than being concerned with discrimination. However, in so far as Directive 92/85 is concerned with overcoming disadvantages experienced by pregnant women in the labour market, it has objectives which are clearly consonant with those of the Equal Treatment Directive and the Sex Discrimination Act.

The Pregnancy Directive 92/85

The Pregnancy Directive provides not only for the protection of pregnant and breast feeding women from noxious substances and working practices which are particularly dangerous to them, but also calls for 14 weeks maternity leave paid at statutory sick pay rates and protection from dismissal by reason of pregnancy from the inception of employment. This Directive was signed by the Council of Ministers in October 1992 and was implemented by the Trade Union Reform and Employment Rights Act (TURERA) 1993, the provisions of which came into effect in October 1994. These include an amended right not be automatically unfairly dismissed by reason of pregnancy under the Employment Rights Act (ERA) 1996, s. 99, for which there will no longer be any qualification period. The removal of compensation limits for sex discrimination cases following *Marshall (No. 2)* means that although dismissal by reason of pregnancy is now automatically unfair, there may still be a case for proceeding under the SDA as well as the ERA.

2-38

The amended provisions with regard to maternity leave (Employment Rights Act 1996, ss. 71–78) provide for a right to return to work at the end of the 14 week period for all pregnant women, but women who have two years service may still benefit from the right to return at the end of 29 weeks

---

[85] Case C-342/93, [1996] I.R.L.R. 214.

from the birth of the baby. The right at the end of 29 weeks is subject to notice provisions and to complex provisions regarding the interaction of statutory and contractual rights (ERA, ss. 79–85).

2-39   The treatment of pregnancy in particular has given rise to similar problems in U.S. legislation, the Supreme Court concluding in *General Electric Company v. Gilbert*[86] that discrimination on grounds of pregnancy was not covered by Title VII of the Civil Rights Act 1964. However, the Pregnancy Disability Amendment to Title VII now prohibits discrimination based on pregnancy, but utilises a comparative approach similar to that espoused in the U.K.

Dress codes

2-40   The same problem of less favourable treatment arises in relation to dress codes. In *Schmidt v. Austicks Bookshop Ltd*[87] the employer required his female employees to wear skirts and to don overalls, whereas there was no comparable requirement placed upon male employees. The EAT concluded that this did not constitute discrimination, because in the absence of any comparable requirement which could be placed upon men, such a rule could not constitute less favourable treatment of women. Nonetheless, the EAT went on to hold that a more fruitful way to formulate such an issue would be to ask if there were comparable rules governing the dress of men or women, although the specific requirements under those rules might not be the same. The *Schmidt* case suggests that the way in which such problems are formulated is important.

Whilst it is necessary to compare like with like changes in fashion can lead to difficulties in matters such as, for example, the wearing of earrings by men or other items of personal jewellery. In considering whether an employer would be acting unlawfully in imposing dress rules which distinguish between men and women it is necessary to bear in mind that the significance of specific items or styles of dress can change over time.[88]

In *Smith v. Safeway Ltd*[89] a male assistant on the delicatessen counter was dismissed when his "pony tail" grew so long as to be no longer capable of being contained under his uniform hat. The EAT concluded by a majority, Mr Justice Pill dissenting, that a rule restricting "pony tails" for men, but not imposing comparable restrictions on women, who could clip long hair back, was inherently discriminatory. The majority distinguished *Schmidt* in that restrictions as to hair length necessarily applied as much outside working hours as within them and that the legitimate requirements of the employer

---

[86] 429 U.S. 125 (1979). Note also the decision of the London South Tribunal in *Reynolds v. Mitsubishi Trust and Banking Corporation* 14003/91, EOR, Case Digest No. 13) that a dismissal of an employee on the ground that she was to undergo an operation for a hysterectomy was on grounds of sex. The London South Tribunal felt itself bound to follow the ECJ decision in *Dekker*, rather than the Court of Appeal in *Webb*. The *Webb* case was also distinguished by the Northern Ireland I.T. in *Scott v. McMullan and McMullan t/a Desmac Stationery*, (Case 1862/90, EOR, Case Digest No. 13) on the basis that the facts in *Webb* were special in that the replacement was needed for a specific period.

[87] [1978] I.C.R. 85.

[88] *McConomy v. Croft Inns* [1992] I.R.L.R. 562, N.I.C.A. I.

[89] [1995] I.R.L.R. 132, EAT, *The Times*, March 5, 1996, C.A.

to maintain a conventional appearance could be met in the case of a pony tail, without distinguishing between men and women. In the Court of Appeal Phillips L.J. held that there was an important distinction between discrimination between the sexes and discrimination against one or other of the sexes. It was not discriminatory to adopt a conventional standard of dress or appearance, as to do otherwise would place whichever sex was forced to appear in an unconventional mode at a disadvantage. Such considerations could extend to more permanent characteristics, such as tattoos or hair length, as well as to ephemera such as clothes and jewellery. Nor should the members of the EAT have substituted their view of what was conventional for that of the employee.

The underlying question remains, however, as to how far the sex discrimination legislation requires an employer to accommodate himself to changing notions of fashion, or to altered conceptions of the conventional roles, or appearance, of men and women. It is clear from the view of the EAT in *Burret v. West Birmingham Health Authority*[90] that the subjective perception of the employee is not decisive here, however. In this case a nurse disliked wearing her uniform cap, which served no functional purpose, but the EAT upheld the Industrial Tribunal's view that the complainant's dislike of her cap did not necessarily constitute less favourable treatment, a topic on which it is for the Tribunal to form a view.[91]

Indirect discrimination

Discrimination is not necessarily the result of prejudice on the part of those with the power of decision making. Often the very fabric of our society constitutes what has been termed an inbuilt headwind[92] for anyone who is not a member of that group which has traditionally been expected to take part in a particular activity. For example, schools and public buildings have generally not been designed with the needs of the handicapped in mind; just to get through the door can be a major achievement, yet those who designed the buildings were not generally animated with a prejudice against the disabled; they simply failed to consider the position of the handicapped person or the effects which their plans might have upon such people. There is still little realisation that the reason that many handicapped people stay at home is the sheer difficulty of going to places planned without reference to their needs.

2-41

So it is with women, the aged, members of racial or other social minorities: their position may not have been allowed for, thus putting them at a disadvantage in any competition for valued cultural, social or economic opportunities. Thus the career pattern of managers in most private or public sector organisations does not allow for a "career break" of any length (though a few organisations are now beginning to take this requirement seriously). The

2-42

---

[90] [1994] I.R.L.R. 7.

[91] Conversely, the subjective view of a manager that he did not like the "discoified" hair style of a subordinate was held to be discriminatory by the I.T. in *Gatehouse v. Stretton Leisure Ltd* (1994) DCLD 21. For further discussion of these issues see L. Flynn "Gender Equality Laws and Employers" Dress Codes in *Industrial Law Journal*, 24.3, 280–85.

[92] *Grigg v. Dukes Power Company* 401 U.S. 424, (1971) 3 FED 75.

absence of any such arrangements for a "career break," a negative practice so widely accepted as to be almost invisible, constitutes an inbuilt headwind against the progress of women in management. Likewise, patterns of educational qualifications or experience may be demanded for jobs which put first generation immigrants at a particular disadvantage, but which have never been critically examined to test whether they are necessary for effective job performance. Even subtle expectations about what is appropriate behaviour in a particular social setting may put newcomers or outsiders at a disadvantage.

2-43   In spite of the widespread existence of discriminatory practices[93] comparatively few tribunal cases are based on the concept of indirect discrimination, and it has not even featured to any great degree as a basis of formal EOC or CRE investigations in the employment field.[94] This may be due to ignorance or lack of will amongst applicants and their advisers, although it may be because no compensation is payable in the industrial tribunals for indirect discrimination if the respondent proves that the requirement or condition was not applied with the intention of treating the claimant less favourably.[95] The EOC has proposed[96] the removal of this limitation, which would make it more attractive to build a case on the indirect discrimination provisions.

Compensation for indirect discrimination

2-44   Under the SDA, s.66(3) or the RRA, s.57(3) it is clear from the decision of the EAT in *London Underground Ltd v. Edwards*[97] that compensation is payable unless the respondents can show that the requirement or condition is not *applied* with the intention of treating the claimant unfavourably on grounds of his or her sex or marital status (or race), rather than that it was not formulated with the intention of treating such claimants unfavourably. In that case a female lone parent was unable to cope with revised shift arrangements and claimed to have been discriminatorily constructively dismissed. London Underground were aware of the potential impact of the new arrangements on parents with primary child care responsibilities, because a scheme to deal with these concerns had been discussed with the unions, although not agreed. Therefore although the new shift patterns were not formulated with the intention of treating women unfavourably, they were applied with the knowledge of their potential adverse impact on single parents, most of whom are women. Consequently, the claimant received compensation for economic loss and injury to feelings, by reason of the intentional application to her of an indirectly discriminatory requirement.

The reasoning in *London Underground v. Edwards* was extended to the sphere of race relations in *J.H. Walker Ltd v. Hussein*[98] in which a clothing company under financial pressure forbad its employees to take any holidays in the busy period of May–June. This requirement was found to be indirectly discriminatory on racial grounds by the Industrial Tribunal, in that it precluded a substantial minority of Muslim employees from celebrating Eid.

---

[93] Dickens, Townley and Winchester, *Tackling Sex Discrimination Through Collective Bargaining* (HMSO, 1988).
[94] McCrudden, Smith and Brown, *Racial Justice at Work, Enforcement of the Race Relations Act in Employment* (Policy Studies Institute, 1991).
[95] Sex Discrimination Act 1975, s.66(3) and Race Relations Act 1976, s.57(3).
[96] *Equal Treatment for Men and Women: Strengthening the Acts* (EOC, 1988).
[97] [1995] I.R.L.R. 355, EAT.
[98] [1996] I.R.L.R. 12, EAT.

The question on appeal was whether this requirement was *applied* with the intention of treating the complainants unfavourably under the RRA, s.57(3). The EAT held that because the employees had protested, the company thereby knew that its decision on holidays would have discriminatory consequences. Therefore in persisting with that policy the company demonstrated that it wanted to bring about those consequences.

The EAT rejected the argument that section 57(3) of the 1976 Act requires an enquiry into the subjective intentions of the respondent or into his state of mind, other than that, knowing that his actions will have indirectly discriminatory consequences, he persists in applying the condition in question. (See below at page 256 in relation to this case.)

It was arguable that the restriction of the availability of compensation under SDA, s.66(3) to cases where the respondent fails to prove that the requirement or condition is not applied with the intention of treating the claimant unfavourably on grounds of his or her sex or marital status was contrary to the requirements of the Equal Treatment Directive. No such limitation upon the scope of remedies can be found in the Directive and in *Marshall v. Southampton and South West Hants Health Authority (No. 2)*[99] the ECJ showed itself capable of requiring that restrictions on compensations in domestic discrimination law which find no parallel in the Directive should be disapplied. Yet the EAT in *McMillan v. Edinburgh Voluntary Organisations Council*[1] concluded that the clear words of section 65(1)(b) and section 66(3) could not be construed to accord with the Equal Treatment Directive without distorting their language. This conclusion was founded upon the decisions of the House of Lords in *Duke v. GEC Reliance Ltd* and *Webb v. EMO (Air Cargo) Ltd*.[2] Only where such a case is brought by a public sector employee, who may rely upon the direct effect of the Directive in respect of a sex discrimination claim, could the limitation in the Sex Discrimination Act, s.66(3) be overcome, without Parliament changing the law. The Sex Discrimination and Equal Pay (Miscellaneous Amendments) Regulations 1996 now provide as from July 31, 1996 that compensation may be paid under SDA s.65(1)(b) as regards an act of *indirect* discrimination, where the respondent proves that the requirement or condition was not applied with the intention of treating the complainant unfavourably. (See below at page 256.)[2a]

The Sex Discrimination Act and the Race Relations Act provisions on indirect discrimination are aimed at the effect of widely accepted practices on minorities. It is these practices which have been termed ''institutional racism'',[3] by which is meant the limiting effect of socially accepted arrange- **2-45**

---

[99] Case C-271/91 [1993] I.R.L.R. 445, ECJ.

[1] [1995] I.R.L.R. 536, EAT.

[2] Discussed at paragraph 1–47 above.

[2a] S.I. 1996 No. 438, which inserts new subsections 65(1a) and (1b) in the SDA 1976.

[3] See the Scarman Report, Cmnd. 8427 (1981) at p. 11 and also Christopher McCrudden, ''Institutional Discrimination'' in 2 *Oxford Journal of Legal Studies*, 303 (1982). For examples of the widely accepted and little understood phenomenon of indirect discrimination, see J. Rosser & C. Davies, ''What Would We Do Without Her? Invisible Women in NHS Administration'' in *In a Man's World. Essays on Women in Male Dominated Professions* (Spence and Podmore eds., Tavistock Publications, 1987); D. Spencer and A. Spencer, ''Gender & The Labour Process: the case of women and men lawyers'' in *Gender and the Labour Process* (Knights & Willmot eds.; Gower, 1986); A. Pollert, *Girls, Wives & Factory Lives* (Macmillan, 1981); Richard Jenkins, *Racism & Recruitment* (Cambridge University Press, 1986).

ments on the aspirations of minorities. There are parallel phenomena which operate in relation to women, which often have the effect of keeping them out of "men's work" and which constitute the stuff of indirect discrimination claims under the Sex Discrimination Act. It was in *Bilka-Kaufhaus GmbH v. Weber von Hartz*[4] that the ECJ first formulated a clear statement of indirect discrimination in Community law, in the United States sense of *disparate impact* discrimination. As explained in chapter 1, indirect discrimination had acquired the connotation of "hidden or disguised" discrimination in the second *Defrenne* case and only returns to the British statutory sense of indirect discrimination, clear of imputations of intentionality, when the ECJ holds in *Bilka* that the respondent employer infringes Article 119 of the EEC Treaty when:

> "it excludes part-time employees from its occupational pension scheme where that exclusion affects a much greater number of women than men, unless the enterprise shows that the exclusion is based on objectively justified factors which are unrelated to any discrimination based on sex."

The elements of indirect discrimination

2-46   The SDA and RRA define indirect discrimination in nearly identical terms.[5] There are four tests of indirect discrimination provided for under the SDA and RRA:

1. Has a requirement or condition been applied equally to both sexes or all racial groups?
2. Is that requirement or condition one with which a considerably smaller number of women (or men) or persons of the racial group in question can comply than those of the opposite sex or persons not of that racial group?
3. Is the requirement or condition justifiable irrespective of the sex, colour, race, nationality, ethnic or national origins of the person in question?
4. Has the imposition of the requirement or condition operated to the detriment of a person who could not comply with it?

---

[4] [1986] I.R.L.R. 317.
[5] SDA, s.1: "A person discriminates against a woman in any circumstances relevant for any purposes of this Act if.(b) he applies to her a requirement or condition which he applies or would apply equally to a man but- (i) which is such that the proportion of women who can comply with it is considerably smaller than the proportion of men who can comply with it, and. (ii) which he cannot show to be justifiable irrespective of the sex of the person to whom it is applied, and. (iii) which is to her detriment because she cannot comply with it." R.R.A., s.1: "A person discriminates against another in any circumstances relevant for the purposes of any provision of this Act if. (b) he applies to that other a requirement or condition which he applies or would apply equally to persons not of the same racial group as that other but- (i) which is such that the proportions of persons of the same racial group as that other who can comply with it is considerably smaller than the proportion of persons not of that racial group who can comply with it; and (ii) which he cannot show to be justifiable irrespective of the colour, race nationality or ethnic or national origins of the person to whom it is applied; and (iii) which is to the detriment of that other because he cannot comply with it."

The majority of indirect discrimination cases in Community employment law **2-47** have been concerned with differences in treatment between full-time and part-time staff with regard to their pay or pensions, as for example, in *Bilka-Kaufhaus*. Consequently the ECJ has been able to point to differences in treatment between predominantly male and female groups, so that:

> "when a measure distinguishing between employees on the basis of their hours of work has in practice an adverse impact on substantially more members of one or other sex, that measure must be regarded as contrary to the objectives pursued by Article 119 of the Treaty, unless the employer shows that it is based upon objectively justified factors unrelated to any discrimination on grounds of sex."[6]

Enderby v. Frenchay Health Authority was, however, an equal pay case in which the claimants sought to establish that differences in the average pay of two NHS professional groups, speech therapists and pharmacists, were discriminatory. The respondent had argued in the EAT and the Court of Appeal, by analogy from the requirements of the Sex Discrimination Act, that it was necessary to identify a "requirement or condition" which the employer had imposed and which had resulted in the differences in pay. The Court of Appeal referred this issue to the ECJ, which concluded that such differences in pay constitute a *primae facie* case of discrimination, which it is for the employer to justify. The ECJ rejected the argument that it is necessary to identify a specific requirement or condition to which the claimant is subject in order for indirect discrimination to be established within the field of equal pay, being more concerned with the resulting patterns of pay. Yet neither does the Equal Pay Act require that there be more than a difference in pay between workers doing like work or work of equal value before the respondent is called upon to establish that any discrepancy in pay is due to a genuine material difference; Lord Slynn in *Ratcliffe v. North Yorks. C.C.*[7] held that:

> "the Equal Pay Act does not draw a distinction between direct and indirect discrimination. We would submit that whilst there may often be an identifiable requirement or condition in equal pay cases, as in the part-timers cases, this need not be so. It can be sufficient to place upon the respondent the obligation to objectively justify any difference in pay if it is established that lower pay is being paid for work of equal value."

Ellis[8] argues that the European Court of Justice has been able to be more flexible in its approach to indirect discrimination than the U.K. courts, because the concept of indirect discrimination is not defined in the same precise manner that it is in the U.K. statutes. She argues that the approach adopted in *Enderby* should also apply to equal treatment cases but it could be argued that it is only likely to be in the sphere of equal pay that it is possible to argue from a difference of result to discriminatory treatment without identifying any causative policy or practice which brings that result about.

---

[6] Case C-127/92, *Enderby v. Frenchay Health Authority*: [1993] I.R.L.R. 595 at para. 14.
[7] [1995] I.R.L.R. 439, H.L.
[8] Evelyn Ellis, "Discrimination in European Community Law" in *European Law Review*, 19,6, pp. 563–579.

Is there a requirement or condition?

2-48   Unlawful indirect discrimination arises from rules or practices which are on their face neutral, but which put protected groups at a disadvantage. For example, an age limit can be an apparently neutral requirement which puts women who have or wish to have children at a disadvantage.[9] Another apparently neutral requirement which can have a disproportionate impact upon women is that of working full-time.[10] Racial minorities may have difficulty in complying with a requirement for "O" level English.[11]

2-49   All the above requirements are clear cut and act as an absolute bar on securing or continuing in employment. It is, however, commonly the case that there is no one absolute bar to gaining employment or access to some other benefit, but a selection procedure which imposes a set of inter-related requirements on which candidates are to be assessed. Whilst the EAT in *Watches of Switzerland v. Savell*[12] held that the need to satisfy the requirements of a promotion procedure could itself be a condition or requirement under section 1(1)(b), the application of this decision is uncertain in view of the subsequent Court of Appeal decision in *Perera v. Civil Service Commission and Department Customs & Excise (No. 2)*.[13] In that case, an applicant for a post as a legal assistant had to be either a qualified solicitor or barrister and had to receive a satisfactory assessment from an interviewing board. The interviewing board was charged with having regard to a number of factors, particularly experience in the United Kingdom. The Court of Appeal held that this procedure could not constitute a requirement or condition because it was not an absolute bar to selection. Candidates could compensate for poor performance on one of the factors by excelling in some other respect, so that no one factor constituted an absolute bar and hence there could be no requirement or condition. This decision tends to reinforce managerial discretion in the balancing of criteria for selection or promotion. Absolute requirements for a job are generally of the more basic sort likely to be possessed by any serious candidate, whilst the actual selection decision will be based on a constellation of factors, one or more of which may be highly detrimental to women. As it is almost invariably the case that candidates are assessed upon a balance of criteria, it would be hard to formulate a requirement or condition which would satisfy section 1(1)(b).[14]

2-50   The requirement that a condition or requirement must be an absolute bar was reiterated by the Court of Appeal in *Meer v. London Borough of Tower*

---

[9] See *Price v. Civil Service Commissioners* [1978] I.C.R. 27.
[10] See *Clarke v. Eley (IMI) Kynock Ltd* [1983] I.C.R. 165; *Home Office v. Holmes* [1983] I.C.R. 165.
[11] See *Raval v. DHSS* [1985] I.C.R. 685.
[12] [1983] I.R.L.R. 141.
[13] [1983] I.R.L.R. 166, C.A.
[14] *Quaere:* Why would the following formulation not suffice. "A requirement that to receive preferential treatment a person should possess one or more of the following characteristics". This would then make s.1(1)(b) correspond to the fact that s.1(a) catches both selecting only whites and preferring whites. Rubenstein makes the point that a requirement or practice constituting an absolute ban may be a derogation from the provisions of the Equal Treatment Directive and could be attacked through that route. See M. Rubenstein, "The Equal Treatment & U.K. Law" in *Women, Employment & European Equality Law* (C. McCrudden ed., Eclipse, 1988).

Hamlets,[15] in which the Court felt bound to follow *Perera*. In *Meer* the Authority had 12 selection criteria for applicants for the post of borough solicitor, one of which was experience in Tower Hamlets. The appellant considered this criterion discriminatory, but because it was not in itself a "must" for appointment to the post, it did not constitute a requirement. The EOC and CRE argue that any practice or policy having an adverse impact on the protected groups should be open to challenge. It is submitted that it is also implicit in the *Danfoss*[16] decision, that if it is sufficient in the context of an equal pay claim under Article 119 for women to show that there is a discrepancy in treatment for the burden of proof to be reversed, there is no need to show that this is brought about by a "requirement or condition" as opposed to a policy or practice. In the earlier case of *Clarke v. Eley (IMI) Kynoch Ltd*[17] the EAT emphasised that the purpose of the legislation is to eliminate established practices which have a disproportionate impact upon minorities. Consequently:

"if the elimination of such practices is the policy lying behind the Act, although such policy cannot be used to give the words any other meaning than they naturally bear it is in our view a powerful argument against giving the words a narrower meaning thereby excluding cases which fall within the mischief which the Act was meant to deal with."[18]

Much of the mischief which this section aims at is beyond its reach, if it is only requirements or conditions which constitute an absolute bar which fall within the purview of section 1(1)(b). There is no basis in the Equal Treatment Directive 76/207, however, for such a limitation. An employee of the State, or one of its organs, could plead that the direct effect of the Directive is to require that the gloss placed upon the terms "requirement or condition" in the U.K. case law be disapplied. An employee of a private sector body bringing a sex discrimination claim could also argue that it is open to the courts to adopt a a more liberal interpretation of the statutory wording without distorting the meaning of the British statute.[19]

2-51

However, this approach has not found favour in the U.K. courts as regards questions of equal treatment. In *Bhudi v. IMI Refiners Ltd*[20] the applicants sought to rely on the decision of the ECJ in *Enderby v. Frenchay Health Authority*[21] to the effect that it was not necessary to establish the application of a precise requirement or condition, if a practice can be shown to have an adverse impact on a group consisting mainly of one gender or the other. The

---

[15] [1988] I.R.L.R. 399, C.A. Balcombe L.J. questioned whether *Perera* was compatible with the purposes of the Act in a significant *obiter*, but arguing that the Court of Appeal is bound by its previous decisions preferred to leave the matter to Parliament.

[16] *Handels-Og Kontorfunktionaerens Forbund I Danmark v. Dansk Arbedjsgiverforening [acting for Danfoss]* [1989] I.R.L.R. 532. Neither can one see in the wording of the Directive any support for the imposition of an absolute requirement as a precondition of establishing indirect discrimination.

[17] [1983] I.C.R. 165.

[18] At 169 *per* Browne-Wilkinson J. It is noteworthy, that this definition of requirement or constitution has been incorporated into the provisions of the Fair Employment Bill 1989 for Northern Ireland, in spite of widespread criticism.

[19] A "knock-on" effect as regards the interpretation of the Race Relations Act would almost certainly follow.

[20] [1994] I.R.L.R. 204.

[21] See above.

EAT held that *Enderby* was a case decided under Article 119 and the Equal Pay Directive and those provisions constitute a distinct regime from that obtaining under the Equal Treatment Directive. Furthermore, the EAT held that as this was not a case brought against an organ of the State, in relation to which the Equal Treatment Directive would have direct effect, it was not possible to interpret the express words of the SDA, s.1(1)(b) so as to obviate the need for there to be a requirement or condition, without distorting the meaning of the statutory language, contrary to the decision of the House of Lords in *Duke v. GEC Reliance*.[22] Thus, as regards the application of the principle of equal treatment in sex discrimination cases, there is at this point still a need for there to be a requirement or condition which acts to the disadvantage of members of the racial group or gender in question, even if in relation to sex discrimination cases the gloss of an absolute requirement can be argued to constitute an illegitimate derogation from the principle of equal treatment in Community law.

Can a considerably smaller proportion of the protected group comply with the requirement or condition?

2-52   Indirect discrimination occurs when a requirement or condition is applied with which a considerably smaller proportion of the members of one sex or of a particular racial group can comply than would be the case for persons not of that sex or racial group.

In order to establish indirect discrimination under the SDA 1975 or the RRA 1976, a considerably smaller proportion of the protected group must be able to comply with the requirement in question than would be the case for non-members of that group.[23] The Equal Treatment Directive provides, however, in Article 2 that the:

> "Application of the principle of equal treatment means that there shall be no discrimination *whatsoever* on grounds of sex either directly or indirectly by reference in particular to marital or family status." (emphasis supplied).

Does this mean that any practice which results in different outcomes for men and women, however small, would give rise to unlawful indirect discrimination in Community law? Such was the argument on behalf of the plaintiffs in *R. v. Secretary of State for Employment, ex p. Seymour-Smith and Perez*,[24] in which judicial review was sought of the two year service qualification

---

[22] [1988] I.R.L.R. 118, *Finnegan v. Clowney Youth Training Programme Ltd* [1990] I.R.L.R. 299 and *Webb v. EMO (Air Cargo) Ltd* [1993] I.R.L.R. 27 discussed above.

[23] Even if that proportion is nil, *i.e.* none "can comply," it was held by the EAT in *Greencroft Social Club v. Mullen* [1985] I.C.R. 796, that it would be contrary to the spirit of the legislation to exclude such a case, *cf.* the unreported case of *Wong v. GLC*, EAT 524/79.

     Some American courts, in interpreting comparable legislation, have used the rule of thumb that if the proportion of the protected group which can comply with a relevant requirement is one fifth smaller than that of the larger group, that is sufficient to establish that a practice has a discriminatory effect, but no settled proportion has been accepted by the courts in Britain as constituting a "considerably smaller" proportion.

[24] [1995] I.R.L.R. 464.

period for unfair dismissal, on the grounds that its impact was indirectly discriminatory. Neil L.J. in the Court of Appeal, giving the judgement of the Court after an extensive review of the authorities in the ECJ[25], concluded that:

"the test laid down by the ECJ is whether a 'considerable difference' exists. But the underlying principle is equal treatment. It will be remembered that by Article 2.1 the principle of equal treatment means that 'there shall be no discrimination whatsoever on grounds of sex.' Accordingly the weight to be attached to the word 'considerable' must not be exaggerated."[26]

Thus the legislative test is not identical as regards E.C. and U.K. law, but the impact of the case law would seem to render the tests of substantial equivalence. In the *Seymour-Smith* case, over a six year period, women were between 88.4 per cent and 90.5 per cent as likely as men to have had two years service, as shown by the Annual Labour Force Survey. On this basis the Divisional Court concluded that that this was not a "considerably" lower proportion of women, whilst the Court of Appeal concluded otherwise.[1]

In this respect it could seem to matter as to whether one looks at the proportions of those who can comply with a particular requirement, as opposed to those who cannot. McCollough J. in the Divisional Court by *Seymour-Smith & Perez* put the matter as follows:

"In considering whether there is a considerable disparity, the court should look at both the relative percentages of those who meet the requirement and the relevant percentages of those who do not. Of these, the more important group will be those who do qualify. The following example makes the point. If 98 per cent of men qualify and 2 per cent do not, and if 96 per cent of women qualify and 4 per cent do not, it would not be right to conclude that the disparity was considerable. But if only 4 per cent of men and only 2 per cent of women qualified the opposite conclusion would be correct."

Proposals have been made for the exemption of small businesses from employment protection measures[28] but the question has been raised as to whether such an exemption of small businesses might be contrary to the

---

[25] Case 96/80, *Jenkins v. Kingsgate Clothing Productions Ltd* [1981] I.R.L.R. 228 ("considerably smaller percentage of women"); Case 170/84, *Bilka-Kaufhaus v. Weber von Hartz* [1987] I.C.R. 110, [1986] I.R.L.R. 317 ("much lower proportion of women"); Case 30/85, *Teuling v. Bedrijfvereniging voor de chemische Industrie* [1988] 3 C.M.L.R. 789 ("considerably smaller proportion of women"); Case 33/89, *Kowalska v. Frie und Hansestadt Hambourg* (1992) I.C.R. 28, [1990] I.R.L.R. 447 ("a considerably lower percentage of men") *Case 184/89, Nimz v. Frie und Hansestadt Hambourg* [1991] E.C.R. 1–297 [1991] I.R.L.R. 222) ("much lower percentage of men"); Case 360/90, *Arbeiterwohlfahrt der Stadt Berlin eV v. Botel* [1992] I.R.L.R. 423 ("considerably lower percentage of women").

[26] At 476.

[27] In *Staffordshire County Council v. Black* [1995] I.R.L.R. 234 the EAT held that the words "considerably smaller" are ordinary words of common usage which are a matter for the industrial tribunals and upheld a Tribunal decision that the proportion of women over 50 who worked full-time (89.5 per cent) was not "considerably smaller" than that for men (97 per cent).

[28] *The Independent*, March 7 and 11, 1995

Equal Treatment Directive. In Germany employees in small businesses employing fewer than five workers are exempt from protection against unfair dismissal. In computing the number of employees, those working less than 10 hours are not counted. In *Kirshammer-Hack v. Sidal*[29] an employee who herself worked over 10 hours contested the exclusion of her firm on the basis that the law itself was contrary to the Equal Treatment Directive as 90 per cent of part-time workers in Germany are women. The ECJ held that the appropriate question was whether small businesses employed considerably more women than men, not whether more women than men worked part-time. Only if small businesses employed more women than men (or vice versa) would their exclusion be indirectly discriminatory, because it is the businesses which are excluded rather than the employees *per se*. The ECJ held that the facts provided to the Court did not establish any such disproportion, but that even if that were the case, the rule would still be potentially capable of justification. However, we would observe that the factual situation might be different in the U.K. and that objective justification would require more than ''generalised statements'' as to the impact of employment measures on the capacity of small businesses to offer employment.

2-53   In the social security case of *Jones v. Chief Adjudication Officer*,[30] Mustill L.J. in the Court of Appeal formulated the following approach to the proportionality test in indirect discrimination.

1. Identify the criteria for selection.
2. Identify the relevant population, comprising all those who satisfy all the other criteria for selection.
3. Divide the relevant population into groups representing those who satisfy the criterion and those who do not.
4. Predict statistically what proportion of each group should consist of women.
5. Ascertain what are the actual male/female balances in the two groups.
6. Compare the actual with the predicted balances.
7. If women are found to be under-represented in the first group and over represented in the second, it is proved that the criterion is discriminatory.

Perhaps the main question is to determine with whom should the protected group be compared. The Sex Discrimination Act, s.5(3)[30a] provides that any comparison between men and women (or in regard to marital status) must be such that the relevant circumstances in the one case are the same, or not materially different, in the other. Thus in *Price v. Civil Service Commission*[31] the Industrial Tribunal considered that the appropriate pool of comparison was the whole population, but the EAT held that it was those people otherwise qualified to apply for the job. In *Kidd v. DRG (U.K.)*,[32] a case in which part-timers were to be selected for redundancy before full-timers, the EAT held that the area for comparison, or pool, is a matter of fact for the Tribunal

[29] Case C-189/91, [1994] I.R.L.R. 185.
[30] [1990] I.R.L.R. 533.
[30a] s.3(4) of the RRA provides similarly in comparisons between members of a particular racial group and persons not of that group.
[31] [1976] I.R.L.R. 405, IT, [1977] I.R.L.R. 291, EAT.
[32] [1985] I.C.R. 405.

in trying to match the circumstances of each case. As the EAT acknowledged, the decisions of tribunals in superficially similar circumstances will differ according to their view as to what are the relevant comparisons which have to be made.[33] Such a decision of fact is, of course, not subject to appeal unless it is "so irrationally inappropriate as to put it outside the range of selection for any reasonable Tribunal," in which case "the Tribunal would have fallen into an error of law which could be corrected in the appellate jurisdiction."[34] Thus in *Greater Manchester Police Authority v. Lea*[35] Knox J. accepted that the pool does not have to be shown to be a statistically perfect match of the persons who would be capable of and interested in the post offered. Having been selected as the most suitable candidate, Mr Lea was refused employment in accordance with the policy of the Police Authority to refuse employment to anyone in receipt of an occupational pension, in order to take account of the needs of the unemployed. In this case statistics for the whole of the economically active population, which must have included many people neither capable of nor interested in a vacancy such as the one in question, showed that whereas 4.7 per cent of men were in receipt of an occupational pension this was true for only 0.6 per cent of women. The EAT accepted that in finding the requirement not to be in receipt of an occupational pension was one with which a considerably smaller proportion of men could comply than women, the Industrial Tribunal had not come to a conclusion which no reasonable tribunal could have reached.

There is a danger, however, of incorporating an act of discrimination into the definition of the pool of comparison, a danger specifically highlighted by Schiemann J. in *R. v. Secretary of State for Education, ex p. Schaffer*,[36] which concerned the allocation of hardship grants for students who were lone parents, only to those who had previously been married. Whilst the proportion of women who were single lone parents was four times that of men, the proportion of lone parents who were single, in the sense of never having been married, was the same for both sexes. The Court took the view that by choosing the latter basis of comparison, an act of discrimination was being built into the ground of comparison.[37]

The choice of the pool for comparison can be a trap for the unwary applicant.   **2-54**
If he or she marshals the available statistics in relation to what is found by the tribunal to be an inappropriate comparison, the case may be lost. The applicant will have failed to prove that indirect discrimination has taken place, even though had the appropriate comparison been made, the statistics might have supported the complaint. Thus in *Pearse v. Bradford Metropol-*

---

[33] Compare, for example, the decision in *Kidd*, with that in the *Home Office v. Holmes* and *Clark & Eley v. IMI*.

[34] *Per* Waite J. at p. 415. In *Kidd* the pool of comparison was held to be all those households in which the need to care for small children makes it difficult for one or both parents to work full time. Waite J. held that a reasonable Tribunal could conclude that it was unsafe to assume that the burden of child care was more likely to prevent married than unmarried women working full-time in those circumstances or for married women as against married men. Statistical proof was required of these matters in view of the changing pattern of child rearing practices.

[35] [1990] I.R.L.R. 372, EAT.

[36] [1987] I.R.L.R. 53.

[37] See also the Court of Appeal decision in *Jones v. University of Manchester* [1993] I.R.L.R. 218.

itan Council[38] the appellant alleged that a college which restricted applications for a counselling vacancy to existing full-time members of staff, indirectly discriminated against part-timers. The appellant produced statistics showing that the ratio of full-time to part-time staff was lower for women than for men. The EAT held, however, that the appropriate comparison was not that of all full-time to part-time staff, but of full or part-time college employees otherwise qualified for this particular post, and, as the appellant advanced no figures in relation to that comparison, even though granted an adjournment in which to compile such figures, the case failed.

2-55   Where statistical proof is required, how elaborate need that be for the parties to prove their case? In *Perera*[39] the EAT accepted that there was no need to produce elaborate statistical evidence to establish that a particular practice has a disproportionate impact upon minorities. If the issue is in dispute the employer can attack the statistical evidence in rebuttal of the original contentions. Statistics may relate to the population at large, if this is the appropriate field of comparison, or to a particular workplace, or to the workforce in question. A Tribunal may, however, take into account its own knowledge and experience in examining such questions, according to the Northern Ireland Court of Appeal in *Briggs v. North Eastern Library and Education Board*.[40] Even though the EAT in *Kidd v.* DRG (U.K.) Ltd had felt that it needed statistical evidence to prove that married women bear a greater responsibility for child-rearing than men,[41] the Court of Appeal in *Meade-Hill v. National Union of Civil and Public Servants*[42] took judicial notice of the fact that a considerably greater proportion of women than men could not comply with a requirement to move house.

Can comply

2-56   It was argued by the employer in *Price v. Civil Service Commission*[43] that as many women as men could comply with an age limit of age 28 for applications to join the executive class of the Civil Service. There are just as many women as men below the age of 28 and if only a smaller proportion of them chose to apply, that, it was argued, was a different matter. Women had the same capacity to apply as men and therefore, in the words of the statute, the proportion of women who could comply was the same as was the case for men. This argument was rejected by Phillips J. in the EAT who stated that[44]:

> "It should not be said that a person 'can' do something merely because it is theoretically possible for him to do so; it is necessary to see whether he can do so in practice."

2-57   Such an approach recognises that in reality particular segments of the popula-

---

[38] EOR 21, p. 35.
[39] See above at para. 2–49.
[40] [1990] I.R.L.R. 181, NICA.
[41] This is, however, more than an academic or even juridical point. In taking its own experience into account, a Tribunal can simply reify its own prejudices and whilst the decision in *Kidd* might seem a little far-fetched on its facts, nonetheless it avoids the trap of stereotyped thinking about family roles.
[42] [1995] I.R.L.R. 478.
[43] See above at para. 2–53.
[44] At 31.

tion live their lives under conditions which render it difficult or effectively impossible for them to meet a particular requirement. The same view of the capacity of Sikhs to comply with a requirement not to wear a turban was taken by the House of Lords in *Mandla v. Dowell Lee*.[45] Lord Fraser of Tullybelton stated[46]:

> "In the context of section 1(i)(b)(i) of the 1976 Act it must, in my opinion, have been intended by Parliament to be read not as meaning 'can physically,' so as to indicate a theoretical possibility, but as meaning 'can in practice' or 'can consistently with the customs and cultural conditions of the racial group'."

It was held by the EAT in *Ravall v. DHSS*,[47] that the ability of the members of a group to comply with a requirement is to be judged at the date of the incident in question, and not at some future date. Thus the argument was rejected that whilst a smaller proportion of people of Asian origins possessed "O" level English, as there was no reason to suppose that they lacked the necessary ability, they could comply by entering the necessary examination at some future date.

It is implicit in many of the decisions of the ECJ, such as *Rinner-Kühn*,[48] that whilst women could, in theory, enjoy the benefits reserved to full-time workers by themselves working full-time, it is accepted that in practice they do not, whether by reason of family commitments or otherwise.

Does the detriment or condition operate to the detriment of the complainant?

Under section 1(1)(b)(iii) of both Acts the complainant must also establish that the requirement or condition is to his or her detriment because he or she cannot comply with it. This sub-section is intended to establish that the complainant has *locus standi*, *i.e.* that he or she is the victim of the alleged discrimination. In *Steel v. Union of Post Office Workers*[49] the EAT held that the time to consider whether a detriment has been suffered is the time when the complainant has to comply with the requirement or condition.[50] In *Clarke*

2-58

---

[45] [1983] I.R.L.R. 209.
[46] At 213.
[47] See now *CRE v. Dutton* [1989] I.R.L.R. 8, C.A. at 13.
[48] *Rinner-Kühn v. FWW Special-Gebäudereinigung GmbH* Case 171/88 [1989] ECR 2743.
[49] [1978] I.C.R. 181.
[50] The issue in *Turner v. Labour Party* [1987] I.R.L.R. 101, C.A. was whether a divorced woman could comply with a requirement to be married in order to receive for her offspring a survivor's pension on the same terms and of the same value as would have been payable to the surviving spouse of a married member of the pension scheme. The majority of the Court of Appeal took the view that as the survivors' benefits of a pension scheme were only payable at the date of the death of the member, it could not be said that a divorced woman could not comply with that requirement before the date at which the requirement would come into operation, *i.e.* before her death. She might not want to marry, nor could she be compelled to marry, but she could marry before then. Ralph Gibson L.J., dissenting, took the view that death might occur at any time and that a member was paying contributions for present cover and not just future benefits and therefore her present incapacity to comply, not now being married, was to her detriment. *Cf.* The decision of the Court of Appeal in *Meade-Hill and NUCPS v. British Council* [1995] I.R.L.R. 485, where it was held by a majority (Stuart-Smith

v. Eley (IMI) Kynoch Ltd[51] the EAT held that it was not relevant that a complainant could have avoided a present inability to comply with a requirement if different action had been taken in the past. The employees could have avoided being selected for redundancy by electing to have worked full-time at some point in the past, but were none the less held to have suffered in detriment.

Can the discriminator justify the discriminatory act?

2-59   An employer or other discriminator may argue that an otherwise discriminatory practice is "justifiable irrespective of the sex (colour, race, nationality, or ethnic or national origins) of the person to whom it is applied" (SDA & RRA, s.1(1)(b)(3)). The principal question which has arisen in the cases is what is meant by "justifiable." In the landmark case of *Steel v. UPW*[52] Philips J. referred[53] to the famous judgement of the U.S. Supreme Court in *Griggs v. Duke Power Co.* in which it was held that[54]:

> "The Act proscribes not only overt discrimination but also practices which are fair in form, but discriminatory in operation. The touchstone is business necessity. If an employment practice which operates to exclude negroes cannot be shown to be related to job performance, the practice is prohibited."

2-60   It is this standard which Philips J. was seeking to adopt, *i.e.* unless a practice is necessary, rather than merely convenient, it is not justifiable in this context and "for this purpose it is relevant to consider whether the employer can find some other and non-discriminatory method of achieving his objective." Subsequent cases tended to weaken this standard, perhaps reflecting the defeat in Parliament during the passage of the legislation of an amendment which would have substituted "necessary" for "justifiable." The standard adopted has been reasonably necessary[55] right and proper in the circumstances[56] reasonably necessary to the party who applies the condition,[57] acceptable to right thinking people as sound and tolerable reasons for adopting the practice in question[58] or merely of marginal advantage to the

---

L.J. dissenting) that discrimination occurred on the inclusion of the relevant mobility clause in the applicant's contract and not on its application.

[51] [1982] I.R.L.R. 482.

[52] [1978] I.C.R. 181. In *Steel* the Post Office had had a practice of allocating postal walks (or rounds) according to the seniority of the established full-time postal workers. Prior to 1976 women had not been eligible to become established postal workers, (remaining "temporaries" no matter how long they worked there), so that even after 1976 they lacked the seniority necessary to be allocated their choice of walks, that is to pick a walk which finished near to their own homes. This was held not to be a justifiable arrangement when the case was remitted to the Industrial Tribunal. On the question as to how far women "can" join the building trades see the EAT decision in *Brooks v. London Borough of Haringey* [1992] I.R.L.R. 478.

[53] At 188.

[54] US 424 (1971), at p. 431.

[55] *Singh v. Rowntree Mackintosh* [1979] I.C.R. 554, EAT.

[56] *Panesar v. Nestle Co.* [1980] I.C.R. 144, C.A.

[57] *Ojutiku and Oburori v. MSC* [1982] I.C.R. 661, C.A. *per* Eveleigh L.J.

[58] *Ibid. per* Stephenson L.J.

employer.[59] This series of definitions showed a consistent tendency over time for the objective standards first enunciated by Philips J. in *Steel v. UPW* to be weakened by the addition of subjective elements.[60]

In *Bilka-Kaufhaus v. Weber von Hartz*[61] a German department store only   **2-61**
provided pensions for full-time staff. The case was referred to the ECJ for a preliminary ruling as to whether this constituted discrimination contrary to Article 119 and as to whether the practice was justifiable. The Court held that a practice which adversely affects a greater number of women than men infringes the policy contained in Article 119 (i.e. it is indirectly discriminatory) unless it is "based upon objectively justified factors which are unrelated to any discrimination based on sex."[62] The Court held that such a practice could be justified:

> "if the national court finds that the means chosen by Bilka meet a genuine need of the enterprise, that they are suitable for attaining the objective pursued by the enterprise and are necessary for that purpose."[63]

This objective standard, though enunciated in the equal pay context of Article 119, has also been applied by the ECJ in the context of equal treatment. The test has been applied directly by the national courts in cases which rely upon the application of Article 119 or the Equal Treatment Directive, most notably for example, by the House of Lords in the judicial review case of *R. v. Secretary of State, ex p. the EOC*.[64]

The test has been applied at the level of legislative and social policy, as well as at the enterprise level. Thus social policies, particularly in the field of social security but also as regards employment, have been required to be justified when they have been found to have an indirectly discriminatory impact as between men and women. Employment policies within the firm, such as distinctions in the pay and conditions afforded to part-time staff have also been found to be indirectly discriminatory and therefore requiring justification. Employment practices, such as piecework, which can result in differences in average pay, have also required to be justified according to the *Bilka* criteria.

The test in *Bilka* of objective justification untainted by sex discrimination   **2-62**
can be seen as comprising the need to identify a genuine need on the part of the discriminator, which can be met by suitable and necessary means. The need for the justification advanced by the discriminator not to be tainted by sex discrimination can be seen in *Arbeiterwolhlfahrt der Stadt Berlin eV v. Botel* in which part-time workers received less by way of compensation under

[59] *Kidd v. DRG (U.K.). supra.*
[60] In *Clarke v. Eley (IMI) Kynoch Ltd* [1983] I.C.R. 165 Browne-Wilkinson J. criticised the extent to which the *Ojutiku* formula leaves the discretion to decide such an emotive matter as racial or sex discrimination within the discretion of the tribunals. Justice Browne-Wilkinson J. opined that it was desirable for tribunals to receive some guidance as to how they were to balance the discriminatory effect of a requirement on the one hand with the reasons urged as a justification for imposing it on the other.
[61] [1987] I.C.R. 110, [1986] I.R.L.R. 317, [1986] 2 C.M.L.R. 701.
[62] Case 170/84, [1986] 2 C.M.L.R. 701 at point 31.
[63] At point 36
[64] [1994] I.R.L.R. 176, H.L.

a statutorily regulated scheme of compensation for attending staff committee training sessions than did full-timers. This discrepancy arose because part-timers received no compensation in respect of hours for which they would not normally have been at work, although they gave up some of their free time to attend. As there were far more female part-timers on the committee than male, this practice was found to be indirectly discriminatory. The employer argued that as the purpose of the payment was to compensate for wages lost in respect of hours not worked whilst attending the training sessions, the difference in compensation levels was objectively justifiable. The ECJ held, however, that:

> "(S)uch a situation is by its nature very likely to dissuade the category of part-time employees, of whom an undoubtedly larger proportion are women, from acting as a member of the staff committee or from acquiring the knowledge and skills required by that office, making the representation of this category of employees by qualified members of the staff committees all the more difficult. To that extent, the difference in treatment in question cannot be considered as justified by objective factors unrelated to any discrimination on grounds of sex, unless the Member state in question can establish the contrary before the national court."[65]

The implications of this decision for the U.K. statutory scheme of paid time off for taking part in union duties is evident, but the point here is rather that the basis of the decision is that the purported justification is rejected as not being free from sex discrimination, rather than that it does not correspond to a real need on the part of the enterprise. Similarly the payment of lower wages to match the conditions offered by private contractors in *Ratcliffe v. North Yorks C.C.*[66] was held to be tainted by sex discrimination, in that it was predicated on the willingness of married women workers in a rural area to accept such inferior terms.

2-63   The second requirement of the test of justification in *Bilka* is that the practice in question shall "correspond to a real need on the part of the undertaking". In *Bilka* itself the firm argued that it had a need to retain a core of full-time staff by paying to them a non-contributory retirement pension in order to ensure that unpopular working times, such as Saturday afternoons, were covered. The ECJ held that it was for the national court to assess if this did in fact correspond to a real need of the undertaking, met by a practice which was both suitable and necessary.

2-64   In *Rinner-Kühn v. FWW Spezial-Gebäudereinigung*,[67] a case concerning the exclusion of part-timers from the German equivalent of statutory sick pay, the German Government had argued that the exclusion of part-timers was justified because such workers "are not intergrated in and connected with the undertaking in a way comparable to that of other workers." These arguments were dismissed as "generalised statements", not meeting the objective standards of justification enunciated in *Bilka*. A legislative provision which in practice gives rise to discriminatory effects may only be justified where

---

[65] Case 360/90, [1992] I.R.L.R. 423 at 426.
[66] [1995] I.R.L.R. 439.
[67] [1989] I.R.L.R. 493, ECJ.

the Member State "can show that the means chosen meet a necessary aim of its social policy and that they are suitable and requisite for attaining that aim" where, as was held to be so in the social security case of *Commission v. Belgium*,[68] the ECJ concluded that supplements paid to those with responsibility to support a family fulfilled a legitimate objective of social policy.

The second requirement of the test of justification in *Bilka*, is that the practice adopted shall be a suitable method of attaining the objective in question. According to the ECJ this is a matter for the national court to decide, although in some instances this does not have appear to have precluded the ECJ from going on to consider the appropriateness of the policies in question. In the Article 169 case cited above, *European Commission v. Belgium*, the Belgian system of unemployment assistance, which gives rise to tiered layers of benefits according to whether the claimant has dependants, was considered a suitable method of achieving the social policy of guaranteeing a minimum subsistence level. **2-65**

In *R. v. Secretary of State for Employment, ex p. EOC*[69] the House of Lords relied upon the test of justification in *Bilka*, as applied to legislative policy in *Rinner-Kühn* (above). In that case the EOC sought judicial review of the question as to whether the differential qualification periods required to be served by full-time and part-time workers in order to be eligible for redundancy and unfair dismissal compensation, constituted unlawful indirect discrimination. Lord Keith of Kinkel put the matter as follows:

> "The bringing about of an increase in the availability of part-time work is properly to be regarded as a beneficial aim of social policy and it cannot be said that it is not a necessary aim. The question is whether the threshold provisions of the Act of 1978 have been shown, by reference to objective factors, to be suitable and requisite for achieving that aim."[70]

Lord Keith went on to hold that the Secretary of State had failed to show that the threshold provisions were suitable in so far as their purpose was to reduce the indirect cost of employing part-time labour. As it would be a gross breach of the principle of equal pay to pay a lower rate so as to reduce the direct costs of employing part-time workers, so it could not be a suitable means of stimulating part-time employment to reduce its indirect costs in this way.

The EOC case clearly exemplifies the third requirement of the test of justification *i.e.* that the practice shall be "necessary" (*Bilka*) or "requisite" (*Rinner-Kühn*). Neil L.J. held that the policy of having different threshold levels for part-time and full-time staff could not be said to be requisite for its purpose, in that the Secretary of State had failed to provide adequate objective evidence that the lower thresholds for part-timers stimulated their employment. Similarly, the Court of Appeal in *R. v. Secretary of State for Employment, ex p. Seymour-Smith and Perez*[71] upheld the decision of the

---

[68] [1991] I.R.L.R. 393, ECJ.
[69] [1994] I.R.L.R. 176.
[70] At p. 181.
[71] [1995] I.R.L.R. 465.

Divisional Court that the Secretary of State had failed, for similar reasons, to justify the two year qualification period for unfair dismissal.

The precise operation of the test of justification in cases concerning social policy measures has now been brought into question by the decisions of the Court of Justice in the joined cases of *Nolte v. Hannover*, and *Megner & Scheffel v. Innungskrankenkasse Vorderpfalz*. Both of these cases concerned the exclusion of workers in "minor employment" (employed for fewer than 15 hours per week and earning less than one seventh of the average wage of workers insured under the German statutory pension system) from the German statutory old-age, sickness and invalidity insurance schemes. It was alleged that such an exclusion was indirectly discriminatory against women under Directive 79/7. The decision of the Court of Justice turns upon the question as to whether such a practice could be justified on the basis that there is a social demand for such employment and that if it were to be made subject to compulsory social insurance provisions, the supply of such jobs would dry up or be driven into the "grey" or "black" economy. The court treated the submissions of the German government with deference, holding that:

> "(I)n the current state of Community law, social policy is a matter for the Member States. Consequently, it is for the Member States to choose the measures capable of achieving the aim of their social and employment policy. In exercising that competence, the Member States have a broad margin of discretion.
>
> It should be noted that the social and employment policy relied on by the German government is objectively unrelated to any discrimination on grounds of sex and that, in exercising its competence, the national legislature was reasonably entitled to consider that the legislation in question was necessary in order to achieve that aim."[71a]

The decisions in *Nolte* and *Megner* clearly are at variance with the views expressed in *Rinner-Kühn*, where reliance on "generalised statements" was not considered to constitute a justification of an otherwise indirectly discriminatory policy. In view of these decisions, the House of Lords may take a more restrictive view of the scope of anti-discrimination law in the *Seymour-Smith and Perez* case. Certainly the observation of Neil L.J. in that case, that henceforth all social policy measures may need to be reviewed for their discriminatory impact, would seem to be somewhat of an overstatement. *Nolte* and *Megner* may spell the end of the judicial review of social policy in terms of its conformity with Community equality law, a policy which has hitherto proved fruitful for the EOC. Whilst one could argue, as did Slynn L.J. in the *Ratcliffe v. North Yorkshire C.C.* case, that where an indirectly discriminatory practice is justified by reliance on a policy which is facilitated by the weak market position of part-time women workers, the purported justification is itself tainted with sex discrimination, this argument is unlikely to have the same force after the *Nolte* and *Megner* decisions.

The *Bilka* test was adopted by the House of Lords in the equal pay case of *Rainey v. Greater Glasgow Health Board*.[72] In an important *obiter dictum*

[71a] Case C-317/93 [1996] I.R.L.R. 225; [1996] All E.R. (EC) 212, ECJ, at points 33–34.
[72] [1987] I.R.L.R. 26 and see *Greater Glasgow Health Board v. Carey* (1987) I.R.L.R. 484, EAT.

the House of Lords expanded its application to the requirements of justification in the Sex Discrimination Act, by holding that:

"there would not appear to be any material distinction in principle between the need to demonstrate objectively justified grounds of difference for the purpose of s.1(3) [of the Equal Pay Act] and the need to justify a requirement or condition under s.1(1)(b)(ii) of the Act of 1975."[73]

In *Duke v. Reliance Systems*[74] the House of Lords held that as the Sex Discrimination Act became law prior to the Equal Treatment Directive, it was not to be interpreted as giving effect to the Directive. On this reasoning it would have been the standard enunciated by the Court of Appeal in *Ojutiku v. MSC*,[75] which constituted the standard of justification in discrimination, though not in equal pay cases. The judges of the Court of Appeal expressed this standard each in a slightly different form, thus: *per* Eveleigh L.J.: if a person produces reasons for doing something which would be acceptable to right thinking people as sound and tolerable reasons for so doing, then he has justified his conduct.[76] *Per* Kerr L.J.: "Justifiable" implies a lower standard than the word "necessary."[77] *Per* Stephenson L.J.: The party applying the discriminatory condition must prove it to be justifiable in all the circumstances on balancing its discriminatory effect against the discriminator's need for it. But that need is what is reasonably needed by the party who applies the condition.[78]

2-66

The Court of Appeal in the race relations case of *Hampson v. Department of Education and Science*[79] adopted the test set out by Stephenson L.J. in *Ojutiku*. The test formulated by Balcombe J., giving the judgment of the court, was that:

2-67

"'justifiable' requires an objective balance to be struck between the discriminatory effect of the condition and the reasonable needs of the party who applies the condition."[80]

How effective is *Hampson* as a reconciliation of the standard formerly enunciated by Stephenson L.J. in *Ojutiku* with the standard in *Bilka*? Certainly the House of Lords approved this formulation in *Webb v. EMO (Air Cargo) Ltd*[81] and it has been relied upon in subsequent Court of Appeal cases, such as *Jones v. University of Manchester*[82] and *Meade-Hill and National Union of Civil and Public Servants v. British Council*.[83–84] In *Jones* the Court of Appeal discussed the application of the test of justification, as set out in

2-68

---

[73] *per* Lord Keith of Kinkel at 31.
[74] [1988] I.R.L.R. 118 and see *Parsons v. East Surrey Health Authority* [1986] I.C.R. 837, E.A.T.
[75] [1982] I.C.R. 661; {1982] I.R.L.R. 418.
[76] At p. 668.
[77] At p. 670.
[78] At p. 674.
[79] [1989] I.R.L.R. 69, C.A.
[80] Approved by the House of Lords in *Webb v. EMO Air Cargo (U.K.) Ltd* [1993] I.R.L.R. 27.
[81] [1993] I.R.L.R. 27.
[82] [1993] I.R.L.R. 218, C.A.
[83–84] [1995] I.R.L.R. 478, C.A.

Hampson, concluding that the Industrial Tribunal in that case had failed to carry out correctly the objective balancing exercise required. The case concerned the application of an age limit of 35 for appointment as a careers adviser, but the I.T. had discounted the arguments put forward by the University concerning the desirability of promoting a wider age spread in the department concerned and ensuring a suitable line of management succession. The Court of Appeal was of the view that something more than the "reasonable" needs of the University were being required by the Tribunal, but the main difficulty in regard to justification arose from the question as to whether it is the discriminatory effect on the applicant (and others like her?) or the effect upon the total array of candidates who might be considered for the post, which should be placed in the balance against the reasonable needs of the respondent. This was put in terms of a "subjective" versus an "objective" balance, but that distinction did not find favour with the Court. Sir Ralph Gibson L.J; giving the leading judgement, held that it was not inappropriate to consider the qualitative effect upon the applicant, *i.e.* how great and long lasting is the damage done, not only to the applicant but to others similarly situated, so long as account is taken of the quantitative effects of the decision, *i.e.* how typical is the applicant's situation of the broader "pool" of candidates.[85] If one were to apply the *Bilka* test to the facts of *Jones*, then the question would be formulated so as to examine (1) whether the University has a "genuine need" to take into account the age profile of its careers department, (2) whether the age limits imposed were "suitable" to achieve that purpose and (3) that it was "necessary" (or in *Rinner-Kühn* "requisite") to impose them. Thus the *Bilka* test is more concerned to establish adverse impact and then to seek for a non-discriminatory explanation of the practice, rather than to enquire into the qualitative extent of the adverse impact and to balance this against the discriminatory effect. However, in *Bilka* the extent of the wrong suffered by the applicant was not in question, nor was her position in any way untypical of part-time workers as a class, nor of the majority of female employees in the company.

2-69   It has been held that it is a question of fact for the industrial tribunal as to whether the circumstances in any individual case meet the standards of justification then prevailing.[86] That justification must be irrespective of the sex, race or nationality, etc. of the person concerned. Thus, where in *Orphanos v. Queen Mary College*[87] the College sought to justify the practice of charging higher fees to non-EEC students on the ground that it was not a legitimate use of public funds to subsidise the education of overseas students, the House of Lords held that this reason was so bound up with the question of the nationality of the appellant that it could not constitute a justification under section 1(b)(ii).

---

[85] Sir David Croom Johnson held that it was incorrect to take account of the sex of the applicant in assessing the impact of the requirement upon the applicant, because justification under section 1(1((b) must be "irrespective of the sex of the person to whom it is applied". However, in this context it is with respect submitted that that phrase refers to the justification offered by the respondent, rather than to the assessment of the impact on the applicant, who is claiming to have been discriminated on grounds of gender.

[86] *Panesar v. Nestle & Co. Ltd* [1980] I.C.R. 144, C.A., *Cobb v. Secretary of State for Employment and the Manpower Services Commission* at 129 n.

[87] [1985] I.R.L.R. 349, H.L.

Victimisation

A separate cause of action in relation to less favourable treatment is set out   **2-70**
in the RRA, s.2 and the SDA, s.4, that of victimisation. The purpose of these
sections is to deter an employer from taking action against those employees
who have brought proceedings under the two Acts or have given evidence
against the employer in the course of such proceedings. In reality, adverse
employer reaction is not uncommon, as is shown by a survey of the experiences of successful claimants undertaken by the EOC.[88] The existence of the
section on victimisation was not effective in preventing the fact of having
taken action under the sex discrimination legislation from having an adverse
effect on the careers and working experience of many of the applicants who
had actually been successful in the tribunals, partly because the pressures to
which they were subject were often subtle and informal.

One reason for the lack of effectiveness of the sections on victimisation is   **2-71**
their complexity. The Race Relations Act, s.2 provides as follows:

> "(1) A person (the discriminator) discriminates against another person
> (the person victimised) in any circumstances relevant for the purposes
> of any provision of this Act if he treats the person victimised less favour-
> ably than in those circumstances he treats or would treat other persons,
> and does so by reason that the person victimised has —
>
> (a) brought proceedings against the discriminator or any other person
>   under this Act; or
> (b) given evidence or information in connection with proceedings
>   brought by any person against the discriminator or any person under
>   this Act; or
> (c) otherwise done anything under or by reference to this Act in relation
>   to the discriminator or any other person; or
> (d) alleged that the discriminator or any other person has committed an
>   act which (whether or not the allegation so states) would amount to
>   a contravention of this Act.
>
> or by reason that the discriminator knows that the person victimised
> intends to do any of these things, or suspects that the person victimised
> has done, or intends to do, any of them."

The Sex Discrimination Act sets out a provision on victimisation in similar
terms.

Article 8 of the Equal Treatment Directive contains a victimisation provision   **2-72**
in connection with the bringing of a complaint of sex discrimination. It provides that:

> "Member States shall take the necessary measures to protect employees
> against dismissal by the employer as a reaction to a complaint within
> the undertaking or to any legal proceedings aimed at enforcing compli-
> ance with the principle of equal treatment."

[88] Alice Leonard, *Pyrrhic Victories* (EOC, 1986).

Thus the provisions of the Directive are simultaneously wider than the U.K. Acts, in that they are more open-textured and less technical, but narrower, in that they protect only against dismissal as a reaction to the victim's having brought a complaint.

2-73 In order for the person victimised to succeed in an action under the Race Relations Act, s.2 or the Sex Discrimination Act, s.4 he or she must show that he or she took one of the "protected acts" set out in subsections (a)–(b) and that, in any circumstances relevant to the purposes of any provision of these Acts, the person victimised has been treated less favourably[89] than in those circumstances the discriminator treats or would treat other persons, by reason of the person victimised having taken that action. Thus in *Cornelius v. University College of Swansea*[90], the appellant had complained of sexual harassment by her boss, the College accountant, and had been transferred to another post in the Arts Centre. She did not like the new job and requested a return to her previous post and when this was not forthcoming she unsuccessfully took proceedings in the industrial tribunal alleging discrimination. Whilst awaiting an appeal in these proceedings she again requested a transfer, and when this was refused on the ground that the College was not prepared to take any action which might seem to prejudge the results of her appeal, the appellant again took proceedings, this time under the Sex Discrimination Act, s.4 alleging victimisation. The original proceedings brought by the appellant constituted a section 4(1)(a) action but the question was whether the subsequent refusal to transfer her or to hear her case under an internal grievance procedure was by reason of the proceedings which she had brought. The Court of Appeal held that this was not the case, and that the actions of the College administration were simply those which they would have taken pending the outcome of any legal proceedings and were not motivated by the fact these were proceedings under the Sex Discrimination Act. The appellant had not, therefore, been treated less favourably in those circumstances than another person would have been treated.

2-74 Somewhat similar issues arose in *Aziz v. Trinity Street Taxis Ltd*[91] in which a taxi driver was expelled from the company which had been set up on a co-operative basis by certain of the taxi drivers in Coventry to operate a radio control system. The driver was to be charged £1,000 to introduce a third taxi into the system, which he regarded as an arbitrary and unfair imposition. He suspected that the decision to levy such charges was racially motivated and began to consider taking action in the Industrial Tribunals. Other drivers had expressed verbal support for his point of view but because the appellant was of the opinion that they might not support him if he took action, he made secret tape recordings of their conversations. The existence of these tape recordings was revealed by an order for discovery during the Industrial Tribunal hearing. Subsequent to the hearing, the members of the company (which was limited by guarantee) voted to expel the appellant on the ground that

---

[89] *Nagarayan v. Agnew* [1994] I.R.L.R. 63, EAT makes clear that the applicant must have been subject to less favourable treatment as defined in either Part II or Part III of the relevant Act, as a result of taking one of the "protected acts."

[90] [1987] I.R.L.R. 147, C.A.

[91] [1988] I.R.L.R. 204, C.A.

making such recordings constituted a gross breach of trust and confidence between the members of the company.

The Court of Appeal held that making the tape recordings was an act done by reference to the Race Relations Act, which fell within section 2(1)(c), but the question was whether the expulsion was undertaken by reason of the fact that the tape recordings were made with reference to the race relations legislation or would have occurred whatever the purpose of the recordings. The comparison as to whether the person discriminated against has been treated less favourably in the relevant circumstances requires comparison to be made with persons who have not done a protected act.[92] Thus in the instant case the relevant circumstances were membership of the company and the comparison was with members who had not made such tape recordings. This led to the conclusion that the appellant had been less favourably treated. The appellant had failed to show, however, that his treatment was by reason of his having done a protected act, in that the fact that the tape recordings were made by reference to the Race Relations Act was not a relevant factor in the minds of the members who voted for his expulsion. They would have voted for the expulsion of any member who made such recordings, whatever their purpose, on the ground that this was an underhand action and a breach of trust.

The fourth type of protected act under the Sex Discrimination Act s.4 (1)(d) or the Race Relations Act s.2 (1)(d) exists where the person complaining that they have been victimised "alleged that the discriminator or any other person has committed an act which would (whether or not the allegation so states) amount to a contravention" of the relevant Act, including the Equal Pay Act. Thus where a woman alleges that she has been subject to sexual harassment and believes that she has been victimised as a result of bringing the original complaint, she will be protected providing that the original allegation is of conduct which would amount to a contravention of the Sex Discrimination Act. However, Part 4 of the Acts is based on the principle that the employer is vicariously liable for acts of unlawful discrimination committed by employees or agents and therefore, if the act in question falls outside the course of employment of the employee in question, the employer would not be liable.[93] There is a danger that the allegation may not be such that it would amount to a contravention of the Act, as the sub-section requires, if the employer cannot be vicariously responsible for it. Thus in *Walters v. Commissioner of Police of the Metropolis*[94] a woman police constable had originally complained of a sexual assault by a fellow constable when both were off-duty and away from their place of work. Her complaint was investigated but did not lead to any disciplinary action. Later she alleged that she had been victimised by reason of that original complaint, but in order to succeed in an action for victimisation she had to show, according to section 4(1)(d), that the discriminator had committed an act which would amount to a contravention of the Sex Discrimination Act. The tribunal had taken the question of whether the harassment had occurred in the course of the male

2-75

---

[92] It would have been simpler for the legislation to use the notion of unfavourable, rather than less favourable, treatment.

[93] See chapter 4.

[94] [1995] I.R.L.R. 531, EAT.

constable's employment as a preliminary point, based on facts agreed by counsel at the hearing. The EAT upheld the tribunal decision that, on the agreed facts, the act in question had occurred outside the course of the male constable's employment. It followed that if the complaint could not therefore amount to a contravention of the Sex Discrimination Act, the necessary legal basis for a victimisation complaint was not made out. The result is that where an employee makes a complaint in respect of conduct, which perhaps because it is particularly outrageous, cannot be construed as a mode of performing his contractual duties, the victim is not protected against victimisation as a result of having brought her complaint. The argument that the Act should be construed in a less restrictive fashion to encompass "a reaction to a complaint within the undertaking" as provided for by Article 7 of the Equal Treatment Directive (*see above*) was rejected, on the basis that there was no warrant to disregard the wording of the Act.

2-76 Therefore a person who seeks to avail themselves of the provisions on victimisation must show:

1. That they have undertaken a protected act within the terms of the Sex Discrimination Act, s.4 or Race Relations Act, s.2, which is one of the four categories of the act specified in subsections (a)–(d), and
2. that they have been treated less favourably in terms of Parts 2 or 3 of the relevant Act than other persons in the relevant circumstances, which circumstances do not include the undertaking of the protected act, and
3. that the discrimination complained of is by reason of their having undertaken a protected act, rather than an act the nature of which would have brought retribution whether or not it was performed with reference to the Sex Discrimination Act or Race Relations Act.

Section 55 of the Disability Discrimination Act provides in similar, but not quite identical terms, in that the protection extends to situations where the employee believes or suspects that the victim has done one of the protected acts.

Discriminatory practices

2-77 Whilst proceedings in respect of direct or indirect discrimination under section 1 of the Race Relations Act or the Sex Discrimination Act require there to be a victim because the discrimination must be to the detriment of the complainant, under the Race Relations Act, s.28 or the Sex Discrimination Act, s.37, the Commissions can deal with the position of an indirectly discriminatory practice found to exist in the course of a formal investigation, notwithstanding the absence of a specific victim of the discrimination.[95] The sections apply to the situation where a requirement or condition is applied which is unlawful by virtue of Parts II or III of the Acts or would do so if

---

[95] Contrast the position when an employer states an intention to discriminate directly (*e.g.* "We don't take Pakistanis") but there is no victim. RRA, s.28 and SDA, s.37 refer back to the indirect discrimination provisions in the two Acts, and do not therefore deal with direct discrimination. See also the Percy Ingle investigation by the CRE.

the requirement or condition were applied to members of the other gender or to a member of a specific racial group. Legal steps may be brought under these sections only by the Commissions in accordance with the requirements of the Sex Discrimination Act, ss.67–71 or the Race Relations Act, ss.58–62, *i.e.* in the context of a formal investigation. Under these procedures a non-discrimination notice may be issued, which could ultimately be enforced by an injunctive measure.

Exceptions to the Principle of Equal Treatment

The Equal Treatment Directive 76/207 contains three qualifications to the universal application of the principle of equal treatment set out in Article 2. Such derogations are to be interpreted strictly and relied upon only to the extent necessary in the context. In *Johnston v. Chief Constable of the Royal Ulster Constabulary* the ECJ held that: **2-78**

> "in determining the scope of any derogation from an individual right such as the equal treatment of men and women provided for by the directive, the principle of proportionality, one of the general principles of law underlying the Community legal order, must be observed. That principle requires that derogations remain within the limits of what is appropriate and necessary for achieving the aim in view and requires the principle of equal treatment to be reconciled as far as possible with the requirements of . . . the context of the activity in question."[96]

Thus all such derogations are to be interpreted strictly and in accordance with the needs of the situation, that is to say, observing the principle of proportionality.

Sex as a determining factor

Article 2(2) provides for a derogation from the principle of equal treatment where "the sex of the worker constitutes a determining factor," as was held to be the case in respect of midwives, in view of the "personal sensitivities" involved.[97] In the *Johnston* case itself, women police officers had been excluded from the service after the Chief Constable of Northern Ireland decided that henceforth all police officers should be armed. The Chief Constable was of the view that it was undesirable on grounds of public safety that women police officers should carry firearms, by reason of the increased risk of assassination and public distaste for such a measure. The Court held that it was for the national court to determine whether in the context in which the activities of a police officer were carried out, the sex of the officer did constitute a determining factor and whether the measures adopted, which had led to the termination of the applicant's contract, were proportionate to the threats to public safety and the frequent risk of assassination. This derogation parallels the inclusion of the "genuine occupational qualifications" in the   **2-79**

---

[96] Case 222/84 [1986] 3 C.M.L.R. 240 at point 38. See also Case 318/86, *European Commission v. France.*
[97] Case 165/82, *European Commission v. U.K.* [1983] E.C.R. 3431, [1984] 1 C.M.L.R. 44.

Sex Discrimination Act which are discussed at paragraphs 5–85 to 5–92 below.

Pregnancy and maternity

2-80   Member States are left with a power to institute measures for the protection of women as regards pregnancy and maternity by Article 2(3), which provides that the Directive "shall be without prejudice to provisions concerning the protection of women, particularly as regards pregnancy and maternity." As was held by the Court of Justice in *Johnston*:

> "It is clear from the express reference to pregnancy and maternity that the directive is intended to protect a woman's biological condition and the special relationship which exists between a woman and her child."

The Court went on to hold that such a derogation, which must be interpreted strictly, does not encompass situations simply where public opinion demands that women be given greater protection against risks which affect men and women in the same way.

It follows that the derogation in Article 2(3) does not require that fathers and mothers be treated in the same way as regards paternity and maternity. It is not intended "to settle questions concerned with the organisation of the family, or to alter the division of responsibility between parents," according to the ECJ in *Hofman v. Barmer Ersatskasse.*[98] Article 2(3), it was held, does not provide any mandate for a claim to paternity leave, being concerned with the "woman's biological condition during pregnancy and thereafter until such time as her physiological and mental functions have returned to normal after childbirth." It also protects the "special relationship between a woman and her child" by preventing that from being disturbed by the simultaneous pursuit of employment.

Note in this context that the Pregnancy Directive now requires that Member states provide for maternity leave.[99]

Equal opportunities

2-81   The third derogation provided is in Article 2(4), which provides that the Directive "shall be without prejudice to measures to promote equal opportunity for men and women, in particular by removing existing inequalities which affect women's opportunities in the areas referred to in Article 1(1)." This derogation allows for the existence at national level of measures designed to promote equality of opportunity, *i.e.* forms of positive action. However, the Court has taken a strict view of this derogation, in accordance with the general view that all such derogations should be limited, holding that the general preservation by France of certain advantages for women after the Directive was implemented, such as compassionate leave when children are ill and shorter working hours for older women, had not been shown to reduce actual instances of inequality.[1] This exception is discussed at paragraph 5–37 in the

---

[98] Case 184/83, [1986] 1 CMLR. 242. In *European Commission v. Italy* Case 163/82 [184] 3 CMLR 169 the Court also held that the refusal of paternity leave to the father of an adoptive child fell outside the ambit of Article 2(3) in that the purpose of the provision in question was to assimilate the conditions of entry into the family of an adoptive child to that of the arrival of a new-born child.

[99] See chapter 11.

[1] Case 312/86, *European Commission v. France* [1988] E.C.R. 6315, [1989] 1 C.M.L.R. 408.

context of discrimination in employment and the permissible extent of positive action.

Power to amend certain provisions of the Acts

The Secretary of State may, by an order which has been laid before Parliament, amend section 9 of the Race Relations Act, which provides an exception for seamen recruited abroad. In spite of a great reduction in the number of seamen recruited in the Indian sub-continent, no such order has as yet been made. Orders may also be made to render lawful acts which are unlawful by selected sections of the Race Relations Act. No such orders have been made to date. Neither have any orders been made in respect of the similar powers to amend the statute contained in the Sex Discrimination Act, s.80.

2-82

3 DISABILITY DISCRIMINATION

3-01   The background to the Disability Discrimination Act 1995 (DDA) was explained in chapter 1. The legislation ends the existing arrangements for registration as disabled and the quota scheme[1] (around the end of 1996). Instead it creates a new ground of unlawful discrimination. It relies quite heavily upon existing concepts and procedures in the sex and race discrimination regimes. But there are some novelties as regards fundamental concepts. The main thrust of this chapter is to explain what is peculiar to disability discrimination law and to point out where use can be made of other parts of this book to supplement that with material of more general application.[2]

The National Disability Council

3-02   *No law enforcement body* Our chapter 9 deals with the National Disability Council (NDC) and the the two Commissions concerned with working towards the elimination of sex and race discrimination. Readers are referred there for detail of the composition and functions of the NDC.[3] In general, however, it should be noted that the NDC has a primarily advisory function *vis-à-vis* the Secretary of State in relation to the functioning of the legislation.[4] It is without law enforcement powers of its own, so that it can neither bring proceedings under the Act nor carry out formal investigations of allegedly unlawful acts. Furthermore it has no power to assist individuals with their own potential or actual cases under the legislation. It is this toothlessness compared with the two Commissions which has been the greatest cause for criticism of the Disability Discrimination Act. The Council is expected to do the preparatory work on codes of practice in relation to the provision of goods and services. The existing National Advisory Council on Employment of People with Disabilities will continue to advise the Secretary of State on those parts of the Act covering employment.

Similarities of the DDA to other discrimination legislation

3-03   However other than in relation to the institutional arrangement above, it has to be said that the Disability Discrimination Act 1995 has much in common with the existing discrimination legislation covering sex and race. Anyone

---

[1] i.e. under the Disabled Persons (Employment) Acts 1944 and 1958.
[2] In particular the chapter on Industrial Tribunal Proceedings and Remedies will apply.
[3] See pages 307–308.
[4] s. 50 DDA.

coming to the new Act with a knowledge of the other legislation has a clear advantage.

Law enforcement Thus so far as law enforcement is concerned individuals can bring employment cases in the industrial tribunals under section 8 of the DDA and non-employment cases in the county courts under section 25 of the DDA.

Employment In employment, save for a provision (in section 7) exempting smaller employers, the coverage has considerable similarities. Employment itself is defined in the same way — see section 68(i). Section 4 of the DDA (discrimination against applicants and employees) reads very much like section 4 of the Race Relations Act 1976 (RRA) or section 6 of the Sex Discrimination Act 1975 (SDA) (without the exemption relating to terms made necessary because of the Equal Pay Act 1970. There are provisions covering contract work and trade organisations.[5] However, there are no provisions in Part II equivalent to sections 13 and 14 of the SDA or sections 12 and 13 of the RRA (qualifying bodies and persons concerned with vocational training),[6] Moreover there are some notable exceptions including the police, prison officers, fire fighters in public service, and the armed forces, as well as employment on board ships, hovercraft or aeroplanes.[7]

Non-employment The range of the coverage in the non-employment area is a good deal more restricted than under the other Acts. But where it does apply, *i.e.* in relation to the provision of goods, facilities and services — see section 19 of the DDA — (excepting transport, public sector education, or any prescribed service) and to premises — see section 22 of the DDA, there are strong echoes of the equivalent provisions in the other Acts.

General provisions Generally there is similar protection from victimisation by virtue of section 55 of the DDA (see chapter 2, paragraphs 2–70 to 2–76 for the detail of the existing law). Under sections 57 and 58 of the DDA the principles relating to aiding unlawful acts and vicarious liability and the employer's statutory defence (of having taken reasonably practicable steps to prevent the act or such acts) apply in the same way (see chapter 5, paragraphs 5–70 to 5–79). The Act applies to the Crown in a similar fashion, and the law on acts done under statutory, etc. authority is similar to the RRA position (see chapter 10). Any Codes of Practice issued will have to be taken into account by courts or tribunals if relevant by reason of section 53 of the DDA. The law on the use of similar fact evidence and on discovery of documents in proving discrimination, and on the general approach of courts and tribunals in view of the difficulties of proving discrimination, all set out in paragraphs 4–29 to 4–35 of chapter 4 on proof, will apply. The special questionnaire procedure set out in paragraphs 4–22 to 4–28 will apply in relation

---

[5] ss. 12 to 15 of the DDA.
[6] But see s. 19 (3) (g) in Part III.
[7] Police are excluded as they have no contract of service and it would therefore take a specific provision to include them and there is none. Some special categories of police, prison officers and categories of firefighters are excluded by s. 64 (5) & (6). Section 68 (3) excludes employment on board a ship, aircraft or hovercraft. S. 63 (7) makes it clear that service in the armed forces is excluded from Part II.

to Part II (employment) cases — see section 56 of the DDA, though not it seems in relation to non-employment cases.

Remedies And the law relating to remedies is generally similar (save that in the non-employment field a power has been given to the Secretary of State whereby a maximum can be prescribed for injury to feelings: see Schedule 3, Part II para. 7). See chapter 7, paragraphs 7–57 to 7–80 for the tribunal position and our chapter 8, paragraph 8–84 for the court position.

Differences of the DDA from other discrimination legislation

3-04   The main differences are as follows.

Who can use law First only a disabled person or a person who has been disabled can bring proceedings (except under the victimisation provisions) whereas under the SDA both men and women, and under the RRA both ethnic minorities and whites, can bring proceedings. There is nothing in the DDA itself therefore to prevent more favourable treatment of the disabled. (In contrast to the position set out in our chapter 2 for race and sex discrimination.) Although the DDA specifically says in section 6(7) that apart from the duties to make adjustments nothing in Part II is to be taken to require an employer to treat a disabled person more favourably than he treats or would treat others, an employer can do so voluntarily. Quotas were supposedly mandatory under the 1944 and 1958 legislation repealed by the 1995 Act. They can still be used voluntarily, although not to set maximum numbers, but are not now compulsory. Similarly, employers generally can advertise posts as "priority for disabled" in the same way after the 1995 Act as before it. (Although it should be borne in mind that in local government law, and it was amongst local authorities where schemes to get disabled persons into post were common, there is a general requirement to appoint on merit, thus making the position completely different after the 1995 Act. In the local government context, therefore, priority interview schemes cannot survive the DDA as they entail the possibility of the choice being made only from the disabled without going on to consider others, whereas guaranteed interview schemes can because appointment is still on merit).[8]

Justifying discrimination Second, it will be possible to justify direct disability discrimination — see sections 5, 17 and 20 DDA — (for the reason that whereas a person's sex or race is treated as an irrelevant consideration for most areas covered by that legislation, the nature of a particular disability may have to be taken into account).

No indirect discrimination: duty to make reasonable adjustments Third, there is no law on indirect disability discrimination. The Government regarded provisions inserting duties to make adjustments for those with disabilities — see sections 6 and 21 DDA — as covering most of the ground that a law on

---

[8] Local Government and Housing Act 1989. See the discussion of this point at EOR No. 65, p. 38.

indirect discrimination would have covered. (Indeed the direct discrimination provisions may prove to be significantly more widely drafted than under the other legislation and thus also catch some matters which would there constitute indirect discrimination.[9])

Discriminatory advertisements, pressure and instructions Fourth, because there is no body with law enforcement powers similar to the Equal Opportunities Commission (EOC) or the Commission for Racial Equality (CRE), there is no body to enforce laws against unlawful instructions or pressure to discriminate or discriminatory advertisements so they have not been made separately unlawful. But discriminatory advertisements do have some consequences — see below.

DDA only a skeleton Finally, whereas the sex and race primary legislation provides a firm base from which to start advising someone as to the way in which the law will apply in practice, the same is not true of the Disability Discrimination Act since in relation to several fundamental areas the Secretary of State is given the power to flesh out definitions in the statute by issuing *Guidance* (in relation to the meaning of disability) — see section 3, or *Regulations* — see sections 5, 6, 17, 20, 21 and 24 and the schedules. Anyone working with the Act will therefore need access to such subsidiary guidance/legislation. The Meaning of Disability Regulations (S.I. 1996 No. 1455) came into effect on July 30, 1996; the Employment Regulations (S.I. 1996 No. 1456) on December 2, 1996.

The practitioner's essential library

Such a variety of documents, apart from those in the case itself, will be required by the practitioner for a disability discrimination case that we may as well set out a checklist. As well as the ordinary regulations relating to tribunal procedure, including the 1996 amendment regulations (S.I. 1996 No. 1578), have you got copies of the DDA, regulations made under the DDA, guidance made under the DDA, the Code of Practice made under the DDA, relevant existing case law under the SDA or RRA, and copies of those Acts to demonstrate the relevance? In the course of time the disability legislation will produce its own case law to add to that. Oh, and in cases of ambiguity in the statute you may need to refer to Hansard! Whether you add a copy of this book to the list is entirely up to you!   **3-05**

The definition of disability

Section 1(1) DDA says that a person has a disability *"if he has a physical or mental impairment which has a substantial and long-term adverse effect on his ability to carry out normal day-to-day activities."* In the paragraphs   **3-06**

---

[9] See the wording of s. 5 (1) (a) and s. 20 (1) (a) where the ground of discrimination is "for a reason which relates to the disabled person's disability". This is capable of embracing a lot, and it will be interesting to see how widely the wording is interpreted.

which follow we have used italics to refer to wording in the basic definition in the hope that it will help the reader keep it in mind.

Schedule 1   The basic definition is qualified by the supplementary provisions in Schedule 1. Schedule 1 deals with the following matters: *impairment, long term effects*, severe disfigurement, *normal day-to-day activities, substantial adverse effects*, effect of medical treatment, persons deemed to be disabled, and progressive conditions. More detail is set out below.

Guidance pursuant to Section 3   Under Section 3 the Secretary of State may (and has done so) issue guidance about the matters to be taken into account in determining whether an *impairment* has *a substantial adverse effect on a person's ability to carry out normal day-to-day activities*; or whether such an *impairment* has a *long term effect*. The guidance may take the form of examples of what it is reasonable to regard in a particular way. The current Guidance gives examples relating to: mobility, manual dexterity, physical co-ordination, continence, ability to lift, carry or otherwise move everyday objects, speech, hearing or eyesight, memory or ability to concentrate, learn or understand and perception of the risk of physical danger. (This coincides with the list in Paragraph 4 of Schedule 1 of the Act.) A court or tribunal is bound to take the guidance into account.

The Meaning of Disability Regulations The current Regulations deal with a variety of matters: addictions, tendencies to certain anti-social acts, hay fever, tattoos and piercings, and the position of babies and young children. More detail is set out below. The list is set out here simply as an indication of where to look on which topics.

A person who has had a disability
Section 2 makes it clear that the discrimination provisions of the Act also apply in relation to a person who has had a disability. Modifications made to the Act by Schedule 2 mean that references in Parts II and III to a disabled person are to be read as including references to a person who has had a disability.

Schedule I to the Act supplementing the basic definition

3-07   Schedule 1 of the Act supplementing the basic definition of disability is summarised below.

Para 1: *Impairment*
Mental impairment where there is or has been a mental illness is included only if the illness is a clinically well-recognised illness.

Regulations prescribe more widely what is and what is not to be treated as an *impairment* and what is meant by "condition". Addictions, other than those arising from medical prescription, whether to alcohol, tobacco or other substances, are excluded but not impairments arising from addiction. The Regulations also exclude various personality disorders: a tendency to set fires, steal, or to physical or sexual abuse of other persons, exhibitionism and voyeurism.

Para. 2: *Long term effects*

The effect of an *impairment* is a *long term effect* if it has lasted or is likely to last at least 12 months, or is likely to last for the rest of the person's life. Where an *impairment* ceases to have *a substantial adverse effect on a person's ability to carry out normal day-to-day activities*, nevertheless if that effect is likely to recur it is to be treated as continuing to have that effect. Guidance under section 3 deals with factors to be taken into account in assessing the likelihood of *long term adverse effect*. Here again regulations prescribe when the likelihood of recurrence is to be disregarded. Severe hay fever (seasonal allergic rhinitis) is excluded except where it aggravates the effect of another condition. Moreover more generally future regulations may prescribe when a *long term effect* is to be treated as such in the Act and when not. Guidance points up the relevance of action the person could reasonably take to avoid a recurrence in assessing the likelihood of recurrence.

Para. 3: Severe disfigurement

A severe disfigurement is to be treated as having *a substantial adverse effect on the ability of the person concerned to carry out normal day-to-day activities*. Despite this Regulations provide otherwise in respect of tattoos and non-medical body-piercing.

Para. 4: *Normal day-to-day activities*

An impairment is to be taken to affect *the ability of the person concerned to carry out normal day-to-day activities* only if it affects mobility, manual dexterity, physical co-ordination, continence, the ability to lift, carry or move everyday objects, speech, hearing or eyesight, memory or the ability to concentrate, learn or understand; or perception of the risk of physical danger. But Regulations may prescribe when *impairments* with those effects are not to be taken to affect the *ability of the person concerned to carry out normal day-to-day activities*; and when *impairments* with other effects are to be taken to affect that ability. The Regulations provide that babies and those under six with disabilities, whose day-to-day activities would in any event be limited whether disabled or not, are specially covered by reference to what the effects would normally be on an older person.

Guidance under section 3 indicates that account should be taken of how far an activity is normal for most people and carried out by most people on a daily or very regular basis. Guidance under section 3 makes clear that indirect effect should also be taken into account *e.g.* where medical advice is to change, limit, or refrain from a *normal day-to-day activity*, or where an *impairment* causes pain or fatigue in performing *normal day-to-day activities*. And where a person has a mental illness such as depression also whether they can, in practice, sustain an activity over a reasonable period is relevant.

Para. 5: *Substantial adverse effects*

Regulations may prescribe when an effect *on the ability of a person to carry out normal day-to-day activities* is to be treated as *a substantial adverse effect*, and when not.

The Guidance, in relation to each of the categories of day-to-day activities set out in Schedule 1 of the Act, gives examples of what should be taken into account, and what would and would not be reasonable to regard as a substantial effect. The details are not set out here as the reader considering the legislation in depth to answer a particular problem will obviously need to look directly at the Guidance. Paragraph 3-06 above lists the matters in respect of which the Guidance provides examples.

Further, under the Guidance *substantial* is more than minor or trivial. The time taken to carry out an *activity* and the manner in which it is carried out should be taken into account. Account should also be taken of how far the person can reasonably be expected to manage the effects of the *impairment* to prevent or reduce the impact on *normal day-to-day activities.*

The Guidance also deals with cumulative effects. Some *impairments* such as breathing difficulties or manic depression could have an *adverse effect* on a number of *activities*, and their cumulative effect should be taken into account. Similarly the cumulative effect of more than one *impairment* should be considered.

Para. 6: *Effect of medical treatment*

Schedule 1 says that in deciding whether an *impairment* is likely to *have a substantial adverse effect on the ability of the person concerned to carry out normal day-to-day activities,* measures taken to treat or correct it, such as medical treatment and the use of a prosthesis or other aid, are in effect disregarded. But there is an exception where spectacles or contact lenses can correct an eyesight *impairment* of a person's sight, or it is correctable in other ways as may be prescribed. And other exceptions may be prescribed for other *impairments.*

Para. 7: *Persons deemed to be disabled*

Any person who, both on January 12, 1995 and on December 2, 1996, is registered as disabled under section 6 of the Disabled Persons (Employment) Act 1944, is under Schedule 1 to be deemed during an initial period of three years from December 2, 1996, to have a *disability,* and hence to be a disabled person; and afterwards, to have had a disability and hence to have been a disabled person during that period. The certificate of registration is conclusive evidence. Regulations may further provide for prescribed descriptions of persons to be deemed to have disabilities, and thus to be a disabled person, and when a person who has been deemed to be a disabled person is to be treated as no longer so deemed.

Para. 8: *Progressive conditions*

A person with a progressive condition (such as cancer, multiple sclerosis or muscular dystrophy or infection by the human immunodeficiency virus), and who has as a result an *impairment* which has (or had) *an effect on his ability to carry out normal day-to-day activities,* but not a *substantial adverse effect,* is dealt with as having an *impairment,* which has such *a substantial adverse effect* if the condition is likely to have that result. Regulations may say when conditions are to be treated as progressive, and when not.

Employment See p 134

3-08   Part II of the Act deals with Employment.

Small employers

[handwritten: Use in Recommendations at end. Rec.]

There is one major difference from the SDA and RRA coverage: there is currently an exemption from Part II of the DDA for an employer who has fewer than 20 employees. (A figure which seems to be a hang-over from the 1944 Act.) The Secretary of State may reduce this number by Order after conducting a review, and if not done before is duty-bound to conduct a review after four years.[10]

Discrimination against applicants and employees

As previously indicated section 4 of the DDA dealing with discrimination against applicants for jobs and employees is similar to section 4 of the RRA (there is no private household exemption as under the RRA, but few households these days are likely to employ 20 or more!). Readers should refer to our chapter 5, paragraphs 5–03 to 5–07, 5–14 to 5–24, and 5–39 to 5–68, for those provisions where the relevant case law is also set out, and also the slight wording difference commented upon. (When reading those passages, however, it needs to be remembered that there is no indirect disability discrimination law.)

It can be taken for granted, for example, that in as much as the SDA/RRA provisions as interpreted in the case law cover harassment on the prohibited grounds so also would section 4 of the DDA cover harassment of a person because he or she is disabled.

There is one point in particular that should be borne in mind by all employers caught by the Act. Any existing employee could become a disabled person whilst still employed. More or less enforced retirement on medical grounds may have been the almost inexorable fate of many such people in the past,[11] but the DDA may now in such cases require a quite different response. Indeed the Code of Practice will specifically refer to some of the steps an employer may have to take under the duty to make reasonable adjustments (see below) if an employee becomes disabled or has a disability which worsens.

Can persons who are not disabled bring a claim?

The wording of section 4 is "discriminate against a disabled person". It should be noted that whereas men and white people can claim discrimination under the SDA and RRA respectively, only a person who is or has been disabled can bring a claim under the DDA unless the claim is one of victimisation under section 55. The consequences for positive action have been referred to previously.

Also an employee who is not disabled seems to have no cause of action under DDA if he is sacked because his employer believes that if his severely disfigured wife waits outside for him from time to time it will put off customers. A white employee who is sacked because his black wife does like-

---

[10] s. 7 DDA.
[11] See Caroline Gooding, *Disabling Laws, Enabling Acts*, Pluto Press 1994, p. 6.

wise with a similar apprehended effect on customers would rightly be regarded as being sacked "on racial grounds".

Forms of discrimination

3-09 There are two forms both of which can be justified: (i) less favourable treatment; and (ii) failure to comply with a section 6 duty to make adjustments.

Less favourable treatment

Under section 5 of the DDA a person discriminates against a disabled person under the Employment Part of the Act if

> "for a reason which relates to the disabled person's disability, he treats him less favourably than he treats or would treat others to whom that reason does not or would not apply, and cannot show that the treatment in question is justified."

A reason which relates to disability could be, for example, objection to use of a wheelchair (even though some temporarily injured persons not within the legal definition of disabled might take to a wheelchair for a while), so the statutory wording here seems wide enough to catch what in other areas of discrimination might fall to be dealt with under indirect discrimination provisions.

Readers are referred to paragraphs 4–10 to 4–21 of chapter 4 on Proof of Discrimination for the assistance which will be provided by case law on the drawing of inferences as to the grounds for less favourable treatment where it has occurred in circumstances consistent with disability discrimination and there is no satisfactory explanation.

In passing it may be noted that the RRA says that segregation on the prohibited grounds is treating a person less favourably. The DDA says no such thing.[12] Nevertheless, segregation on grounds of a person's disability could be less favourable treatment. But clearly much will depend on the circumstances and limited segregation because of access problems to the main workspace might be the only way of complying with a duty to make adjustments.

The notion of justifying direct discrimination is unique to this Act: there is authority at the highest level that it is not possible to justify direct discrimination under either the SDA or RRA (although debate has recently opened up on that subject).[13]

Failure to comply with section 6 duty

3-10 An employer also discriminates against a disabled person if he fails to comply with a section 6 duty to make adjustments imposed on him in relation to the

---

[12] Gooding, *op. cit.*, p. 130.
[13] *James v. Eastleigh Borough Council* [1990] I.R.L.R. 288, H.L.

disabled person; and he cannot show that his failure to comply with that duty is justified. The content of the section 6 duty is set out in some detail later in the text at paragraph 3–12.

Justified discrimination

Less favourable treatment treatment is justified under section 5(3) only if the **3-11** reason for it is both *material to the circumstances of the particular case and substantial*. Similarly failure to comply with the duty to make adjustments is justified under section 5(4) only where the reason is of the same nature. At some future stage regulations may say more about what can and cannot amount to justification particularly by reference to the cost of affording any benefit.

Current Regulations provide that an an employer will be regarded as justified in relation to less favourable treatment of a disabled person in accession to an occupational pension scheme in applying eligibility requirements for receiving any benefit in relation to termination of service, retirement old age or death, accident, injury, sickness or invalidity where the person has a health condition making it likely that the cost of providing the benefit to that person would be substantially greater and the employer has obtained medical evidence. The steps which employers ought to take to satisfy themselves of the likelihood of greater costs will appear in the Code of Practice. Regulations also make special provision in relation to contributions under occupational pension schemes to enable uniform rates to be maintained even though the disabled person may be ineligible for some benefits.

Terms or practices linking pay to performance are specifically treated as justified if applied to all employees or all employees in a class. This leaves intact the duty to make adjustments in respect of aspects of arrangements or premises producing a substantial disadvantage, but the duty could not be used to compel higher pay if low performance due to disability could not be improved.

It is important for employers to appreciate that the *circumstances of the particular case* involve not just those pertaining to the job itself but also those of the individual concerned. Not only do disabilities differ widely in their impact on people's abilities to perform tasks, but also persons with very similar disabilities may, for a variety of reasons such as new technology skills or even sheer will-power, be at widely different levels in their abilities to cope with or overcome the difficulties posed. So even if an employer has shown a level of foresight and considered in general terms whether in a particular work context persons with a particular type of disability would be able to carry out the work bearing in mind all possible aids and adjustments the employer could make and come to the conclusion that it would not be feasible, that employer should not apply that conclusion as a rigid policy but should consider the circumstances of the individual.

It is a reasonably safe assertion to say that *materiality* must have as its underlying assumption the employer's need to carry out the job safely and effectively. Future regulations may flesh out what cost effectively might mean in this context, having regard to the underlying themes of the Act, one of which is that employers can expect to bear some cost in achieving its aims.

The reason must also be *substantial*. This would mean that it must have a basis in facts provable by evidence rather than unsubstantiated theories or opinion. Moreover it is possible to read into such a word the notion that marginal considerations would not suffice.

The reason put forward must also be *the reason for the treatment* where less favourable treatment applies, or *the reason for the failure* where the employer has failed to make adjustments. So reasons devised after the event will not appear to suffice and in this respect in particular the legislation is more tightly drafted than the indirect discrimination provisions in the SDA and RRA.

So advocates and tribunals should beware that there is as much scope for employers to put forward pretextual reasons under the guise of justifying discrimination as there is when trying to explain less favourable treatment in circumstances which point to grounds related to a person's disability. Thus before discovering whether the reason put forward is material, etc. and substantial the tribunal will want to ask itself the question whether the reason *was* the reason for the treatment or the failure as the case may be. If it was not whether it is material or substantial is irrelevant.

It would seem to follow also that if an employer runs a pretextual reason for less favourable treatment in the first place and fails on that, that employer will not be able to justify the less favourable treatment found to be on grounds related to disability because his purported reason for that treatment will have been disbelieved. He cannot turn round and substitute another reason.

By virtue of section 5(5) an employer cannot justify less favourable treatment where there is also an unjustified failure to make adjustments unless he could have done so even if he had complied with the section 6 duty.

Duty of employer to make adjustments

3-12 Section 6 of the DDA sets out the duty to make adjustments on an employer in certain circumstances. They relate (i) to arrangements and (ii) to a physical feature.

The duty applies first where any *arrangements* made by or on behalf of an employer for determining who should be offered employment or in relation to any term condition or arrangements on which employment, promotion, a transfer, training or any other benefit is offered or afforded, or second any *physical feature* of premises occupied by the employer, place the disabled person concerned at a substantial disadvantage in comparison with persons who are not disabled.

The duty applies only in respect of an actual job applicant or one who has notified the employer that he may be a job applicant so far as selection arrangements are concerned, and otherwise only to an actual job applicant or employee. And then not if the the employer does not know or could not reasonably be expected to know that the person is or may be a job applicant, or that the person has a disability and is likely to be affected in the way mentioned.

The duty of the employer is to take such steps as it is reasonable, in all the circumstances of the case, for him to have to take to prevent the arrangements or feature having that effect.

The Act usefully gives examples of steps which an employer may have to take to comply with the duty: making adjustments to premises; allocating some of the disabled person's duties to another person; transferring him to fill an existing vacancy; altering his working hours; assigning him to a different place of work; allowing him to be absent during working hours for rehabilitation, assessment or treatment; providing training; acquiring or modifying equipment; modifying instructions or reference manuals; modifying procedures for testing or assessment; providing a reader or interpreter; and providing supervision.

The Act sets out a number of factors which have to be taken into account in deciding whether it is reasonable for an employer to have to take a particular step: the extent to which taking the step would prevent the effect; the extent to which it is practicable for the employer to take the step; the financial and other costs involved in taking the step and the extent to which it would disrupt any of his activities; the extent of the employer's financial and other resources; and the availability to the employer of financial or other assistance with respect to taking the step. The Government's view is that most adjustments will cost relatively little.

However it should be noted that what is set out in the preceding two paragraphs may be modified under a wide-ranging power to make regulations particularly to reflect the cost of taking any steps concerned. The intention is, at least initially, to leave judgements as to costs to the industrial tribunals taking into account the Code of Practice, and to use this power only if it becomes necessary. The Act does, though, make it clear that the regulations could have the effect of adding to the section 6 duty to make adjustments.

Regulations specifically include a number of matters under the heading of "physical feature of premises" whether temporary or permanent namely features arising from the design or construction of a building on the premises, features on the premises of any approach or access to a building, fixtures, fittings, furnishings, furniture, equipment or materials in or on premises, and any physical element or quality of any land comprised in the premises.

In an exclusion brought about by the Regulations (which may prove to be exceptionally wide in practice and do much to discredit the new provisions since it will exclude all reference to the particular circumstances of the disabled person or how simple adaptation would be), there is excluded from the duty to make reasonable adjustments cases where the feature was specifically covered by Part M of the Building Regulations in force.[14]   **3-13**

Regulations set out when it it is reasonable for an occupier under a lease not to make adjustments, where the terms of the lease affect the position, namely, if he has applied to the lessor for consent setting out the section 6 duty circumstances, and that consent has been withheld, and the occupier has informed the disabled person of the situation. (A lessor can be joined in industrial tribunal proceedings under Part I of Schedule 4.)

Candour on the part of disabled job applicants

The provisions really impose a need for a degree of candour on the part of disabled persons as to what their disability actually entails in practice and how particular problems may be encountered and indeed can be overcome. The reality is that it will also pay employers to scrutinise applications with some care to extract the relevant information.   **3-14**

It may be useful to consider this at a very basic level. How would the law

[14] Or in Scotland Part T of the Technical Standards.

work in relation to a very common stipulation that job applicants should apply by sending a covering letter in their own handwriting accompanied by a typed or printed cv? There may well be interested blind and other persons who would find it difficult to maintain legibility in a handwritten letter and who normally type. Suppose such an applicant sends a cv with a type-written covering letter explaining the disability and why the letter is typewritten. Suppose also an employer who at first sift does not read the letters of application or the cv but simply discards all those who sent in typewritten letters as a rough and ready way of reducing the numbers with some basis in the thought that people who do not obey instructions are not wanted anyway.

If there was a law against indirect discrimination in the disability field the answer would be simple (if the employer could not justify the requirement it would be unlawful), but there is no such law. The facts do not amount to less favourable treatment of the disabled person contrary to section 5(i) because nothing has been done "for a reason which relates to a person's disability". Does it amount to prima facie unlawful discrimination requiring justification as a failure to comply with the duty to make adjustments imposed by section 6? It is likely that any tribunal would hold that this an area to which the duty to make adjustments applies (and unlikely that any regulations would say otherwise) and easy to see that the disabled person is placed at a substantial disadvantage. But if the employer has not read the letters of application at first sift he or she will not know that the person is disabled so the application of the duty to make adjustments will turn on whether the employer could be reasonably expected to know of the disability and how the person would be affected. It is difficult to imagine any tribunal concluding that an employer could not be reasonably expected to know what is explicitly stated in a letter of application. Justifying the handwriting requirement in the absence of reasoning which paid no attention to the circumstances of the particular case seems doomed to failure.

It may be that generally in British habits of thought there is quite a strong tendency to see problems as reasons for not doing things when they should properly be perceived as obstacles to be overcome, or to see what is customary as equivalent to what is necessary although the original reasons for so acting have long been largely irrelevant to the modern era. If that is so, adjusting to the duty to make adjustments could not infrequently start to change ways of thinking more generally than just in relation to disabled persons.

Less favourable treatment and/or failure to make adjustments

3-15 It may often be necessary to run a case in the alternative as discrimination by way of less favourable treatment and/or by way of failure to make adjustments. An example; although it is hypothetical because there is no existing case law, it has been made as real as possible by making use of an extract from an actual person's cv. Let us suppose that a blind lawyer has applied for a legal job and has been turned down without interview. He hears that a rather less well qualified and experienced lawyer who is not disabled has been called for interview. In the blind lawyer's cv he had summed up the likely effect of his disability in the following way:

"Whilst I am registered as blind this has not so far proved a problem in my studies and work experience. I have had the opportunity of working with a range of blind solicitors and thereby gained valuable insight into the way to handle any day-to-day challenges. I am also a student member of the Society of Blind Lawyers, which allows me to keep up to date with the latest changes and developments. A range of specialist equipment is available for the accessing of printed material including a Versabraille 2 plus which facilitates note taking and conversion to print (this machine I already own) and scanners and access software (for which Employment Service grants are available). In short there would be very little I could not undertake in an employment situation and such extra assistance as may be required would represent no cost to my employer."

The applicant has sent off a questionnaire seeking explanations and supporting documents. The reply in essence is that the other person had some experience of a particular legal speciality which (according to his cv) the applicant had not, and this speciality was amongst the firm's needs. The applicant is highly suspicious of this reason because it was not mentioned in the advertisement or the job specification or the very brief shortlisting notes: in short it looks like a pretext. But if that was not the true reason for his being turned down what was? Did the employers see the references to his blindness and simply switch off (less favourable treatment); did they not believe his claims as to what he was capable of doing when they were prepared to believe the claims of those not disabled as to their capabilities (less favourable treatment); could they not be bothered to apply for grants (failure to make adjustments)? The applicant probably would not know the answer to these questions when he commences proceedings so claiming both grounds would be appropriate. Indeed if the law in *Quarcoopome v. Sock Shop Holdings Ltd*[15] is applied here — and why not? — a general claim of disability discrimination should be held to cover both forms of disability discrimination (less favourable treatment and failure to make adjustments). But appropriate amendment should be made at some stage because a tribunal can only rule on a claim actually made (see chapter 7 on this point).

It should of course be noted that if there is apparent less favourable treatment and the applicant, but not the comparator, is disabled then the applicant will be able to rely on established law that in the absence of a satisfactory explanation from the employer the tribunal may draw the appropriate inference (see chapter 4). If the general impression was that the employer simply could not be bothered to get involved with a blind person it would seem open to the tribunal to draw the inference that a mixture of both grounds was involved.

The Code of Practice

From the draft code it appears that much of what will be in the Code particularly with regard to the practical guidance with a view to eliminating discrimination will be self-evident to anyone who has read the Act, the Regulations, and the Guidance. But the guidance offered on eliminating dis-   **3-16**

---

[15] [1995] I.R.L.R. 353.

crimination more widely looks to be particularly useful. Some of the major points are:

- Do not make assumptions but talk to the disabled person
- consider whether expert help is needed
- be imaginative
- plan ahead because improvements to help the disabled might be achieved more cheaply, etc. if implemented along with other changes rather than if implemented later (though anticipatory changes are not required for disabled people who may appear on the scene at some stage)
- consult other employees to gain co-operation.

Discriminatory advertisements

3-17   As no Commission with enforcement powers exists as in the case of sex and race discrimination there is no statutory body to enforce a duty not to publish a discriminatory advertisement as there is in relation to discriminatory advertisements in those areas. The upshot is that a discriminatory advertisement is not itself unlawful.

However, in relation to sex and race discrimination, an advertisement showing a discriminatory intention can also be led as evidence in support of a claim by an applicant that there was discrimination on the prohibited grounds in relation to his or her job application, although this is not expressly stated in the statutes. The Disability Discrimination Act expressly adopts this latter approach in section 11, although it is open to doubt whether the provision really achieves any more than the Tribunals would have read into the law in any event.

Section 11 applies if a disabled person has applied for employment and the employer has refused to offer, or has deliberately not offered him the employment and the disabled person has presented a complaint against the employer. It creates a rebuttable presumption where the employer has advertised the employment (whether before or after the disabled person applied for it) and the advertisement indicated, or might reasonably be understood to have indicated, that any application for the advertised employment would, or might, be determined to any extent by reference to the successful applicant not having any disability or any category of disability which includes the disabled person's disability or the employer's reluctance to make adjustments. The tribunal shall assume, unless the contrary is shown, that the employer's reason for refusing to offer or deliberately not offering, the employment to the applicant was related to the complainant's disability.

However, it should be borne in mind that in such a case it is open to the employer to run the defence that the discrimination was justified. Thus there might well be circumstances in which an employer could openly say in an advertisement that unfortunately the nature of the job is such that it is not possible to accommodate certain forms of disability.

Discrimination against contract workers

3-18   Section 12 of the DDA applies Part II to a principal for whom contract work is done in much the same way as section 9 of the SDA and section 7 of the

RRA apply those Acts (except that those sections have Genuine Occupational Qualifications (GOQ) exceptions) and readers are referred there (see chapter 5, paragraphs 5–93 to 5–95). It is unlawful for a principal to discriminate against a disabled person in the terms on which he allows him to do the work, by not allowing him to do it or continue to do it, in the way he affords him access to any benefits or by refusing or deliberately omitting to afford him access to them, or by subjecting him to any other detriment. Case law on the existing provisions establishes that the protection applies to refusing to take on a contract worker as in the case of *BP Chemicals Ltd v. Gillick*.[16]

Regulations clarify the extent of the duty of reasonable adjustment as between employer and principal. The aim is to ensure that the duty applies to the employer if the reasonable adjustment would be needed irrespective of the principal concerned. A principal would have to co-operate with any reasonable adjustment by the employer, *e.g.* use of a special portable computer. A principal would have to make reasonable adjustments which may be necessary because of a feature of the premises which the principal occupies.

Discrimination by trade organisations

Section 13 of the DDA starts off in similar terms to section 12 of the SDA and section 11 of the RRA. (See chapter 5, paragraph 5–100.) It is unlawful for a trade organisation (*i.e.* an organisation of workers, or of employers or any other organisation whose members carry on a particular profession or trade for the purposes of which the organisation exists.) to discriminate against a disabled person in certain circumstances. Those are: in the terms on which it is prepared to admit him to membership or by refusing to accept, or deliberately not accepting, his application for membership; and in the case of a disabled member in the way it affords him access to any benefits or by refusing or deliberately omitting to afford him access to them, by depriving him of membership, or varying the terms on which he is a member, or by subjecting him to any other detriment.

3-19

Thereafter in sections 14 to 15 of the DDA the provisions follow very closely the provisions of sections 5 and 6 of the DDA[17] in detailing the two forms of discrimination by way of less favourable treatment, and by way of failure to make adjustments, both of which can be justified by a reason which is both material and substantial; see paragraphs 3–09 to 3–12 above. However there is no provision equivalent to subsection 6 (3) setting out examples of steps which may have to be taken to comply with the duty to make adjustments. Once again there is a wide-ranging power to make regulations.

Adjustments where premises are leased

The duty to make adjustments imposed on employers by section 6 and on trade organisations by section 15 could pose particular problems where the lease of the premises makes special provision. The lease has effect as though it entitled the occupier to make the alteration with the consent of the lessor

3-20

---

[16] [1995] I.R.L.R. 128, EAT.
[17] Though confusion is sown by a wrong side-note to section 15 in the HMSO copy of the Act from which we are working!

such consent not to be unreasonably withheld and only reasonable conditions to be imposed. Under Schedule 4 to the DDA there is further provision to join the lessor as party to tribunal proceedings, and if the tribunal finds consent to alterations has been refused or conditions imposed it may determine the reasonableness of the refusal or the conditions. There is power to make a declaration, to order an alteration, and to make the lessor pay compensation to the complainant but only where no such compensation order is made against the occupier. There is also power to make regulations on this subject, and the power has been used to spell out when a landlord is deemed to have withheld consent, and cases where the withholding or a condition imposed would be deemed unreasonable, or in some cases reasonable.

Occupational pension schemes and insurance services

3-21   Section 17 deems every occupational pension scheme to include a paramount provision called "a non-discrimination rule" relating to the terms on which persons become members of the scheme and members of the scheme are treated. The rule requires the trustees or managers of the scheme to refrain from any act or omission which, if done in relation to a person by an employer would amount to unlawful discrimination under Part II. However regulations can modify the impact of Part II in this area.

Section 18 applies where a provider of insurance services enters into arrangements with an employer under which his employees, or a class of his employees receive insurance services or are given an opportunity to receive such services. Those services must be of a prescribed description for the provision of benefits in respect of termination of service, retirement, old age or death, accident, injury, sickness or invalidity, or any other prescribed matter. The insurer is to be taken, for the purposes of Part II, to discriminate unlawfully against a disabled person who is such an employee or a prospective employee if he acts in relation to that employee in a way which would be unlawful discrimination for the purposes of Part III (provision of services to members of the public).

Non-employment provisions

Goods, facilities and services

3-22   Part III of the DDA deals with discrimination in the provision of goods facilities or services. Section 19 of the Act has much in common with sections 29 of the SDA and 20 of the RRA and reference should be made to our treatment of those provisions where relevant case law on the meaning of some of the common phrases (*e.g.* "to the public or a section of the public") is set out (see chapter 8, paragraphs 8–20 to 8–39).

It is unlawful for a provider of services (which includes goods or facilities) to the public, or a section of the public, to discriminate against a disabled person by refusing to provide, or deliberately not providing, any service which he generally provides, or is prepared to provide, to members of the public in failing to comply with a section 21 duty to make adjustments in circumstances in which the effect of that failure is to make it impossible or unreasonably difficult for the disabled person to make use of the service; in the standard of service provided or the manner of its provision; and in the terms on which it is provided. The same is true whether or not the services are provided for payment.

The list of examples of the services covered by these provisions of the DDA is similar to that under section 29 of the SDA and section 20 of the RRA,[18] with the following differences.

First, the DDA adds two new examples: access to and use of means of communication and information services (but there is no reason to suppose that the other Acts would not in fact cover these matters). It includes two that in the other Acts would be dealt with under the employment provisions: facilities provided by employment agencies or under section 2 of the Employment Training Act 1973.

Second, the DDA excludes from the list two examples that are present under the other Acts: facilities for education and for transport or travel. The reasons are apparent from subsection 19 (5). Except in prescribed circumstances publicly funded education, and that run by voluntary agencies, is excluded from the operation of these provisions. But Part IV of the DDA has separate provisions on education. So also is excluded any service so far as it consists of the use of any means of transport. But Part V deals with public transport.

Section 20 then goes on to set out the meaning of discrimination in this context. As with the employment provisions, there are two forms of discrimination: unjustified less favourable treatment for a reason which relates to the disabled person's disability where the reason does not apply to others or where others would not be so treated[19]; and unjustified failure to comply with the duty to make adjustments (here imposed by section 21).[20]

3-23

Treatment (here referring both to less favourable treatment and failure to comply with a section 21 duty to make adjustments) is only justified where in the opinion of the provider of services one or more of five listed conditions are satisfied and it is reasonable for him to hold that opinion in all the circumstances of the case. Obviously this formulation gives considerable weight to the opinion of the provider of services, with a court only able to take a different view if it concludes that an opinion is unreasonably held. But there is something of a catch if the service provider does not take into account all the circumstances: there is a real risk that a court might conclude the resulting opinion is unreasonable if something highly material has been overlooked. (However regulations may spell out the circumstances when it is reasonable to hold an opinion and when not.) The wording of the corresponding employment provision in section 5 of the DDA seems to make it abundantly clear that the reason put forward by way of justification must be the actual reason

---

[18] See chapter 8, paragraph 8–26.

[19] The Government's "Brief Guide to the Act" gives a number of examples of unlawful discrimination: a supermarket owner refuses to serve someone whose disability means that they shop slowly; a restaurant owner insists that a person with a facial disfigurement sits out of sight of other customers; a travel company asks a disabled person for a bigger deposit when booking a holiday.

[20] The "Brief Guide" gives as examples: a restaurant which does not allow animals in will have to allow in a disabled person with a guide dog; a library with a reference section upstairs without a lift, entailing that staff could quite well have to bring reference books to the disabled person.

at the time. Section 20 is not so clear in this respect, but it would be odd if section 20 was held to lend itself to *ex post facto* reasoning to supply justification whereas section 5 does not.

The conditions are:

- that the treatment is necessary in order not to endanger the health or safety of any person and that can include the disabled person;
- that the disabled person is incapable of entering into an enforceable agreement, or of giving an informed consent and for that reason the treatment is reasonable in that case. But regulations may disapply this in certain circumstances where the law gives another the power to act on that person's behalf;
- in a case of refusal or failure to provide the services, that the treatment is reasonable because the provider of services would otherwise be unable to provide the service to members of the public;
- in a case relating to the standard or manner of the service or the terms on which it is provided, that the treatment is necessary in order for the provider of services to be able to provide the service to the disabled person or to other members of the public;
- in a case relating to different terms of service, that the difference reflects the greater cost to the provider of services in providing the service to the disabled person. But this does not include the cost of complying with a duty to make adjustments under section 21.

Regulations made under the Act may add to this list.

The section 21 duty to make adjustments

3-24   The section 21 duty to make adjustments arises in two circumstances, set out below. But it should be noted that nothing in the section requires steps which would fundamentally alter the nature of the service in question or the nature of the provider's trade, profession or business.

Nothing is to require steps which would involve expenditure over the appropriate prescribed limit. Having a prescribed limit is probably sensible, inasmuch as courts are not well-equipped to say overall what kind of expenditure could be expected, but a lot depends on what is actually prescribed. It may not be an actual figure but a figure to be calculated by reference to some such criterion as turnover. There is considerable flexibility built into the power, or more realistically, the duty to prescribe.

Practice, policy or procedure

3-25   Where a provider of services has a *practice, policy or procedure* which makes it impossible or unreasonably difficult for disabled persons to make use of a service which he provides, or is prepared to provide, to other members of the public, it is his duty to take such steps as it is reasonable, in all the circumstances of the case for him to have to take in order to change that practice, policy or procedure so that it no longer has that effect.[21]

---

[21] It is interesting to note that in this context the legislators have eschewed use of the unfortunate words "requirement or condition", found in the indirect discrimination provisions under the SDA and RRA, in favour the broader and more flexible test involved in the words "policy, practice or procedure which makes it impossible or unreasonably difficult", which has similarities to proposals for changing the SDA and RRA put forward by the EOC and CRE.

Physical feature

Where a *physical feature* (e.g. arising from the design or construction of a **3-26** building or the approach or access to premises) makes it impossible or unreasonably difficult for disabled persons to make use of such a service, the provider of that service also has a duty. It is to take such steps as it is reasonable, in all the circumstances of the case, for him to have to take in order to: remove the feature; alter it so that it no longer has that effect; provide a reasonable means of avoiding the feature; or provide a reasonable alternative method of making the service available to disabled persons.

Regulations may prescribe what matters are to be taken into account in determining whether any provision is reasonable; and exempting categories of providers of services from the duty to make adjustments in respect of physical features.

Leased premises and adjustments

Section 27 of the DDA provides for the situation where a provider of services **3-27** under a duty to make adjustments holds the premises under a lease and is in similar terms to section 16 of the Act where an employer is in a similar situation with regard to a section 6 duty. The only substantial difference, set out in Schedule 4, is if the matter is litigated when the matter will be dealt with in the county court or the sheriff court in Scotland.

Discrimination in relation to premises

Part III also makes unlawful discrimination in the disposal or management **3-28** of premises and in relation to a licence or consent to a subletting. The basic provisions detailing the application of the law are in sections 22 and 23 of the DDA and are very similar to sections 30 and 31 of the SDA and sections 21 and 22 of the RRA, including a small premises exception.[22]

The meaning of discrimination in this context is of course rather different, and section 24 of the Act sets out that meaning. The main point to note is that only unjustified less favourable treatment on the prohibited ground is unlawful here. (There is no duty to make adjustments.)

Justifying less favourable treatment

The approach of section 24 of the DDA to justification is similar to that **3-29** taken under section 20 of the Act. A person can justify his less favourable treatment only if in his opinion one or more of a list of conditions is satisfied and it is reasonable in all the circumstances of the case for him to hold that opinion. Here the conditions are:

- that the treatment is necessary in order not to endanger the health or safety of any person (which may include the disabled person);
- that the disabled person is incapable of entering into an enforceable

---

[22] See chapter 8, paragraphs 8–46 to 8–54.

agreement, or of giving an informed consent and for that reason the treatment is reasonable in that case;

● in a case concerning the way in which the disabled person was permitted to make use of the benefits or facilities of managed premises, the treatment is necessary in order for the disabled person or the occupiers of other premises forming part of the building to make use of the benefit or facility;

● in a case concerning the refusal or deliberate omission to permit the disabled person to make use of the benefits or facilities of managed premises, the treatment is necessary in order for the occupiers of other premises forming part of the building to make use of the benefit or facility.

Regulations making further provision in relation to matters concerning premises may well be issued.

Enforcement of Part III

General scheme

3-30   The enforcement provisions are similar to those in existence under the SDA and RRA with proceedings to be brought in the county court in England and Wales and the sheriff court in Scotland (although there is no provision for assessors to sit with judges as under the RRA and therefore no need for designation of courts).[23]

Time limits/conciliation

The time limits are similar to those under the SDA, with a similar discretion to allow in late claims.[24] But there is provision in section 28 of the DDA for the Secretary of State to make arrangements for the availability of advice and assistance with a view to settling disputes other than by going to court. Two months are added to the basic time limit where within that six months a person appointed under these arrangements is approached.

Remedies/ injury to feelings

The position with regard to remedies is as for claims under the SDA or RRA, except that under the DDA there is power to prescribe a maximum amount for injury to feelings. Here it seems that a straightforward figure is contemplated, rather than one to be calculated by reference to any criteria.[25] Awards for injury to feelings in non-employment cases under existing discrimination legislation have not been particularly high with no examples of county court judges and sheriffs running amok (even a couple whose wedding night was ruined by being turned away on racial grounds from their booked hotel were

---

[23] See chapter 8, paragraphs 8–79 to 8–87.
[24] See chapter 8, paragraph 8–82.
[25] Sched. 3, para. 7.

awarded only £4,000 each), so one wonders why there was felt to be a need to restrain judges and sheriffs here.

Validity and revision of certain agreements

Terms in contracts are void which require an unlawful act, or exclude or limit the operation of Part III, or prevent claims under it (except settling a claim), and application may be made to the court for an order modifying the agreement accordingly.[26]

Education

The provisions of Part IV of the DDA relating to education do not create **3-31** rights under which individuals can claim that they have been unlawfully discriminated against. Instead they impose obligations in the publicly funded area of education on the institutions primarily to publish information about the ways in which they are dealing with the education of disabled persons. Section 29 deals with schools, and sections 30 and 31 deal with further and higher education.

Schools

The Education Act 1993 is amended so that the annual report for each county, voluntary or grant-maintained school has to contain a report containing information as to the arrangements for the admission of disabled pupils; the steps taken to prevent disabled pupils from being treated less favourably than other pupils; and the facilities provided to assist access to the school by disabled pupils. The Education Act 1994 is also amended so that the Teacher Training Agency, in exercising their functions, are to have regard to the requirements of disabled persons.

Further and higher education

The Further and Higher Education Act 1992 is amended so that the conditions imposed by the further education funding councils on financial support are to include a requirement that the governing body publish "disability statements" with both the content of the statements and the intervals prescribed by regulations, and may also include conditions relating to provision for disabled persons. Those funding councils themselves are required to make annual reports as to progress and plans with regard to provision of further education for disabled students. Local Education Authorities (LEAs) too are to publish disability statements as to further education with prescribed contents and at prescribed intervals.

The higher education funding councils are put under a duty in exercising their functions to have regard to the requirements of disabled persons, and their funding conditions are to require funded institutions to publish "disability statements" with both the content of the statements and the intervals to be specified in the conditions.

---

[26] s. 26 of the DDA.

Public transport

3-32   The provisions of Part V of the DDA are dealt with very briefly here. Consultation on the new standards has already occurred.

Taxis
Essentially section 32 enables the Secretary of State to make regulations, backed up by criminal sanctions, as to accessibility to taxis for disabled persons and section 33 gives power to extend regulation to contracted hire car services at ports, airports, railway or bus stations. Section 34 stops licensing authorities licensing non-conforming taxis, but the following section allows for exemption orders to be sought after consultation but only if there would be an unacceptable reduction in the number of taxis in its area. Section 36 imposes duties on drivers in respect of carriage of and incidental assistance to passengers in wheelchairs, but drivers can gain exemption from the licensing authority on medical grounds or other grounds relating to personal physical condition. Section 37 relates to the carrying of guide and hearing dogs, but again with provision for exemption on medical grounds. Section 38 provides for appeals to magistrates against refusal of exemption certificates. Section 39 gives power to make regulations for Scotland in this area.

Public service vehicles
Section 40–45 give the Secretary of State power, after consulting the Disabled Persons Transport Advisory Committee, to make regulations, backed up by criminal sanctions and by certificates issued by vehicle examiners appointed under the Road Traffic Act 1988, as to accessibility to public service vehicles. There is provision for special authorisations, reviews, appeals, and fees to be charged.

Rail vehicles
Sections 46–47 give power to the Secretary of State, after consulting the advisory committee and representative organisations, to make accessibility regulations for rail vehicles, but only for those first brought into use after December 31, 1998. Once again there is provision for exemption, but the Secretary of State has to consult the advisory committee before making a decision.

Commencement and application of the DDA

The operative parts of the 1995 Act are to be brought into operation on appointed days,[27] but the Secretary of State is allowed to do any required consultation before the particular appointed day. The Act also applies to Northern Ireland — see Schedule 8 — for which there is a separate Disability Council. Reference to the Arbitration, Conciliation Advisory Service (ACAS) should be read as the Labour Relations Agency there.

---

[27] The employment provisions are operative from December 2, 1996.

4 PROOF OF DIRECT DISCRIMINATION

Characteristics of direct discrimination

In this chapter we deal with matters relating primarily to proof of direct **4-01** discrimination. Some direct discrimination has overt features and proof is straightforward, but most is predominantly covert and proof is problematical.

Overt discrimination, in the sense of discrimination where the discriminatory ground is made manifest, is more common than may be imagined. The blatant discriminator, who knows full well he or she is discriminating, in making decisions and is prepared to let the victim know it too, may be, nowadays, the exceptional case. (But overt sexual harassment may be quite widespread). There, however, are cases where the discriminator relies on supposed white or male solidarity and expresses his discriminatory reasoning in the presence of another person, who then blows the whistle on him, and becomes the principal witness against him. There are also cases where the discriminator, believing that what he is doing is lawful because he himself is not prejudiced, acknowledges the discrimination (*e.g.* "I'm not prejudiced but I cannot appoint a black/woman/disabled foreman, because the shopfloor staff would not accept it.") to the victim or somebody else, and indeed sometimes in response to questionnaires under the Acts, only to find that he has in fact admitted a breach of the law.

Certain unlawful acts under the legislation, it should be noted, necessarily **4-02** consist of overt discrimination, witting or unwitting. For example, instructions or pressure to discriminate under the Sex Discrimination Act 1975 (SDA) or the Race Relations Act 1976 (RRA). The main evidence in these cases will usually be that of the person who was on the receiving end of the instructions or pressure, and the cases will stand or fall according to whether the person is believed and what construction the court or tribunal places upon what is proved to have been said. Unlawful advertisements are a special case of overt discrimination. Except in these particular cases where the nature of the unlawfulness so requires, proof of an overt manifestation of a discriminatory ground is not a necessary feature of a discrimination case. Clearly, however, where that manifestation is present, proving discrimination is far less problematical than where it is not.

Proving *covert* discrimination generally involves overcoming several **4-03** obstacles.[1]

---

[1] For an account of these difficulties see Alice Leonard, *Judging Inequality* (Cobden Trust, 1987). See also the excellent article, "Proof of Discrimination in the United Kingdom and the United States" by Steven L. Willborn, 1986 in *Civil Justice Quarterly* 321 (but written before *Singh v. WMPTE*).

The true ground of the alleged discriminator's decision is in his or her mind at the time of his decision. Proof of a state of mind is necessarily difficult. The alleged discriminator's own evidence as to state of mind is likely to be unreliable. There will generally be a wish to avoid liability. Even where there is an attempt to be totally honest in denying discriminatory grounds for the decision, he or she may be unaware of the discriminatory influences affecting the decision. Discrimination occurs not only because of views which are so outrageous that persons holding them are aware that they are racist or sexist or whatever politically correct word comes to be used in respect of the disabled. Persons may make unfounded assumptions about the reactions of others to black people or women or the disabled; they may have unfavourably stereotyped views of the characteristics of black people or women or the disabled; they may unconsciously prefer a person of their own race or sex or a person who is not disabled because they feel more comfortable with such a person.

Further, the documentary evidence which would assist in proving that a discriminatory ground was the substantial cause of less favourable treatment is likely to be in the control of the alleged discriminator. Examples are notes relating to decisions concerning the applicant and others and documents such as references which were relied on.

4-04 The statements of law and discussion which follow concern attempts to find solutions to these difficulties, and the working out of the problems in relation to: the treatment of the burden of proof; the questionnaire procedure; the discovery rules; and testing. Each of these topics will be dealt with in turn. There will be reference throughout to a typical characteristic of much discrimination. There will often have been other opportunities for the alleged discriminator to have discriminated either against the same complainant or against others. What use can be made of evidence relating to these other instances?

4-05 If a coin which is tossed one hundred times comes down 95 times heads, and 5 times tails, one could be pretty certain that something was wrong, without being able to say on which particular extra occasions it should have come down tails, or indeed even exactly how many extra times it should have come down tails. All that one can say is that over a large number of instances one could have expected the number of heads and the number of tails to be roughly the same. The reasoning in a race or sex discrimination case is much the same. The following quotation from a tribunal case illustrates the process:

> "The table shows that despite about one quarter of the workforce being from members of ethnic minorities, only one has been promoted into a supervisory position. We find that the statistical evidence, given that it represents a pattern of at least 16 years duration, is logically probative of the impression held by the Asian Community in Derby that Derby City Transport was not a workplace within which Asians were able to achieve promotion, if they sought it. There was evidence before us that many did apply, and whilst we were bound to accept that many were rejected for reasons other than race, some were not."[2]

---

[2] *Joshi and Whittaker v. Derby City Transport and Booker* 20017/91 & 20021/91 Nottingham Tribunal.

The relevance of evidence arising from ethnic monitoring of decision-making is generally that it has a supporting role in a case from which an inference may be drawn. The law on admissibility is looked at below and there is also a further look at the monitoring process and its advantages at the end of this chapter.

Such monitoring data may play more than a supportive role where a Commission serves a non-discrimination notice in an investigation. Here the evidence on which the Commission wholly relies may be an analysis of a large number of instances of decision-making.[3] The analysis reveals such disparities in the decisions in favour of the different sexes or races at the receiving end that, in the absence of any satisfactory explanation, it is possible to infer sex or race discrimination on the balance of probabilities. Here the evidence is central to the finding of discrimination. It appears to be the case that a Commission can find discrimination on this basis even though it cannot with certainty point to an individual case of discrimination.

    4-06

    The argument would be that the Commission accepts that it might, on close examination, be possible to explain away on non-discriminatory grounds a small part of the disparity, but that the disparity is so great between decisions in favour of one sex or race as compared with those of another that it is not going to be possible to explain it all away, and it is enough for the Commission's purposes to be satisfied that the person "is committing, or has committed" unlawful acts.

Codes of practice

The assumption of the RRA, SDA and DDA (Disability Discrimination Act 1995) is that there are steps which can be taken by employers to prevent racial discrimination occurring. The Acts provide for the making of codes of practice by the Commissions or the Secretary of State in the case of the DDA, and state that the codes:

    4-07

> "may include such practical guidance as the Commission [or the Secretary of State] think fit as to what steps it is reasonably practicable for employers to take for the purpose of preventing their employees from doing in the course of their employment acts made unlawful by this Act."[4]

An employer can avoid liability by showing that such steps have been taken. Tribunals are bound to take into account a provision in a code if it appears relevant to a question in the proceedings.[5] It should ensue that if an applicant proves a failure to follow a relevant part of the code tribunals could well see this as making it more likely that discrimination will have occurred. On the whole, however, we have been struck by how little reference there is in the case law to the codes. We have decided to deal with the essential features of the codes in the context of proof of discrimination to try to redress the balance.

---

[3] See for the example the CRE's formal investigation into Hackney LBC.
[4] RRA, s.32(3), SDA, s.41(3), DDA, s.53(3).
[5] RRA, s.47(10), SDA, s.56A(10), DDA, s.53(6).

The standard of proof

4-08 Discrimination cases are civil cases. (Do not be misled by the statement of one of the Law Lords in *Mandla v. Lee*[6] who wrongly said they were criminal.) Accordingly, the standard of proof is no higher than the balance of probabilities. Tribunals are therefore able to find sex, race, or disability discrimination even when they are unsure about it if the applicant has established that it more probably happened than not. Perhaps there is a need for tribunals to be reminded on appeal that certainty is not required. The success rate in discrimination cases is low. In 1985 the Commission for Racial Equality (CRE) said in the Review of the Act:

> "The probability is that tribunals are dismissing cases involving genuine discrimination."[7]

If they are correct, is it that many tribunals are unfamiliar with the subject-matter? Or is it that tribunals regard discrimination as extremely serious and so in practice, whatever they say, find discrimination only when they are sure that it exists precisely because they think it so serious?

The burden of proof

4-09 The burden of proof is distributed as follows in discrimination cases:

1. In direct discrimination cases it falls upon the party alleging discrimination.
2. In an indirect race or sex discrimination case it falls upon the party alleging discrimination, except as to the question of justifiability where the burden is upon the party attempting to justify the requirement or condition. Similarly in a disability discrimination case the burden of justifying either less favourable treatment or failure to comply with a section 6 duty (under the DDA) falls to the employer.
3. Where a party alleges that the case falls within one of the exceptions to the Acts, that party assumes the burden of establishing that this is so.
4. Where a non-discrimination notice has been issued in a formal investigation conducted by one of the Commissions, the burden falls upon the party alleging that a Commission requirement is unreasonable (because it is based on an incorrect finding of fact or some other reason).

The United Kingdom Government has blocked a proposed E.C. Directive modifying the burden of proof in sex discrimination and equal pay cases.[8] Both the CRE and the Equal Opportunities Commission (EOC) have recom-

---

[6] [1983] 2 A.C. 548.
[7] CRE *Review of the Race Relations Act 1976 Proposals for Change* (1985). Similar views were stated in the 1992 Review.
[8] But there is now an effort to resurrect the Directive under the Social Protocol without applying it to the U.K. Without U.K. opposition the proposal would have gone through previously. But see the *Danfoss* case [1989] I.R.L.R. 532, ECJ.

mended that in circumstances consistent with direct racial or sex discrimination or victimisation the evidential burden of establishing an innocent
explanation should shift to the respondent.[9] The Northern Ireland courts seem
to have reached that position already.[10]

Treatment of the burden of proof

We have set out above where, formally, the burden of proof lies, but it is
impossible to understand the position in discrimination cases without taking
into account the gloss which case law has put upon this topic. Although the
burden of proof is on the individual alleging discrimination it has been recognised that explanation for the respondent's behaviour is best looked for from
the respondent. At the same time, notions of burdens shifting to the respondent were rejected as unduly complicating the matter for industrial tribunals.

4-10

4-21

We wish that we could set the matter out simply by reference solely to recent   **4-11**
Court of Appeal authority, see page 120 for the *China Centre* case, but in
practice earlier EAT authority is still referred to in the tribunals and it is as
well to run through the background of this central issue of discrimination
law. Quotations from the cases are self-explanatory for the most part.

In *Khanna v. Ministry of Defence* Browne-Wilkinson J. said:

> "The right course in this case was for the Industrial Tribunal to take
> into account the fact that direct evidence of discrimination is seldom
> going to be available and that accordingly in these cases the affirmative
> evidence of discrimination will normally consist of inferences to be
> drawn from the primary facts. If the primary facts indicate that there
> has been discrimination of some kind, the employer is called on to give
> an explanation and, failing clear specific explanation being given by an
> employer to the satisfaction of the Industrial Tribunal, an inference of
> unlawful discrimination from the primary facts will mean the complaint
> succeeds."[11]

In *Chattopadhyay v. Headmaster of Holloway School* Browne-Wilkinson J.
again presiding in the EAT said:

> "the law has been established that if an applicant shows that he has
> been treated less favourably than others in circumstances which are con-
> sistent with that treatment being based on racial grounds, the Industrial
> Tribunal should draw an inference that such treatment was on racial
> grounds, unless the respondent can satisfy the Industrial Tribunal that
> there is an innocent explanation."[12]

It may be appropriate to draw inferences both of race and sex discrimination   **4-12**
as happened in the case of *Noone v. South West Thames Regional Health
Authority*.[13] The EAT rejected an appeal against liability, where the *Khanna*

---

[9] Proposals made by the CRE in 1985 and again in 1992, and by the EOC in 1988.
[10] See *Dorman v. Belfast City Council* [1990] I.R.L.R. 179, N.I. C.A.
[11] [1981] I.R.L.R. 331 at 333 and compare the Northern Ireland case *Wallace v. South Eastern
Education & Library Board* [1980] I.R.L.R. 193.
[12] [1982] I.C.R. 132 at 137 and [1981] I.R.L.R. 487.
[13] Referred to in the report of *North West Thames RHA v. Noone* [1987] I.R.L.R. 357 and [1977]
I.R.L.R. 225.

principle had been applied to the case of failure to short-list an Asian origin woman for the post of consultant microbiologist, despite her qualifications. Inferences of both race and sex discrimination had been drawn by the industrial tribunal and were upheld by the EAT. In an appropriate case an inference might also be drawn of disability discrimination.

The question of when the primary facts will be such that it is appropriate to raise an inference of discrimination needing a satisfactory answer has been left vague. In most cases it does not matter because no shifting of the burden occurs, and it has been held that it is not normally appropriate to dismiss a complainant's case without hearing the respondent's evidence unless the case is exceptional or frivolous.[14] Accordingly, what the cases amount to is not the definition of a turning point (and quite possibly the courts do not wish to focus attention on such an artificial matter), but a way of analysing the whole of the evidence received in the case. Do the circumstances call for explanation? Did we get an explanation? Are we satisfied with it? What is the inference to be drawn?

4-13   Where the employer has appointed an apparently less well qualified person instead of the applicant, and that person is of a different race or sex or not disabled, the tribunals will no doubt take the view that an explanation is called for.

However, the trickier situation is where there are equally well qualified persons. In *Saunders v. Richmond-upon-Thames LBC*[15] qualifications were found to be roughly the same and the EAT took the view that an inference of discrimination was inappropriate. The position may be different, however, if the complainant is able to demonstrate a pattern of decisions by the employer against women or black persons or disabled persons.[16] In these circumstances it may be reasonable to infer discrimination even though the person appointed is equally well qualified, because the decision between equally well qualified people must be based on some criterion, and failing an explanation of that criterion it looks as though sex or race or disability is being used as the determining factor.

4-14   In *Noone v. North West Thames Regional Health Authority*,[17] the Court of Appeal held that where there is a finding that a black candidate for a post has not been selected despite superior qualifications, usually the proper inference will be that the discrimination was on racial grounds if the employer fails to provide a satisfactory explanation.

Dr Noone was of Sri Lankan origin and had applied for a post as consultant microbiologist with the respondents. She had superior qualifications, greater experience and more publications than the successful applicant but was not appointed. The industrial tribunal found discrimination on the grounds of race: the interview procedure amounted in their view to "little more than a sham," and the decision was so subjective as virtually to be arbitrary. The EAT allowed an appeal against liability by the health authority. There was evidence entitling a conclusion that the decision of the appointments panel

[14] *See Oxford v. DHSS* [1977] I.C.R. 884, EAT.
[15] 1978 I.C.R. 75.
[16] See *West Midlands Passenger Transport Executive v. Singh* [1988] 2 All E.R. 873, [1988] 1 W.L.R., C.A., 730, [1988] I.R.L.R. 186, [1988] I.C.R. 614.
[17] [1988] I.R.L.R. 195.

was unsatisfactory and unreasonable, indeed revealing personal bias, but the EAT found no positive evidence that that was attributable to race, and therefore nothing to justify an inference that the discrimination was on the prohibited ground. The Court of Appeal restored the tribunal's finding on liability. May L.J. said:

> "In these cases of alleged racial discrimination it is always for the complainant to make out his or her case. It is not often that there is direct evidence of racial discrimination, and these complaints more often than not have to be dealt with on the basis of what are the proper inferences to be drawn from the primary facts. For myself I would have thought that it was almost common sense that, if there is a finding of discrimination and of a difference in race and then an inadequate or unsatisfactory explanation by the employer for the discrimination, usually the legitimate inference will be that the discrimination was on racial grounds."

He went on:

> "If there is no evidence or material from which an Industrial Tribunal can draw the inference of racial discrimination then, of course, they should not do so. On the other hand, one must not forget that it is the Industrial Tribunal who see and hear the persons actually involved. Perhaps more than in most cases the assessment by the Industrial Tribunal of the thinking of the person or persons against whom the allegation of racial discrimination is made is most important. As is well known, appeals lie from an Industrial Tribunal to the Employment Appeal Tribunal only on a point of law, and it is only when the latter is satisfied that there was no material upon which the former could reach the conclusion they did that the Appeal Tribunal should entertain the appeal ... I do not find the Employment Appeal Tribunal's reasoning on this aspect of the case convincing. If in the circumstances of the instant case the discrimination is held to have been based on a personal bias or personal prejudice, it seems to be only a very small step to go on and conclude that the discrimination was racial."[18]

The *Noone* position that where there is a difference in race, less favourable treatment of the applicant, and an unsatisfactory explanation by the respondent, then "*usually*" the legitimate inference will be racial discrimination, appeared to represent some backtracking from the *Khanna* and *Chattopadhyay* position that in those circumstances the tribunal "*should*" infer racial discrimination.   **4-15**

Shortly after the *Noone* case in the Court of Appeal, the EAT in fact held in *Barking and Dagenham L.B.C. v. Camara*[19] that the *Khanna* and *Chattopadhyay* formulations were wrong in law. Instead, an industrial tribunal having found the primary facts should make such findings as it thought   **4-16**

---

[18] At p. 198.

[19] [1988] I.C.R. 865, and see also a further attempt to restate the law in *British Gas v. Sharma* [1991] I.R.L.R. 101 which the CRE describes as the EAT being reluctant to bow to the view of the Court of Appeal in *Baker v. Cornwall C.C.* in their consultative document for the 2nd Review of the RRA.

"fair", having regard to the difficulty of putting forward a case of discrimination, and thereafter, bearing in mind the burden of proof on the applicant, decide whether discrimination had been established. An appeal was allowed against a finding of discrimination based on the industrial tribunal's understanding that they *"should"* draw an inference of racial discrimination when the primary facts had established a difference in race, less favourable treatment and there was an unsatisfactory explanation for that treatment. The case was remitted for rehearing. The *Camara* decision was, in our view inconsistent with the restatement of *Khanna* in *West Midlands Passenger Transport Executive v. Singh*[20] and the Court of Appeal has twice looked at the whole question again.

The *China Centre* guidelines

4-17   In *Baker v. Cornwall County Council*,[21] the Court of Appeal held that if discrimination takes place in circumstances which are consistent with the treatment being based on grounds of sex or race, the tribunal *"should be prepared"* to draw the inference that the discrimination was on such grounds unless the employer satisfies the tribunal that there was some innocent explanation. In *King v. The Great Britain-China Centre* Neill L.J. stated the following:

> "(1) It is for the applicant who complains of racial discrimination to make out his or her case. Thus if the applicant does not prove the case on the balance of probabilities he or she will fail.
> (2) It is important to bear in mind that it is unusual to find direct evidence of racial discrimination. Few employers will be prepared to admit such discrimination even to themselves. In some cases the discrimination will not be ill-intentioned but merely based on an assumption 'he or she would not have fitted in'.
> (3) The outcome of the case will therefore usually depend on what inferences it is proper to draw from the primary facts found by the Tribunal. These inferences can include, in appropriate cases, any inferences that it is just and equitable to draw in accordance with s.65(2)(b) of the 1976 Act from an evasive or equivocal reply to a questionnaire.
> (4) Though there will be some cases where, for example, the non-selection of the applicant for a post or promotion is clearly not on racial grounds, a finding of discrimination and a finding of different race will often point to the possibility of racial discrimination. In such circumstances the Tribunal will look to the employer for an explanation. If no explanation is then put forward, or if the Tribunal considers the explanation to be inadequate or unsatisfactory, it will be legitimate for the Tribunal to infer that the discrimination was on racial grounds. This is not a matter of law but, as May L.J. put it in *Noone*, 'almost common sense'.
> (5) It is unnecessary and unhelpful to introduce the concept of a shifting evidential burden of proof. At the conclusion of all the evidence the Tribunal should make findings as to the primary facts and draw such inferences as they consider proper from those facts. They should then

---

[20] [1988] I.R.L.R. 186.
[21] [1990] I.R.L.R. 194, C.A.

reach a conclusion on the balance of probabilities, bearing in mind both the difficulties which face a person who complains of unlawful discrimination and the fact that it is for the complainant to prove his or her case."[22]

In the hands of tribunal panels experienced in discrimination cases, the *China Centre* formulation is capable of producing a just result. However, in the hands of tribunal panels unfamiliar with the subtle ways in which discrimination occurs, and too ready to accept at face value assertions by employers relating to nebulous matters such as "wrong personality", "lack of leadership qualities," in the face of the contrary evidence of qualifications, experience, and references, injustice may well still occur.   **4-18**

It is often the case that an applicant will be able to point to failures on the part of respondents to follow their own procedures. In the case of *Qureshi v. London Borough of Newham*,[23] which involved failure to follow equal opportunity procedures, the Court of Appeal held that an employer's incompetence does not, without more, become discrimination merely because the person affected by it is from an ethnic minority. If there is overt racism it would be different. In practice, the effect of this decision is to relieve the employer of the necessity to demonstrate similar incompetence also in the case of men or white applicants.   **4-19**

Although, following *Qureshi*, incompetence without more is not discrimination, the *China Centre* framework should be remembered, and if there is less favourable treatment and a difference in sex, race or whether disabled the tribunal should consider whether they are satisfied with the respondent's explanation for less favourable treatment. If they reach the conclusion that the incident looks more like a response targetted at the applicant than incompetence they would be free to draw the appropriate inference.   **4-20**

It is always wise for the tribunal to look at what has happened in the round as well as at each incident that makes up the whole picture, because explanations which individually seem satisfactory on balance may seem far-fetched when viewed together.   **4-21**

Questionnaires

The questionnaire procedure   **4-22**

The discrimination statutes, and orders made thereunder, make provision for the service of a questionnaire on a potential or actual respondent (in a tribunal case within 21 days of the commencement of proceedings or thereafter with leave; the county court position is different, see chapter 7):

"With a view to helping a person ('the person aggrieved') who considers s/he may have been discriminated against in contravention of this

---

[22] [1991] I.R.L.R. 513 at 518.
[23] [1991] I.R.L.R. 264.

Act to decide whether to institute proceedings and, if he does so, to formulate and present his/her case in the most effective manner, the Secretary of State shall by order prescribe

(a) forms by which the person aggrieved may question the respondent on his reasons for doing any relevant act, or on any other matter which is or may be relevant; and

(b) forms by which the respondent may if he so wishes reply to any questions . . .''.

A person aggrieved may question a (proposed) respondent without using the prescribed forms.[24]

4-23   In practice, the length of time taken to respond to the questionnaire means that tribunal proceedings (the time limit is three months) are often commenced only to be withdrawn when the respondent provides what the aggrieved person regards as a satisfactory explanation for his act or decision. Sometimes tribunals underestimate the importance of the questionnaire procedure and list cases for hearing before the complainant has received the response to the questionnaire. Quite often the answers to the questionnaire will satisfy an applicant and he or she will withdraw the case.

4-24   The question and any reply are admissible in evidence, subject in the case of court proceedings to being able to apply prior to the hearing for a determination as to admissibility. In theory there is a considerable incentive for a respondent to give a prompt and full reply to the questionnaire because the Acts say:

> ''if it appears to the court or tribunal that the respondent deliberately, and without reasonable excuse, omitted to reply within a reasonable period or that his reply is evasive or equivocal, the (court or) tribunal may draw any inference from that fact that it considers just and equitable to draw, including an inference that he committed an unlawful act.''[25]

4-25   In practice, tribunals are sometimes reluctant to draw inferences except in extreme circumstances, as in *Virdee v. EEC Quarries Ltd*[26] where the answer completely evaded all the questions save a partial answer to one. The statute says ''may draw any inference . . . that it considers just and equitable to draw.'' If it is just and equitable to draw an inference, it is difficult to see what else the court or tribunal might take into account in deciding whether to draw an inference. In the *China Centre* case, referred to above, an inference of racial discrimination was drawn from the questionnaire response taken together with other material.[27]

4-26   It is unclear whether the questionnaire procedure under section 74 of the Sex Discrimination Act applies also to proceedings under the equal pay legisla-

---

[24] SDA, s.74, RRA, s.65, DDA, s.56.
[25] SDA, s.74(2)(b), RRA s.65(2)(b), DDA, s.56(3)(b). The questionnaire procedure under the DDA applies only to employment matters, not to matters to which court proceedings apply.
[26] [1978] I.R.L.R. 295, I.T.
[27] [1991] I.R.L.R. 513 at 516.

tion, although there is no good reason why a similar procedure should not apply.

The Commissions do not have the power to use the questionnaire procedure in cases where only they have the right to bring proceedings since the power is limited to persons who believe they may have been discriminated *"against"*.

In practice, an individual can often get assistance from the Commissions in drafting an appropriate questionnaire under their discretionary power to provide assistance, but the National Disability Council has no such power to provide assistance.

Since under the discovery rules (see below) it is not possible to order a party to create a schedule of evidence where the documents are not already in existence, the questionnaire procedure may sometimes be used to achieve this. Thus the EAT in *Carrington v. Helix Lighting Ltd* suggested the use of a supplementary questionnaire served with leave of the tribunal to get data on ethnic make-up of the workforce, where documents relating to ethnic monitoring were not already in existence.[28]   **4-27**

The questionnaire procedure can also be used, for example, to probe for reasons for the prospective (or actual) respondent's acting or not acting in certain ways and what criteria if any have been applied in making decisions, or to find out how others have been treated in similar circumstances, or indeed what other comparators there might be, or to get the respondent to say what documents exist.

It is surprising how often at trial the respondent's case does differ from replies to the questionnaire so as to provide fertile ground for cross-examination. Lack of consistency in the explanation put forward by the respondent is likely to lead to the tribunal not being satisfied with the explanation. Conversely, too detailed and thorough a questionnaire on some matters can simply alert a respondent in advance to areas of difficulty, giving ample opportunity to invent answers thus making cross-examination more difficult. Thus we have heard some advocates express the view that questions about the Codes of Practice are best left for cross-examination, since putting them in the questionnaire may prompt a mastery of the relevant code which would not otherwise have existed.   **4-28**

It should not be forgotten that the rules now permit the use of interrogatories by order of the tribunal. However failure to answer the questionnaire without proper reason can lead to the drawing of adverse inferences, so there may, depending on the circumstances, be little point in forcing an answer by applying to use an interrogatory if the questionnaire has been used.

Discovery

The discovery rules

In *British Library v. Palyza and Mukherjee* Nolan J. in the EAT said: **4-29**

"that Parliament has seen fit to place upon the complainant of racial or

---

[28] [1990] I.R.L.R. 6 at 9 and [1990] I.C.R. 125.

sexual discrimination the burden of proving his or her case, notwithstanding that the bulk of the relevant evidence is likely to be in the possession of the respondent to the complaint. The procedure of discovery is designed to offset the probative disadvantage which the complainant would otherwise suffer."[29]

Whereas the questionnaire procedure is available before as well as after proceedings are commenced, discovery of documents is a process applicable only after proceedings have been commenced. The parties on discovery can be made to disclose all documents necessary for fairly disposing of the issue in dispute. The House of Lords set out the principles in relation to two cases which reached them at the same time, one under the Sex Discrimination Act, the other under the Race Relations Act: *Science Research Council v. Nasse, Leyland Cars v. Vyas*[30]:

1. The information necessary to prove discrimination cases is normally in the possession of the respondents so making discovery essential if the case is to be fairly decided.
2. Confidentiality of the material is not, of itself, a reason for refusing discovery, but is a factor to be considered. In the case of confidential documents the court or tribunal should examine them to see whether disclosure really is necessary, and if so to consider whether it is possible fairly to preserve confidence by covering up irrelevant parts.
3. The test in both the courts and tribunals is whether discovery is necessary for fairly disposing of the proceedings or for saving costs.

4-30   In discrimination cases, discovery and inspection is frequently sought of material for the purposes of comparing the complainant's case with that of other persons, especially those who have been treated more favourably than the complainant. This material is often viewed as confidential by the authors and by the employer from whom it is sought: for example references, and other assessments of the people concerned. If discovery is necessary for fairly disposing of the proceedings, discovery must be ordered notwithstanding the documents' confidentiality. In deciding whether discovery is necessary for that reason the tribunal should first inspect the documents and consider whether justice could be done by taking special measures, such as covering up confidential but irrelevant parts of the documents, substituting anonymous references for specific names, or, in rare cases, a hearing *in camera*. In both the *Nasse* and *Vyas* cases discovery which had been ordered of confidential documents without such inspection was held to be wrong.

4-31   Lord Salmon commented on the relationship between the questionnaire procedures under the Acts and the right to discovery and inspection:

"I do not think that the importance to the complainant of the right to claim an order for inspection of the relevant documents is diminished by the statutory machinery which exists to allow the complainant and indeed the industrial tribunal to question the employer and at an early stage to obtain answers relating to whether the employer has unlawfully

---

[29] [1984] I.C.R. 504 at 507 and [1984] I.R.L.R. 306.
[30] [1979] I.C.R. 921, [1980] A.C. 1028.

discriminated against his employee. It is, no doubt, possible that the answers, if reliable, might establish or negative the alleged unlawful discrimination and therefore make inspection of any documents unnecessary. On the other hand, there is the danger that the answers may be exiguous or unreliable and misleading. The only way of testing the accuracy of the employer's answers may often be by comparing them with the reports and records in their possession. The statutory machinery for obtaining early information from the employers was not, in my view, intended to be a substitute for, but an addition to the complainant's rights of discovery and inspection of documents.''[31]

Generally, where it is necessary for fairly disposing of the case information relating to comparators such as a statement of the sex or race as the case may be, qualifications, and description of work experience, is revealed only in anonymous form without the names or addresses of those concerned. Often a list form is used with the comparators being referred to as A, B, C, D, etc., but if a complainant seeks verification, the tribunal system may provide the means of verification.[32]   **4-32**

Discovery and the fairness test

Discovery, even though relevant, will not be granted if it is oppressive. It   **4-33**
will fail the fairness test. In *West Midlands Passenger Transport Executive v. Singh*[33] the Court of Appeal suggested two ways in which a discovery claim might be oppressive: it may require the provision of material not readily to hand, which can only be made available with difficulty and at great expense; or the effect of discovery may be to require the party ordered to make discovery to embark on a course which will add unreasonably to the length and cost of the hearing.

In *Selvarajan v. Inner London Education Authority*,[34] a lecturer claiming racial discrimination after the Race Relations Act 1976 came into force sought discovery of documents relating to various occasions between 1961 and 1976 during his employment when he had failed to obtain various jobs. His case was that there was continuing discrimination. The industrial tribunal had limited discovery to events after 1973, but the EAT could see no logic in this cut-off date. The events going back to 1961 could be probative, so the EAT held, of the allegation of discrimination after the Act. Thus the issue was whether there was oppression or unfairness. Because of the limited nature of the documents sought, and further safeguards which were available, the EAT held there was none. The application was limited to the application forms of the candidates who were appointed, and of the applicant, minutes of appointment and minutes of governors' meetings on certain dates, and the applicant's own file. As regards matters prior to 1971, however, it was left open to the respondents to apply to the tribunal that the applicant should not be allowed to go into those matters if a lapse of time meant explanations and so forth were unobtainable.

---

[31] At p.933 in the I.C.R. version.
[32] See *Oxford v. DHSS* [1977] I.R.L.R. 225, EAT; [1977] I.C.R. 884 EAT. and *Williams v. Dyfed* [1986] I.C.R. 449, EAT.
[33] [1988] I.R.L.R. 186.
[34] [1980] I.R.L.R. 313, EAT; there is no relevant distinction between hostility pointing to a racialist attitude before the act complained of and such hostility shown afterwards, and evidence relating to both is admissible, see *Chattopadhay* [1981] I.R.L.R. 487, EAT.

4-34   Discovery in the *Selvarajan* case related to previous incidents concerning the complainant himself, but an applicant may seek discovery of evidence relating to the treatment of others to establish a discriminatory pattern into which the applicant's case fits. The law here was established by the Court of Appeal in *West Midlands Passenger Transport Executive v. Singh*. Balcombe L.J. stated the issue as follows:

> "The issue is whether evidence that a particular employer has or has not appointed any or many coloured applicants in the past is material to the question whether he has discriminated on racial grounds against a particular complainant; and whether discovery devoted to ascertaining the percentage of successful coloured applicants with successful white applicants should be ordered."[35]

4-35   The Court went on to observe that in considering the relevance of the material sought to be adduced, it was to be noted that cases based on racial discrimination had a number of special features:

1. That the law had established that if the applicant could show that he had been treated less favourably than others in circumstances consistent with that treatment being based on racial grounds, an industrial tribunal should infer that such treatment was on racial grounds, unless the employer could show the contrary;
2. That evidence adduced in such cases was not required to show decisively that the employer had acted on racial grounds, but was required to tend to prove the case;
3. Since discrimination involved an individual not being treated on his own merits, but as receiving unfavourable treatment because he was a member of a particular group, statistical evidence might establish a discernible pattern which might give rise to an inference of discrimination against the group;
4. If a practice were being operated against a group, in the absence of a satisfactory explanation, it was reasonable to infer that the complainant, as a member of the group had himself been treated less favourably on the ground of race;
5. There was an approved practice in such cases for employers to provide evidence of a non-discriminatory attitude which could be accepted as having probative force, and in consequence, any evidence of a discriminatory attitude on their part would also have probative effect;
6. Suitability of candidates for posts was rarely measured objectively, and if there was evidence of a high percentage rate of failure to achieve promotion by members of a particular racial group, that fact might indicate a condition of unconscious racial attitude by employers.[36]

The Court was satisfied that the statistical material was relevant to the issues. Having decided that the discovery was relevant, the test of whether the dis-

[35] [1988] I.R.L.R. 186.
[36] At p.188.

covery was necessary for fairly disposing of the case was applied, but there was no evidence to suggest oppression.

Testing

In this section we discuss providing similar fact evidence by artificially creating applications made in similar circumstances.   **4-36**

Suppose a black person applies for a job and is told that the job has gone, but disbelieves that explanation. One option open to him is, as soon as possible, to get white friends to make comparable applications to that employer citing the same qualifications. Sometimes a local racial equality council can arrange such a test. If it is established by the testing that the job is still open to the white applicant, the inference that the employer's statement to the complainant that the job had gone was a pretextual reason given for a racially discriminatory decision is strong.

The CRE commonly uses "testing" evidence of this sort in cases supported   **4-37** by it of the sort outlined above. Other examples are cases of refusal of entry to a nightclub, or of a drink in a public house. In these situations the number of reasons other than race which can be offered by way of explanation are limited. In both cases age, dress or behaviour may be cited and therefore it is essential for the testers to be of the same age, wear comparable clothes and to behave similarly. In the case of a nightclub, whether or not the person is a member is also likely to be relevant. These precautions serve to narrow the alleged discriminator's scope for pretextual explanations.

In recent years courts and tribunals have generally been happy to accept   **4-38** supporting evidence of the testing kind. It may or may not be backed up by evidence relating to the way other genuine applicants/customers were treated. However, it is one thing artificially to create a situation for the purposes of comparison. It may be quite another thing artificially to create a complainant/plaintiff in a case by putting forward a person who is not genuinely interested in a job or the provision of a service, certainly if there is any attempt to claim damages for loss or injury to feelings.

Where there is a contemporaneous test using a comparator, the evidence   **4-39** would be admitted by direct reference to section 3 (4) of the Race Relations Act 1976 (or the equivalent provision in the Sex Discrimination Act 1975, s.5 (3) as the case may be). (Subs. 3 (4) RRA reads "A . . . comparison of the case of a person of a particular racial group with that of a person not of that group under section 1(1) must be such that the relevant circumstances in the one case are the same, or not materially different in the other." That the relevant circumstances have been artificially created would appear to be immaterial for this purpose.) However if the tests are not contemporaneous, since the surrounding circumstances may have changed, it is better to consider the evidence as relevant by virtue of the third special feature listed in *West Midlands Passenger Transport Executive v. Singh*[37] and provide both black and white comparable testers on the new occasion.

---

[37] [1988] I.R.L.R. 186.

4-40   In any event it should be added that testing depends for its efficacy on the simple nature of the situation. In more complex situations where the number of comparable features which have to be controlled increases, it is decreasingly useful as a tool. This is particularly so where the actual presentation of people is called for. It may be possible to test certain complex situations if, for example, the test takes the form of a comparable written application form. An industrial tribunal found racial discrimination against an applicant for solicitors' articles who was of Sri Lankan origin where she reapplied using an English sounding name. She was rejected on her application under her real name Dharani Thiruppathy, but invited for interview under the name Jane Thorpe. It did not amount to a perfect test because there were some small differences other than race in the two application forms, but the rejection rate for ethnic minority candidates was much higher than for white candidates and the tribunal found racial discrimination.[38]

4-41   In some types of situations testing may be decreasingly useful as the nature of discrimination changes in society. If discrimination takes the form not of a complete ban on women or members of ethnic minorities, but instead acceptance of only those who are way above their male or white counterparts who are being accepted with lower qualifications, then the level at which the qualifications are pitched in the test becomes all-important. If high, then all the applicants male, female, white and ethnic minority will be accepted. If low, then all the female and ethnic minority applicants will be rejected. The Commissions will need to bear this in mind if they carry out wide-scale testing as part of formal investigations. Indeed, it may well be that the investigations would only give a true picture if matched testers were used at several different levels of qualification in respect of each potential discriminator.[39]

Codes of Practice

4-42   In this edition of the book, as in the last, we have decided to put material relating to the Codes of Practice and monitoring alongside material on proof of discrimination. We are conscious that the future of equal opportunities may well lie in giving legal content to the concept of equal opportunity in its own right as a positive matter and creating specific associated duties such as that to monitor, rather than concentrating wholly on avoiding racial discrimination. That is really the way Northern Ireland law on religious discrimination has gone.[40] Dealing with the material on the codes and monitoring in this chapter should not be seen as blinkering ourselves to that possibility, but rather as a way of drawing attention to its relevance to proof.

---

[38] *Thiruppathy v. Steggles Palmer* Equal Opportunities Review Discrimination *Case Law Digest* No. 8 1991, p. 7.

[39] With hindsight it is quite possible to see that the CRE's formal investigation "Sorry It's Gone" may well have been bedevilled by these factors. The testers all had a high level of "respectability" in their appearance and story-lines.

[40] See Fair Employment (Northern Ireland) Act 1989.

The employment codes

On the status and general purpose of the Employment Codes produced under the relevant legislation the Acts say:

4-43

"A failure on the part of any person to observe any provision of a code of practice shall not of itself render him liable to any proceedings; but in any proceedings under this Act before an industrial tribunal any code of practice issued under this section shall be admissible in evidence, and if any provision of such a code appears to the tribunal to be relevant to any question arising in the proceedings it shall be taken into account in determining that question."[41]

There is a defence for an employer to prove that he took such steps as were reasonably practicable from doing the act in question or acts of that description, and the Acts contemplate guidance on the appropriate steps as being one of the functions of the Codes.[42]

4-44

Both the EOC and CRE Codes recommend that equal opportunity policies should be monitored.[43] In the basic discrimination legislation, there was no power in the Commissions to produce Codes outside the area of employment with the same status, but the CRE has now been given power in the field of housing to make codes (see chapter 8). The CRE has also produced a "quasi-code" in education (having been refused a code-making power in that area, although oddly the Secretary of State then endorsed the "quasi-code").[44]

4-45

CRE employment code
The CRE Employment Code says:

4-46

"In order to ensure that an equal opportunity policy is fully effective, the following action by employers is recommended:

(a) allocating overall responsibility for the policy to a member of senior management;
(b) discussing and, where appropriate, agreeing with the trade unions or employee representatives the policy's contents and implementation;
(c) ensuring that the policy is known to all employees and if possible to all job applicants;
(d) providing training and guidance for supervisory staff and other relevant decision makers (such as personnel and line managers, foremen, gatekeepers and receptionists) to ensure that they understand their position in law and under company policy;
(e) examining and regularly reviewing existing procedures and criteria and changing them where they find that they are actually or potentially discriminatory;

---

[41] RRA, s. 47 (10), SDA, s. 56A (10), DDA, s. 53(4)–(6).
[42] RRA, s. 32 (3), SDA, s.41 (3).
[43] CRE Employment Code paras. 1.4f and 1.33 to 1.42; EOC Code paras. 37 to 40.
[44] *Code of Practice for the Elimination of Racial Discrimination in Education* (CRE, 1989), there is a separate version for Scotland. The EOC now has power to produce a code relating to equal pay and has produced a draft code.

(f) making an initial analysis of the workforce and regularly monitoring the application of policy with the aid of analysis of the ethnic origins of the workforce and of job applicants.''[45]

4-47   There was nothing very new about these recommendations. It will be seen that the essential features of what is stated would need but slight modification to be appropriate as a *management programme* for the personnel aspects of, say, a car manufacturing company introducing a new model on a new production line allocating responsibility for policy; getting agreement on implementation; ensuring everyone knows what is happening; providing proper training; keeping procedures under review; and keeping a check on production figures, hours worked, etc. The various parts of the programme would be interrelated. If, for example, production figures were below expectations, this would lead to an enquiry as to the cause, procedures would be checked, as would the sufficiency of training, guidance, etc., if procedures were found to be faulty, and ultimately if the matter was not put right, responsibility would be laid at the door of a particular manager.

4-48   Whilst some tribunals patiently listen to questions about the codes from the applicant's representative, others are dismissive and succeed in implying that the Codes really are not all that important. Yet in any other context they would probably accept the simple proposition that things are likely to go wrong in the absence of proper management. Just as an employer can show in defence that he has taken steps to avoid discrimination, so an employee should be able to rely on a failure to take such steps as making it more likely that discrimination did occur. Because of the *Qureshi* case (see above at page 122) failure to follow an equal opportunity policy will not, without more, prove racial discrimination, but that does not mean it is irrelevant to proof.

4-49   To take an example, specific recommendations in the CRE Code say that staff responsible for shortlisting, interviewing and selecting candidates should be clearly informed of selection criteria and for the need for their consistent application; given guidance or training on the effect which generalised assumptions and prejudices about race can have on selection decisions; made aware of the possible misunderstandings that can occur in interviews between persons of different cultural background; and wherever possible, shortlisting and interviewing should not be done alone but should at least be checked at a more senior level. If a completely untrained and unguided person acts alone to make an employment decision involving persons from different races and has no selection criteria established to be applied and no monitoring has ever been done of such decisions, does not this make racial discrimination likely?

Monitoring

4-50   The Codes recommend monitoring on the basis of sex, or on the basis of ethnic origin[46] in situations such as appointments to jobs, or recipients of a

---

[45] CRE Code para. 1.4.
[46] See the booklet by Mary Coussey and John Whitmore, *Jobs and Racial Equality* (British Institute of Management 1987); Mary Coussey and Hilary Jackson, *Making Equal Opportunities Work* (Pitman Publishing, 1992).

service, or admission to educational courses. There is one immediate and obvious difference between monitoring on the basis of sex and monitoring on the basis of ethnic origin. It is that records have traditionally been kept in such a way that it has been possible to distinguish male from female. This applies to personnel records, housing department records and education records. The same is not true of ethnic origin records. Where those same records did contain comments about ethnicity it was usually haphazard and sometimes with malevolent intent or effect. Thus systematic ethnic monitoring has had to be introduced.

Most discrimination these days is covert and indeed it is often, though by no means always, unintentional. Most managements, when first asked to carry out monitoring, will at first respond by saying: "We don't need to because we do not discriminate and nobody has ever proved that we have." That discrimination will not have been established by litigation would not be surprising. Relatively few individual cases have succeeded, and for the very good reason that it is often not difficult in an isolated instance to advance plausible reasons for decisions unconnected with sex or race. However, when large numbers of similar decisions are looked at and analysed, a common discovery is that these reasons, plausible in the individual case, start to look highly implausible when multiplied as explanations for wide disparities in male/female, or white/black success rates. **4-51**

Comparisons

Monitoring data can be used to make the following types of comparison: **4-52**

1. To compare the proportion of black people/women in the appropriate labour market with their proportion as applicants for particular jobs as employees; with adaptations the same can be applied to potential recipients of services/candidates applying for services, education places.
2. To compare the proportion of black people/women in grades, jobs and departments and branches in similar areas; the same can be done in the case of recipients of housing from a local authority (*e.g.* are black people predominantly in inferior quality housing; or to educational courses (*e.g.* are women predominantly, on certain types of courses?).
3. To compare the application and success rates of blacks/women whites/men for vacancies and promotion: the same can be done in the case of recipients of housing from local authorities (*e.g.* are black people on a waiting list less successful than white people?); or to admission to, say, a university: are black people/women less successful than white people/men?).

Disparities and barriers

Disparities in any of these comparisons may indicate where there are barriers to equal opportunities. The points at which more than minor disparities appear are those where reasons should be sought. It is here that an understanding of the various hurdles in the way of equal opportunity is crucial, because without such an appreciation the identification of particular hurdles **4-53** present in the circumstances under review will be very difficult. The removal of one barrier may lead to another being created. Suppose that an all-white workforce is reproducing itself by reliance upon word-of-mouth recruiting. If open advertising of jobs is substituted as a practice, it may well be found that black applicants are disproportionately rejected upon receipt of written applications, or at interview because those responsible for selection still feel happier with persons in their own image; and this will need proper training and guidance, and criteria that are as objective as possible.

Targets and quotas

Numerical targets differentiated from quotas

4-54   In ordinary business management understanding of the techniques, proced-ures, etc. necessary to achieve an objective is very important, but in practice targets are set in numerical terms, *e.g.* to achieve a production or sales of so many cars per week. That gives both management and managed a measure of performance against which judgements can be made. The target will be based upon what can reasonably be expected to be achieved if things are running smoothly. If the target is not reached, questions will be asked about whether things are running smoothly.

4-55   Numerical target-setting is in fact implicit in certain of the voluntary provi-sions of the Sex Discrimination Act 1975 and the Race Relations Act 1976: those permitting positive action with regard to training and encouragement to take up particular work (see chapter 5). The statutory conditions in which they may apply relate to underrepresentation; and it follows that the provi-sions cease to apply when that state of underrepresentation is at an end. An employer applying section 38 of the Race Relations Act 1976 should there-fore be thinking something like "when the numbers of black workers in this work reach such and such a number we shall no longer need or be able to use these provisions." This point is mentioned to illustrate the contention that setting numerical targets is consistent with the overall aims of the two pieces of legislation.[47]

4-56   The Codes of Practice do not, however, deal with target-setting and, arguably, need updating in this respect. In contrast, the Department of Employment's guide "Ten Point Plan for Employers"[48] is more realistic and advocates action plans which include targets.

4-57   The argument for setting numerical targets goes beyond the case where spe-cial positive action provisions apply. Indeed they are then more relevant to proof of discrimination. If, for example, it is possible to estimate what would be the likely numbers of black persons or women taken on as employees in a given period assuming that equal opportunities are being provided, there

---

[47] see also SDA, s.48.
[48] *Equal Opportunities—Ten Point Plan for Employers* (Department of Employment, 1992). This guide is highly recommended.

is a management case for setting that figure as a target against which to measure whether equal opportunities are being provided.

Care must be taken, however, to ensure that the target is not regarded as a **4-58** fixed quota which must be reached willy nilly and not exceeded. A quota will be unlawful under the SDA or RRA. Targets are lawful so long as it is understood that they are to be achieved by lawful means. That is to say that (except in those rare cases which form exceptions to the general principles of the legislation) decisions must not be taken on the prohibited grounds of sex, marital status, or race. Failure to reach targets will lead to questions as to whether discriminatory decisions are being made preventing the appointment of blacks or women, as the case may be; or whether there are unnecessary barriers being placed in their way. Where very small numbers are concerned, it is probably unwise to set numerical targets, but the larger the numbers involved the wiser it becomes to have numerical targets in view. The position under the Disability Discrimination Act 1995 is different, however. Since the right to complain of less favourable treatment on grounds related to disability is given only to disabled persons or those who have been disabled, there is nothing in the Act to prevent more favourable treatment of the disabled. Although the Act specifically says in section 6(7) that apart from the duties to make adjustments nothing in Part II is to be taken to require an employer to treat a disabled person more favourably than he treats or would treat others, an employer can do so voluntarily. Quotas were the norm under the 1944 legislation repealed by the 1995 Act. Quotas setting minima (but not maxima) can still be used voluntarily, unless the employer is required to appoint on merit as in the case of local authorities, but are not now compulsory.

Target setting

To give an example of target setting, suppose that an employer aims to recruit **4-59** 1,000 unskilled staff in a travel-to-work locality known to have a 25 per cent black population of working age. It is reasonable to suppose that somewhere around 250 of those appointed will be black, and that figure could be set as a target. If only 50 black people are appointed some very searching questions should be asked; if 220 or 280 so be it.

This is an example of target setting related to a particular recruitment exer- **4-60** cise. It is large enough to make that a sensible approach. Other methods might be to set a percentage target of 25 per cent black recruitment generally in this locality, to cover both this exercise and vacancies occurring from time to time. It may make sense to look at the overall results, though little sense to try and draw conclusions from each small-scale recruitment to fill casual vacancies. Another method might be to look at the ethnic breakdown of the existing workforce and at the recruitment potential over a period of years and set a target of reaching a 25 per cent black workforce in the locality within a determinate number of years.[49]

---

[49] The last census contained questions relating to ethnic origin and sex and provides a data base against which the monitoring returns of employers and others can be compared. The Labour Force Surveys published in the Department of Employment's *Gazette* are another useful source of data.

5 DISCRIMINATION IN EMPLOYMENT

5-01 Section 6 of the Sex Discrimination Act (SDA) and section 4 of the Race Relations Act (RRA) set out a number of specific heads of potential discrimination in relation to work. The provisions of the two Acts are in nearly identical terms and broadly comparable to section 4 of the Disability Discrimination Act 1995 (DDA), (except in so far as the Race Relations Act includes an additional head of discrimination, namely discrimination in the terms of employment under section 4(2)(a). This provision concerns contractual benefits, an area covered by the Equal Pay Act (EqPA) in relation to sex discrimination.)

5-02 Complaints under Part II of the Race Relations Act or the Sex Discrimination Act or in respect of the liability of principals or of aiding unlawful acts, are to be heard in the industrial tribunals, (RRA, s.54, SDA, s.63, DDA, s.8) except in relation to a qualifying body, from the decision of which an appeal may be brought under any enactment.

Employment in Great Britain

Definition of employment

5-03 Where an employee seeks to bring a complaint under Part II of the Sex Discrimination Act, the Race Relations Act or the Disability Discrimination Act which pertains to discrimination in employment, the complainant must be employed at an establishment in Great Britain. "Employment" means employment under a contract of service or of apprenticeship or a contract personally to execute any work or labour and related expressions shall be construed accordingly.[1] The EAT in *Quinnen v. Hovells*[2] held that a "contract personally to execute any work or labour" was intended to have a wider connotation than "employment" so as to include persons outside the master and servant relationship, *i.e.* the self-employed.[3]

Although the rights in part II of the Sex Discrimination Act are headed "Discrimination in the Employment Field" and section 6 provides that it is

---

[1] RRA, s.78(1), SDA, s.82(1), DDA, s.68(1). A J.P. is the holder of an office and not employed, *Knight v. A.G.* (1979) I.C.R. 194, EAT.

[2] [1984] I.R.L.R. 227.

[3] This broader connotation does not, however, extend to those who are working under a contract to supply services other than their own labour. Thus in *Mirror Group Newspapers v. Gunning* [1986] I.C.R. 145, C.A., a contract between the newspaper company and an independent wholesale distributor fell outside the terms of the comparable section of the SDA, because the contract did not contemplate that the work was necessarily to be performed personally by the contractor.

unlawful "in relation to employment at an establishment in Great Britain, to discriminate against a woman," the EAT in *Leighton v. Michael and Charalambous*[4] held that a claim under the Act is not precluded by the fact that the employee is a party to an illegal contract. Whilst knowing participation in an illegal contract to defraud the Inland Revenue has precluded unfair dismissal claims, the EAT upheld a claim of alleged sexual harassment, on the basis that the rights in question are statutory and any reference to the contract of employment was only for the purposes of determining whether the person is "employed". Such an interpretation was also held to be in accord with the broad scope of "working conditions" in Article 5(1) of the Equal Treatment Directive 76/207.

For these purposes, employment is to be regarded as being at an establishment in Great Britain unless the employee does his work wholly or mainly outside Great Britain.[5] The exclusion contained in the Sex Discrimination Act, s.10(1) does not apply to employment on a British registered ship, nor to an aircraft or hovercraft registered in Britain and operated by a person who has his principal place of business, or is ordinarily resident in, Great Britain, unless the work is done wholly outside Great Britain. Thus in *Haughton v. Olau Line (U.K.) Ltd*[6] the employee was excluded from the coverage of the Act because the ship on which she worked was registered in Germany and operated mainly outside British territorial waters.[7]

5-04

The Race Relations Act, s.8(1) provides that employment is to be regarded as at an establishment in Great Britain unless the employee does his work wholly or mainly outside Great Britain: section 8(2), however, provides that in the case of employment on a British registered ship or an aircraft or hovercraft registered in the United Kingdom and operated by a person who has his principal place of business or is ordinarily resident in Great Britain, the word "mainly" in section 8(1) shall be omitted. In other words, the employment is deemed to be at an establishment in Great Britain unless the applicant does his work wholly outside Great Britain. In *Deria v. The General Council of British Shipping*[8] three British registered Somali seamen were refused work on a British ship requisitioned for service in the South Atlantic at the time of the Falklands war. The vessel unexpectedly completed its voyage in Southampton, rather than Gibraltar. In spite of the fact that the employment would not have been wholly outside Great Britain, the Court of Appeal found against the seamen on the ground that the wording of section 8(2) was apt to cover existing employment, and if it is to be applied to selection for employment, must be read as applying where the applicant "does or is to

5-05

---

[4] [1996] I.R.L.R. 67. (The respondents refused to deduct tax and N.I. when they took over the fish and chip shop at which the applicant worked, even though she protested.)

[5] SDA 1975, s.10 and RRA, s.8; also the DDA s.68(2), but here employment on ship, aircraft or hovercraft is excluded.

[6] [1986] I.R.L.R. 465, C.A.

[7] It was argued on behalf of the appellant that her case was governed also by the provisions of the Equal Treatment Directive 76/207 which does not specify whether it applies extraterritorially. This argument was ruled out on the basis that the British statute was unambiguous and that there was therefore no place for the application of the Directive. In the light of the dicta of the ECJ in the *Marleasing* case, some doubt must now be cast on this aspect of the decision. See chapter 1 for further discussion of questions of interpretation in the light of Community law.

[8] [1986] I.R.L.R. 108, C.A.

do'' his work wholly outside Great Britain. As the voyage was intended to terminate in Gibraltar, on this construction the employment was excluded from the jurisdiction of the Race Relations Act. This construction was said to have the virtue of enabling the parties to know whether or not any element of unlawful discrimination was taking place at the time of the acts complained of, rather than leaving the matter at large and uncertain until the period of the employment is complete.[9]

5-06   Under the Race Relations Act, s.9, there is an exception for seamen recruited abroad, an exception which is subject to a saving in respect of off-shore oil workers. This exception allowed the continuing recruitment of a substantial part of the crews of British registered shipping abroad, often in the Indian sub-continent. Those seamen recruited overseas have normally earned only a fraction of the wages paid to crewmen recruited in the United Kingdom, but it was feared that if this practice were ended it would have a seriously damaging effect on the economics of British registered shipping. The off-shore oil industry was brought within the scope of the two Acts as regards employment matters in 1987.[10]

As concerns access to employment, In *Meyers v. Adjudication Officer*[11] the ECJ held that family credit, which is paid as a supplement to those in work at low wages, was concerned with access to employment and working conditions and therefore fell within the scope of the Equal Treatment Directive 76/207.

Recruitment and selection

5-07   It is unlawful under the Sex Discrimination Act, s.6(1)(a), the Race Relations Act, s.4(1)(a) and the Disability Discrimination Act s.4(1)(a) for an employer to discriminate in the arrangements made for the purpose of determining who should be offered employment. This provision covers recruitment and selection practices, both clearly vital if equal opportunities are to be made available to all classes of potential employees. Such discrimination could be either direct or indirect in the case of race or sex, as where, say, unjustifiable language or other tests, which have a disproportionate impact on the ability of women or minorities to secure employment are imposed on applicants. The provisions on discriminatory advertising contained in section 38 of the Sex Discrimination Act and section 29 of the Race Relations Act are also relevant in this context.[12]

Article 3 of the Equal Treatment Directive 76/207 provides that "there shall be no discrimination whatsoever on grounds of sex in the conditions,

---

[9] In *Wood v. Cunard Line* [1991] 281, C.A.; [1989] I.R.L.R. 431, EAT, a case occurring under comparable provisions of the Employment Protection (Consolidation) Act 1978, s.141(5), the EAT held that a British seaman working on a British registered ship which only ever plied in the Caribbean was excluded from the coverage of the Act, as his employment was wholly outside Great Britain, notwithstanding that he was given money for the fare home for his leaves which he normally took in the U.K.

[10] The Race Relations (Off-shore Employment) Order (S.I. 1987 No. 920) and The Sex Discrimination and Equal Pay (Off-shore Employment) Order (S.I. 1987 No. 930).

[11] Case C-1116/94 [1995] I.R.L.R. 498, ECJ.

[12] It therefore follows that a person may prove discrimination in a case, even though he or she cannot show that he or she would have got the job. There is also the question as to how to assess compensation for the loss of a chance, see chapter 00.

including selection criteria, for access to all jobs or posts, whatever the sector or branch of activity, and to all levels of the occupational hierarchy.''

Advertising

In this context, section 29(1) of the Race Relations Act provides that: **5-08**

> "It is unlawful to publish or cause to be published an advertisement which indicates or might be reasonably understood as indicating, an intention by a person to do an act of discrimination, whether the doing of that act would be lawful or, by virtue of Parts 2 or 3, unlawful."[13]

Section 38(1) of the Sex Discrimination Act restricts the ambit of the parallel   **5-09** provision on advertising to those acts which indicate an intention of doing an unlawful act only, although section 38(3) further provides that:

> "the use of a job description with a sexual connotation (such as 'waiter', 'salesgirl', 'postman', or 'stewardess') shall be taken to indicate an intention to discriminate, unless the advertisement indicates an intention to the contrary."

Proceedings in relation to a contravention of those sections[14] can only be   **5-10** brought by the Equal Opportunities Commission (EOC) or the Commission for Racial Equality[15] (CRE), as, for example, in the case of *London Borough of Lambeth v. CRE*.[16] The justification for restricting the right to bring proceedings in respect of advertising is presumably to avoid potential action by a multitude of readers, who need not necessarily have been intending to apply for the vacancy. The Race Relations Code of Practice advises employers not to advertise vacancies in such a way that minority candidates are excluded or disproportionately reduced, and that recruitment literature should include a statement that they are equal opportunity employers.[17] Similar advice is also given in the EOC Code.[18]

The Race Relations Act provides for exceptions to the provisions on discrim-   **5-11** inatory advertising particularly where:

> 1. The advertisement indicates that persons of any class defined other

---

[13] See chapter 9 for further discussion of role of the Commissioners.

[14] SDA, s.72 and RRA, s.63, although the Commission may also proceed by way of a formal investigation and the issuing of a non-discrimination notice under SDA, s.67(1)(c) or RRA, s.58(1)(c).

[15] *Cardiff Women's Aid v. Hartup* [1994] I.R.L.R. 390, in which the EAT held that placing an advertisement is not an act of discrimination rendered unlawful by Part II of the SDA or RRA, but may show an intention to do an act of discrimination contrary to the RRA s.29(1) or the SDA s.38(1).

[16] [1989] I.R.L.R. 379, EAT, [1990] I.R.L.R 231, C.A.

[17] Code of Practice para. 1.5–1.7.

[18] The Sex Discrimination Code para. 19, which enjoins employers not to present recruitment material in such a way that it reinforces stereotyped roles or the tendency to occupational segregation of the sexes.

than by reference to colour, ethnic or national origins are required for employment outside Great Britain.[19]

2. The advertisement is for a job in which there are genuine occupational qualifications for employing a person of a particular race, colour, ethnic or national origin or sex.

See the Chapter on Disability Discrimination for the very different position on advertising.

Recruitment practices

5-12   The importance of recruitment practices is testified by the attention given to them in the Codes of Practice for the SDA and RRA. The Codes enjoin employers not to discriminate directly or indirectly in recruitment, selection or interviewing practice. The CRE Code of Practice advises employers that:

> "to avoid indirect discrimination it is recommended that employers should not confine recruitment unjustifiably to those agencies, job centres, careers offices and schools which, because of their particular source of applicants, provide only or mainly applicants of a particular racial group."[20]

Furthermore the Code states that it is unlawful to use recruitment methods which cannot be shown to be justifiable and which are indirectly discriminatory in that they disproportionately reduce the numbers of applicants from a particular racial group.[21] Thus the practice of "head hunting" for managerial and professional posts, which favours those already in relevant work, may be indirectly discriminatory and difficult to justify objectively unless the vacancy has been openly advertised first.

5-13   The CRE Code recommends that employers should not rely on word of mouth recruitment, where the workforce is predominantly composed of the members of only one racial group, nor should employees be recruited mainly through a trade union where this means that only the members of a particular racial group come forward.[22] The CRE Code also recommends that gate staff should be instructed not to treat applicants from particular racial groups less favourably than others, that staff involved in recruitment should be clearly informed of the selection criteria, given guidance and training on the effects of generalised assumptions about race on selection decisions and made aware of the possible misunderstandings that can occur in interviews between persons of different cultural backgrounds. It recommends that shortlisting and interviewing should not be done by one person alone but at least be checked at a more senior level.[23] The EOC Code contains similar, though less detailed provisions on recruitment, but emphasises that interview questions should relate to the requirements of the job and not include questions about marriage

---

[19] RRA, s.29(3). The origin of this provision lies in the concern not to permit racially discriminatory advertisements to appear for jobs abroad.

[20] See para. 1(9).

[21] See para. 1.10.

[22] See para. 1.10(*a*) & (*b*).

[23] See para. 1.14.

plans or family intentions, as these may be construed as showing bias against women.[24]

Arrangements for selection

It is unlawful for an employer to discriminate on a prohibited ground in the arrangements which he makes for the purpose of determining who should be offered employment.[25] It is no defence for an employer to argue that the arrangements were not made with the intention of discriminating, if they operate so as to discriminate in practice. It was held by the EAT in *Brennan v. Dewhurst (J.H.) Ltd*[26] that the argument that the discrimination has to be found in the making of the arrangements rather than in the operation of the arrangements would leave a gap in the plain policy of the Act. In that case, applicants were referred to the shop manager as a first filter, although appointments would have been made by the district manager. The intention of the shop manager not to employ women meant that no women would get through to the final interview. The Act relates to the arrangements made, not the making of the arrangements, so that when the first selector conducted the interview in such a way as to discriminate against women, this was held to be unlawful under section 6(1)(a).

5-14

Refusing or deliberately omitting to offer employment

In the *Brennan* case it was held that the employer's shop manager who conducted the interview could not be said to be "making arrangements" himself. The style and content of an interview may, none the less, constitute evidence of direct discrimination under the SDA, s.6(1)(c) and the RRA, s.4(1)(c) — "refusing or deliberately omitting to offer her that employment". Thus in *Saunders v. Richmond Borough Council*[27] a lady golf professional was asked, amongst other questions, "Do you think men respond as well to a woman golf professional as to a man?" She argued that the asking of such questions was in itself discriminatory, in so far as they were questions which may not have been asked of a male candidate. The EAT took the view that the asking of such gender related questions was not in itself discriminatory and may be entirely appropriate where they are related to real aspects of capacity to do the job. Whilst an employer may not assume that all women with small children are unreliable, he may on this reasoning legitimately raise questions about the arrangements which such a woman has made to enable her to attend work regularly.[28] The asking of such questions may constitute evidence of

5-15

---

[24] See para. 23(c).
[25] RRA, s.(4)(1)(a), SDA, s.6(1)(a), DDA,s.4(1)(a).
[26] [1983] I.R.L.R. 357.
[27] [1978] I.C.R. 75, EAT.
[28] *See Hurley v. Mustoe* [1981] I.R.L.R. 208, EAT and *McGuire v. Greater Glasgow Health Board*, I.T. Case No. 2869/89. In *Johnston v. Fultons Fine Furnishings*, Case No. 02087/94 the I.T. found that to ask a woman if she intended to have any more children and whether working on Saturdays would cause child-minding problems was discriminatory, as the questions were intended to filter out those women candidates of child-bearing age who were perceived as likely to have more children. On the other hand, in *Twilley v. Tomkins* Case No. 27506/92 a woman candidate for a pools collection vacancy, questioned about her child-minding arrangements and the attitude of her husband to her working four evenings per week, was found not to have been discriminated against, because such questions were asked of both male and female candidates and because regular evening work depended on the co-operation of partners.

discriminatory attitudes or it may be an entirely appropriate way of testing the suitability of the candidate to perform the duties of the job. The inferences to be drawn from the evidence of questions asked at interview are matters of fact for the tribunal, but tribunals have not been unwilling to draw an inference that discrimination has occurred where a selection panel has been obtrusive or persistent in questioning female candidates about their family responsibilities and child care arrangements.[29]

5-16   Where an employer asks the same questions of all candidates, even though the questions may offend the susceptibilities of one candidate more than another, there is no discrimination. In *Simon v. Brimham Associates*[30] a Jewish candidate for a job in the Middle East objected to being asked about his religion. The employer explained that the question was asked because if he were of the Jewish faith this might preclude his selection for the post. At this point the candidate withdrew from the interview and took proceedings under the Race Relations Act. The Court of Appeal held that whilst words or acts of discouragement could constitute less favourable treatment, the complainant (surprisingly in the view of the authors) had not established that this question, which would have been asked of any candidate for the post, meant that the candidate had been treated less favourably than the interviewer would have treated some other non-Jewish person. If the candidate in *Simon* had not been appointed, rather than withdrawing, the action would have fallen under section 6(1)(c) refusal to offer employment.

5-17   It is discriminatory contrary to the RRA, s.4(1)(c) or SDA 6(1)(c) to assume that a particular job is "women's work" or "men's work" or that a member of the other sex, or a person of a different race, would not "fit in". In *Noone v. North West Thames RHA*[31] the Court of Appeal held that the Industrial

---

[29] *cf. Adams v. Strathclyde Regional Council*, EAT Case No. 456/88 in which a woman candidate for a teaching post claimed that she was so upset by a question as to how many children she had and of what age that she could not perform properly during the rest of the interview. Her application was dismissed by the industrial tribunal on the ground that the question was designed to put her at ease. The EAT upheld the decision holding that there was nothing inherently adverse in such questions and that this was a question which could equally well have been asked of a man. Caution should be exercised in this respect, however, for as the EAT observed, such questions can give the impression of discrimination to candidates, whether or not it is intended. Some public bodies frame their equal opportunity policies so as to restrict the ambit of such questions. In the I.T. case of *O'Driscoll v. The Post Office*, Case No. 25671/89, the interviewer asked an Irish applicant "Do you have a problem with the drink over here?" meaning, so he said, is the Guinness as good. The applicant, who understood the question as arising from the common stereotype of the Irish as being prone to drink problems, was awarded £600 for injury to feelings because the arrangements made for the interview (*i.e.* the questions asked) gave the impression of racial stereotyping and could have resulted in a poorer subsequent interview performance. Likewise a woman candidate for the post of education adviser in *Makija v. Borough of Haringey*, Case No. 03023/89, who was asked the question at interview "Given your opinions on equal opportunities and as a woman how would you deal with reactionary male teachers?" was upheld in her claim that a question phrased in that way was inherently discriminatory and revealed the operation of stereotyped assumptions as to the capabilities of men and women. Equally, questions may reveal a racially prejudiced attitude, as for example in *Richards v. Hodgson and Riceview Restaurants Ltd*, Case No. 7086/93, when a black man with mini-dreadlocks who had applied for a position as waiter in an American style restaurant, was asked if he would be prepared to cut his hair, having already been informed that Filipino applicants would not have been welcome.

[30] [1987] I.R.L.R. 307, C.A.

[31] [1988] I.R.L.R. 195, C.A.

Tribunal had been entitled to conclude that a well-experienced Sri Lankan candidate for a post of consultant microbiologist who was rejected because she would not "fit in", was rejected on racial grounds. Such feelings about the gender or race of an appropriate candidate can lead to stereotyped selection decisions.[32]

It is not necessary for race or sex to be the only factor in the decision to refuse employment for the case to fall within either the Race Relations Act, s.4(1)(c) or the Sex Discrimination Act, s.6(1)(c).[33] In *Owen & Briggs v. James*,[34] the complainant was refused employment on her first interview but seeing the post advertised again she re-applied and was again granted an interview. Though the employer put forward as reasons for her refusal that she had been unemployed for three years and that she had not disclosed the fact of her earlier interview, the fact that the job was offered to a white girl with inferior qualifications, to whom the employer expressed racist sentiments, was held by the EAT to constitute a sufficient ground on which the Tribunal could conclude that the refusal to offer employment was contrary to section 4(1)(c). The RRA, s.4(1)(c) does not cover the situation where a dismissed employee is applying to be re-instated on appeal according to the EAT in *The Post Office v. Adekeye (No. 2)*.[35]

5-18

The terms on which employment is offered

It is the offer of employment which is caught under either the Sex Discrimination Act, s.6(1)(b) or the Race Relations Act, s.4(1)(b). Once an offer which is discriminatory on grounds of sex is accepted, the terms of the resulting contract become governed by the Equal Pay Act, whereas under the Race Relations Act the matter is subject to section 4(2)(a). The result is that whereas under the Equal Pay Act there is need of an actual male comparator to establish a claim for equal pay, under the Race Relations Act the treatment likely to be afforded to a hypothetical person not of the complainant's racial group, etc. would found a claim.[36]

5-19

The terms on which employment is offered may include pensions. In *Barclays Bank v. Kapur*,[37] employees of East African Asian origin complained that their service in an associated company in Kenya was excluded for pension purposes when they were transferred to the U.K. due to the policy of "Africanisation" in that country. By contrast, the service of expatriate employees who had served in East Africa was included, so that the

5-20

---

[32] In *Bishop v. The Cooper Group*, Case No. 60910/92, a well qualified girl rejected for an apprenticeship because she would not "fit in" was found to have been subject to discrimination. Equally a man in *Croyston v. Texas Homecare Ltd*, Case No. 63658/94, who applied for a job as personnel assistant in a company where almost all the branch staff managers were female was held to have been discriminated against, after having been told by the manager to whom he made his application that her staff would be extremely surprised if a man were appointed.

[33] There is no reason to suppose that "a reason which relates to the disabled person's disability" need be the only reason under s.4(1)(c) of the DDA.

[34] [1982] I.R.L.R. 502, C.A.

[35] [1995] I.R.L.R. 297.

[36] See para. 5.50, on the hypothetical male.

[37] [1991] I.R.L.R. 136, H.L.; [1989] I.R.L.R. 387, C.A.; [1989] I.R.L.R. 57, EAT.

appplicants were offered employment on disadvantageous terms, Lord Griffiths holding that "a man works not only for his current wage but also for his pension."

5-21   Another important term of employment likely to give rise to discrimination claims is working hours. Although the EAT held in *Clymo v. Wandsworth Borough Council*[38] that an employer who stipulated full-time work was not imposing a "requirement" on employees, the question of working hours remains contentious. Many women returning from maternity leave would prefer to work part-time. In the *Clymo* case, for example, a professional librarian was refused "job-share" terms on returning from maternity leave, a facility available to lower grades in the library service of the Borough, but not to the professional grades. The EAT took the view that full-time work was inherent to the way in which the post was specified and not therefore a "requirement", even though in *Home Office v. Holmes*,[39] Waite J. had taken the view that:

> "Words like 'requirement' and 'condition' are plain clear words of wide import fully capable of including any obligation of service, whether full-time or part-time."

In *Briggs v. North Eastern Education and Library Board*,[40] the Northern Ireland Court of Appeal held that the fact that the employer requires the employee to carry out the job she is employed to do does not mean that there is not a requirement. It is for the employer to objectively justify the requirement to work full-time in such cases[41] or to refuse to operate flexi-time.

Dismissed employees

5-22   Discrimination against applicants for employment is rendered unlawful by the SDA s.6(1) and RRA s.4(1), whereas discrimination during an employment is rendered unlawful by the SDA s.6(2) and RRA s.4(2). Former employees whose contracts no longer subsist do not fall within the protection of Part 2 of the Acts. In *Nagarajan v. Agnew*[42] an employee complained that a refusal to re-employ him for reasons which related to his previous employment,

---

[38] [1989] I.R.L.R. 241.

[39] [1984] I.R.L.R. 299, approved by the N.I.C.A. in *Briggs v. North Eastern Education and Library Board* [1990] I.R.L.R. 181, which declined to follow the EAT in *Clymo v. Wandsworth Borough Council* (see above).

[40] In *Briggs v. North Eastern Education and Library Board* (see above) the employers were held to have justified a requirement that a teacher supervise school games for an hour after the finish of normal lessons, rather than at lunchtime. It is for the employer to justify such a requirement in accordance with the circumstances of the case.

[41] For example, in *Todd v. Rushcliffe Borough Council*, Case No. 11339/90, (EOR Discrimination Case Law Digest No. 8) a housing department employee was found to have been indirectly discriminated against by the requirement to return full-time, whereas in *Gill and Oakes v. Wirral Health Authority*, Case No. 1615/90, a requirement that midwives returned full-time was held to be justifiable even though it had a disproportionate impact on married women. The I.T. in *Watt v. Ballantyne & Copeland*, Case No. 5/1262/94, preferred to follow *Briggs*, rather than *Clymo* in finding a requirement that a former job share return from maternity leave full-time was indirectly discriminatory.

[42] *Nagarajan v. Agnew, Nagarajan v. Swiggs and London Regional Transport, Swiggs and London Regional Transport v. Nagarajan* [1994] I.R.L.R. 61.

which had been terminated over a year before, constituted victimisation. The EAT held that the RRA s.4(2) was couched in the present tense and that, as of the five heads of unlawfulness set out there, the first three could only occur during employment, the remaining two heads (refusal of benefits and the subjection of the employee to a detriment), should be construed similarly. Yet there seems little warrant for such a restrictive construction; would Parliament have intended that a racially motivated refusal to provide a reference be excluded from the coverage of the Act? Even though this possibility was explicitly canvassed, the decision in *Nagarajan* was approved in *The Post Office v. Adekeye*[43] in which an employee complained of racial discrimination in the conduct of her appeal against summary dismissal. Relying upon the decision of the Court of Appeal in *J. Sainsbury Ltd v. Savage*[44] that, in the absence of an express provision preserving her contract of employment, employment ceases at the date of summary dismissal, the EAT held that as the complainant was no longer an employee at the time of her appeal, she fell outside the scope of s.4(2). Smith J. expressed the view that had Parliament thought about the matter it would have wanted to encompass appeals as well as dismissals, but that it did not do so. Where an employee is dismissed with notice and the appeal falls within the notice period, it would be within the compass of the Acts, as would also be the case if the contract expressly preserves employment pending an appeal against dismissal, even if no work is done nor wages paid.

Promotion, transfer or training opportunities

It is unlawful for an employer to discriminate in the way in which he affords access to opportunities for promotion, transfer or training under the Sex Discrimination Act, s. 6(2)(a) or the Race Relations Act, s.4(2)(b). The protection of the Sex Discrimination Act, s.6(2) and the Race Relations Act, s.4(2) extends only to those currently employed and not to former employees (see paragraph 5–22 above). Thus promotion systems need to be open equally to all groups, irrespective of their gender, race, etc. Therefore the EAT held in *Mecca Leisure Group Ltd v. Chatprachong*[45] that the employer had not discriminated against a chinese croupier in not providing special language training which would have enabled him to prepare himself better for the oral promotion examinations held by the Betting and Gambling Board, since the employer would not have given special language training to other employees who had difficulties in communication. The EOC Code recommends that promotion and career development patterns are reviewed, especially where employees of one sex are concentrated in sections from which transfers are traditionally restricted without real justification. Where this is the case the EAT in *Francis v. British Airways Engine Overhaul Ltd*,[46] which concerned the lack of promotion prospects for a certain all-female grade of aircraft worker, recommended that where there are no promotion opportunities from a particular grade which is predominantly composed of women (or

5-23

---

[43] [1995] I.R.L.R. 297.
[44] [1980] I.R.L.R. 109.
[45] [1993] I.R.L.R. 531. Note the conditions governing special training or encouragement for underrepresented minorities discussed at paragraph 5–25 *et seq.*
[46] [1982] I.R.L.R. 10.

minorities), that an indirect discrimination claim could be formulated as follows: looking at the employees in the job categories from which promotion is possible as one class, in order to be eligible for promotion on the basis of their service and experience, an employee must be a member of that class.

In *Clymo v. Wandsworth Borough Council*[47] the EAT held that s.6(2)(*a*) of the SDA refers to the employer's acts or omissions in affording *access* to opportunities for promotion, etc., which already exist. In that case the applicant was wished to job share but her request was refused by the employer. The EAT held that as the facility to job share did not exist in her grade she could not be refused access to it, contrary to s.6(2)(*a*). It is for this reason that the Disability Discrimination Act, s.4(2)(*b*) refers to discrimination in the opportunities afforded for promotion, etc. (that is to say, whether these opportunities take the form of an existing facility or not), whilst s.4(2)(*c*) refers to a refusal to afford him any such opportunity, that is to say, to an existing opportunity.

5-24   It is possible that an employer may discriminate directly in allocating opportunities for promotion, or that a requirement or condition may be imposed within the promotion procedure which has an adverse impact on women or members of minorities, *i.e.* which could give rise to the possibility of indirect discrimination. Thus in *Watches of Switzerland v. Savell*,[48] the need to comply with the requirements of a promotion system was held to be capable of constituting a requirement or condition for the purpose of establishing indirect discrimination, but in *Perera v. The Civil Service Commission and Department of Customs and Excise (No. 2)*,[49] it was held that any such requirement or condition must constitute an absolute bar, if it is to ground a claim that promotion was denied on the basis of indirect discrimination. In all such cases the problem is often that of proof,[50] especially where there is an attempt to rely on statistical evidence on which to found the inference of discrimination. An exception is provided in the Race Relations Act, s.6, which provides that nothing in section 4 shall render unlawful training which is intended to provide skills which are to be exercised overseas.

Readers should note that there is no indirect discrimination provision under the Disability Discrimination Act. Instead there is, under section 6, a duty to make reasonable adjustments. The triggering words are much less restrictive than those triggering the indirect discrimination provisions in the SDA and RRA. Readers are referred to chapter 3 on the section 6 duty.

Special encouragement and training

5-25   Neither the Sex Discrimination Act nor the Race Relations Act permit the use of sex or race as a criterion for appointment to a post except where one of the closely-defined genuine occupational qualifications (GOQS) applies. However, in fact neither the Sex Discrimination Act nor the Race Relations Act requires appointment on merit. It is perfectly legitimate to use the tossing of a coin as a method of selection, which may of course result in the least

---

[47] [1989] I.R.L.R. 249, EAT.
[48] [1983] I.R.L.R. 141, EAT.
[49] [1983] I.C.R. 428, C.A.
[50] See chapter 3.

meritorious person being appointed. So appointment on merit is not mandated, but appointment by reason of sex or race is prohibited.

So much for the actual point of selection for a post. Prior to that point, certain **5-26** derogations from the non-discriminatory approach are permitted both in the sex and race fields to deal with underrepresentation. These are conveniently summarised as being intended to overcome chill and bring about skill.

Until the Sex Discrimination Act 1986, the Sex Discrimination Act and the **5-27** Race Relations Act were in similar terms. But without any clear explanation for a different approach the law diverged on the question of what discriminatory training is permitted. Probably the general public was rather more tolerant of women-only training than of training restricted to a particular race. Hence the former was freed from ministerial control which a scheme of designated training orders still ensured in the race field, until this too was altered in the Employment Act 1989.

Overcoming the chill factor

Even where discrimination at the point of recruitment has been removed, **5-28** women, or black people as the case may be, may not apply for particular posts if that employer is perceived to have been discriminating in the past either generally or in relation to the particular sort of work ("the chill factor" is a convenient expression). There is only one way of overcoming chill and that is by warmth. Accordingly, both the Sex Discrimination Act, s.48, and the Race Relations Act, s.38, in circumstances of underrepresentation permit the encouraging of women only, or men only, or only persons of a particular racial group to take advantage of opportunities for doing that work. Apparently the Sex Discrimination Act provision is wider because it allows the encouragement to extend to "that work" generally, whilst the Race Relations Act provision restricts the encouragement to "that work at that establishment", and the definition of what constitutes underrepresentation is similarly different.

Definitions of underrepresentation

The Sex Discrimination Act definition of underrepresentation is: **5-29**

"where at any time within the twelve months immediately preceding the doing of the act there were no persons of the sex in question among those doing that work or the number of persons of that sex doing the work was comparatively small."

The Race Relations Act definition is:

"(a) that there are no persons of the racial group in question among those doing that work at that establishment; or
(b) that the proportion of persons of that group among those doing that work at that establishment is small in comparison with the proportion of persons of that group

(i) among all those employed by that employer there; or

(ii) among the population of the area from which that employer normally recruits persons for work in his employment at that establishment.''

5-30   Where the conditions of underrepresentation apply, the encouragement can, for example, take the form of specific words of encouragement to the groups concerned to apply for jobs in advertisements (experience shows that there are fewer complaints if the relevant section of the Act is also quoted), or specific advertisements in parts of the press largely restricted to women or ethnic minorities. Section 6 of the Sex Discrimination Act and section 4 of the Race Relations Act would, without these exemptions catch these ''arrangements'' as discriminatory in themselves. But taking sex or race into account in making a selection decision as to particular people goes beyond mere encouragement. So where a council considered only black and ethnic minority applicants for two gardening apprenticeships (an apprenticeship is treated as employment) the council acted unlawfully: *Hughes and Gissing v. Hackney LBC*.[51] It is thought that this is also true of a selection decision as to the composition of a short-list.

If the pitfalls are avoided, use of appropriate encouragement can do much to overcome adverse perceptions.

Discriminatory training for employees

5-31   An employer may, in the conditions of underrepresentation set out above, make provision affording female employees only, or male employees only or only employees of a particular racial group (as the case may be) access to facilities for training which would help to fit them for the work in question. The only difference in the Sex Discrimination Act and the Race Relations Act provisions is that the Race Relations Act refers to employees ''at that establishment'' whereas the Sex Discrimination Act is not so restricted.

5-32   An employer cannot go so far as to guarantee appointment to particular work post-training if the employee embarks on training, because this would in effect amount not only to lawfully discriminatory training but also unlawful discrimination in appointment to jobs.

5-33   Obviously the special training provision has great potential for career development in cases where there are clear patterns of employment such as women only in secretarial and clerical positions, or blacks only in manual positions. The scope for training to fit persons for supervisory and managerial positions is likely to be considerable, particularly if the training is carried out along with a review of the appointment criteria relating to those higher grade posts. For example, it will often be necessary to ensure that the internal training and previous experience is treated as equivalent to higher academic qualifications if that has been the normal qualification in the past for a supervisory or managerial post.

5-34   There is a real risk that special training schemes will be set up to cater for ethnic minorities and women when the real problem is not that they lack

[51] [1987] EOR 27.

training, but that there was a reluctance to appoint them to supervisory positions because of their race or sex. If the persons on such training schemes look to be already well qualified, the chances are that the organisation concerned has expected ethnic minority or women managers to be better qualified than whites or men, as the case may be, appointed to managerial positions. It is not uncommon when appointments of ethnic minorities or women to managerial positions first take place to appoint only those who are seen as utterly safe appointments so that the rest of the workforce feels reassured.[52]

Discriminatory training generally

In defined conditions of underrepresentation of particular groups, both the Sex Discrimination Act and the Race Relations Act permit discriminatory training to help fit people for particular work. Apart from certain specified training bodies other organisations once needed designating as training bodies before being permitted to offer such training. The designation requirement however was removed in the field of sex by virtue of the Sex Discrimination Act 1986 and for race by the Employment Act 1989. This relaxation, however, was accompanied by a qualification that it does not legalise anything prohibited by section 6 of the Sex Discrimination Act 1975 or section 4 of the Race Relations Act 1976. Thus it makes clear that any training actually regarded as employment by the Acts, *e.g.* apprenticeship, is excluded.

    Where it is possible to offer discriminatory training it is also possible to provide encouragement to take advantage of opportunities to do particular work.

5-35

The conditions of underrepresentation are, in essence, that in the preceding twelve months either no women/men/members of a particular racial group (or comparatively few) were doing that work in Great Britain, or an area of Great Britain.

    These "chill and skill" provisions have one thing in common: they are voluntary in nature. There is no power to require their implementation, even in cases where discrimination has been proved. The CRE has recommended that the possibility of ordering such training to take place should be amongst the remedies available to industrial tribunals.

5-36

Positive action and the principle of equal treatment

The question has arisen as to whether affirmative or positive action is compatible with the Equal Treatment Directive. Article 2(1) of the Directive states that "the principle of equal treatment shall mean that there shall be no discrimination whatsoever on grounds of sex either directly or indirectly by reference in particular to marital or family status." However, Article 2(4) provides that the principle of equal treatment shall be "without prejudice to

5-37

---

[52] s.8 of the Employment Act 1989 allows for the making of orders to exempt discrimination in favour of lone parents in connection with training. S.I. 1989 No. 2140 & S.I. 1991 No. 2813 so provide.

measures to promote equal opportunity for men and women, in particular by removing existing inequalities which affect women's opportunities' as regards *inter alia* access to employment, promotion and training.[53] However, the Court of Justice has taken a strict view of this derogation, in accordance with the general view that all such derogations should be limited, holding that the general preservation by France of certain advantages for women after the Directive was implemented, including compassionate leave when children are ill and shorter working hours for older women, had not been shown to reduce actual instances of inequality.[54] All derogations from the principle of equal treatment are to be interpreted strictly, in accordance with the principle of proportionality, according to the Court of Justice in *Johnston v. Chief Constable of the Royal Ulster Constabulary.*[55]

In *Kalanke v. Bremen*[56] a German domestic law enacted in the State of Bremen provided that where women are under-represented in a particular grade or category of the public service and a male and a female candidate for a post are equally qualified, the job in question is to go to the woman. Under-representation was defined as existing where women constitute less than half of the employees in the grade or category in question. Advocate General Tresauro distinguished between three models of affirmative action:

(a) Programmes which aim to overcome disadvantage in the labour market, by taking selective action with regard to vocational guidance and training.

(b) Programmes which aim to foster balance between career and family responsibilities, placing emphasis on such measures as those which relate to the arrangement of working hours, child care facilities, easing re-entry into work by those women who have completed their families and fiscal or social security policies which take account of family duties.

(c) Programmes which aim to overcome the effects of historical disadvantage through the utilisation of quotas and goals.

In the first two models substantive equality is to be reached via the realisation of equal opportunities, whilst in the third model, equality of outcome is sought directly. The Advocate General Tresauro argued that the terms of Article 2(4) of the Equal Treatment Directive are only apt to legitimate programmes of the first two types, in that a programme aiming directly at equality of outcome goes further than ensuring that competition takes place on a level playing field, in so far as that may be achieved by legislative actions.

---

[53] The Agreement annexed to the Social Protocol of the Treaty of European Union, which does not bind the U.K., also provides that it "shall not prevent any Member state from maintaining or adopting measures providing for specific advantages to make it easier for women to pursue a vocational activity or to prevent or compensate for disadvantages in their professional careers."

[54] Case 222/84, [1986] 3 C.M.L.R. 240, in which the ECJ held that "in determining the scope of any derogation from an individual right such as the equal treatment of men and women provided for by the directive, the principle of proportionality, one of the general principles of law underlying the Community legal order, must be observed. That principle requires that derogations remain within the limits of what is appropriate and necessary for achieving the aim in view and requires the principle of equal treatment to be reconciled as far as possible with the requirements of . . . the context of the activity in question." (at pt 38).

[55] Case 222/84, [1986] I.R.L.R. 263, ECJ.

[56] Case C-450/93, [1995] I.R.L.R. 660, ECJ.

The aim of programmes intended to ensure an equal starting point is said to be "first to identify barriers and then to remove them, using the most suitable instruments for the purpose." Such measures would be discriminatory only in appearance, leading to substantive equality between the sexes, as opposed to purely formal equality. The Council Recommendation on Positive Action 84/365/EC, which whilst not being legally binding can be adopted as an aid for legislative interpretation, is also cast in terms of promoting measures to encourage the vocational progress of women.

The Court of Justice adopted an analysis akin to that of the Advocate General and concluded that "such a system substitutes for the equality of opportunity envisaged in Article 2(4) the result which is only to be arrived at by providing such equality of opportunity."[56a]

There is a clear distinction between the special encouragement and training provided for under the Sex Discrimination Act, s.48 and the Race Relations Act, s.38 and the type of "positive action" considered in *Kalanke*. Such "positive action" departs from the merit principle, under which the best qualified candidate is to be appointed, irrespective of race or gender. By contrast the object of the special encouragement and training permissible under U.K. law is to enable under-represented minorities to acquire "merit" and so to achieve advancement on the basis of equal competition. Indeed there is an inherent conflict between the proscription of discrimination against individuals and the practice of positive action.[57] Nonetheless, it is questionable as to whether an equal opportunities plan for women which fell within the bounds of *Kalanke*, but which operated even when the number of women performing the function was not "comparatively small" as required by SDA, s.48(1) or (2), could be categorised as unlawful.

The Department of Employment *Ten Point Plan for Employers* encourages management to review its practices and to develop an equal opportunities

---

[56a] The European Commission has issued a communication on the *Kalanke* decision, fearing that it may tend to stifle the development of equal opportunity plans. The Commission takes the view that it is only rigid numerical quotas, which make no allowance for the particular circumstances of the case, which are touched by *Kalanke* and proposes that Article 2(4) of the Equal Treatment Directive be amended to reinforce this interpretation. The Commission communication sets out a number of forms of "positive action" policies short of an absolute quota, which in its view remain lawful after *Kalanke*.

The 50 per cent rule in *Kalanke* is a part of the problem, seeming to be based on the notion of "sameness" between men and women, and making no allowance for any differences between men and women which might be expressed in their orientation to the type of work. Would it not have been more appropriate to give preference to women in this way when the proportion of women employed in the grade in question is less than the proportion of suitably qualified women in their sector of the labour market? For further discussion of the "sameness" "difference" debate and its application to hiring policies, see "Deconstructing Equality -versus- Difference; or, the Uses of Post Structuralist Theory for Feminimism", Joan W. Scott, Feminist Studies 14, pp. 33–50 and on the balance between individual rights and group interests in the context of equal opportunity policies, see "Preferential Treatment in the Labour Market after *Kalanke*; Some Comparative Perspectives", Titia Loenen and Albertine Veldman, International Journal of Comparative Labour Law and Industrial Relations, 12,1, pp. 43–53. See also C. Hakim, *Key Issues in Women's Work*, 1995.

[57] In the USA, where the concept of affirmative action originated, it has come under increasing criticism of late. Not only must such plans be transitional in nature but are subject to the principle of critical scrutiny, *i.e.* they must serve a compelling government interest and be narrowly tailored to that end, *i.e.* proportionate. Private plans must also be proportionate to their ends, though not serving governmental interests. See David K. Terpstra, "Affirmative Action: A Focus on the Issues," in *Labor Law Journal* (May, 1995) pp. 307–313; "Affirmative Action Under Attack in the USA", *EOR 63*, (September/October 1995) pp. 31–33.

plan, including numerical targets. A clear distinction is, however, drawn between numerical targets, in pursuit of which candidates are still selected on merit, and quotas, which would be likely to entail unlawful discrimination. The emphasis in the Department's Ten Point Plan is on actions to overcome disadvantage in the labour market by paying attention to selection processes, training and vocational guidance, though there is also some emphasis on the reconciliation of work and family life via greater flexibility in working hours and practices.[58]

Positive action and the DDA

5-38   For the position under the Disability Discrimination Act see chapter 3. Broadly, a reason connected with the persons disability should not be used as a reason for less favourable treatment unless justifiable. However, since a person who is not disabled (and has not been) cannot bring proceedings under that Act (except for victimisation) there is nothing to prohibit more favourable treatment of a disabled person.

Access to benefits, facilities and services

5-39   The Race Relations Act, s.4(2)(b) encompasses discrimination in the provision of benefits, facilities or services, whether contractual or non-contractual, whereas under the Sex Discrimination Act all contractual matters are brought within the purview of the Equal Pay Act. Thus the Sex Discrimination Act, s.6(6) excepts all money payments from the category of benefits in section 6(2)(a). Correspondingly the Race Relations Act, s.4(2)(a) covers discrimination in the terms of employment, again a topic which falls within the Equal Pay Act.

Benefits, facilities or services also provided to the public

5-40   Those benefits, facilities and services provided by an employer to the public which are also supplied to employees are excluded from these provisions by the Sex Discrimination Act, s.6(7), the Race Relations Act, s.4(4) and the Disability Discrimination Act, s.4(3), unless the benefits, facilities or services differ in some material respect from those supplied to employees, or their supply is regulated by the employee's contract of employment or the benefits, facilities or services relate to training.

---

[58] The Social Partners reached a Framework Agreement on Parental Leave in December 1995 under the Social Protocol and Agreement appended to the TEU at Maastricht, which will have effect as regards all other Member States except the U.K. This agreement provides for a right to three months non-transferable parental leave for both parents, to be taking during the first eight years of a child's life. Such a right will be subject to notice provisions and to a right of postponement by the employer on operational grounds. The agreement has been passed to the Commission to seek a "decision" from the Council to implement the agreement, in accordance with the procedures agreed at Maastricht, and it is proposed that the terms of this agreement be incorporated into a directive (COM(96)29 final) which will give legislative effect to the framework agreement.

Dismissal

Discriminatory dismissals are unlawful under the Sex Discrimination Act,   **5-41**
s.6(2)(b), the Race Relations Act, s.4(2)(c) and the Disability Discrimination
Act, s.4(2)(d). These provisions overlap with those of the Employment Rights
Act (ERA) 1996 on unfair dismissal, although the differences in qualifying
service and in levels of compensation would often suggest an application be
made under both statutes. In relation only to sex discrimination, the Equal
Treatment Directive 76/207 provides in Article 3 that men and women shall
be guaranteed the same conditions without discrimination on grounds of sex
as regards conditions governing dismissal.

The ERA 1996 requires a two year qualifying service, whilst the SDA and   **5-42**
RRA contain no such limitations. In *R. v. Secretary of State for Employment,
ex p. EOC* the House of Lords held that the longer qualifying periods for
unfair dismissal protection required of part-time employees were indirectly
discriminatory against women and amending legislation has now been introduced to remove the hours requirements completely, with the result that any
week in which the employee has a contract of employment counts as qualifying service.[59] The two year qualification period itself has now been successfully challenged in the Court of Appeal in *R. v. Secretary of State, ex p.
Seymour-Smith and Perez*,[60] as being indirectly discriminatory. However, the
proportion of women who enjoy two years continuous service, as against the
proportion of men who have such service, continues to rise. At present it is
impossible to say what period of service might be justifiable and it is unlikely
that legislation will be introduced until either the House of Lords has reached
a decision which it regards as *acte claire*, or the matter has been referred to
the ECJ. However, the EAT in *Clifford v. Devon County Council*[61] held that
a part-time County Council employee was entitled to bring an action for
unfair dismissal, even though at times she worked for less than eight hours
a week, on the basis that Lord Keith in the *EOC* case had spoken of "the
thresholds" in the 1978 Act. *Clifford v. Devon C.C.* precedes the decision
of the Court of Appeal in *Seymour-Smith and Perez* but it serves to demonstrate that public sector employees may rely on the direct effect of the Equal
Treatment Directive in this context as regards applications for unfair dismissal. The question as to whether unfair dismissal compensation is "pay"
for the purposes of Article 119 was left open by the Court of Appeal in
Seymour-Smith and Perez, in spite of an expression of sympathy for the EAT
decision to that effect in *Mediguard Services Ltd v. Thame*.[62] Should it be
held by the House of Lords or the European Court of Justice that unfair
dismissal compensation is "pay" for the purposes of Article 119, it would
put those who complain of unfair dismissal in the same position as those
seeking a redundancy payment, which was held to constitute pay in the
Barber[63] case and which is therefore directly effective for both public and
private sector employees.

---

[59] [1994] I.R.L.R. 176 and the Employment Protection (Part-time Employees) Regulations (S.I.
1995 No. 31).
[60] [1995] I.R.L.R. 464, C.A.
[61] [1994] I.R.L.R. 628, EAT and see *Warren v. Wylie* [1994] I.R.L.R. 316, I.T.
[62] *Mediguard Services Ltd v. Thame* [1994] I.R.L.R. 504, EAT.
[63] Case C-262/88, *Barber v. Guardian Royal Exchange* [1990] E.C.R. 1–1899, [1990] 2
C.M.L.R. 513, [1990] I.R.L.R. 240.

Following the implementation of the Pregnancy Directive 92/85 there is no qualifying service for a dismissal which occurs for a reason connected with pregnancy. Thus where a woman suffers dismissal for a pregnancy related reason, there is no service requirement for unfair dismissal, but the absence of a maximum level of compensation and the possibility of injury to feelings within the award suggests that application should be made under both statutes. For dismissals on grounds related to gender or family status, other than pregnancy, for which the question of service qualification is still not entirely resolved, both causes of action should be pleaded wherever appropriate.[63a]

5-43   Dismissal of a woman on grounds that she marries[64] or on grounds of her marital status is contrary to the SDA. In *Coleman v. Skyrail Oceanic Ltd,*[65] the employer dismissed a female employee when she married a man who worked for a rival travel firm. The two employers colluded and decided to dismiss the woman in preference to the man because he was assumed to be the breadwinner, an assumption held by the majority of the Court of Appeal to be based on sex.

5-44   To fall within the scope of the Acts, a dismissal has to take place on one of the prohibited grounds. In *Berrisford v. Woodard Schools (Midland Division) Ltd,*[66] an unmarried matron of a girls' boarding school run by a Church of England foundation was dismissed, not, as the Industrial Tribunal found, by reason of her pregnancy, but because her pregnancy was a manifestation of extra-marital sex. The Tribunal found that a male teacher, who had had a woman living with him who had a child, had been instructed to regularise the position and that another male teacher who formed a liaison with the mother of a pupil was given the choice of leaving the school or terminating the relationship. On this basis, the EAT upheld the Tribunal decision and dismissed the argument that because a man cannot become pregnant there must necessarily be discrimination in any dismissal connected with pregnancy. Since it was said to be the example given to pupils which was objectionable, in the view of the EAT, there was evidence upon which the Tribunal could conclude that a man so situated would also have been dismissed if there were comparable visible signs of extra-marital sexual activity. In such cases it is the drawing of the framework of comparison which tends to frame the conclusions.[67] The decision in *Berrisford* must now be regarded as being of doubtful authority following the refusal of the EAT in *O'Neil v. Governors of St. Thomas More RCVA School* to distinguish between pregnancy *per se* dismissals and dismissals which arise from the particular consequences attendant on the pregnancy (see paragraph 2-06).

Where an employer lacks any form of equal opportunities policy, industrial

---

[63a] Readers should note that the decision of the ECJ in *Nolte* (see paragraph 2–65) now makes it somewhat less likely that the House of Lords will strike down the two year qualification period for unfair dismissal as discriminatory.

[64] *North East Midlands Co-operative Society v. Allen* [1977] I.R.L.R. 212.

[65] [1981] I.R.L.R. 398.

[66] [1991] I.R.L.R. 247.

[67] See chapter 2 for a discussion of pregnancy cases and the drawing of the framework of comparison.

tribunals are more likely to draw the inference that a disputed dismissal was on racial grounds.[68]

An example of the effects of a dismissal arising from a common retirement **5-45** age is given by *Bullock v. Alison Ottley School*,[69] in which the school had provided for a common retirement age of 60 for teaching, administrative and domestic staff, but a retirement age of 65 for the gardening and grounds staff, all of whom were men. The EAT held that such a division of the staff into groups was contrary to the "but for" test enunciated by the majority of the House of Lords in *James v. Eastleigh Borough Council*,[70] but it is not obvious as to why this should be so as, had the complainant been a man, it is not clear that her situation would have been any different. It is likely, though not decided by the EAT, that the requirement to be a groundsman in order to stay on to age 65 was indirectly discriminatory, as all the grounds and maintenance staff were men and all but two of the teaching, administrative and domestic staff were women. Thus, it can be argued that the *Bullock* case does not rule out differential retirement ages for different groups of staff, though these may, in certain circumstances, be indirectly discriminatory, a view subsequently espoused by the Court of Appeal,[71] which held that the later retirement age for outside staff was objectively justified by the genuine need to recruit and retain this group of staff.

Selections for redundancy

Where an employer is engaged upon some form of reorganisation in which **5-46** jobs are re-allocated and some employees may be made redundant, discrimination may occur in the process. If the discrimination occurs in omitting to offer continued employment, the Sex Discrimination Act, s.6(1)(c), or the Disability Discrimination Act, s.4(1)(c) the Race Relations Act s.4(1)(c) come into effect. In *Timex Corporation v. Hodgson*,[72] the employer was engaged in a redundancy exercise and wished to reduce the total of three supervisors to only one. The employers chose to retain the one female supervisor, because they felt that only a woman supervisor would in certain respects be able to look after the women working in the factory, although the two men dismissed had longer service. If the discrimination lay in omitting to offer employment under section 6(1)(c), that subsection falls within the ambit of the genuine occupational qualifications set out in section 7, whereas discriminatory dismissals under section 6(2)(b) do not. The EAT held that[73]:

> "There are two stages inherent in any selection for redundancy where the job content of the remaining jobs is to be altered: first, the selection of the employees to carry out the revised job and secondly, the dismissal of those not selected to do the revised job . . . In our view the correct

---

[68] See the I.T. cases of *Cocking v. Newey & Lyre Ltd*, Case No. 14577/91 and *Danty v. Brittania Assurance plc*, Case No. 3875/92.
[69] [1991] I.R.L.R. 324. For a discussion of the common basis of comparison aspects of this see chapter 2.
[70] [1990] I.R.L.R. 288, H.L.
[71] [1992] I.R.L.R. 564, C.A.
[72] [1982] I.C.R. 63, EAT.
[73] *Per* Browne-Wilkinson J. at p. 67.

analysis is that the employers discriminate against the man by selecting the woman to do the revised job, not in dismissing the man who is not selected for the revised job. The discrimination lies therefore either in "deliberately omitting to offer" the man employment in the revised job. Once the selection for the revised job has been made, the dismissal of those selected necessarily follows. But the dismissal of those not selected is not itself discriminatory: any employee, whether male or female, who has not been selected for the revised job will be dismissed because there is no job for him or her to do."

5-47 Redundancy exercises carried out utilising last-in-first-out (LIFO) may well be indirectly discriminatory under the SDA or RRA, as also may be the equally common practice of dismissing part-timers first. In *Clarke and Powell v. Eley (IMI Kynoch) Ltd*,[74] part-timers were dismissed before full-timers, who were then selected for dismissal according to a LIFO criterion, in the course of a redundancy exercise. The EAT held that whilst selection of part-timers first was grossly discriminatory in its effects, selection according to a LIFO criterion had a lesser discriminatory effect which might be more easily capable of justification. The use of LIFO criteria were similarly considered to be capable of being contrary to the SDA or RRA in individual cases, according to the High Court in *R. v. London Borough of Hammersmith, ex p. NALGO*.[75]

Other detriments

5-48 Whether or not a person has suffered a detriment contrary to the Sex Discrimination Act, s.6(2)(c), the Race Relations Act, s.4(2)(c) or the Disability Discrimination Act, s.4(2)(d) is a question of fact, although it is possible that the detriment could be of such an insubstantial nature as to fall within the *de minimis* rule, as in *Peake v. Automotive Products Ltd*[76] (where women were allowed out five minutes before finishing time to facilitate their access to the buses).

The ECJ held in *Arbeiterwohlfarht der Stadt Berlin v. Botel*[77] that the refusal of payment to workers working part-time for attendance at that part of a trade union training course held outside their normal working hours was discriminatory contrary to Article 119.

Sexual harassment

5-49 Harassment is not a term defined in the domestic Statutes but constitutes a species of "detriment" under the Sex Discrimination Act, s.6(2)(b), the Race Relations Act, s.4(2)(c) or the Disability Discrimination Act, s.4(2)(d). However, the European Commission Recommendation on The Protection of the

---

[74] [1982] I.R.L.R. 482, EAT, [1982] I.R.L.R. 131, I.T.
[75] [1991] I.R.L.R. 249 See chapter 9 for a discussion of the judicial review aspects of this case.
[76] [1978] 233 Q.B. In this case the disabled were also allowed to leave early. As there is no protection for the able-bodied under the DDA, no discrimination would have occurred on these facts.
[77-79] Case 360/90, [1992] I.R.L.R. 423.

Dignity of Men and Women at Work[80] provides that conduct of a sexual nature, or other conduct based on sex affecting the dignity of women and men at work is unacceptable if it is:

1. unwanted, unreasonable and offensive to the recipient;
2. used as a basis for employment decisions, such as promotion, or is
3. such as to create an intimidating, hostile or humiliating work environment for the recipient.

The Commission Recommendation notes that such conduct may be contrary **5-50** to the principle of equal treatment contained in Directive 76/207, specifically Articles 3 (access to jobs, etc.), 4 (access to training) and 5 (working conditions, including the conditions governing dismissal). The Recommendation is accompanied by a Code of Practice on measures to combat sexual harassment, which was issued following resolutions of the Council of Ministers[81] and the European Parliament[82] on the protection of the dignity of men and women at work and forms part of the Commission's Third Action Programme on Equal Opportunities for Men and Women.

In *Grimaldi v. Fonds des Maladies Professionelles*,[83] the ECJ held that whilst **5-51** Article 189(5) provides that recommendations have no binding force and do not in themselves confer rights on individuals:

> "(N)ational courts are bound to take Recommendations into consideration in order to decide disputes submitted to them, in particular where they clarify the interpretation of national provisions adopted in order to implement them or where they are designed to supplement Community measures."

Whilst the Sex Discrimination Act was passed 15 years before the Code was adopted, as Docksey and Fitzpatrick[84] note, the U.K. has agreed that the Sex Discrimination Act represents its obligations under Directive 76/207. It is therefore arguable that the Recommendation and its associated Code of Practice can be prayed in aid as an interpretative device when considering sexual harassment claims brought under the Sex Discrimination Act.

The nature of sexual harassment

Although British law does not expressly proscribe sexual harassment, the **5-52** E.C. Code of Conduct defines it as:

> "unwanted conduct of a sexual nature, or other conduct based on sex affecting the dignity of men and women at work. This can include unwelcome physical, verbal or non-verbal conduct."

---

[80] [1992] O.J. C27/4.
[81] [1990] O.J. C157. The Resolution calls upon the Member States and the institutions and organs of the European Communities to develop positive measures designed to create a climate at work in which women and men respect each others human integrity.
[82] [1991] O.J. C305.
[83] [1990] I.R.L.R. 400.
[84] C. Docksey and B. Fitzpatrick, "The Duty of National Courts to interpret Provisions of National Law in Accordance with Community law" in I.L.J., 20, 2, pp. 113–120.

The EC Code of Conduct states in Article 2 that sexual harassment can include unwelcome physical, verbal or non-verbal contact and goes on to provide that "it is unacceptable if such conduct is unwanted, unreasonable and offensive to the recipient" whether it forms a basis for employment decisions, or it "creates an intimidating or hostile work environment for the recipient." The Code further provides that

> "it is for each individual to determine what behaviour is acceptable to them and what they regard as offensive. Sexual attention becomes sexual harassment if it is persisted in once it has been made clear that it is regarded by the recipient as offensive, although one incident of harassment may constitute sexual harassment if it is sufficiently serious. It is the unwanted nature of the conduct which distinguishes sexual harassment from friendly behaviour, which is welcome and mutual."

In *Wadman v. Carpenter Farrer Partnership*[85] the EAT referred to the guidance to be found in the European Commission Recommendation and Code of Practice and commended them to tribunals. It is now commonplace for tribunals to make reference to the Code in sexual harassment cases as setting a standard by which both the conduct of the parties and the arrangements made by the employer for dealing with such complaints, may be judged.

In the Scottish case of *Strathclyde Regional Council v. Porcelli*[86] the Lord President of the Court of Session expressed the view that sexual harassment is a "particularly degrading and unacceptable form of treatment which it must be taken to be the intention of Parliament to restrain." Sexual harassment has been considered to be "legal shorthand for activity which is easily recognised as subjecting her to any other detriment"[87] under the Sex Discrimination Act 1975, s.6(2)(b). What then are the hallmarks of this easily recognisable activity and what remedies does the Act place in the hands of those who feel that they have suffered some form of sexual harassment?

5-53   It was held in the racial harassment case of *De Souza v. Automobile Association*[88] that: "before an employee can be said to have been subjected to some "other detriment" that the court or Tribunal must find that by reason of the act or acts complained of a reasonable worker would or might take the view that he had thereby been disadvantaged in the circumstances in which he had thereafter to work."[89]

5-54   The standard of behaviour which might constitute racial or sexual harassment is therefore to be viewed from the point of view of the victim, rather than the alleged perpetrator. What might be acceptable behaviour to one person, may not be to another. Standards will vary as to what constitutes sexual harassment. In *Wileman v. Minilec Engineering Ltd*[90] a director's secretary complained that she had been the victim of sexual harassment by her boss

[85] [1993] I.R.L.R. 374, EAT.
[86] [1986] I.R.L.R. 134 at 137.
[87] *Wileman v. Minilec Engineering Ltd* [1988] I.R.L.R. 145.
[88] [1986] I.R.L.R. 103 *per* May L.J. at 107.
[89] Note the correspondence between this approach and the E.C. Resolution referred to above with its reference to conduct which creates an intimidating, hostile or humiliating work environment.
[90] [1988] I.R.L.R. 145.

over a period of four and a half years. The complainant sought aggravated damages, and in support of the claim endeavoured to introduce evidence of the director's conduct towards other women, which was not admitted. In discussing the relevance of this evidence Popplewell J. stated that.[91]

> "If this gentleman made sexual remarks to a number of people, it has to be looked at in the context of each person. All the people to whom they are made may regard them as wholly inoffensive; everyone else may regard them as offensive. Each individual then has the right, if the remarks are regarded as offensive, to treat them as an offence under the Sex Discrimination Act 1975."

Sexual harassment cases have been considered as constituting a species of direct discrimination under section 1(1)(a), *i.e.* as treating the woman less favourably on the grounds of her sex and more specifically in the employment context, as subjecting her to any other detriment under section 6(2)(b). In order to constitute a detriment under section 6(2)(b), treatment need only be such that:

5-55

> "the putative reasonable employee could justifiably complain about his or her working conditions or environment, whether or not these were so bad as to constitute dismissal or even if the employee is prepared to work on and put up with the situation."[92]

The essential test is therefore whether the woman has been treated less favourably on grounds of her sex than a comparable man would have been treated and that she has thereby suffered a detriment.

Thus in *Insitu Cleaning Co. Ltd v. Heads*[93] the EAT held that it was absurd to compare some passing reference to a bald head or a beard with the situation when the son of the two of the directors of a small company greeted a woman supervisor at the beginning of a meeting with the phrase "Hiya, big tits". The EAT made specific reference to the notion contained in the E.C. Code of an "intimidating, hostile or humiliating work environment" in reaching their conclusions. Even one such incident could be of sufficient gravity to found a successful claim, according to the EAT, which relied upon its previous decision in *Bracebridge Engineering Ltd v. Darby*.[94] In *Bracebridge* a woman was subject to an indecent assault by her charge hand and the works manager. The EAT held that a single incident of sexual harassment, provided that it is serious enough, can be a sufficient "detriment" to result in a successful discrimination claim.

The expression "subjecting to any other detriment" does not mean anything

5-56

[91] At p. 147.
[92] May L.J. in *De Souza v. Automobile Association (supra*, p. 87 at 107. The American EEOC guide-lines on sexual harassment likewise enjoin sexual harassment not only when compliance with unwelcome requests is made a condition of employment, or the employee has been disciplined or dismissed for refusing to comply with persistent and unwanted sexual overtures, but also where the "conduct has the effect of unreasonably interfering with an individual's work performance or creating an intimidating, hostile or offensive working environment."
[93] [1995] I.R.L.R. 4, EAT.
[94] [1990] I.R.L.R. 3, EAT.

more than "putting under a disadvantage."[95] An employee could be said to be suffering a detriment if she is disadvantaged in the circumstances in which she has to work. The question is whether the reasonable employee would feel she has been put at a disadvantage in her working life, rather than whether she has been subject to a detriment of some type because she refused to comply with demands which had been made upon her. The EOC Code of Practice provides that:

> "all reasonably practical steps should be taken to ensure that a standard of conduct or behaviour is observed which prevents members of either sex from being intimidated, harassed or otherwise subject to unfavourable treatment on the grounds of their sex."[96]

5-57   What if the employer argues that in view of the expressed attitude of the employee towards sexual matters, the conduct complained of cannot be to her detriment? In *Wileman v. Minilec Engineering Ltd*[97] the EAT held that there were grounds for the Industrial Tribunal to take into account the fact that the complainant often wore scanty and provocative clothing at work in assessing whether the harassment to which she was subjected constituted a detriment. In the view of the EAT, an industrial tribunal is entitled to look at the circumstances in which remarks are made which are said to constitute a detriment. In *Wileman* the extent of any such detriment was also held to be relevant in assessing injury to feelings.

5-58   For a claim to succeed under the SDA, s.6(2)(b) or the RRA, s.4(2)(c) an employee has to have been treated less favourably on grounds of her sex or race. Such action must be directed towards the employee or intended to affect her in some way. In the *De Souza*[98] case, a manager made a racially insulting remark to a fellow manager in respect of one of the office staff, who did not herself hear the remark, nor from the evidence did it appear that she was intended to do so. May L.J. held that he did not think she could:

> "properly be said to have been treated less favourably by whomsoever used the word, unless he intended her to overhear the conversation in which it was used, or knew or ought reasonably to have anticipated that the person he was talking to would pass the insult on or that the appellant would hear of it in some other way."[99]

Thus the conduct in question must be directed towards the complainant or it must be considered to be reasonably likely to have an effect on the sensibilities of the person in question. For example, a display of "pin ups" might not be directed towards any other person, but if it is reasonably likely that they would be seen by someone who might consider that they were offensive, such a display could constitute less favourable treatment of that person.

---

[95] *Ministry of Defence v. Jeremiah* [1980] I.C.R. 13, C.A.
[96] See para. 32(e).
[97] [1988] I.R.L.R. 144.
[98] [1977] I.R.L.R. 365, C.A. The *de minimis* ground of the decision in *Peake* was held to be the only valid ground for that decision in *Ministry of Defence v. Jeremiah* [1980] I.C.R. 13, C.A., a case in which the rule that only men had to work in dirty conditions was held to constitute a detriment.
[99] [1986] I.R.L.R. 134 at 137.

However, even though Article 2 of the Recommendation of the E.C. Commission enjoins Member States to "create a climate at work in which women and men respect one another's human integrity" the EAT in *Stewart v. Cleveland Guest (Engineering) Ltd*,[1-2] upheld a Tribunal decision that a display of pin-ups in the workplace was "neutral" in its effect as between men and women, in that men might also object to such a display.

In *Strathclyde Regional Council v. Porcelli*,[3] two laboratory male technicians **5-59** had pursued a course of harassment towards a female colleague whom they disliked and whom they hoped would thereby apply for a transfer or leave. This campaign included sexual innuendoes, suggestive remarks and intimidating conduct. The question arose as to whether such treatment was on the grounds of the respondent's sex. Emslie L.J. held that section 1(1)(a) is concerned with "treatment" and not with the motive or objective of the person responsible for that treatment. There need not be a sex related purpose in the mind of a person who indulges in unwanted and objectionable sexual overtures to a woman or exposes her to offensive sexual jokes. It is enough if the treatment occurs because she is a woman. In that case Grieve L.J. spoke of the weapons used against the complainer[4]:

> "if any could be identified as what I called 'a sexual sword', and it was clear that the wound it inflicted was more than a mere scratch, the conclusion must be that the sword had been unsheathed and used because the victim was a woman."

The treatment has, however, to occur on the grounds of the complainant's **5-60** sex. In *Porcelli*, it was argued on behalf of the employer that the treatment was not on the grounds of the sex of the complainant, because an equally disliked man would have received perhaps different but no less objectionable treatment. The Court of Session held, however, that where the treatment includes a significant sexual element to which a man would not be vulnerable, it is based upon the sex of the woman. It is no answer to the question posed by section 1(1)(a) that a man would have received different but equally unpleasant treatment. In *Balgobin v. London Borough of Tower Hamlets*,[5] the employer had held an investigation into alleged sexual harassment by a cook in a hostel run by the Council. The investigation was inconclusive and the alleged perpetrator and victims of the sexual harassment returned to work together. The victims complained that this action itself constituted a separate head of adverse treatment on ground of their sex, but this argument was rejected by the EAT. The employer would have taken the same action on the completion of an inconclusive disciplinary inquiry into, say, unwelcome homosexual advances by one man towards another. The treatment of, or requiring the employees to work together again was not on grounds of their sex; it was because they were employees, even if the consequence of the treatment was an intolerable situation.

[1-2] [1994] I.R.L.R. 440, EAT.
[3] [1986] I.R.L.R. 134.
[4] At p. 139. But note the 1-T-decision in *Goodwin v. Watkins*, Care No. 18694/94, that a general outburst by a chief about "fucking waitresses" did not constitute sexual harassment, because his comment was not based on sexual considerations, especially as he had apologised for his bad language.
[5] [1987] I.R.L.R. 401.

Specific problems of evidence in harassment cases

5-61   One of the problems facing both industrial tribunals, and indeed internal
disciplinary hearings, is the extent to which evidence may be admitted of
other consensual sexual activity by the victim, as tending to show how far
advances or sexual banter were likely to have been acceptable at the time.
The EAT in *Wileman v. Minilec Engineering* held that "a person may be
happy to accept the remarks of A or B in a sexual context, and wholly upset
by similar remarks made by C", nor was it considered relevant or of probative value that the complainant subsequently posed for a newspaper in a flimsy
costume. The EAT in the earlier case of *Snowball v. Gardner Merchant*[6] did,
however, admit evidence about the general sexual content of the complainant's conversation as being relevant to whether or not she had suffered detriment. The argument that this was a collateral matter which went only to
credit and on which answers in cross examination are final, was rejected.
This decision could be subject to the criticism that, if followed, it would
have the effect of deterring complainants, who might fear that their entire
sexual life could be subject to examination.

Questions of credibility emerge as important in cases where objection is
taken to "office banter", with emphasis being placed by industrial tribunals
on whether the complainant had made it sufficiently clear at the time that
she objected to the conduct in question.[7]

5-62   The previous or related conduct of the perpetrator can also be relevant. The
I.T. in *Groundrill v. Townhill and Pinefleet Ltd*[8] found that the previous
conduct of the perpetrator in respect of two other former women employees
was relevant and admissible. Evidence of similar conduct in a new job to
which the perpetrator was transferred was admitted as fresh and previously
unavailable evidence in a review of the decision in *Larpiniere v. Young*,[9] the
matter in this case seen as going to credit.

5-63   The EAT in *Bracebridge Engineering v. Darby*[10] held that a failure to investigate adequately complaints of sexual harassment could undermine the relationship of mutual trust and confidence between employer and employee. It
is clearly important for employers to make it clear that complaints of harassment, whether sexual or racial, fall within the scope of disciplinary proceedings, although it is clearly a sensitive matter for both the victim and the
alleged perpetrator as to when the employer should turn from a counselling
type of response to formal disciplinary proceedings.[11]

---

[6] [1987] I.R.L.R. 397.
[7] See, for example, *Hepburn v. Gordon and Day Partnership*, Case No. S/4429/91; *Stagg v. PSA* Case No. 7313/90.
[8] Case No. 21269/90.
[9] Case No. 191/90.
[10] [1990] I.R.L.R. 3.
[11] See also the I.T. case of *Mullan v. Department of Employment* [1991] in which a small female
employee was held upside down by a male colleague who simulated oral sex with her, but
whose case was reluctantly and only partially investigated by the Department of Employment.
Note that under the Rules of Procedure I.T.'s and the EAT may impose reporting restrictions
to protect the identity of individuals involved in cases of sexual misconduct. Note that the
E.C. Code of Practice advocates clear and distinct sexual harassment procedures be put in
place.

Where it is likely that evidence of a sensitive or salacious nature may be **5-64** led, industrial tribunals have powers to make a restricted reporting order under Rule 14, Schedule 1 of the Industrial Tribunal (Constitution and Rules of Procedure) Regulations 1993[12] but not to clear the tribunal of the press and public, according to the EAT in *R. v. Southampton Industrial Tribunal ex p. INS News Group and Express Newspapers plc.*[13] In that case the respondent and applicant both objected that a restricted reporting order made on the first day, which was intended to prevent the parties being identified, had been broken by a newspaper article and by a radio broadcast. As the Tribunal did not consider that in these circumstances it had powers to order that the proceedings be taken in private under Rule 8(3), the Tribunal made its order to exclude the press under the general powers provided by Rule 9 "to conduct the hearing as it considers most appropriate for the clarification of the issues before it". The EAT was of the view that, as a general principle of statutory construction, wider powers could not be used to modify the specific powers set out to deal with this situation in Rule 14. The EAT advised that such restricted reporting orders should clearly specify what is meant in the circumstances by "the publication of identifying matter."

Provisions of the E.C. Code

The E.C. Code of Practice makes several recommendations to employers **5-65** to facilitate a climate of opinion at work which inhibits sexual harassment, including:

(a) the issuing of a policy statement which makes clear that such behaviour will not be permitted or condoned and that employees have a right to complain about it;

(b) ensuring that the contents of the policy are communicated to all employees;

(c) promoting the policy in such a way that local management is responsive and supportive to such complaints; and

(d) providing both "awareness" training and more specific training for those responsible for operating the complaints procedure.

The Code advocates that a clear and precise procedure for dealing with com- **5-66** plaints of harassment will have the following features:

(a) A first stage, in which an effort is made to resolve the problem informally.

(b) A "sympathetic friend" or "confidential counsellor" designated as a first port of call for victims of alleged harassment.

(c) A special procedure may be necessary where the normal grievance procedure is not suitable, either because of problems of confidentiality or where, perhaps, the employee's line manager is the alleged perpetrator.

(d) The investigation should be independent and objective, with respect

---

[12] SI 1993 No. 2687 and the Industrial Tribunal (Constitution and Rules of Procedure) (Scotland) Regulations (SI. 1993 No 2688).
[13] [1995] I.R.L.R. 247, EAT.

for the rights of both the complainant and the alleged perpetrator to be properly heard and represented by a friend, colleague or trade union representative.

(e) The range of disciplinary penalties should be clearly specified in advance and where consideration is given to transferring one of the parties, wherever practicable, the complainant should be allowed to choose to stay where they are or to opt for a transfer.

The European Commission has issued a guide to implementing its Code on the Dignity of Men and Women at Work. The CRE have issued (1995) a guide to employers an racial harassment on broadly similar terms to the EC Code of the Dignity of Men and Women at Work. The EOC has also issued a guide to how to deal with sexual harassment as has the Irish Department of Equality and Law Reform.

Whilst it is not appropriate in a volume on discrimination law to pursue such matters in any detail, it is worth noting in this context that the Criminal Justice and Public Order Act 1994 creates a new offence of intentional harassment, which could cover racial and sexual harassment, as well as harassment on grounds of disability or sexual orientation. A person could be liable if he causes harassment, alarm or distress by using threatening, abusive or insulting words or behaviour or displays any sign or writing which is threatening, insulting or abusive. The provision covers conduct in a private as well as in a public place, although not in a dwelling house, in relation to other people in that house. Harassing behaviour could also give rise to liability in the torts of personal trespass.

Racial harassment

5-67   The issues which arise in cases of racial harassment are essentially similar to those which occur in relation to sexual harassment, with the proviso that complaints of racial harassment are likely to centre on the creation of a hostile, threatening or demeaning work environment. For example, in *British Leyland Cars Ltd v. Brown*,[14] the management feared that a black employee who had been arrested for theft in the plant and granted bail would try to re-enter the premises, perhaps under a false name. The management therefore issued instructions to the security guards to stop every black person and institute a thorough identity check; this instruction resulted in a certain amount of newspaper publicity. A group of black employees sought to establish that they had suffered a detriment under section 4(2)(b), albeit that the CRE also commenced proceedings under section 30 in connection with the issuing of such instructions. On a preliminary point, it was held by the EAT that the circulation of the instructions and the setting up of a regime under which black employees would have to undergo special checks was capable of constituting a detriment under section 4(2)(d) of the Race Relations Act, even if no employees had, by the time of the complaint, presented themselves for admission at the gate. The actual detriment suffered was a question of fact for the tribunal, which depended on the knowledge which each employee had of the instructions, his own intentions, etc.

[14] [1983] I.R.L.R. 193, EAT.

Stereotyped views may result in stereotyped insults and the CRE Code of   **5-68**
Practice warns against ignoring, or treating lightly, grievances from members
of particular racial groups on the assumption that they are over-sensitive
about discrimination. The widespread and unchecked use of racial banter may
result in the creation of a hostile, threatening, or more particularly, demeaning
work environment leading to complaints of discrimination.[15] The test as to
whether the actions complained of were on racial grounds is answered by
analogy with the sex discrimination cases, by considering whether a person
not of that racial group would have been vulnerable to the action in question.
Whilst the E.C. Code of Practice has no legal status in cases of racial harassment, it can have an indirect impact in so far as it is bound to influence the
standard which an employer must reach to be seen as "taking such steps as
were reasonably practicable" under section 32(3) to prevent acts of racial
discrimination.

Liability of employers for the actions of their employees

Whilst employers are liable for the actions of employees in respect of dis-   **5-69**
criminatory acts undertaken within the scope of their employment, the
employer is afforded a defence under the SDA, s.41(3) (or RRA, s.32(3)) if
he can "prove that he took such steps as were reasonably practicable to
prevent the employee from doing that act, or from doing in his employment
acts of that description". In cases of sexual harassment, it is clear that an
employer is much more likely to be successful in establishing a defence under
section 41(3) if there is a suitable policy in place, which conforms to the
main points of the Code.

Vicarious liability

Whilst Part 1 of the Act defines what is meant by discrimination, it is Part   **5-70**
2 which regulates the extent to which such discriminatory acts are unlawful

---

[15] In the I.I. case (Case No. 08807/88) of *Surinder Chima Singh v. The Chief Constable of Nottinghamshire Constabulary* a detective constable of West Indian origins, Glen Williams, eloquently expressed the reality of what such racial banter can entail.

"Sir there are certain ways that as a black person you have to deal with it. The CID tends to be a very close working group.

Now imagine the situation where a black man in a predominantly white office who for quite a while everyone saw as 'Good old Glen, he hasn't got a chip on his shoulder, he's one of the lads, I don't see him as a black man', that sort of attitude. 'He is just Glen.' It wasn't until the point where I started saying, 'I don't want to listen to these remarks anymore, they are offensive. I don't want to hear them', that the atmosphere changed.

The reality is that anybody who refers to a black man as a 'nigger' 'coon' or 'spook', whether it be in jest or not, if that person went up to some ordinary black guy in the street and said that to his face, he would be looking at a fist in the mouth, never mind a grin or a smile or an acceptance.

Regardless of whichever way I might have dealt with those particular comments being made, I guaranteed my survival within the CID. Unfortunately for me it also meant losing my dignity and I reached a point where I could not take that any more." References to an "Irish Paddy" in *McAuley v. Alloys Foundry*, Case No. 62824/93, and to a "Paki" in *Mann v. Woody*, Case No. 10361/91, were also had to be discriminatory.

in the employment context. The Sex Discrimination Act, s.6(1) provides that:

> "It is unlawful for a person, in relation to employment by *him* at an establishment in Great Britain, to discriminate against a woman . . ." (emphasis added).[16]

Thus the Acts are rendering unlawful the actions of the employer and not those of workers in the firm. However, it, is in the nature of things that discrimination can only occur as the result of the behaviour of individual employees and the question therefore arises as to the extent of the employer's liability for such action by employees. In this context, it is important that the Race Relations Act, s.32 and the Sex Discrimination Act, s.41 provide that:

> "(1) Anything done by a person in the course of his employment shall be treated for the purposes of this Act as done by his employer as well as by him, whether or not it was done with the employer's knowledge or approval.
> (2) Anything done by a person as agent for another person with the authority (whether express or implied, and whether precedent or subsequent) of that other person shall be treated for the purposes of this Act (except as regards offences thereunder) as done by that other person as well as by him."

The Disability Discrimination Act is in similar terms.

5-71   Whilst liability of the employer under Race Relations Act, s.32, the Sex Discrimination Act, s.41 and the Disability Discrimination Act, s.58 is a direct liability, the question nonetheless arises as to whether an employee who engages in some form of racial or sexual discrimination is acting within the course of his employment. The passage from the 9th edition of Salmond on Torts,[17] approved by the Privy Council in *Canadian Pacific Railway v. Lockhart*,[18] sets out the general principles:

> "It is clear that the master is responsible for acts actually authorised by him; for liability would exist in this case, even if the relationship between the parties was merely one of agency, and not one of service at all. But a master, as opposed to the employer of an independent contractor, is liable even for the acts which he has not authorised, provided they are so connected with acts which he has authorised that they might rightly be regarded as modes . . . although improper modes . . . of doing them. In other words a master is responsible not merely for what he authorises his servant to do, but also for the way in which he does it . . . On the other hand, if the unauthorised and wrongful act of the servant is not so connected with the authorised act as to be a mode of doing it, but is an independent act, the master is not responsible: for in such a

---

[16] And Sex Discrimination Act s.6(2) provides similarly in relation to employments in being at the time of the act in question. The Race Relations Act, s.4(1) and (2) provides similarly.
[17] At p. 95.
[18] (1942) A.C. 591, at 599.

case the servant is not acting in the course of his employment, but has gone outside it.''

This passage was more recently approved and applied by the Court of Appeal in *Aldred v. Nacanco*,[a19] a case concerning vicarious liability for injury, and in the racial harassment case of *Irving v. The Post Office*,[20] in which a letter sorter nourished a grudge against his West Indian neighbours over a question of street parking. When the letter sorter came across a Christmas card addressed to his next door neighbours he wrote on the back of the envelope ''Go back to Jamaica Sambo'' and underneath it he drew a cartoon of a smiling face. When the identity of the letter sorter was discovered he was disciplined but not dismissed. Perhaps because the neighbours were not satisfied with the disciplinary penalty imposed by the Post Office (dismissal suspended for a year), they sought a declaration under the Race Relations Act that the Post Office and its servants and agents had unlawfully discriminated against them. After reviewing the authorities on vicarious liability, the Court of Appeal held that the letter sorter's action could not be regarded merely as an unauthorised way of performing the duties for which he was employed. His employment provided the opportunity for his misconduct, but the misconduct formed no part of the performance of his duties as a letter sorter, even though he was authorised to write on envelopes for postal purposes.

5-72

Often the fact of employment will have provided the opportunity or occasion for a discriminatory act such as racial harassment to take place, but that does not necessarily make the employer vicariously liable. It is only if the actions complained of constitute a mode of carrying out the authorised tasks that the employer will be liable. For example, in *Heasmans v. Clarity Cleaning Co. Ltd*[21] the defendant company were under contract to the plaintiffs to provide cleaning services. One of their cleaners, whose honesty they had no reason to doubt, ran up a £1,400 bill on the plaintiff's telephone account in three months by making a series of unauthorised international calls. Even though his employment provided the opportunity for his wrongdoing, it was held that he was not acting in the course of his employment.

5-73

Applying these principles to cases of sexual or racial harassment at work, where an employee is in a supervisory position and takes advantage of that position to engage in some form of harassment, as in *Bracebridge Engineering v. Darby*,[22] such abuse of authority would be sufficiently closely connected with the task of supervision as to constitute a mode of performing the duties of the post. Following the *Irving* case, it is less clear that an employee who makes unwelcome advances to a fellow employee with whom he enjoys no working relationship is doing so in the course of his employment. The conduct complained of must be sufficiently closely connected with the employment of the person in question as to constitute an improper way of performing his or her job, if it is to give rise to vicarious liability on the part of the employer.

5-74

---

[19] [1987] I.R.L.R. 292.
[20] [1987] I.R.L.R. 289.
[21] [1987] I.R.L.R. 286.
[22] [1990] I.R.L.R. 3, EAT.

In the racial harassment case of *Tower Boot Co. Ltd v. Jones*[23] a young black employee was subject to racial abuse from two fellow workers, being called a "monkey" and a "chimp", his arm was burned by a hot screwdriver, his legs whipped with a piece of welt and bolts were thrown at his head. The EAT, by a majority, held that this action was not such that it was possible to describe it as an improper mode of performing an authorised task. Consequently the employer was held not to have been vicariously liable for the actions of its employees. Ironically, on this analysis, the more bizarre and outrageous the conduct the less likely it is that the employer could be found to have been responsible. Arguably the overriding obligation in the contract of employment to have regard to employees' health and safety,[24] could be used as the foundation of direct responsibility for abusive actions which cause distress and injury. Alternatively, such actions could be argued to be contrary to the implied term in the contracts of fellow employees to have regard to the health and safety of fellow employees, in which the actions of the employees, being an improper mode or performing that obligation, would give rise to vicarious liability on the part of the employer. Such approaches would preserve the contractual analysis of the problem, whilst extending the scope of employer responsibility. The more radical alternative would be to construe "in the course of employment" as synonymous with "during" the employment, thus making the employer responsible for all acts of sexual or racial harassment or any other discriminatory act perpetrated by employees whilst they are at work.

However, although the Tribunal in *Tower Boot* had found as a fact that the complainant's foreman was aware of the problem and that the action which he took was wholly inadequate, this had not been used as the basis of a separate head of complaint when the case was first heard. The EAT therefore remitted the case for consideration on this alternative basis by another Tribunal. The employer is under an obligation to take complaints of this nature seriously, according to the EAT in *Bracebridge Engineering Ltd v. Darby*,[25] in which Wood J. observed that where sexual discrimination and investigation are concerned it is extremely important not to undermine the trust and confidence of female staff. It follows that such a failure is a breach of the contractual obligation to maintain mutual trust and confidence between the parties to the employment relationship. Therefore such a failure to investigate complaints can lead to a potential liability on the part of the employer arising from constructive dismissal, contrary to the Sex Discrimination Acts, s.6(2)(b). However, even if the employee stays in her job, such a failure to investigate a complaint seriously could equally constitute a "detriment" contrary to s.6(2)(b).

An interesting example of the effect of applying the "course of employment" test in the sensitive context of allegations of sexual harassment is provided by *Waters v. Commissioner of Police of the Metropolis*.[26] In that case a woman police constable had originally complained of a sexual assault by a fellow constable when both were off-duty and away from their place of work. Her complaint was investigated but did not lead to any disciplinary

---

[23] [1995] I.R.L.R. 529, EAT.
[24] *Johnstone v. Bloomsbury Health Authority* [1991] I.C.R. 269. [1991] I.R.L.R. 118, C.A.; see Smith and Wood "Industrial Law" (Butterworths, 1993) pp. 98–99.
[25] [1990] I.R.L.R. 3, EAT.
[26] [1995] IRLR 531, EAT.

action. Later she alleged that held that she had been victimised by reason of that original complaint, but in order to succeed in an action for victimisation she had to show, according to s.4(1)(d) that "the discriminator or any other person has committed an act which would amount to a contravention" of the Sex Discrimination or Equal Pay Acts. The EAT upheld a decision on a preliminary point, based on facts agreed by counsel at the hearing, that the act in question had occurred outside the course of the employment of the male constable[27] and that as the complaint could not amount to a contravention of the Sex Discrimination Act, the necessary legal basis for a victimisation complaint was not made out. The result is that where an employee makes a complaint in respect of conduct, however outrageous, which cannot be construed as a mode of performing the contract of employment, the victim is not protected against victimisation as a result of having brought her complaint. The argument that the Act should be construed in a less restrictive fashion to accord with the provisions of Article 7 of the Equal Treatment Directive (see paragraph 2–75 above) was rejected.

The fact that this conduct may be unknown to the employer is not material, **5-75** so long as it is taking place within the course of the employment, for the Race Relations Act, s.32 and the Sex Discrimination Act, s.41 provide that such an act shall be treated as done by the employer, whether or not it was done with the employer's knowledge or approval. However, the Race Relations Act, s.32(3) and the Sex Discrimination Act, s.41(3) provide a defence for any employer who can:

"prove that he took such steps as were reasonably practicable to prevent the employee from doing that act, or from doing in his employment acts of that description."

In *Balgobin and Francis v. London Borough of Tower Hamlets*[28] a cook **5-76** sexually harassed two of the female cleaners employed in a hostel over a period of three months. As soon as the cleaners complained, the cook was suspended whilst the complaints against him were investigated. The complaints were not substantiated and the employees concerned returned to their original duties, after which there were no further complaints of improper conduct by the cook. Having found that the allegations had not been made known to management, that there was proper and adequate staff supervision and that the employers had made known their policy of equal opportunities, the EAT upheld a decision by the Industrial Tribunal that the employers had established a defence under the Sex Discrimination Act, s.41(3). The majority of the EAT took the view that it was very difficult to see what steps in practical terms the employers could reasonably have taken to prevent that which occurred from occurring. The minority took the view that the employers had taken little positive action to bring the provisions of the equal

---

[27] *cf.*, *Van Den Berghen v. Nabarro Nathanson and others*, Case No.20779/91, in which conduct at an office Xmas lunch was found to have taken place "in the coure of employment". However, a remark made walking down the street after dinner, was regretfully found not to be in the course of employment, in *Cumberbatch v. Hickson* and the DSS, Case No. 3221/94. It could be argued that where communication between workers is a normal requirement of their jobs, then racially or sexually abusive comments are a mode of such communication and take place in the course of employment.

[28] [1987] I.R.L.R. 401, EAT.

opportunity policy to the notice of employees or to make it clear that sexual harassment was an offence. It is much more likely now, post the promulgation of the E.C. Code on the Protection of Dignity of Women at Work,[29] that were the circumstances of this particular case to be repeated, the minority view would prevail.[30] Thus an employer who has promulgated a policy to protect the dignity of men and women at work, and undertaken training to bring its provisions to the notice of all concerned, would be more likely to succeed in a defence under section 41(3).[31] Without that the mere absence of complaints does not mean that a problem does not exist; it may simply indicate that employees fear complaining or think there is no point in it.

5-77   An employer may be responsible for the consequences of a discriminatory act performed by an employee, although the effects of that act arise from a step taken by an intermediary employee who may not himself be motivated by racial considerations or considerations of gender. Thus in *Kingston v. B.R.*[32] a transport policeman was found to have engaged in a form of racial harassment. To avoid further difficulties between the policeman and the employee concerned, a decision was taken by the local manager to transfer the employee to other duties. Although the manager who took the decision to transfer the employee was himself innocent of racial motivation, the employers were nonetheless liable for the consequences of an act of which the original cause was the discriminatory conduct of the policeman.

Aiding unlawful acts

5-78   A person who knowingly aids another person to do an act made unlawful by the Sex Discrimination Act or the Race Relations Act is himself to be treated as doing an unlawful act of a like description. Where a person is acting within the course of his employment so as to fall within the Race Relations Act, s.32, the Sex Discrimination Act, s.42 of the Disability Discrimination Act, s.5 (or would do but for subsection 3 of the relevant Act), he shall be deemed to be aiding the act of the employer, *i.e.* to be liable personally for the act. The Race Relations Act, s.33, Sex Discrimination Act, s.43 and the Disability Discrimination Act, s.57 make individual liability for aiding an unlawful act contingent upon the direct liability of the employer under section 32 or section 42 or section 58 respectively.

Therefore if the employee acts outside the course of his employment, with the result that the employer is not vicariously liable for his action, the

---

[29] see chap 4 for details of the Code.

[30] In *Coyle v. Cahill Motor Engineering Ltd* (Case No. 1808/87) a male supervisor who had been previously disciplined in respect of sexual harassment was placed in charge of a young female trainee. The management were held not to have taken all reasonable steps to prevent future incidents because they had at no point specifically invited the girl in question to comment on the way she was being treated.

[31] Thus in the I.T. case of *Taylor v. Asda Stores Ltd*, Case No. 41315/93, the respondent was able to sustain a defence under s.32(3) of the Race Relations Act because, in the Chairman's view it not only had an equal opportunities policy but carried it out. By contrast the company failed to establish such a defence in *Cooley v. BRS Ltd*, Case No. 4890/94, in which complaints of racial harassment were not properly dealt with. In the current climate of opinion, it may be insufficient for companies to have a policy on harassment which is simply a paper-tiger; it needs to be followed up.

[32] [1984] I.R.L.R. 147; [1984] I.C.R. 781, C.A.; affirming [1982] I.R.L.R. 274, EAT.

employee cannot be deemed to be liable for aiding the doing of the act in question. Only where the employer is responsible for the actions of the employee under the Sex Discrimination Act, s.41 or Race Relations Act, s.31, do the provisions of s.42 or s.32 respectively deem the employee to be personally responsible for aiding the employer's act of unlawful discrimination. It has, nonetheless, been suggested[33] not only that there could be personal liability in the torts of personal trespass, in particular where the action in question has involved physical contact or restraint, but that the emergent tort of harassment *simpliciter* could be utilised in this context.

Where a person relies on an assurance by the person whose act he is aiding that the act in question is not an unlawful discriminatory act, subsection 3 provides that he is not knowingly aiding that other, providing that it is reasonable for him to rely on the statement. A person who makes such a statement knowingly, or recklessly, which is in a material respect false is liable to a level 5 fine on summary conviction, under the Race Relations Act, s.32(4) or the Sex Discrimination Act, s.42(4).

5-79

Exclusions from the SDA

There are a small number of occupational groups excluded from the provisions of the Sex Discrimination Act, namely ministers of religion, so as to comply with the doctrines of the religion or avoid offending the religious susceptibilities of a significant number of its followers,[34] and prison officers in relation to height requirements.[35]

5-80

Exclusions in relation to death and retirement under the SDA

Whilst the Race Relations Act makes no provision for any exclusion of the provisions of the Act in relation to death or retirement, the Sex Discrimination Act originally excluded all such provisions.[36] This blanket exclusion of provisions in relation to death and retirement was held to be contrary to the Equal Treatment Directive Article 5(1) in *Marshall v. Southampton and South West Hants Area Health Authority*.[37]

In the *Marshall* case, the policy of the employer was that "normal retirement age will be the age at which social security pensions become payable", *i.e.* age 60 for women and 65 for men. Miss Marshall contended that the application of this policy constituted less favourable treatment under section 1(1)(a) of the Sex Discrimination Act, but her case was dismissed in the Industrial Tribunal and in the EAT because it was held to fall within the exception then provided by the Sex Discrimination Act, s.6(4), as a provision made in relation to death or retirement. Miss Marshall had made an alternat-

5-81

---

[33] Sexual Harassment: Moving Away from Discrimination, J. Dine and B. Watt, *MLR* (1995) 58:3, pp. 343–363.
[34] SDA, s.19.
[35] SDA, s.18.
[36] SDA 1975, s.6(4).
[37] [1986] I.R.L.R. 40, ECJ.

ive claim that her compulsory retirement at the age of 62 was contrary to Article 5(1) of the Equal Treatment Directive.[38] This claim had been upheld in the Industrial Tribunal, but rejected in the EAT on the grounds that the Directive could not be relied on before a United Kingdom court or tribunal. The case was referred to the ECJ which distinguished between the concept of retirement and pension ages and went on to hold that a compulsory retirement age fell within the concept of dismissal under Article 5(1) of the Directive, even if it was also the occasion of the granting of a pension. It was argued that the determination of pension ages for the purpose of social security was a matter which States could reserve to themselves under the EEC Social Security Directive 79/7, but the ECJ distinguished between the determination of pensionable age for the purpose of social security and the imposition of a retirement age within a contract of employment, holding the latter to fall within the Equal Treatment Directive. Whilst in *Burton v. British Railways Board (No. 2)*[39] the ECJ had held that the age of access to a voluntary redundancy scheme could be linked to state pension ages without violation of Article 5(1), the situation in *Burton* could be distinguished from that in the *Marshall* case, in that whilst the one had concerned access to voluntary early retirement, the other was concerned with the age of compulsory retirement

5-82 Since a directive is only of direct effect against an organ of the state, which a Health Authority was held to be, the rights available to public and private sector employees differed.[40] The result was the decision to enact the Sex Discrimination Act 1986, which narrowed the exclusion contained in the Sex Discrimination Act 1975, s.6(4). Whilst it is lawful to discriminate in provisions made with regard to death, as regards sub-sections 6(1)(b) and (2),[41] it is unlawful for a person to discriminate against a woman in relation to retirement with regard to access to opportunities for promotion, transfer or training, or by subjecting her to any detriment, demotion or dismissal.[42]

5-83 It is interesting to note that the words "any other benefits, facilities or services, or by omitting to afford her access to them" and "any other detriment" are omitted from the areas in which discrimination in relation to retirement is unlawful. One of the purposes of these omissions was to permit the continued payment of differential pension benefits, although following the Social Security Act 1975, ss.53–56, access to pension scheme membership has had to be equalised since 1978. Differential pension ages under the State social security system are permitted under the EEC Social Security Directive 79/7, but following the ECJ case of *Barber v. Guardian Royal Exchange Assurance*,[43] pension benefits are now seen as "pay" under Article 119.[44] In holding that differential pension ages did not constitute a question of access to pensions, as had been held in the *Burton* case, but one of pay under Article

---

[38] Directive 76/207.
[39] [1982] I.R.L.R. 116. See *Roberts v. Cleveland Area Health Authority* (1979) I.R.L.R. 244, C.A.
[40] See chapter 1.
[41] s.6(1)(a) and (c) are concerned with the making or of omitting to make, of offers of employment.
[42] SDA 1975, s.6(4) as amended by SDA 1986, s.2(1).
[43] [1990] I.R.L.R. 258.
[44] But only benefits accured by virtue of service after May 1990, according to the Protocol on Article 119 appended to the Treaty on European Union concluded at Maastricht.

119, the ECJ was reaching a conclusion contrary to the exclusionary provisions of section 6(1A)(b) of the Equal Pay Act, which are in similar terms to section 6(4) of the 1975 Act. The amendments made by the Sex Discrimination Act 1986 to the the Equal Pay Act 1970 and the Sex Discrimination Act 1975, in the light of the *Marshall* case, did not therefore take account of the post *Barber* status of pensions as pay under Article 119. Pensions matters are discussed in chapter 6 on Equal Pay.

Following the *Barber* case a number of matters with respect to the way in which the principle of equal pay applied to pensions were left undecided or unclear and further cases were referred to the Court of Justice in Luxembourg. These cases are discussed in chapter 6 on equal pay, but their broad effect has been to mandate equal treatment between men and women in pensions matters. The result is that it is no longer appropriate to maintain exceptions to the application of sub-sections 6(1)(b) & (2) as regards the provisions of benefits, facilities and services in relation to death or retirement, in order to allow for the payment of differential pensions. The Pensions Act 1995, s.62 will introduce an equal treatment rule into occupational pensions which do not already contain one. An equal treatment rule will govern both membership of pensions schemes and the treatment of members of the scheme, in a way analogous to the operation of the statutory equal pay term in the Equal Pay Act (see chapter 6). The Pensions Act, s.66(3) will amend the Sex Discrimination Act, s.6(4) from a date to be appointed (probably in 1997) to provide that it is only lawful to discriminate against a woman in relation to her membership of, or rights under, an occupational pension scheme where the equal treatment rule introduced by the Pensions Act does not apply. Therefore it will be lawful to discriminate in relation to provisions concerning pensions only where the comparisons provided for by the Equal Pay Act do not apply, *i.e.* there is neither like work, work rated equal nor work of equal value, or there are genuine material differences other than sex between the cases being compared. We submit, however, that this restriction to the defined cases of comparison in the Equal Pay Act is unwarranted in view of the absence of any reliance on such matters in the *Barber v. Guardian Royal Exchange Assurance* case itself.

5-84

Genuine occupational qualifications

Both the Race Relations Act and the Sex Discrimination Act provide for a number of "genuine occupational qualifications", under which an otherwise discriminatory act would not be unlawful.

5-85

The Race Relations Act, s.5 provides that where the genuine occupational qualifications apply, section 4(1)(a) (selection arrangements) or section 4(1)(c) (refusal or omission to offer employment) are excluded, as are the provisions on promotion, transfer and training in section 4(2)(*b*). The exclusions provided for are where, for reasons of authenticity, dramatic performances require a person of a particular racial group,[45] as also for artistic or

5-86

---

[45] RRA, s.5(2)(a).

photographic modelling,[46] employment in an ethnic restaurant,[47] and where the holder of the job will be providing personal services to members of a racial group promoting their welfare, and those services can most effectively be provided by a person of that racial group.[48] In *Tottenham Green Under Fives' Centre v. Marshall*,[49] Wood J. in the EAT held that where an employer is seeking to rely on the personal services genuine occupational qualification, then:

> "(a) The particular racial group will need to be clearly and, if necessary, narrowly defined because it will have to be the holder of the post and also that of the recipient of the personal services.
> (b) The holder of the post must be directly involved in the provision of the services — to direct others so to do is insufficient as the service must be personal. It does not seem to us that it need necessarily be on a one-to-one basis.
> (c) If the post holder provides several personal services to the recipient, then provided that one of those genuinely falls within the subsection, the defence is established.
> (d) "Promoting their welfare" is a very wide expression. The facts of each case are likely to vary enormously and different considerations will apply. It would be undesirable to seek to narrow the width of those words.
> (e) "Those services can most effectively be provided by a person of that racial group" — the words are not "must be provided" or "can only be provided". The Act assumes that the personal services could be provided by others, but can they be "most effectively provided". Would they be less effective if provided by others?"

5-87   The *Tottenham Green* case concerned the provision of nursery services to Afro-Caribbean children within the context of an explicitly multi-cultural nursery. When an Afro-Caribbean helper left, the Committee decided to advertise for another Afro-Caribbean worker, with a view to maintaining the cultural background link for Afro-Caribbean children, dealing with parents, reading and talking in dialect where necessary and generally looking to the skin care and general health of the Afro-Caribbean children. The Industrial Tribunal found that it was only the dialect requirement which could be most effectively provided by an Afro-Caribbean worker and decided that as that was only a marginal requirement — a desirable extra — found that the requirements of section 5(2)(a) were not satisfied. The case was remitted from the EAT to the same Tribunal after the above guidance was given but the decision remained the same. On a second appeal,[50] Mr Justice Knox held that it is not open to an industrial tribunal to disregard a duty in determining whether a genuine occupational qualification exception applies, unless the matter is *de minimis* or a sham duty invented for the purpose of qualifying for the exception. As neither was the case in this matter, the section 5(2)(d) exception necessarily applied.

[46] RRA, s.5(2)(b).
[47] RRA, s.5(2)(c).
[48] RRA, s.5(2)(d).
[49] [1989] I.R.L.R. 147.
[50] *Tottenham Green Under-Fives Centre v. Marshall (No. 2)* [1991] I.R.L.R. 162.

In *London Borough of Lambeth v. CRE*,[51] over half of the Borough's tenants **5-88** were of Asian or Afro-Caribbean origins. When vacancies arose for a head of housing benefit and a group manager within the housing department, it was decided to advertise the posts confining applications to Asian or Afro-Caribbean applicants and relying on section 5(2)(d). The CRE challenged the discriminatory advertisement under section 29, the Borough relying on the personal services exception. The decision of the EAT that these appointments fell outside the terms of section 5(2)(d) was upheld by the Court of Appeal on the ground that these were managerial appointments, whilst the section appears to contemplate either face-to-face or direct personal physical contact between the giver and receiver of the services. The Court of Appeal rejected the argument on behalf of the Borough that the sub-section contemplated a form of positive action in the fields to which it relates. The Court did, however, conclude that as section 3(1) provides that a racial group can be defined by colour, it is open to an industrial tribunal to find that the provider and receiver of the personal services could be of the same colour, even though not of the same ethnic group.

The above exceptions apply even where the person will be performing such **5-89** duties for only a part of his working time,[52] although they do not apply in relation to the filling of a vacancy if the employer already has sufficient employees of the racial group in question who are capable of carrying out the duties, and whom it would be reasonable to employ without undue inconvenience to the employer.[53]

The range of genuine occupational qualifications under the Sex Discrimina- **5-90** tion Act is much wider, although as with the Race Relations Act provisions, it is only the sections on selection, refusal to offer employment, transfer, training and promotion which are excluded. The qualifications embodied in section 7(2) are as follows:

"Being a man is a genuine occupational qualification for a job only where —

(a) The essential nature of the job calls for a man for reasons of physiology (excluding physical strength or stamina) or, in dramatic performances or other entertainment, for reasons of authenticity, so that the essential nature of the job would be materially different if carried out by a women; or

(b) the job needs to be held by a man to preserve decency or privacy because —

(i) it is likely to involve physical contact with men in circumstances where they might reasonably object to its being carried out by a woman, or

(ii) the holder of the job is likely to do his work in circumstances where men might reasonably object to the presence of a woman because they are in state of undress or using sanitary facilities; or

---

[51] [1989] I.R.L.R. 379, EAT; [1990] I.R.L.R. 231, C.A.
[52] RRA, s.5(3).
[53] RRA, s.5(4)(a), (b), (c).

(ba) the job is likely to involve the holder of the job in doing his work, or living, in a private home and needs to be held by a man because objection might reasonably be taken to allowing a woman —

(i) the degree of personal or physical contact with a person living in the home, or
(ii) the knowledge of intimate details of such a person's life, which is likely, because of the nature or circumstances of the job or of the home, to be allowed to, or available to, the holder of the job, or[54]

(c) the nature or location of the establishment makes it impracticable for the holder of the job to live elsewhere than in premises provided by the employer, and —

(i) the only such premises for persons holding that kind of job are lived in, or normally lived in, by men and not equipped with separate sleeping accommodation for women and sanitary facilities which could be used by women in privacy from men, and
(ii) it is not reasonable to expect the employer either to equip those premises with such accommodation and facilities or to provide other accommodation for women; or

(d) the nature of the establishment, or the part of it in which the work is done, requires the job to be held by a man because —

(i) it is, or is part of, a hospital, prison or other establishment for persons requiring special care, supervision, or attention, and
(ii) those persons are all men (disregarding any woman whose presence is exceptional), and
(iii) it is reasonable, having regard to the essential character of the establishment or that part, that the job should not be held by a woman; or

(e) the holder of the job provides individuals with personal services promoting their welfare or education, or similar personal services, and those services can most effectively be provided by a man, or
(f) (repealed by the Employment Act 1989)
(g) the job needs to be held by a man because it is likely to involve the performance of duties outside the United Kingdom in a country whose laws and customs are such that the duties could not, or could not effectively, be performed by a woman, or
(h) the job is one of two to be held by a married couple.''

5-91   The genuine occupational qualifications are not operative in relation to dismissals or other detriments or in relation to the offer of other benefits, facilities or services. Consequently in *Timex Ltd v. Hodgson*,[55] the supervisory structure was reorganised in the overall context of a redundancy. A male supervisor was selected for redundancy, whilst a woman supervisor of less experience was retained in the context of a reorganisation in which her job was given additional duties of a welfare type for remaining female members

---

[54] s.7(e)(ba) was inserted by the SDA 1986.
[55] [1981] I.R.L.R. 530, EAT and see paragraph 5–46.

of the workforce, which could more effectively be performed by a woman. The EAT held that any discrimination occurred not in the dismissal from the previous job but in the failure to be offered the revised job, *i.e.* the discriminatory act was the omission to offer employment rather than the dismissal, which therefore fell within the scope of the genuine occupational qualifications in section 7(2)(c). The EAT also held that, provided the Industrial Tribunal was satisfied that the additional duties were genuine, it was not for the Tribunal to instruct the employer how to manage his business.

The provisions as to decency and privacy in the Sex Discrimination Act, s.7(2)(b)(ii) cover not only the state in which the actual duties of the job are performed, but also all matters reasonably incidental to the performance of the job. Thus in *Sisley v. Britannia Security Systems Ltd*,[56] women working twelve hour shifts in a security control centre, who often spent up to five hours resting in a state of undress on the bed provided for that purpose by the employer, fell within the Sex Discrimination Act, s.7(2)(b)(ii) even though resting was not strictly part of their job duties. The genuine occupational qualifications relating to decency and privacy, along with the provisions in paragraphs (a), (c), (d), (f) or (g), are qualified by the Sex Discrimination Act, s.7(4), which provides that they do not apply to   **5-92**

> "the filling of a vacancy when the employer already has male employees —
>
> (a) who are capable of carrying out the duties falling within that paragraph, and
> (b) whom it would be reasonable to employ on those duties, and
> (c) whose numbers are sufficient to meet the employer's likely requirements in respect of those duties without undue inconvenience."[57]

A man applied for a post as sales assistant in a dress shop in *Etam plc v. Rowan*[58] and was refused. His claim that that the refusal to employ him was discriminatory was defended by the employer on the grounds of decency and privacy, in that a sales assistant may be required to work in the fitting rooms and to measure women who are uncertain of their size. The EAT upheld a finding that the refusal to employ a man was discriminatory, in that it would have been possible to ensure that those aspects of the job could have been executed by one of the 16 existing female staff without great inconvenience.

Special cases

Contract workers

Under the Sex Discrimination Act, s.6(1) the Race Relations Act, s.4(1) and Disability Discrimination Act, s.12 it is unlawful "for a person, in relation   **5-93**

---

[56] [1983] I.R.L.R. 404, EAT.
[57] RRA 1976, s.5(4) is in similar term in respect of the genuine occupational qualifications contained in that Act.
[58] [1989] I.R.L.R. 150, EAT.

to employment by him at an establishment'' to discriminate against a woman or any person on racial grounds or by reason of a person's disability. Whilst this section would make the employer of contract workers liable, it leaves untouched the principal for whom the work is being undertaken and who controls many of the terms on which it is done. Consequently, the Sex Discrimination Act, s.9 or the Race Relations Act, s.7 place analogous responsibilities on such principals to those placed upon employers generally, except for the functions of selection, engagement and dismissal which would remain with the person who is in strict law the employer. The section requires the existence of a contract for the supply of labour between the contractor and the principal,[59] although the individuals performing the work may be either employed or, following the expanded definition of employment in the Sex Discrimination Act, s.82(1) or the Race Relations Act, s.78(1), self-employed.

5-94   The three sided relationship between worker, employment agency and principal was explored in *BP Chemicals Ltd v. Gillick and Roevin Management Services Ltd*[60] in which a contract worker employed by R carried out work on behalf of the appellant principals, BP. Following a short period of maternity leave, the respondent worker sought to return to her previous job with BP, but was only offered alternative work at a lower salary, which she refused. She was subsequently dismissed by the employment agency R. The EAT held that although the extended definition of ''employment'' in section 82 applied only where there was a direct contractual relationship between the worker and her ''employer'', section 9 was apt to cover this situation. The appellant principal had argued that it was not liable because section 9(2) provides only that:

> ''It is unlawful for the principal, in relation to work to which this section applies, to discriminate against a woman who is a contract worker—
> (a) in the terms on which he allows her to do that work, or
> (b) by not allowing her to do it or continue to do it, or
> (c) in the way he affords her access to any benefits, facilities or services or by refusing or deliberately omitting to afford her access to them, or
> (d) by subjecting her to any other detriment.''

The employer argued that the section only applied to contract workers who are actually working, but did not cover a refusal to take them into employment. The EAT took the view, however, that there is no mention of selection or dismissal in the sub-section, only because these are contractual functions to be performed by the agency who is the direct employer of a contract worker. They held that it would be contrary to the scheme of the Act to imply such a limitation upon the scope of the section, which embraces the refusal to allow a woman to do the work or to continue to do so.

5-95   Although the contractual status of such workers is open to doubt,[61] they

---

[59] See *Rice v. Fon-A-Car* [1980] I.C.R. 133, EAT in which it was held that a taxi driver who responded to requests for taxi services passed on through a central agency was not a contract worker because there was no contract between the agency and the customer for the supply of taxi services

[60] [1995] I.R.L.R. 128.

[61] ''Where A contracts with B to render services exclusively to C, the contract is not a contract for services (or of services) but a contract sui generis a different type of contract from either

nonetheless fall within the scope of the Act, provided they are engaged under a contract to execute personally any work or labour.[62] Persons undertaking training under the ET scheme are not contract workers within the meaning of this section. In *Daley v. Allied Suppliers Ltd*,[63] the EAT held that YTS trainees were under a contract of training and not a contract to execute work.

Vocational training

Section 13 of the RRA and Section 14 of the SDA, as amended by the Employment Act 1989, provide that it is unlawful to discriminate on grounds of gender, marital status or race in the terms on which training to help fit a person for employment is offered, or by refusing or deliberately omitting to offer training, terminating training or subjecting a trainee to any other detriment.[64] These provisions are subject to the proviso in sub-section 2 of the respective sections that they do not apply to discrimination rendered unlawful by the RRA, s.4(1) or (2) or s.6(1) or (2) of the SDA, or to provisions which would be rendered unlawful by any of those provisions but for the operation of other provisions of the Acts, *i.e.* sections 47 and 48 of the RRA and sections 37 and 38 of the SDA allowing special encouragement and training in conditions of under representation. These sections are therefore without prejudice to the operation of discriminatory training undertaken to remedy under representation of women or of minority employees.

5-96

Partnerships

Whereas under the Race Relations Act, s.10 only partnerships of six or more partners are brought within the Act in relation to the appointment of partners, following the enforcement proceedings brought by the European Commission against the United Kingdom,[65] the Sex Discrimination Act 1986, s.2(2) amended the Sex Discrimination Act 1976, s.11 to include all partnerships, no matter what the number of partners involved.

5-97

These sections render it unlawful to discriminate in the arrangements made for determining who should be offered partnerships, the terms on which partnerships are offered, or refusing or deliberately omitting to offer a partnership.[66] In a case where a person is already a partner it is also unlawful to discriminate in the provision of access to benefits, facilities or services or in expelling a person from a partnership, or subjecting him or her to any other detriment.[67]

5-98

---

of the familiar two." *Construction Industry Training Board v. Labour Force Ltd* (1970) 3 All E.R. 220, *per* Cook J. at 225. *Cf. McMeecham v. Secretary of State for Employment* [1995] I.R.L.R. 461.

[62] See *Mirror Group Newspapers v. Gunning* [1986] I.C.R. 145, C.A., *Tanna v. Post Office* (1981) I.C.R. 374, EAT.

[63] (1983) I.C.R. 90, EAT.

[64] The Training and Enterprise Councils (TECS) which are now responsible for providing such training are required to have equal opportunity policies as a condition of their funding.

[65] *Commission of the European Communities v. United Kingdom* (Case No. 61/81) [1982] E.C.R. 2601.

[66] RRA, s.10(1)(a)–(c), SDA, s.11(1)(a)–(c).

[67] RRA, s.10(1)(d)(i),–(ii) SDA, s.11(1)(d)(i).–(ii).

5-99   The Sex Discrimination Act adds the proviso that sections 11(11)(b) and (d) do not apply to provisions in relation to death and retirement except in so far as they apply to the terms on which a woman is offered a partnership, or to the expulsion of a woman from a partnership, in order to accommodate the effects of the Marshall case as implemented by the Sex Discrimination Act 1986.

Trade unions and employers' organisations

5-100   Trade unions and employers' associations are covered by the Race Relations Act, s.11, the Sex Discrimination Act, s.12 and the Disability Discrimination Act, s.13 which proscribe discrimination in the terms on which membership is offered, refused, or varied, or in the way in which access is provided to benefits, facilities and services or in subjecting the applicant or member to any other detriment.

5-101   Positive action in regard to training members to assist them to take up office in such organisations or encouraging only members of a particular racial group to take advantage of opportunities for holding such posts in the organisation is permitted under the Race Relations Act, s.38(3) where there are no persons of a particular racial group holding such posts or where the proportion of persons of that racial group holding such office is disproportionately small. A similar provision exists in the Sex Discrimination Act, s.48(2) in relation to positive action in favour of women.

5-102   Under the Sex Discrimination Act, s.49, provision is made for reserving seats for women on any elected bodies of organisations covered by section 12 or to create extra seats for women where, in the opinion of the organisation, it is needed to secure a reasonable minimum of members of that sex serving on the body concerned.

5-103   Under Article 4(b) of the Equal Treatment Directive[68] Member States must take measures to ensure that:

> "any provisions contrary to the principle of equal treatment . . . in rules governing the independent occupations and professions shall be, or may be, declared null and void or may be amended."

The European Court of Justice held that the United Kingdom was in breach of this obligation in enforcement proceedings[69] as regards the rules of trade unions, professional bodies and traded associations. No enforcement machinery exists as yet, however, through which aggrieved members or would-be members may enforce their Community rights.[70]

5-104   Discriminatory terms contained in collective agreements, employers' rule

---

[68] Directive 76/207.
[69] Case 165/82, *Commission of the E.C. v. U.K.*: [1983] E.C.R. 3431; [1984] 1 C.M.L.R. 136, [1984] I.C.R. 192; [1984] I.R.L.R. 29, ECJ.
[70] Note that this right arising under a Directive is only enforceable as against as organ of the state, which is unlikely to be the case for this type of body. See p. ? for discussion of the legal status of E.C. Directives.

books or the rules of qualifying bodies are rendered void by the Sex Discrimination Act 1986, s.6. This section was also passed following the successful enforcement proceedings brought by the Commission against the United Kingdom Government, an action which succeeded even though collective agreements in the United Kingdom are almost invariably not legally enforceable, following upon the Trade Union and Labour Relations Act 1974, s.18. The Government chose to implement the ECJ decision by declaring such terms void rather than amending them, and indeed took this opportunity to repeal section 3 of the Equal Pay Act 1970. That section conferred upon the Central Arbitration Committee the power to amend collective agreements which contained terms which were not inclusive as between men and women. The CAC had, prior to the decision of the Court of Appeal in *R. v. C.A.C. ex p. Hy-Mac*,[71] taken a liberal view of its powers to amend agreements, but the *Hy-Mac* decision had largely nullified those powers. By virtue of the Sex Discrimination Act 1986, s.6(5), any term which has been incorporated into the terms of an individual's contract of employment and which are beneficial to her, although discriminatory, are unaffected by the avoidance of the relevant term of the collective agreement and may be modified in the county court by virtue of the Sex Discrimination Act, s.77(5). Thus the only remedies available to a person who experiences discrimination as the result of a discriminatory term in a collective agreement, which has been incorporated into her contract of employment, is to apply to an industrial tribunal under section 2 of the Equal Pay Act 1970, if the term is unlawful by virtue of that Act, or to a county court under the Sex Discrimination Act, s.77(5), if it is discriminatory by virtue of the Sex Discrimination Act.

However, the Trade Union Reform and Employment Rights Act 1993 amends the SDA 1986 and introduces a new sub-section 6(4A) into that Act. This provides for such actions to be brought in an Industrial Tribunal, although the new provisions are, however, limited to actions by which the offending term may be declared void. The new sub-section provides a right of action in the Industrial Tribunals for individuals who may be affected by unlawfully discriminatory terms of collective agreements, unlawfully discriminatory rules made by employers, trade unions, employers associations, professional organisations or qualifying bodies under SDA 1986, 6(1)–(2). Section 4A(a) applies this right to persons who believe that such a rule may have effect in relation to them at some future time and that the rule could lead to an act being done to him or her which would be unlawful if done at the present time. (A person who was actually affected could take direct action in respect of any detriment suffered.) Section 4A(b) applies this new right to those seeking employment as respects rules made by or on behalf of an employer or employers association. Section 4A(c) applies this right to those seeking membership of, or authorisation from, a qualifying body. It remains true, however, that there is no forum in which discriminatory terms of a collective agreement may be amended, a state of affairs lamented by the EOC.

Qualifying bodies

Under the Race Relations Act, s.12 and the Sex Discrimination Act, s.13, it **5-105** is unlawful for a body which can confer an authorisation or qualification

---

[71] [1979] I.R.L.R. 461.

which is needed for, or facilitates, engagement in a particular profession or trade to discriminate against a person in the terms upon which the authorisation or qualification is conferred, by refusing or deliberately omitting to grant an application or withdrawing or varying the terms upon which the authorisation or qualification is awarded. Article 3 of the Equal Treatment Directive provides that there shall be no discrimination in "access to all jobs or posts, whatever the sector or branch of activity." The DDA does not cover qualifying bodies at all. In *British Judo Association v. Petty*,[72] the EAT held that section 13 of the SDA was apt to cover the refusal to award a licence to women to referee national men's judo competitions, even though the Judo Association argued that it was not awarding a qualification to facilitate the candidates' entry into the occupation, but simply upholding standards of refereeing. The test is whether the qualification in fact facilitates entry into the profession or occupation, whether it is intended to do so or not. In early 1996 the Labour Party Policy of "woman only" shortlists was declared unlawful by an industrial tribunal, on the basis that it contravened the SDA, s.13, in *Jepson and Dyas-Elliot v. The Labour Party*.[73]

5-106   The Sex Discrimination Act goes further than the Race Relations Act, and in section 13(2) provides that where a body is required to satisfy itself as to the good character of a potential member before awarding a qualification which facilitates entry into a trade or profession, it shall have regard to any evidence that the applicant has practiced unlawful discrimination in carrying on any trade or profession. The jurisdiction of industrial tribunals is excluded where an appeal, or proceedings in the nature of an appeal, can be bought under any statute against the decision of a qualifying body under the SDA, s.65(2) and the RRA, s.54(2). The General Medical Council was held to be such a body in *Khan v. GMC*[74] because it had a power to review its decisions on registration.

5-107   In the enforcement proceedings taken against the United Kingdom[75] the European Court of Justice held that s.13 did not satisfy Article 4(6) of the Equal Treatment Directive, which requires Member States to legislate to ensure that the internal rules of qualifying bodies can be amended or declared null and void where they are incompatible with the provisions of E.C. law. The Sex Discrimination Act, s.6(2) now renders void non-contractual rules of qualifying bodies which would be unlawful by virtue of the Sex Discrimination Act 1975.

The Trade Union Reform and Employment Rights Act introduces a new section 6(4)(c) into the SDA 1986 which gives a right of action in respect of such rights in the industrial tribunals, but note the observations in paragraph 5–104 above.

Employment agencies

5-108   Discrimination by employment and vocational guidance agencies is unlawful under the Race Relations Act, s.14 and the Sex Discrimination Act, s.15.

---

[72] [1981] I.R.L.R. 484, EAT.
[73] [1996] I.R.L.R. 116.
[74] [1994] I.R.L.R. 646.
[75] Case 165/82, [1984] 1 All E.R. 353; [1984] I.R.L.R. 29.

The services provided by employment agencies fall within the scope of the DDA, s.19 which forms a part of the non-employment provisions. Reference should be made to chapter 3 for coverage of this issue. Discriminatory activities undertaken by local education authorities under the Employment and Training Act 1973 are rendered unlawful by subsection 2, as these would otherwise be saved by the provisions in the Race Relations Act, s.41, although the amended Sex Discrimination Act, s.51, does not save prior statutory provisions, except in so far as these are concerned with the protection of women.

An employment agency is defined as a person who, for profit or not, provides services for the purposes of finding employment for workers or supplying employers with workers.

Police

For the purpose of the SDA and RRA, the holding of the office of constable is to be treated as employment by the chief officer of police, or police authority, in relation to actions taken by them respectively under the Race Relations Act, s.16, and the Sex Discrimination Act, s.17(2). The Sex Discrimination Act, s.17(2), provides that men and women shall not be treated differently except as to uniform, equipment or height requirements and in relation to special treatment accorded to women in connection with pregnancy or childbirth, or in relation to pensions paid in respect of special constables or police cadets. There is no equivalent provision in the DDA.

5-109

Barristers

In view of the fact that barristers fell without Part 2 of the Acts because they work neither under a partnership agreement nor under a contract, whether of service or for services, a gap was exposed in the legislation. The Courts and Legal Services Act 1990, ss.64 and 65 inserted a new section in each of the Acts[76] as respects barristers in England and Wales and advocates in Scotland, which provide that it is unlawful to discriminate on grounds of race or sex as regards the making of offers of pupillage or a tenancy, the terms on which pupillages or tenancies are offered, or in the giving, withholding or accepting of briefs. But although akin to the work provision, the new sections are inserted in Part 3 of each Act and therefore the proceedings are brought in the county courts (or sheriff courts in Scotland).[77]

5-110

---

[76] RRA 1976, s. 26A & B, SDA 1975, s.35A &B.
[77] By virtue of being placed within Part 3 of the Acts, legal aid is available in county courts and there is no statutory limit on compensation, but on the other hand, married barristers do enjoy protection on grounds of their marital status.

6 EQUAL PAY

The legal framework

6-01　The Equal Pay Act (EqPA) was first passed in 1970, but employers were given five years in which to implement equal pay. The Equal Pay Act did not come into force until the end of 1975, by which time the Sex Discrimination Act 1975 had been passed and the Equal Pay Act was re-enacted as Schedule 1 to the Sex Discrimination Act. The two Acts are intended to "provide in effect a single comprehensive code" in the field of employment,[1] although the two Acts have not been consolidated.[2] The distinction between the two Acts is that the Equal Pay Act is concerned with equalising terms and conditions of employment between men and women, whereas the Sex Discrimination Act is concerned to eliminate discrimination in relation to non-pay matters, such as access to training or promotion opportunities, although these clearly could be the subject of implied terms in the contract of employment. However, since Britain acceded to the Treaty of Rome, Article 119, which enshrines the principle of equal pay for work of equal value, has become an important source of law in this area.[3]

6-02　There are three types of explanation for the persistence of the overall gap of 20 per cent between the hourly rates of pay earned by full-time women workers and those earned by full-time male workers.[4] They are (a) the occupational segregation of men and women, (b) differences in pay for the same or similar work and (c) the under-valuation of female-dominated jobs. Whereas (a) can be attacked by the Sex Discrimination Act, and (b) is subject to the like work of the Equal Pay Act 1970, (c) is appropriate for review under the equal value amendments to the 1970 Act introduced in 1983. The comparable worth provisions contained in section 1(2)(c) of the 1970 Act are capable of achieving an improvement in the relative position of women workers without needing to wait until women have had time to work their way into a wider range of occupations and reach the higher levels of the occupational hierarchy. This would more certainly be the case were those provisions contained in the type of pro-active pay equity system which exists in Ontario, under which employers are required to develop and post a plan to achieve comparable worth between male and female dominated groups in the labour force within a set period. Nonetheless, the British provisions, though cumbersome and slow, have had and are having an effect on the earnings differential between men and women, with the result that whereas

---

[1] *Shields v. E. Coomes (Holdings) Ltd* [1978] I.C.R. 1159, *per* Bridge L.J. at 1178.
[2] One of the proposals for change contained in the EOC review of the sex discrimination legislation, "Equal Pay for Men and Women" (EOC, 1990) was that the two Acts should be consolidated to avoid problems of overlap.
[3] See chapter 1 for a further discussion of the relation between domestic and European law relating to equal pay.
[4] Jill Rubery, "The Economics of Equal Value" (EOC, 1992).

women received 73 per cent of gross male earnings in 1984, by 1994 that figure was 80 per cent.

Article 119

Article 119 enshrines the principle of equal pay, which the ECJ in the second   **6-03**
Defrenne[5] case declared "forms part of the foundations of the Community."
Article 119 provides as follows:

> "Each member state shall during the first stage ensure and subsequently maintain the application of the principle that men and women should receive equal pay for equal work."

The principle of equal pay was restated in the Equal Pay Directive 75/117, Article 1 of which provides as follows:

> The principle of equal pay for men and women outlined in Article 119 of the Treaty, hereinafter called the 'principle of equal pay,' means for the same work or for work to which equal value is attributed, the elimination of all discrimination on grounds of sex with regard to all aspects and conditions of remuneration. In particular, where a job classification system is used for determining pay, it must be on the same criteria for men and women and so drawn up as to exclude any discrimination on grounds of sex."

The Equal Pay Act, as enacted, failed to provide for equal value claims except   **6-04**
where the employer had voluntarily undertaken a job evaluation study. Following upon enforcement proceedings brought by the Commission against the United Kingdom Government,[6] the Equal Pay (Amendment) Regulations 1983 (often referred to as the Equal Value Regulations) were introduced to provide a right to equal value claims. These Regulations were introduced under the European Communities Act 1972 and amend the provisions of the Equal Pay Act 1970.

The rights arising under Article 119 in respect of direct and overt discrimina-   **6-05**
tion were held to be directly effective by the ECJ in *Defrenne (No. 2)*. As the ECJ in *Jenkins v. Kingsgate (Clothing Productions) Ltd*[7] held that Article 1 of the Equal Pay Directive simply restates the principle of equal pay contained in Article 119 and "in no way alters the content or scope of that principle," it follows that Article 1 of the Directive, with its explicit reference to work of equal value, can be seen as directly effective both vertically and horizontally, *i.e.* it applies to workers in both the public and private sectors. In *Jenkins*, the ECJ also held that the concept of direct effect applies "to all forms of discrimination which may be identified solely with the aid of the criteria of equal work and equal value referred to by the Article in question, without national or Community measures being required to define them with

---

[5] Case 43/75, *Defrenne v. Sabena*: [1976], ECJ 455 at p. 473. and see chapter 1 generally for a discussion of the relation between Community and national law.
[6] Case 61/81: [1982] E.C.R. 2061 and Case 61/82: [1982] E.C.R. 3431.
[7] [1981] I.R.L.R. 228 at 234.

greater precision in order to permit their application.''[8] Nonetheless, doubts were expressed by Lord Oliver in *Pickstone v. Freemans*[9] that a right which is dependant for its exercise upon the complex national provisions of the Equal Value Regulations could be of direct effect.

6-06 Applicants can rely on the direct effect of rights which arise under Article 119 and, according to the Court of Appeal in *Biggs v. Somerset County Council*,[9a] the Equal Pay Directive confers no new or separate rights. It is not possible to found a claim on the Directive to the exclusion of Article 119 in order to circumvent the procedural rules applicable under domestic law, according to the EAT in *Preston v. Wolverhampton NHS Healthcare Trust*.[10]

The European Commission produced a Memorandum on Equal Pay for Work of Equal Value[11] which set out the main principles of Community law in this area. An E.C. Code of Practice on Equal Pay for Work of Equal Value, is under discussion at the time of writing. The EOC produced a draft Code of Practice on Equal Pay in April 1995 & hopes to made available a final version early in 1996, to be placed before Parliament in later 1996.

The Equal Pay Act 1970

6-07 The Equal Pay Act operates by implying into the contract under which a woman is employed an equality clause[12] whenever a woman is engaged in like work with a man,[13] work rated as equivalent[14] or work to which equal value is attributed.[15] Section 1 of the Equal Pay Act provides as follows:

> "1. If the terms of a contract under which a woman is employed at an establishment in Great Britain do not include (directly or by reference to a collective agreement or otherwise) an equality clause they shall be deemed to include one.
>
> 2. An equality clause is a provision which relates to terms (whether concerned with pay or not) of a contract under which a woman is employed (the woman's contract), and has the effect that
>
> (a) where the woman is employed on like work with a man in the same employment
>
> (i) if (apart from the equality clause) any term of the woman's contract is or becomes less favourable to the woman than a term of a similar kind in a contract under which that man is employed that term of the woman's contract shall be treated as so modified as not to be less favourable, and

---

[8] At 234.
[9] [1988] I.R.L.R. 357 at 364.
[9a] [1996] I.R.L.R. 203.
[10] [1996] I.R.L.R. 484 and see paragraph 6–40 for a discussion of the effect of time limits on Treaty procedures and directives in national law.
[11] COM (94) 6 final.
[12] Case 61/81: [1982] E.C.R. 2061 and Case 61/82: [1992] E.C.R. 3431.
[13] EqPA 1970, s.1(2)(a).
[14] EqPA 1970, s.1(2)(b).
[15] EqPA 1970, s.1(2)(c).

(ii) if (apart from the equality clause) at any time the woman's contract does not include a term corresponding to a term benefiting that man included in the contract under which he is employed, the woman's contract shall be treated as including such a term.''

Similar provisions covering women doing work rated as equivalent are contained in subsection 1(2)(b) and for work of equal value in subsection 1(2)(c).

The Act applies to a woman of any age[16] working at an establishment in Great Britain[17] under a contract of service or of apprenticeship or a contract personally to execute any work or labour.[18] The EAT in *Quinnen v. Hovells*[19] held that a ''contract personally to execute any work or labour'' was intended to have a wider connotation than ''employment'' so as to include persons outside the master and servant relationship, *i.e.* the self-employed[20] The Act applies to Crown employments as it applies to private employments.[21]   **6-08**

The Equal Pay Act and the Sex Discrimination Act

The Equal Pay Act and Sex Discrimination Act are complementary to each other and are to be construed as one code. Bridge L.J. in *Shields v. E. Coomes (Holdings) Ltd*[22] put the matter as follows: **6-09**

''In the sphere of employment the provisions of the Sex Discrimination Act 1975 and the Equal Pay Act 1970 aimed at eliminating discrimination on grounds of sex are closely interlocking and provide in effect a single comprehensive code. The particular provisions designed to preclude overlapping between the two statutes are complex, and it may often be difficult to determine whether a particular matter or complaint falls to be addressed under one statute or the other. But what is abundantly clear is that both Acts should be construed and applied as one harmonious whole and in such a way that the broad principles are not frustrated by a narrow interpretation or restrictive application of particular provisions.''

The Equal Pay Act was passed five years prior to the Sex Discrimination Act but, was re-enacted in 1975 as a schedule to the later Act with considerable consequential amendment. Nonetheless the two Acts operate on somewhat   **6-10**

---

[16] EqPA 1970, s.11(2).
[17] An employee is to be regarded as being employed in Great Britain unless the employee does her work wholly or mainly outside Great Britain. For an extended definition of employment in Great Britain, both for the purposes of the EqPA and the SDA see the SDA 1976, s.10. and paras.
[18] EqPA 1970, s.1(6).
[19] [1984] I.C.R. 525.
[20] This broader connotation does not, however, extend to those who are working under a contract to supply services other than their own labour. Thus in *Mirror Group Newspapers v. Gunning* [1986] I.R.L.R. 27, C.A., a contract between the newspaper company and an independent wholesale distributor fell outside the terms of the comparable section of the SDA 1975, because the contract did not contemplate that the work was necessarily to be performed personally by the contractor.
[21] EqPA 1970, s.1(9)(10).
[22] [1987] I.C.R. 1159, C.A. at 1178.

different principles. The Equal Pay Act is restricted to contractual terms and conditions of employment and implies an equality clause into the contracts of all women engaged upon like work, work rated as equivalent or work of equal value. Whilst section 6(6) of the Sex Discrimination Act provides that section 6(2) of that Act does not apply to benefits consisting of the payment of money which are regulated in a woman's contract of employment, the Equal Pay Act is not restricted to payments of money only. The Equal Pay Act, s.1(2) provides that:

> "An equality clause is a provision which relates to terms (whether concerned with pay or not) of a contract under which a woman is employed."

6-11   SDA, s. 8(5) also excludes from the SDA, s. 6(2) any contractual terms modified or included by virtue of an equality clause. Thus the statutory equality clause applies to contractual terms and conditions of employment other than money where the woman is employed on like work, work rated as equivalent or work of equal value with a male comparator. The Sex Discrimination Act has an advantage for applicants in that it does not call for the existence of an actual comparator and defines discrimination as existing where the discriminator "treats her less favourably than he treats or would treat a man", *i.e.* hypothetical comparisons can be made. The effect is, therefore, that a woman suffering discrimination in respect of the payment of money under her contract of employment may only proceed under the Equal Pay Act (SDA, s.6(6)). She must proceed under the Equal Pay Act in relation to other contractual terms if like work, work rated as equivalent or work of equal value to an actual comparator exists. She may proceed under the Sex Discrimination Act in relation to contractual terms, except those related to the payment of money, if like work or work of equal value does not exist. Thus, a woman experiencing discrimination in fringe benefits is restricted to the Equal Pay Act if she falls within the ambit of comparison laid down by that Act, but otherwise she could proceed under the Sex Discrimination Act alleging that she has been treated less favourably than a man would have been treated.

6-12   The terms on which employment is offered are regulated by Sex Discrimination Act, s.6(1)(b) where, had the offer been accepted, the term would have fallen to be modified by an equality clause under the Equal Pay Act (SDA, s.8(3)), providing that the employer would not have been able to mount a successful genuine material difference defence under the Equal Pay Act, s.1(3) (SDA, s.8(4)). Therefore, an offer of employment containing discriminatory terms outside the scope of the Equal Pay Act, perhaps because there are no males engaged upon any form of comparable work, does not contravene Sex Discrimination Act, s.6(1)(b).

6-13   The defences which may be mounted by the employer are different under the two Acts. Whereas under the Equal Pay Act there is a defence that the inequality is due to a genuine material factor other than sex, the Sex Discrimination Act provides no comparable defence for direct discrimination under section (1)(1)(a), whilst providing a defence that any occurrence of indirect discrimination under section (1)(1)(b) may be justifiable. The defence of justifiability was held in *Rainey v. Greater Glasgow Health Board*[23] to be equivalent to the genuine material factor defence under the SDA, s.1(1)(b).

Only the Sex Discrimination Act can apply to non-contractual matters, as **6-14** also to any alleged discrimination on grounds of marital status. Allegations of victimisation under both the Sex Discrimination Act and the Equal Pay Act are to be heard under the Sex Discrimination Act, s.4. Unsurprisingly, the EOC in its document "Legislating for Change", proposed that the two Acts be integrated as one Equal Treatment Act incorporating the hypothetical comparisons presently contained only in the Sex Discrimination Act.

Equal Pay and Equal Treatment Directives

Article 119 encompasses any "consideration, whether in cash or in kind, **6-15** which the worker receives, directly or indirectly, in respect of his employment." This broader definition of pay encompasses non-contractual benefits, such as post-retirement travel concessions in *Garland*. The question arises, therefore, as to whether it is more appropriate in such situations to allow the matter to be adjudicated under the Sex Discrimination Act or to interpret the Equal Pay Act so as to conform with the definition of pay in Article 119. Where the question turns on a hypothetical comparison of the sort which is permissible under the Sex Discrimination Act but not under the Equal Pay Act, the issue is far from academic. However, as the ECJ held in *McCarthy's v. Smith* it is not possible to rely on purely hypothetical comparisons under Article 119, which therefore has no application in the absence of comparators, whether or not these are contemporaneous. Equally, Article 1 of the Equal Pay Directive 75/117 applies the "principle of equal pay" only to situations where men and women are undertaking the same work, or work to which equal value is attributed. Non-contractual matters outside the scope of concrete comparisons of equal work or equal value are therefore matters of equal treatment under Community law and fall within the Equal Treatment Directive, which, though it only has vertical direct effect, may have a wider indirect interpretative effect, as discussed in chapter 1.

Exclusions in relation to death and retirement

The Act does not apply to provisions in relation to death or retirement, other **6-16** than a term which, in relation to retirement, affords access to opportunities for promotion, transfer or training or provides for a woman's dismissal or demotion.[24] Prior to the Sex Discrimination Act 1986 all provisions in relation to death or retirement were excluded by the Act but following the decision of the ECJ in *Marshall v. Southampton and South West Hants Health Authority*[25] such a blanket exclusion could not be maintained. The *Marshall* case was initially brought under the Sex Discrimination Act because the Health Authority's rules as to retirement did not constitute a term of the contracts of their employees, but were a retirement policy or practice handed

---

[23] [1987] I.R.L.R 26, H.L.
[24] EqPA 1970, s.6(1)(b) as amended by the SDA 1986.
[25] [1986] I.R.L.R. 140 and see paras.

down to employees. Had the rules as to retirement constituted a term of the employees' contracts, the facts of the case would have fallen to be decided under the Equal Pay Act, rather than the Sex Discrimination Act. The ECJ held that the Authority's practice was contrary to Article 5(1) of the Equal Treatment Directive, as would equally have been the case had the retirement rules constituted a term of the employee's contract. Therefore, the Sex Discrimination Act 1986 modified the exclusionary rules as to death and retirement in the Equal Pay Act, s.6(1)(b), as stated above, to reflect the amendments made to section 6(4) of the Sex Discrimination Act 1975.

The scope of the equality clause

6-17 An equality clause can relate to any term in the contract under which a woman is employed, not merely in relation to pay,[26] except for those terms excluded by section 6(1). Thus the equality clause does not operate in relation to terms which are affected by the laws which regulate the employment of women,[27] although the scope of these laws has been reduced by the Sex Discrimination Act 1986, s.8 and section 6 of the Employment Act 1989.[28] Neither does an equality clause extend to those contractual provisions under which a woman is afforded access to special treatment in connection with pregnancy or childbirth,[29] (a provision present also in Article 2(3) of the Equal Treatment Directive) although in other respects the Act applies to men as to women.[30]

Contractual terms

6-18 An equality clause can only operate where there is a contractual term relating to the matter in dispute.[31] In *Hayward v. Cammell Laird*,[32] the House of Lords held that the natural and ordinary meaning of a term in a contract of employment is a distinct provision or part of a contract, which has sufficient content to make it possible to compare it from the point of view of the benefits which it confers with a similar provision in another contract. In the *Hayward* case, the employers had argued that in considering whether the appellant cook was receiving equal pay with her selected comparators (shipyard painters, laggers and joiners), regard should be had to the whole package of benefits which constituted her remuneration, including sick pay, holiday entitlements and the like. The EAT and the Court of Appeal had decided in favour of the employer's argument in view of the potential for

---

[26] EqPA 1970, s.1(2).
[27] s.6(1)(a).
[28] See paragraph 10–61 for details of the protective legislation which has been retained following the Employment Act 1989.
[29] EqPA 1970, s.6(1)(b).
[30] EqPA 1970, s.1(13). Thus there is no statutory right to paternity leave, although this has been advocated by the EOC and the TUC.
[31] *Pointon v. University of Sussex* [1979] I.R.L.R. 119, C.A. Quaere within whether a contractual term as to pay relates to appointment at the discretion of management according to skill, ability and experience as in *Pointon* or is a term relating to the salary earned, as in *Benveniste v. University of Southampton*.
[32] [1988] I.R.L.R. 257, H.L.

leap-frogging, which they said was a probable consequence if employees were able to compare separately, say, provisions on pay, holidays, entitlement to a car allowance, etc., allowing both men and women to reach equality at a new and higher level than either had enjoyed separately. The House of Lords held, however, that it would be wrong to depart from the natural and ordinary meaning of the word "term", because of the difficulty of its application to particular examples, especially when those examples do not arise in actual cases. A further difficulty arises if a broad construction is adopted, equivalent to remuneration as a whole. Section 1(2)(c)(ii), which deals with the situation where a woman's contract lacks a particular term (the absent term), would be deprived of any ground on which to operate, in that all contracts of employment necessarily contain a term relating to pay in that broader sense. Thus the statutory equality clause is to be applied to the individual terms of a contract and not to the overall package of employee benefits.[33] A similar view of the need to consider each element of the employee's total remuneration separately was enunciated by the ECJ in the pensions case of *Barber v. Guardian Royal Exchange*.[34]

Validity and revision of contracts

A term of a contract is void by SDA, s.77 or RRA, s.72 where its inclusion **6-19** renders the contract unlawful by virtue of either the Equal Pay or Sex Discrimination Acts or where it provides for the doing of an act which is thus unlawful. Where a contract includes an unlawful discriminatory term but is otherwise beneficial to a complainant, that term shall be unenforceable against that party. On the application of an aggrieved party to a contract containing such an unenforceable term, a county or sheriff court may make such order as it thinks just for modifying or removing any such term, under subsection 5 of the relevant section of each Act. For example, if a contract included discriminatory sick pay terms, if those terms were simply rendered void there would be no entitlement to sick pay at all.

Under the SDA, s.77(3) a term which purports to exclude the operation of the Equal Pay Act (or the SDA itself) is rendered unenforceable, except, according to section 77(4), where it is made with the assistance of an ACAS conciliation officer or is a compromise agreement made under the terms of the SDA, s.66(3).

---

[33] It was argued on behalf of the employer that the broad definition of pay contained in Article 119 "the ordinary basic or minimum wage or salary and any other consideration in cash or in kind, which the worker receives, in respect of his employment" suggests a broad reading of pay. In respect of s.1(2)(c), however (the equal value provisions under which the *Hayward* case was brought), which was intended to give full effect to the U.K. obligations under the Treaty of Rome following the decision of the ECJ in *Commission of the European Communities v. U.K.* [1982] I.R.L.R. 133, Article 1 of the Equal Pay Directive (held to be simply declaratory of the meaning of Article 119 and not to add to or change its meaning in any way in *Jenkins v. Kingsgate (Clothing Productions) Ltd* [1981] I.R.L.R. 228, ECJ) provides that "the principle of equal pay calls for the elimination of all discrimination on grounds of sex with regard to all aspects and conditions of remuneration . . .". It is therefore perfectly consistent with Article 119 to compare one aspect of remuneration with another in the application of the EqPA.

[34] [1990] I.R.L.R. 240, ECJ.

Non-contractual terms

6-20   Whilst the Equal Pay Act is restricted to contractual terms, Article 4 of the Equal Pay Directive applies the principle of equal pay not only to individual contracts of employment, but also to the provisions of collective agreements, wage scales and wage agreements, notwithstanding that their terms may not be legally enforceable in the U.K. unless incorporated in the individual contract of employment. The European Commission brought enforcement proceedings against the U.K.[35] in respect of the Equal Treatment Directive. The ECJ held that the obligations arising under the Equal Treatment Directive extended to non-legally-binding collective agreements, as such agreements have important *de facto* consequences for the employment relationships covered by them. Consequently, the Sex Discrimination Act 1986, s.6(1) applies section 77 of the SDA 1975 to the terms of unenforceable collective agreements, administrative rules applied in an employer's undertaking or to the rules of trade unions, employer's associations or qualifying bodies.

The criticism was raised, however, that it was unrealistic to vest county courts with such jurisdiction in relation to collective agreements, employers' internal rules or trade union rules. Consequently the Trade Union Reform and Employment Rights Act 1993 amended section 6 of the SDA 1986 to vest such jurisdiction in the industrial tribunals. Complaints may be made concerning the terms of a collective agreement or an employer's internal rule under section 6(4B) or by trade union members or candidates for membership in regard to the rules of the union under sections 6(4C)(*a*), or by those holding a professional qualification under s.6(4C)(*b*), or seeking such a qualification under s.6(4C)(*c*). Subsection 6(4A) provides that a person to whom subsections 6(4B) and (4C) above apply may present a complaint to an industrial tribunal that a term or rule which is rendered void by the SDA 1975, s.77(1) may at some time have effect in relation to her or that a term or rule which is void by virtue of s.77(1)(*c*) provides for the doing of an act which would be unlawful in relation to her.

The irony of this situation is that it was section 9 of the SDA 1986 which repealed section 3 of the EqPA 1970, *i.e.* it brought to an end the jurisdiction of the Central Arbitration Committee in equal pay matters.

In *Ruzius-Wilbrink*[36] the ECJ held that in a case of indirect discrimination the disadvantaged group, men or women, are entitled to have the same system applied to them as other workers, in proportion to their working hours. This dictum was applied to collective agreements in *Kowalska*.[37] However, industrial tribunals, like the county courts in relation to contractual terms, only have power to render void the terms of employer, trade union or qualifying body rules, or concective agreements, and not to amend them.

The concept of pay

6-21   Whilst the concept of pay has been restricted to contractual terms under the EqPA 1970, Article 119 defines pay in broader terms.

---

[35] Case 165/82, *Re Equal Treatment: E.C. Commission v. United Kingdom* [1983] E.C.R. 3413, [1984] 1 C.M.L.R. 43.
[36] Case 102/88, ECJ.
[37] Case 33/89: [1990] I.R.L.R. 447, ECJ.

Article 119

"For the purpose of this Article, 'pay' means the ordinary basic or minimum wage or salary and any other consideration whether in cash or in kind which the worker receives, directly or indirectly, in respect of his employment from his employer. Equal pay without discrimination based on sex means:

(a) that pay for the same work at piece rates shall be calculated on the same unit of measurement;
(b) that pay for the same work at time rates shall be the same for the same job."

Payment by Results

In, *Specialarbejderforbundet i Danmark* and *Dansk Industri*, formerly *Industriens Arbejdsgivere*, acting for Royal Copenhagen A/S[38] the ECJ, in considering whether piece work falls within the scope of Article 119, referred to the third paragraph of the Article, which provides that "pay for the same work at piece rates shall be calculated on the basis of the same unit of measurement", thus clearly bringing piece work within its scope. Furthermore, the Court held that Article 1 of Directive 75/117 refers to the elimination of discrimination on grounds of sex "with regard to all aspects and conditions of remuneration".

The central issue in *Royal Copenhagen* was the application of Article 119 to differences in average piece work remuneration as between male and female work groups, when those averages concealed a wide dispersion of individual earnings. The Court concluded that a mere finding that there is an average difference in pay between two groups of workers, each predominantly of opposite sexes, is not sufficient to establish discrimination between them. Even where the unit of measurement is the same, the Court held that that does not preclude individual differences in pay being based upon differences in output. It is for the national court to decide whether any difference in average pay is due to differences in the unit of measurement or to differences in output.

Fringe benefits

The phrase "directly or indirectly in respect of his employment" shows that Article 119 is not limited to contractual terms and conditions of employment. In the first *Defrenne* case, the ECJ held that "pay" extends "to all emoluments, in cash or kind, paid or payable, on condition that they are paid, even indirectly, by the employer to the worker as a result of the latter's employment."[39] In *Garland v. British Rail Engineering*,[40] one of the earlier cases heard with reference to Article 119, "pay" was held to include post-retirement travel facilities granted, as an extension of the terms and conditions enjoyed whilst working, to the wives and dependant children of railway-

6-22

---

[38] Case C-400/93, [1995] 648, [1995] All (EC) 577, noted by Bourn in *European Law Review* (1995), 20, 6, 612–617.
[39] Case 80/70 [1974] 1 C.M.L.R. 108 at ground 6.
[40] Case 12/81 [1982] 1 C.M.L.R. 696; [1982] E.C.R. 359; ECJ, [1982] 2 C.M.L.R. 174, H.L.

men, but not to the dependants of railwaywomen. It is notable that this
conclusion was unaffected by the fact that the travel facilities were a conces-
sion to which retired staff had no contractual or other legal right.

Sick pay

6-23   The scope of "pay" under Article 119 has been held to include the German
equivalent to statutory sick pay in *Rinner-Kühn v. FWW Spezial-
Gebäudereinigung*.[41] Under the relevant German legislation employers were
only obliged to pay sick pay to workers employed for 10 hours or more a
week. Mrs Rinner-Kühn's employers, an office cleaning firm, refused to pay
her wages during a short period of absence due to illness. The ECJ held that
"the continued payment of wages in the event of illness falls within the
definition of pay within the meaning of Article 119"[42] and went on to hold
that such a legislative

> "provision as the one in question results in practice in discrimination
> between male and female workers and is, in principle, to be regarded
> as contrary to the objective pursued by Article 119 of the Treaty. It
> would only be otherwise if the different treatment between the two cat-
> egories of workers is justified by objective factors unrelated to any dis-
> crimination on grounds of sex."

Maternity pay

6-24   Maternity pay is manifestly pay for the purposes of Article 119 and Directive
75/117, according to Advocate General Leger in *Gillespie v. Northern Health
and Social Services Board* in which the claimant sought to show that it was
discriminatory not to pay a woman her normal salary during maternity leave.
The Advocate General was, however, of the opinion that discrimination consists either in the application of different rules to the same situation or in
the application of the same rule to different situations (as per the dictum in
Schumaker).[43] As the ECJ in *Webb* had held that pregnancy and maternity
are unique to women, it follows that no comparison could be made between
a woman on maternity leave and a man who is still at work. This view was
endorsed by the full Court, subject to the proviso that the amount of maternity
allowance paid should not be so low as to undermine the purposes of maternity leave. The provisions of the Pregnancy Directive 92/85 did not apply at
the time of the facts of this case.

Payment in lieu of notice

6-25   The basis of the decision of the EAT in *Clark v. Secretary of State for
Employment*[44] is that payment in lieu of notice is "pay" for the purposes of

---

[41] [1989] I.R.L.R. 493, ECJ.
[42] At ground 8.
[43] Case 279/93, [1995] All E.R. (E.C.) 319, ECJ.
[44] [1995] I.R.L.R. 421.

Article 119. Until June 1994, where a woman was dismissed whilst away on maternity leave, she was not entitled to payment in lieu of notice, under section 122(3) of the Employment Protection (Consolidation) Act 1978 (EP(C)A). That subsection provides that the Redundancy Fund administered by the Secretary of State is liable to pay the employee where the employer would be liable in respect of any period of notice under section 49(1) or for any failure to give such notice. The liability of the employer is governed by Schedule 3, para. 2(1) which, at the time, provided that the employer is obliged to pay the employee, provided that she is (a) ready and willing to work, or (b) incapable of work because of sickness or injury or (c) absent from work on holiday. Absence in connection with pregnancy or maternity was not provided for and the EAT held that this constitued direct discrimination. Following *Dekker* and *Webb* the EAT held that it is not possible to assimilate the position of pregnant women to sick men. The argument of the Secretary of State that this was a statutory payment and outside Article 119 was rejected on the ground that the payment was connected with the employment relationship and depended on its terms. The EAT therefore had little difficulty in holding that the discriminatory terms of Schedule 3 must be set aside and pregnant women must be afforded the same advantages as are enjoyed by other persons. The Trade Union Reform and Employment Rights Act 1993 amended Schedule 3 para. 2(1) to include pregnancy as a further ground on which the employer would be liable to pay employees absent from work during their period of statutory notice.

Overtime pay

Where part-timers work overtime, is it indirectly discriminatory not to pay **6-26** them an overtime premium unless they work hours in excess of the normal working hours of full-time staff? This was essentially the question posed in *Stadt Lengerich v Helmig*,[45] which the ECJ answered in the negative. In *Helmig* a collective agreement excluded premium payments for overtime to part-timers, except where they worked a total of hours in excess of the normal working hours of a full-time worker. The ECJ reasoned that full and part-time workers were being treated equally, in that they received the same pay for the same number of hours worked. Thus if a part-timer, whose normal working week was 18 hours, worked for 19 hours, she would receive the same pay as a full-time worker who worked for 19 hours and consequently there would be no discrimination.

Even though there is no right to receive a premium payment for hours spent on a training course outside of a part-timers normal hours, it is indirectly discriminatory not to pay such a worker at all, according to the European Court of Justice in *Arbeiterwohlfahrt der Stadt Berlin eV v. Botel*[46] and *Kuratorium für Dialyse und Nierentranplantation v. Johana Lewark*.[47] A worker engaged in statutory works council training which took place outside of her normal working hours was held in both cases to have been the subject of discrimination when she did not receive the statutorily prescribed compensa-

---

[45] Cases C-399/92, 409/92, 452/92, 34/93, 50/93 and 78/93, [1995] IRLR 217 *cf. Kuratorium für Dialyse und Nierentransplantation v. Johana Lewark*, ECJ (unreported).
[46] Case 360/90, [1992] I.R.L.R. 423 at 426.
[47] Case C-457/93, unreported at the time of writing.

tion for loss of normal pay. Even though the payment did not derive from the employees contract of employment, the right to receive such compensation arose from the employment relationship.

In all three of these cases the part-time worker concerned would have received the same pay for the same number of hours worked as would have been received by an equivalent full-time worker.

Redundancy and unfair dismissal compensation

6-27   The ECJ has taken the view that statutory redundancy payments are a form of pay in *Barber v. Guardian Royal Exchange*,[48] the ECJ held that in which "where the worker is entitled to receive the benefit in question from his employer by reason of the existence of the employment relationship",[49] the fact that a benefit is in the nature of pay cannot be called into question because it also reflects "considerations of social policy," although this aspect of the decision has been subject to criticism.[50] Statutory redundancy pay was held to be a form of pay made in respect of the employee's former employment in order to facilitate his adjustment to the loss of his job and to provide him with a source of income whilst seeking new work.[51] In *Barber*, as in *Garland*, it was the employment nexus which was seen as decisive, even if, as the Court had already held in *Defrenne (No. 2)*,[52] the discrimination arises directly from legislative provisions. The EOC commenced judicial review proceedings in respect of the "decision" of the Secretary of State not to amend domestic law with respect to the discriminatory hours and service requirements for eligibility for redundancy pay and unfair dismissal.[53] In *R. v. Secretary of State for Employment, ex p. EOC*,[54] the House of Lords concluded that redundancy pay, is pay under Article 119. Whilst the Lords held that there is much to be said for the view that unfair dismissal is pay for the purposes of Article 119,[55] as it was not necessary to decide the point at issue, no firm view was taken. In *R. v. Secretary of State, ex p. Seymour-Smith & Perez*,[56] the Court of Appeal held that there was a "very strong argument" that unfair dismissal compensation was pay. Althought the Court of Appeal did not hold the matter to be *acte claire*, it did not refer the matter to the ECJ, but preferred to await the decision of the House of Lords.

---

[48] Case 262/88, [1990] I.R.L.R. 240, ECJ.
[49] At ground 18.
[50] Shrubsall, *Barber v. Guardian Royal Exchange*, Industrial Law Journal, 19, at pp. 244–250.
[51] Whilst the Employment Act 1989 equalised the maximum age for redundancy benefit, it did not apply to the facts of the *Barber* case, nor obviously did it provide that a statutory redundancy benefit is a part of pay. In Case 33/89, *Kowalska v. Frei und Hansestadt Hamburg*: [1990] I.R.L.R. 447, the ECJ held that severance "payments constitute a form of deferred remuneration to which the worker is entitled by virtue of his employment, but which is paid to him at the time of the termination of the employment relationship."
[52] [1976] E.C.R. 455 at para. 40.
[53] Should the Article 100A draft directive on part-time work be adopted it will provide that employees working over eight hours per week enjoy social protection and occupational social security rights *pro rata* to their hours.
[54] [1991] I.R.L.R. 493, H.C. at 500, [1993] I.R.L.R. 10, C.A.
[55] See *Mediaguard Services Ltd v. Thane* [1994] I.R.L.R. 504, EAT.
[56] [1995] I.R.L.R. 465 at 472.

Merit pay

The scope of Article 119 "extends to agreements which seek to regulate **6-28** wage-earning work collectively, as well as to contracts between individuals" according to the ECJ in *Kowalska v. Frei und Hansestadt Hamburg*.[57] In the *Danfoss* case,[58] the ECJ had brought within the scope of the equal pay principle not only substantive pay rates but also the processes by which pay is determined. The case concerned a collectively bargained pay structure, within which there was a system of discretionary pay awards to individuals within each grade. This system resulted in an average difference of 6.85 per cent between the pay of men and women and was characterised by the ECJ as having a total lack of "transparency", *i.e.* the employees could not readily check the basis on which their pay was calculated.[59] In those circumstances the ECJ argued that the burden was thrown upon the employer to justify the average difference in pay which had been shown. Many pay and merit rating systems in Britain are far from "transparent" in this sense and if they produce differences in pay between men and women could be open to challenge. In the subsequent *Nimz*[60] case, the ECJ held that a system of rules (in this case contained in a collective agreement) governing the passage of employees to a higher salary grade also fell within the concept of "pay" contained in Article 119.

Pensions

On average women live some seven years longer than men. This basic fact **6-29** gives rise to difficulties in ensuring the application of precisely the same rules to men as to women in regard to pensions. In a defined benefit or final salary scheme (under which pensioners receive a certain proportion of their final salary according to their length of pensionable service), it must on average cost more to provide the same monthly pension for women as for men. For similar reasons, the same contributions to a defined contribution, or money purchase, scheme will accumulate a capital sum which would buy men a higher rate of monthly pension than women. Equal pensions imply unequal contributions or equal contributions imply unequal pensions, even if the pension age for men and women is the same. If, according to the ECJ,[61] discrimination can only consist in the application of different rules to comparable situations or else in the application of the same rule to different situations, what does "equality" mean in this situation? If the same rule is applied as regards pension benefits, contributions must differ, whereas if contributions are the same, pension benefits must differ. Where the pension age

---

[57] Case 33/89, [1990] I.R.L.R. 447.
[58] Case 109/88 *Handels-og Kontorfunktionaerernes Forbund i Danmark v. Danmark v. Dansk Arbedjsgiverforening (acting for* Danfoss) [1989] I.R.L.R. 532, ECJ.
[59] Thus giving effect in part to the failed directive on the burden of proof in discrimination cases COM (88) 269. And see *Royal Copenhagen* above at n.38.
[60] [1991] I.R.L.R. 222. In this case the rather special facts of the situation were that the rules of a collective agreement provided that only half the service of part-time workers was to be taken into account in qualifying for movement to the next grade, where a part-timer worked between half and three-quarters time and the part-timers comprise a considerably smaller group of men than women.
[61] *Ruckdeschel* [1977] E.C.R. 1753; *Schumaker* [1995] All E.R. (E.C.) 319.

for women is lower than that for men, as is the case for the U.K. state pension and, until recently, for the majority of occupational pensions, the inevitable difficulties are compounded. The circle has normally been squared for final salary, or defined benefit, schemes, by paying the same pensions and requiring employees to contribute the same proportion of their salary, whilst the employer makes a larger contribution on behalf of female employees. In this way a larger capital fund can be built up so as to match the prospective liabilities of the pension fund. Against this background, in *Barber v. Guardian Royal Exchange*[62] [1990], the ECJ held, however, that pensions are pay for the purposes of Article 119, with the consequence that for occupational pensions discriminatory pension ages as between men and women are unlawful. In placing pensions firmly within the orbit of Article 119, the *Barber* case gave immediate effect to the principle of equal pay with regard to pensions.

6-30   The facts of the *Barber* case were that Mr Barber was made redundant at age 52. He was only entitled to receive a lump sum, together with a deferred pension at age 62, when a woman in similar circumstances would have been entitled to be treated as "retired" and would have received an immediate pension. Mr Barber's claim was dismissed by the tribunal. The Court of Appeal referred the question of whether pensions are "pay" under Community law to the ECJ, the principal question being whether a U.K. contracted-out pension is a part of "pay" for the purposes of Article 119.

6-31   The U.K. Government had contended that pensions which are contracted-out of SERPS are a matter of social security and subject to Article 118, which is not of direct effect. Indeed, the Occupational Social Security Directive 86/378 introduced the principle of equal treatment in pensions matters, but left a number of crucial exceptions for later action, such as differential pension ages and the provision of survivors' benefits. Although the explanatory memorandum attached to the Commission's first draft of the proposal recognised that occupational pension schemes generally fall within the scope of the second paragraph of Article 119, the Occupational Social Security Directive 86/378 adopted an approach to the introduction of the principle of equal treatment in this area which recognised that pension scheme managers and others had made their arrangements on the basis that differentiation in pensions matters was permissible and that time would be needed to adjust.

In *Defrenne (No. 1)*[63] the ECJ held that a pension which is directly imposed by law without any element of consultation within the industry or undertaking concerned, and to which the employer contributes as a matter of legal, rather than contractual, duty falls outside the scope of Article 119. The pension scheme in *Defrenne (No. 1)* was excluded from the ambit of Article 119 because it was a special scheme for staff of SABENA which was wholly determined by legislation, even though its scope was restricted to civil air crew. In *Liefting v. Academish Ziekenhuish bij de Universiteit van Amsterdam*,[64] the ECJ did not rely on that distinction when it held that differential sums which public authorities are required to pay under a legislatively deter-

[62] Case 262/88, [1990] E.C.R. 1889; [1990] 2 C.M.L.R. 513; [1990] I.R.L.R. 240.
[63] Case 80/70, [1971] E.C.R. 445, ECJ.
[64] (1984) E.C.R. 3225, ECJ.

mined occupational pension scheme for civil servants may be contrary to Article 119, if they are included within the computation of gross pay.[65]

In the German case of *Bilka Kaufhaus v. Weber von Hartz*,[66] however, the   **6-32**
ECJ held that an occupational pension scheme which supplemented social security provisions, and which was based on an agreement between an employer and its staff committee, on which the firm's employees were represented, constituted deferred remuneration received by the worker in respect of his employment. In other words, it constituted "pay" within Article 119. The way was open, therefore, for the ECJ in *Barber* to conclude that contracted out occupational pension schemes are a part of "pay" and fall within the directly effective provisions of Article 119, notwithstanding that they are fitted within a statutory framework. The basis of such schemes is:

> "an agreement between workers and employees or a unilateral decision taken by the employer. They are wholly financed by the employer or by both the employer and the workers without any contribution being made by public authorities in any circumstances. Accordingly, such schemes form part of the consideration offered to workers by their employer."

Such schemes are not of general application "with the result that affiliation to those schemes derives of necessity from the employment relationship with a given employer." In the United Kingdom all occupational pensions have to seek the approval of the Occupational Pensions Board in order that they can achieve "contracted out" status. To achieve this status they must provide benefits at least as good as those available under SERPS, for which they substitute for a contracted-out employee. All occupational pension schemes in the United Kingdom are therefore cast within a statutory framework, so that the question arose as to whether or not they constitute pay under Article 119.

The *Barber* case itself concerned a contracted out occupational pension scheme and the Court in *Moroni*[67] held that the German type of supplementary occupational scheme is also included within the scope of Article 119. Non-contracted-out occupational schemes were included within the scope of

---

[65] A similar result was achieved in *Worringham and Humphries v. Lloyds Bank*, ([1981] I.R.L.R. 68, ECJ) in which the Bank required male staff to contribute to the pension scheme at a younger age than female staff. In order to ensure equal net pay, a sum was added to the gross pay of male employees, this addition being held to be contrary to Article 119 by the ECJ. In *Newstead v. Department of Transport*, ([1988] I.R.L.R. 68, ECJ) the ECJ held that contributions to a contracted-out pension scheme did not fall within Article 119, being matters of social security governed by Article 118. *Newstead* was concerned with the deduction of contributions to a widows' pension scheme which were demanded only of male civil servants and which led to a difference of net, but not of gross, pay, between male and female civil servants. The contributions of unmarried civil servants, such as Mr Newstead, were returned with interest on death or retirement. *Worringham* and *Liefting* were distinguished on the grounds that in those cases the making up of the net pay of male employees to compensate for the employee's contribution to a pension scheme increased their gross pay. The effect of that increase in gross pay, although subsequently deducted into a pension scheme, was to increase pay for the purpose of other salary-related benefits such as redundancy, unemployment benefits and family allowances.
[66] Case 170/84, [1986] I.R.L.R. 317, ECJ.
[67] Case C-110/91, [1994] I.R.L.R. 131.

Article 119 in *Coloroll*, on the basis that they complied with the criteria set out by the Court in *Bilka*.

A civil service pension, though embodied in legislation, may fall within the scope of Article 119 where it is paid to the worker by reason of the employment relationship. According to the Court in *Beune*[68] conflicting considerations of social and fiscal policy which may have influenced the establishment of the scheme cannot prevail if the pension concerns only a particular category of workers, is directly linked to the period of service and its amount calculated by reference to the civil servant's last salary. Such a pension is entirely comparable to that paid by a private employer to his former employees and the temporal limitations in *Barber* and Protocol No. 2 apply to benefits payable under it. *Beune* renders doubtful the decision of the EAT in *Griffin v. London Pension Fund Authority*[69] that a local government pension, as a creature of statute, fell outside Article 119. The local government pension scheme would seem to satisfy all the criteria set out in *Beune*, even though the details of contributions and benefits are prescribed by statute.

The ECJ took the view that this approach was not affected by the interposition of the pension fund trustees between the employer and the worker, even if this means acting in ways contrary[70] to the trust deed, according to the Advocate General in *Coloroll*. In *Coloroll* the Court of Justice held that trustees of an occupational pension scheme are obliged to observe the principle of equal treatment in order to eliminate all discrimination in the matter of pay. The trustees of an occupational pension must exercise their powers and perform their obligations in such a way as to realise the principle of equal treatment, including, if need be, recourse to the national courts. The national court is bound to ensure correct implementation of Article 119, taking into account the respective liabilities of the employers and trustees under the rules of domestic law. Any problems arising because the funds held by the trustees are insufficient to equalise benefits must be resolved on the basis of national law and such problems cannot affect the implementation of the principle of equal pay, according to the Court of Justice.

6-33   As regards the imposition of a discriminatory pension age, the ECJ had held in *Defrenne (No. 3)* which concerned the compulsory retirement of an air hostess at age 40, that[71]:

> "the fact that the fixing of certain conditions of employment — such as a special age limit — may have pecuniary consequences is not sufficient to bring such conditions within the field of application of Article 119, which is based on the close connection which exists between the nature of the services provided and the amount of remuneration."[72]

---

[68] Case C-7/93, *Bestur van het Algemeen Burgerlijk Pensioenfonds v. Beune*: [1995] I.R.L.R. 103.

[69] [1993] I.R.L.R. 248; [1993] OPLR 49.

[70] Case C200/91 [1994] I.R.L.R. 686 at ground 57.

[71] [1981] 3 C.M.L.R. 100, EAT; [1982] 2 C.M.L.R. 136, E.C.J; [1982] E.C.R. 555, ECJ. See also *Roberts v. Tate and Lyle Industries*, Case 151/84, [1986] 1 C.M.L.R. 714 [1986] E.C.R. 703, *Marshall v. Southampton and South West Hants Health Authority*, Case 152/84 [1986] E.C.R. 723; [1986] 1 C.M.L.R. 688, ECJ; *Beets-Proper v. van Lanschot Bankiers NV*, Case 262/84, [1986] E.C.R. 773, [1987] 1 C.M.L.R. 616, ECJ.

[72] The ECJ reasoned that as the age for early retirement was tied to the state pension age, and that as Article 2 of of the Equal Treatment Directive makes the 1976 Directive subject to the later Social Security Directive E.C. 79/7, Article 7 of which reserves to the Member States

In *Barber* the Court, in reasoning criticised as "weak" by Honeyball and Shaw,[73] simply held that:

> "Art. 119 prohibits any discrimination with regard to pay between men and women, whatever the system which gives rise to such inequality. Accordingly, it is contrary to Art. 119 to impose an age condition which differs according to sex in respect of pensions paid under a contracted-out scheme, even if the difference between the pensionable age for men and that for women is based on the one provided for by the national statutory scheme."[74]

Per "item" comparison

One argument advanced by the employers in *Barber* was that if it were possible in the instant case to weigh the value of a greater lump sum and a deferred pension against the right to an immediate pension, the value of the overall remuneration package would not be greatly affected. The ECJ took the view, however, that equality is mandated in respect of each element of the remuneration package, so that it is not possible to set-off an advantage in one respect against a disadvantage in another, on the basis that "genuine transparency, permitting an effective review, is assured only if the principle of equal pay applies to each of the elements of remuneration granted to men and women." Exactly what would constitute a discrete item in such a review remains unclear and would be open to argument. This aspect of the case is, of course, consonant with the views previously expressed by the Lords on the need for a term by term review of the remuneration package under the Equal Pay Act in *Hayward v. Cammel Laird*, even despite what the Lords saw as the hypothetical danger of leap-frogging claims.

6-34

The time limitation

The consequences of the *Barber* decision for pension schemes were mitigated only by the limitation of the ruling to claims in being or arising as from the date of the judgement (May 17, 1990), the ECJ holding as follows:

6-35

---

the determination of pensionable age, that the differential age for early retirement was not discriminatory.

[73] S. Honeyball and J. Shaw, "Sex, Law and the Retiring Man" in *European Law Review* (1991), pp. 47–58.

[74] The U.K. Government and the respondents in Barber argued that, following *Burton v. British Rail*, a differential pension age was a condition of access to a benefit and therefore fell within the scope of the equality directives. Were that to be the case, there could be no question of direct effect as against a private employer such as the Guardian Royal Exchange. In *Burton* British Rail had offered early retirement to all employees within five years of their normal retirement age, i.e. 60 for men and 55 for women. It was held by the ECJ that this was a question of working conditions under Directive 76/207. Advocate General Walter van Gerven reconciled the approach of the ECJ in *Bilka* with *Burton* by distinguishing between an age condition or limit which governs the selection of employees for dismissal, as in *Burton*, and a condition which governs the grant of a terminal payment to those employees whose dismissal has already been decided. *Bilka* concerned the conditions for the grant of a pension, as *Rinner-Kühn* concerned the conditions for the grant of sick pay.

"The Member States and the parties concerned were reasonably entitled to consider that Article 119 did not apply to pensions under contracted out schemes and that derogations from the principle of equality between men and women were still permitted in that sphere.

In these circumstances, overriding considerations of legal certainty preclude legal situations which have exhausted all their effects in the past from being called into question where that might upset retrospectively the financial balance of many contracted out pension schemes. It is appropriate, however, to provide for an exception in favour of individuals who have taken action in good time in order to safeguard their rights. Finally, it must be pointed out that no restriction on the effects of the aforesaid interpretation can be permitted as regards the acquisition of entitlement to a pension as from the date of this judgement.

It must therefore be held that the direct effect of Article 119 of the Treaty may not be relied upon in order to claim entitlement to a pension with effect from a date prior to that of this judgement, except in the case of workers or those claiming under them who have before that date initiated legal proceedings or raised an equivalent claim under applicable national law."[75]

This aspect of the decision caused great uncertainty because it was not clear whether the provisions on equality in pension schemes applied only to persons:

(a) beginning to contribute to a pension after May 17, 1990, or
(b) in receipt of pensions benefits only in respect of periods of service after May 17, 1990, or
(c) beginning to receive pension benefits after May 17, 1990, whether referable to service before of after that date, or
(d) in receipt of any pension payment made after May 1990, whether referable to service before of after that date.

The decision of the Court in *Barber* left many questions unanswered, not least that of the temporal limitation. Subsequently the following protocol was appended to the Treaty of European Union signed at Maastricht, with the intention of clarifying the effect of the *Barber* judgement:

"For the purposes of Article 119 of the Treaty establishing the European Community, benefits under occupational social security schemes shall not be considered as remuneration if and in so far as they are attributable to periods of service prior to 17 May 1990, except in the case of workers or those claiming under them who have before that date initiated legal proceedings or introduced an equivalent claim under the applicable national law".

In *Ten Oever*[76] the Court of Justice held that *Barber* may be relied upon

[75] Points 43–45.
[76] Case C-109/91, *Ten Oever*: [1993] I.R.L.R. 601; Case C-110/91, *Moroni v. Firma Collo GmbH: [1994] I.R.L.R. 131 and Case C-200/91, Coloroll Pension Trustees v. Russel*: [1994] I.R.L.R. 586.

only in respect of periods of employment subsequent to May 17, 1990, in view of the fact that "there is a time lag between the accrual of entitlement to a pension, which occurs gradually throughout an employee's working life, and its actual payment, which is deferred until a particular age." The Court also took into consideration the accounting link between the periodic contributions and the future amounts to be paid.

Basing its reasoning upon the proposition in *Nimz v. Freie und Hansestadt Hamburg*[77] that "a court must set aside any discriminatory provision of national law without having to request its prior removal by collective bargaining or any other constitutional procedure, and to apply to members of the disadvantaged group the same arrangements as those enjoyed by other employees" the Court in *Coloroll* concludes that "so long as measures for bringing about equal treatment have not been adopted . . . the only proper way of complying with Article 119 is to grant to persons in the disadvantaged group the same advantages as those enjoyed by persons in the favoured class."[78] Therefore, if a scheme has calculated women's pension rights with reference to a pensionable age of 60, the pensions of male employees must also be calculated with reference to such a pensionable age for the period in between the date of the *Barber* judgment and the date at which equalisation is achieved.

In *Ten Oever* the Court of Justice held that a survivors pension fell within the scope of Article 119, notwithstanding that by definition it cannot be paid to the worker him or herself. A survivors benefit is derived from the survivor's spouse's employment and is vested in and paid to the survivor by reason of the spouses employment. In *Coloroll* the Court reasoned that if the survivor were to be deprived of this benefit, Article 119 would be devoid of effectiveness in this situation. However, the temporal limitation which applies in relation to pensionable service applies also to survivors' benefits. Thus if the payment of such benefits relies upon the equalising effect of Article 119, survivors' benefit is payable only in respect of service post May 17, 1990, until the date of equalisation, and thereafter, assuming that both sexes then enjoy the right to a survivors benefit.

6-36

The Court in *Coloroll* went on to apply the temporal limitations in *Barber* to benefits not linked to length of service (such as a death in service benefit), such benefits being available by reason of Article 119 only where the operative event occurred after May 17, 1990. Thus if a female employee died in service before May 1990, and her pension scheme provided no survivor's pension for women, that position would be unchanged, but if she died after that date a survivor's benefit must be provided on the same basis as would be the case for a man.

Equalisation measures

Article 119 does not preclude an employer from taking measures to comply with the judgement in *Barber* by raising the retirement age for women to that of men in relation to periods of service completed after May 17, 1990.

6-37

---

[77] C-184/89, [1991] E.C.R. 1–297, [1991] I.R.L.R. 222.
[78] At pts. 31–32 and see Case C-28/93 *Van denakker v. Stichting Shell Pensioenfonds*: [1994] I.R.L.R. 616.

Whilst it can be inferred from *Defrenne (No. 2)*[79] that equality can only be achieved in Community law by upward harmonisation, *i.e.* lowering the pension age for men rather than increasing that for women, the Advocate General in *Coloroll* argued that this does not preclude new scheme rules being introduced which would equalise benefits at a lower level in relation to future service,[80] a view endorsed by the court in *Smith v. Adrel Systems Ltd.*[81]

The temporal limitation of *Barber* to May 1990 means that, as the Court stated in *Smith v. Advel Systems*, "Community law imposed no obligation which would justify retrospective reduction of the advantages which women enjoyed" as regards service prior to the date of the *Barber* judgment, but equally it does not preclude such a reduction, although women would be able to rely upon their contractual rights under national law to contest such an occurrence.

Equalisation cannot be accompanied by transitional measures designed to limit the adverse consequences which such a step may have for women, according to the Court in *Smith v. Advel Systems*. Thus any form of "red circling" to protect the position of women is not permissible and the transition must be complete and immediate. In *Akker* women had previously been offered an option to retain their previous pension age of 55 when in 1985 equalisation had taken place at age 60. The Court held that, in view of the mandatory nature of Article 119 as regards not only the acts of public authorities but also contracts between private individuals or collective agreements, a lower pension age could not be maintained as regards service after the date of equalisation of the scheme in 1991, even though it was the result of a prior election by the employees. Thus the terms of an existing contract of employment or pension trust deed could be overridden by the principle of equal pay contained in Article 119.

6-38 In *Roberts v. Birds Eye Walls*[82] a larger bridging pension was paid to male

---

[79] "Since Article 119 appears in the context of the harmonisation of working conditions while the improvement is being maintained the objection that the terms of this Article may be observed in other ways than by raising the lowest salaries may be set aside," ground 15, n. 76. The first para. of Article 117, with which the social provisions of the Treaty, as amended by the 1986 Single European Act, commence, provides that "Member States agree upon the need to promote improved working conditions and an improved standard of living, so as to make possible their harmonisation while the improvement is being maintained." The third preamble of the Treaty refers to constant improvement of the living and working conditions of their peoples as the essential objective of its signatories.

[80] Clearly if pensions matters form a term of the contract of employment, (see *Parry v. Cleaver* [1970] A.C.1, *The Halcyon Skies* [1977] Q.B. 14) downward harmonisation may give rise to contractual remedies or alternatively to remedies in trust. The SSA 1989, Sched. 5, para. 3(1) required that equality is to be achieved by a process of levelling-up. Pension fund trustees must act in conformity with Community law, according to the Advocate General in *Coloroll*.

[81] C-408/92, [1994] I.R.L.R. 604 and *Vanden Akker v. Stichting Shell Pensioenfonds* Case C-28/93 [1994] I.R.L.R. 616.

[82] Case C-132/92, [1994] I.R.L.R. 29. See chapter 2 for discussion of the connection between discrimination and justification. In *Roberts v. Birds Eye Walls Ltd* the Court faced a situation in which the complainant had in fact paid a married woman's reduced National Insurance contribution, with the result that she was not actually eligible to receive a full state pension in her own right, but nonetheless receive a widow's pension. The employer successfully argued that for the purpose of calculating the compensatory bridging pensions it was right to take a deemed state pension into account, for otherwise some women would "gain a twofold benefit, namely by paying contributions at a reduced rate and receiving a bridging pension that compensates for the corresponding reduction in the state pension". *A fortiori* the same reasoning applies to the taking into account of a state widows pension.

than female ill-health early retirees to compensate for the absence of the state pension. Such payments were claimed to be discriminatory, the parties being agreed that such a bridging pension constituted pay for the purposes of Article 119. Even though the Advocate General had invited the Court to conclude that such a payment, though arguably constituting direct discrimination, was justified, the Court preferred to base itself on the view that as male and female pensioner were differently situated as regards the resources to which they were otherwise entitled, any differences in the supplementary bridging pension were not discriminatory.[83] Thus the mandatory nature of Article 119 does not preclude differences in pension payments, where these arise from relevant differences in the situation of those being compared. However, the payments in *Birds Eye Walls* were "top-up" payments made to compensate for the absence of other resources and where a bridging pension does not have such an explicit compensatory purpose, it may yet be found to fall within Article 119. A bridging pension offered to male early retirees between the ages of 60 and 65 in order to make up an attractive early retirement package, might fall outside the ratio of *Birds Eye Walls*, unless its purpose is to compensate for differences in entitlement to state pension in the particular circumstances of early retirement. Thus in *Beune* the occupational pension scheme of Dutch civil servants was calculated to provide an income based upon a certain proportion of final salary according to length of service, from which any state pension received was deducted. Prior to equalisation in 1986, married men were entitled to a maximum of 100 per cent of the prevailing minimum wage as a state pension, whilst married women were deemed to be entitled only by virtue of that which their husbands received. Unmarried men and women both received a maximum of 70 per cent of the minimum wage in state pension. As married women were deemed to receive the same 70 per cent state pension as single people, the sums deducted from the pay of married male civil servants in respect of service prior to 1986 was greater than was the case for comparable married women. This difference in net occupational pension was held to be contrary to Article 119, even though the aim, if not the reality, of the system was to produce equal net incomes, by taking into account the respective entitlements to state and occupational pensions.

The right to join a pension scheme

The right to join an occupational pension scheme falls within the scope of Article 119 and is therefore covered by the prohibition on discrimination. Furthermore, according to the Court in *Vroege*[84] and *Fisscher*[85] the temporal limitation in *Barber* does not apply to the right to join such a scheme and neither does the Protocol on Article 119 impose any analogous limitation. The ECJ reasoned that the temporal limitation in *Barber* was necessary because employers and pension funds had formed a reasonable expectation that compulsory implementation of the principle of equal treatment could be deferred according to the provisions of the Occupational Social Security

6-39

---

[83] See Evelyn Ellis, "The Definition of Discrimination in European Sex Equality Laws", *European Law Review*, (1994), 19,6, pp. 563–579.

[84] Case C-57/93, *Vroege v. (1) NCIV Instituut voor Volkshuisvesting BV and (2) Stichting Pensioenfonds NCIV.*

[85] Case-128/93, *Fisscher v. (1) Voorhuis Hengelo BV and (2) Stichting Bedrijfspensioenfonds voor de Detailhandel.*

Directive 86/378, but that it was not necessary to limit similarly the right to join an occupational pension scheme because it has been clear since the judgment in *Bilka* that the right to join a pension scheme was covered by Article 119. As *Bilka* contained no limitation in time, the right to join a pension scheme can be relied upon retrospectively as from the date of the judgment in *Defrenne (No. 2)* in 1976.

A worker excluded from a pension scheme by virtue of, say, working only part-time, would be likely to have been the victim of indirect discrimination. Whilst excluded part-timers are likely to be predominantly women, excluded temporary and fixed term workers may show no such gender bias and may be unable to establish a right to join a pension scheme, even though they have suffered an identical loss.

A worker who can claim retroactively to join an occupational pension scheme does not, according to the Court in *Fisscher*, thereby avoid the obligation to pay contributions relating to the period of membership in question. Equal treatment is to be achieved by placing the worker who has suffered discrimination in the same position as a worker of the opposite sex. To grant membership of an occupational scheme free of obligations to make the relev ant contributions would be to confer more favourable treatment than she would have experienced had she been duly accepted as a member.

Time limits on retrospective claims

6-40 The national rules relating to time limits for bringing actions under national law may be relied on against workers who assert their right to join an occupational pension scheme, according to the Court in *Fisscher*, provided that they are not less favourable for that type of action than for actions of a domestic nature and that they do not render the exercise of rights conferred by Community law impracticable in practice. The principle of effectiveness embodied in Article 5 of the Treaty implies that it is for the national courts to give effect to Community law rights, subject to the normal procedural rules of each legal system. Furthermore the Court in *Rewe-Zentralefinanz and Rewe-Zentral AG v. Landwirtschaftskammer fur das Saarland*[86] held that though Community law must be exercised in accordance with national procedural rules and time limits, unless such conditions render impossible the exercise of Community law rights, "this is not the case where reasonable periods of limitation are fixed." In *Rewe* the applicant had paid customs duties which were subsequently held by the ECJ to be in breach of Community law, but by the time the applicant companies were able to seek reimbursement they were out of time for making such a claim under German national law. It was in a second reference on those strong facts, in which the applicant companies could not have known of their rights until the relevant limitation period had passed, that the ECJ set out its proposition as to the application of national time limits. The general rule was restated in the sex discrimination context by the ECJ in *Emmot v. Ministry of Social Welfare and the Attorney General*[87] that:

---

[86] Case 33/76, *Rewe-Zentralefinanz and Rewe-Zentral AG v. Landwirtschaftskammer fur das Saarland*: [1976] E.C.R. 1989, [1977] 1 C.M.L.R. 533; Case 45/76, *Comet BV v. Pruktschap voor Siergewassen*: [1976] E.C.R. 2043, [1977] 1 C.M.L.R. 533.

[87] Case C-2-208/90, [1991] I.R.L.R. 387. Whilst the ECJ in *Emmot* held that time does not begin to run until such time as a directive has been fully transposed into national law, pensions are a question of pay under Article 119.

"in the absence of Community rules on the subject, it is for the domestic legal systems of each Member State to determine the procedural conditions governing actions at law intended to ensure the protection of the rights which individuals derive from the direct effect of Community law, provided that such conditions are not less favourable than those relating to similar actions of a domestic nature nor framed so as to render virtually impossible the exercise of rights conferred by Community law".

In regard to the second limb of the precept in *Emmot* as to whether national time limits might render the exercise of Community rights impossible, the Court in *Fisscher* held that whereas those responsible for pensions matters might reasonably have considered that Article 119 did not apply pensions paid under contracted-out schemes, in view of the derogations permitted by Directive 86/378,

"as far as the right to join an occupational pensions scheme is concerned, there is no reason to support that the professional groups concerned could have been mistaken about the applicability of Article 119. Indeed it has been clear since the judgment in the *Bilka* case that a breach of the rule of equal treatment committed through not recognising such a right is caught by Article 119".

It follows that national rules on time limits will normally govern the actions brought by individuals to make both current and retrospective claims, both as a matter of general principle and in the particular circumstances of the right to join a pension scheme. Such time limits were applied against the applicant in *Biggs v. Somerset County Council*,[88] in which, following *R. v. Secretary of State, ex p. EOC*, a part-time teacher made an unfair dismissal claim in respect of her dismissal in 1976. The EAT held that her claim was out of time, in that she had three months following her dismissal during which she could have brought her claim, relying upon the direct effect of Article 119, as established in the second *Defrenne*[89] case. The Court of Appeal upheld the EAT on the basis that the judgment of the Court of Appeal in the *EOC* case was declaratory of the state of the law since the supremacy of Community law was established by section 2 of the European Communities Act 1972. In consequence there had been no legal impediment to the bringing of a claim for unfair dismissal on the basis that the service qualifications were indirectly discriminatory, at least since the decision in *Defrenne v. Sabena*. The applicant's mistake was a mistake of law, rather than fact.

The other aspect of national time limits which is relevant in this context, is that of the retrospective reach of the claim itself. The Equal Pay Act 1970 imposes a maximum of two years back pay and, in the absence of any contrary Community rule, that limitation would apply in this context. A similar restriction applies in regulation 12 of the Occupational Pension Schemes (Equal Access to Membership) Regulations 1976, which provides that a tribunal may make a declaration that an applicant has a right to be admitted to a pension scheme from a date no earlier than two years before the institution of the proceedings in question. Such rules on the extent of retrospection have

---

[88] [1995] I.C.R. 811, [1995] I.R.L.R. 452, EAT, *The Independent*, February 1, 1996, C.A.
[89] [1976] I.C.R. 547.

been upheld in the social security references of *Steenhorst-Neerings v. Bestuur van de Bedrijfsverereniging* Case[90] and *Johnson v. Chief Adjudication Officer (No 2)*.[91] Thus a claimant for retrospective pension rights faces two procedural obstacles, first that of the time limit for making an application, and second that, even if successful, such claims do not result in more than two years retrospective rights according to the EAT in *Preston v. Wolverhampton Health Care NHS Trust*.[92] Only employees who are still employed in the relevant employment or who have made a claim within six months of leaving the employment seem likely to succeed in retrospective claims and then only in respect of the immediate two years prior service. However, a majority in the EAT (Mummery J. dissenting) referred the two year limit on retroactivity in equal pay claims to the ECJ in *Levez v. T.H. Jennings (Harlow Pools) Ltd*, on the basis of comparison with the position under the Sex Discrimination Act, where there is no maximum limit on compensation after the ECJ decision in *Marshall (No. 2)*.[92a]

The Pensions Act 1995

6-41   The Pensions Act 1995, s.62, in giving legislative effect to the implications of the *Barber* judgment, applies in s.62(1) an "equal treatment rule" in respect of pensionable service after May 17, 1990, which section 62(2) relates to the terms on which (a) "persons become members of the scheme" and (b) "members of the scheme are treated." An equal treatment rule applies in section 62(3) only where a woman is engaged in like work, work rated equal or work of equal value. In parallel with the provisions of the Equal Pay Act section 62(4) provides that where trustees or managers of a pension scheme show that differences in treatment are genuinely due to a difference which is not the difference of sex, the rule shall not operate. Any powers of discretion which are reserved to the trustees or managers are brought within the scope of section 62 by section 62(5) & (6), as is the treatment of dependants by section 63(1)&(2). In line with the temporal restriction of the judgement in *Barber*, section 63(6) provides that section 62 is to be treated as having effect only in relation to service after May 17, 1990.

Section 63(4) provides that section 62 shall be construed as one with section 1 of the Equal Pay Act 1970 and therefore made subject to the procedural provisions of sections 2 and 2A of that Act. Section 63(4) modifies section 2(4) of the Equal Pay Act so as impose a time limit of six months after leaving the employment in question for the making of applications based upon the application of the equal treatment rule to occupational pensions, a limit similar to that which applies generally in the Equal Pay Act. Section 2(5) of the Equal Pay Act provides that a woman shall not be entitled to any award in respect of arrears of remuneration in respect of a time more than two years before the proceedings were instituted, a rule which therefore encompasses claims in respect of pensions under the equal treatment rule contained in the Pensions Act 1995, s.62.

---

[90] C-338/91, [1994] I.R.L.R. 244, ECJ.
[91] C-410/92, [1995] I.R.L.R. 157, ECJ.
[92] [1996] I.R.L.R. 484, EAT. The EAT held that the six months time limit runs from the end of a fixed term contract where such contracts are separated by a genuine break.
[92a] [1996] I.R.L.R. 499, ECJ.

The Occupational Pension Schemes (Equal Access to Membership) Regulations 1976[93] govern the terms on which men and women may gain entry to an occupational pension scheme as a matter of equal access. The Regulations provide that damages are not a remedy for a failure to comply with the equal access requirements, but regulation 12 provides that an industrial tribunal may declare that an employee has the right to be admitted to a scheme. Such a declaration may not be made with effect from a date more than two years before the date of the application. The Occupational Pension Schemes (Access to Membership) Amendment Regulations 1995[94] amend the 1976 Regulations by repealing the reference contained therein to an upper age limit and amends section 118 of the Social Security Pensions Act 1975 to extend the concept of discrimination in respect of membership to include both direct and indirect discrimination. The 1976 Regulations oblige the employer to make available sufficient funds to secure for the employee prospective entitlement to benefit since the deemed entry date of the employee into the scheme (*i.e.* for up to two years previously). The Amendment Regulations extend this obligation in respect of employees admitted into membership by virtue of the inclusion of indirect discrimination within the scope of section 118 of the Social Security Pensions Act 1975, but only in respect of service from May 31, 1995 or from a later date, as determined.

The 1995 Act, s.64(3) does not, however, in line with the decision in *Coloroll*, require that unisex actuarial tables are used to calculate scheme liabilities. The decision in *Roberts* is reflected in the provision in section 64(2) that different benefits may be provided for men and women where those differences relate to differences in state retirement pension benefits under sections 43 to 55 of the Social Security Contributions and Benefits Act 1992.

Financing of defined benefit pension schemes

There are two types of pension scheme, namely, defined benefit schemes or defined contribution schemes. A defined benefit scheme is otherwise known as a final salary scheme, under which the employer undertakes to provide a pension equal to a certain proportion of final salary. A defined contribution scheme is otherwise known as a money purchase scheme, under which the employer and/or employee agree to contribute a certain proportion of income to accumulate a capital sum on behalf of the individual, out of which a pension can be financed.[95] On average women live seven years longer than men, so it will be more expensive to provide an identical pension for a woman, than for a man with comparable service. Therefore if a woman wanted to provide herself with a given income during retirement by the purchase of an annuity, it would cost her more than it would cost a man. This is because the insurance company would know that it would, on average,

6-42

---

[93] S.I. 1976 No. 142.
[94] S.I. 1995 No. 1215.
[95] Under a defined benefit scheme the employer is liable to make up any shortfall to ensure that the scheme can meet its liabilities, but is generally seen as the beneficial owner of any surpluses in the pension fund. Hence the not uncommon phenomenon of employers taking "pensions holidays" when a fund is over-capitalised in relation to its liabilities. By contrast under a money purchase or defined contribution scheme, it is the employee who takes the risk that the sums accumulated will be inadequate to provide him or her with the expected level of pension on retirement, but who stands to gain if the investments made on his behalf have done better than expected.

have to pay a female pensioner for seven years longer than it would a male. Therefore in a money purchase, or defined contribution scheme, under which men and women make equal contributions, the capital sum available on retirement would buy a woman a smaller monthly income than it would a man. Thus equal contributions imply unequal pensions, or equal pensions imply unequal contributions.

In a final salary or defined benefit scheme, the employee is guaranteed a certain proportion of his or her final salary, depending on the number of years pensionable service. Such a pension must cost more for a woman than a man and if the employees make equal contributions, the contributions made by the employer in respect of the woman must be greater. This seems unproblematic until one considers an employee who leaves his or her job and wishes to transfer to another scheme. In those circumstances, is it consistent with Article 119 for a woman to take a larger capital sum into her new pension scheme than would be the case for a similarly situated man? When an employee commutes a part of his or her pension into a capital sum, is it consistent with Article 119 for a woman to take a larger sum than a man with comparable service? These were the issues in *Neath v. Hugh Steeper Ltd,*[96] raised also in *Coloroll,* in which the Advocate General was against the use of sex based actuarial tables, arguing first that differential treatment of pension contributions on behalf of men and women is not justified because average differences in life expectancy between the sexes do not determine how long any individual may live, second that the financial balance of pension schemes will not be upset if schemes do not distinguish between men and women in their *external* relations with their members and third that subsidies between one group and another are not in any case uncommon.[97] The Court of Justice distinguished, however, between the employer's commitment to pay a periodic pension, which it held fell within Article 119, and the funding arrangements chosen to secure the periodic payment of the pension, which it held were outside the scope of Article 119. In the Court's view it follows that "the use of actuarial factors distinguishing according to sex is not struck at by Article 119. That conclusion necessarily extends to ... the conversion of part of the periodic payments into a capital sum and the transfer of pension rights, the value of which can be determined only by reference to the funding arrangements chosen." The Court and the Advocate General agreed as regards the *internal* use of actuarial tables to calculate potential liabilities, but differed as to their application to the payment of part of the

---

[96] Case C-152/91, [1994] I.R.L.R. 91.

[97] The Advocate General quotes from the U.S. Supreme Court case of *City of Los Angeles v. Manhart,* 435 U.S. 677 at p. 710, 55 L Ed 2d 657, at 666 that "... when insurance risks are grouped, the better risks always subsidise the poorer risks. Healthy persons subsidise health benefits for the less healthy; unmarried workers subsidise the pensions of married workers; persons who eat, drink, or smoke to excess may subsidise pension benefits for persons whose habits are more temperate. Treating different classes of risk as though they were the same for the purpose of group insurance is a common practice which has never been seen as inherently unfair. To insure the flabby and the fit as though they were equivalent risks may be more common than treating men and women alike; but nothing more than habit makes one 'subsidy' seem less fair than the other."

For a further discussion of the issue of the application of sex based actuarial tables to pensions see D. Curtin, "Occupational Pension Schemes and Article 119: Beyond the Fringe" in *CMLRev.* 216 (1987), who is against their application in this context and B. Jones, "Sex Equality in Pension Schemes" in *Trends in European Social Policy,* (J. Kenner ed, Dartmouth, 1995), pp. 85–144 who favours their use.

pension as a capital sum or in the computation of transfer values, these being part of the *external* relations of the scheme, according to the Advocate General. Section 64(3) of the Pensions Act 1995 allows for the utilisation of actuarial factors in the calculation of employer contributions to a pension scheme.

Where an employee has transferred his pension rights to another fund owing to a change of job, according to the decision of the Court of Justice in *Coloroll*, the second scheme is obliged to increase the benefits it undertook to pay him on accepting the transfer so as to eliminate any effects suffered by the worker in consequence of the inadequacy of the capital transferred, where this is due to discriminatory treatment suffered under the first scheme with respect to periods of service subsequent to May 17, 1990.

Additional voluntary contributions

It follows from the above reasoning that equality is mandated by Article 119 as regards all benefits paid by a pension scheme, without distinguishing according to whether those benefits arise from contributions made by the employer or the employee. According to the Court of Justice in *Coloroll* once made, the employers and employees' contributions are managed as a single fund and it is no longer possible to distinguish them. However, the Court of Justice in *Coloroll* held that employee financed additional voluntary contributions (AVCs) are not covered by Article 119, as these are calculated separately, solely on the value of the contributions paid.

6-43

The Occupational Social Security Directive

Little seems to be left, therefore, of the reservations and exceptions from the principle of equality permitted under the Occupational Social Security Directive 86/378. Once pensions are seen as pay under Article 119 and can be resolved by legal analysis on that basis, the direct effect of the Treaty article displaces any relevant directive to a supplementary or extending effect only. In so far as the Directive qualifies rights established under Article 119 it is displaced.[98] The Directive requires that the principle of equal treatment be implemented by January 1, 1993.

6-44

In so far as the Directive is wider than occupational pensions as commonly understood, it remains a valid point of reference; Articles 3 and 4 provide that the principle of equal treatment applies to sickness and invalidity benefits as well as to old age and retirement benefits. It also applies to schemes which offer protection in cases of industrial accident, occupational disease and unemployment in respect of any member of the working population and not simply those engaged under a contract of employment. Article 5 requires that there shall be no discrimination in the scope of such schemes or in access to them, the obligation to contribute or the calculation of contributions and benefits. Article 6 applies the provisions of the Directive to direct and indirect discrimination by reference to sex, marital or family status and specifies the

6-45

---

[98] Advocate General's opinion in *Coloroll*, etc., para. 32.

requirements of the Directive in greater detail. Article 7 requires that the provisions of legally compulsory collective agreements, staff rules and other arrangements relating to occupational schemes are or may be declared null and void or be amended.

An amended Occupational Social Security Directive

6-46   There is currently under discussion a draft proposal to amend the Directive on Occupational Social Security[99] to reflect the impact of *Barber* and the post-*Barber* decisions. The amended Directive will restrict most of the former qualification to the application of the principle of equal treatment to self-employed workers, who fall outside the scope of *Barber*. Following *Moroni*, it extends the right to equal treatment to survivors benefits in Article 3. In response to *Neath*, it allows differential contributions by the employer to equalise benefits in defined contribution schemes under the revised Article 6, and allows for greater employer contributions to defined benefit schemes where these are intended to ensure the adequacy of funds to cover the cost of benefits to be provided. In exercising any discretion the trustees are to observe the principle of equal treatment. The qualifications to the date at which the principle of equal treatment must be realised contained in Article 9 are confined to the self-employed by the amended Directive. The amended Article 13(1) provides that in transposing the directive into national law, the transposition must apply retrospectively to 1976 (for states then in membership) but Article 13(2) provides that such transposition shall not affect national rules relating to time limits, providing these are not less favourable than those for a similar domestic action.

State pensions

6-47   Article 7 of Directive 79/7 on the implementation of the principle of equal treatment in matters of social security allows Member States to determine pensionable age for the purpose of granting old-age and retirement pensions, but Member States are required from time to time to examine "in the light of social developments . . . whether there is justification for maintaining the exclusion concerned."[1] The U.K. Government, having examined the financial, demographic and administrative dimensions of the problem determined to equalise the state pension age at 65 by the year 2020. The decision to equalise the state pension age by stages is contained in Schedule 4 to the Pensions Act 1995, by which a woman born in 1950 will qualify for her pension at age 60, but by stages, a woman born in 1955 will not qualify until age 65. The Act gives a "green light" to equalisation of occupational pensions at age 65, even though only two in five men between 60 and 65 are currently employed (in 1975 the figure was four out of five). Thus whilst the notion of a decade of flexible retirement has been rejected as an option for the state pension, practice seems to point in a different direction.

---

[99] Directive 86/378.
[1] The U.K. Government is equalising the state pension age by year 2020 in stages, in Schedule 4 of the Pensions Act 1995.

The burden of proof in equal pay cases

The issue of the burden of proof in equal pay cases was first considered by the ECJ in *Danfoss*,[2] which concerned a difference in average remuneration between men and women workers under a complex merit rating system. The ECJ held that where a system lacked "transparency" it was for the employer to show that differences in pay were not discriminatory.

> "When an undertaking applies a system of pay which is characterised by a total lack of transparency the burden of proof lies on the employer to show that his pay practice is not discriminatory, where a female worker establishes, by comparison with a relatively large number of employees, that the average pay of female workers is less than that of male workers." (Point 16).

The reasoning behind the above proposition is that otherwise the women "would be deprived of any effective means of ensuring the respect of the principle of equal pay before the national court." Thus reliance is placed upon the principle of effectiveness in reaching this conclusion. This principle was also material in the reasoning of the Court of Justice in *Enderby v. Frenchay Health Authority*[3] in which NHS speech therapists sought equal pay with pharmacists. The EAT had held that unless a requirement or condition could be established, indirect discrimination could not be shown even in the equal pay situation, but the ECJ held that:

> "Where there is a prima facie case of discrimination, it is for the employer to show there are objective reasons for the difference in pay. Workers would be unable to enforce the principle of equal pay before the national courts if evidence of a prima facie case of discrimination did not shift to the employer the onus of showing that the differential is not in fact discriminatory."

In *Royal Copenhagen*[4] the central issue was the application of Article 119 to differences in average piece work remuneration as between male and female work groups, when those averages concealed a wide dispersion of individual earnings. The Court held, however, that a difference in the pay of two groups of piece workers does not necessarily raise an inference of discrimination, because the differences in pay may reflect differences in output. Nonetheless, if the factors which determined the differences in pay cannot be identified, the burden may shift to the employer. It is for the national court to determine whether the conditions for burden-shifting are satisfied.[5] Should the national court conclude that there is a primae facie

6-48

---

[2] Case 109/88, *Handels-ogs Kontorfunkionaerernes Forbund i Danmark v. Dansk Arbejdsgiv-erforening* (acting for *Danfoss*): [1989] I.R.L.R. 532.
[3] Case 127/92, [1993] I.R.L.R. 591.
[4] Case C-400/93, *Specialarbejderforbundet i Danmark* and *Dansk Industri*, formerly *Industriens Arbejdsgivere*, acting for Royal Copenhagen A/S.
[5] In adopting this approach, the Court largely followed Advocate General Leger, who argued that Article 3 of the (now withdrawn) draft Directive on the Burden of Proof COM (88), 88/C 176/09 was based on the principles drawn from the case law of the Court. Article 3 proposed a rebuttable presumption of discrimination, to be based upon a fact or a series of facts which, if they cannot be refuted, imply the existence of direct or indirect discrimination.

instance of discrimination, then the Court concludes that Article 119 "requires" the employer to justify the difference.[6]

In *Royal Copenhagen* the Court was modifying its conclusion in *Enderby* that a purely statistical difference between male and female groups may give rise to an inference of discrimination, for which the respondent employer must furnish an explanation.[7] In *Royal Copenhagen* the Court allows for prior consideration of the reasons for a pay disparity before raising an inference of discrimination, rather than simply confining such matters to the realm of justification, so that differences in the quantity of work between men and women appear to be conceivable, whereas differences in the overall quality of work were beyond contemplation in *Danfoss*.[8]

Operation of the equality clause

6-49   Whilst Article 119 simply requires that Member states shall ensure and maintain the principle of equal pay for equal work, which the Equal Pay Directive restates as requiring the elimination of all discrimination based on sex with regard to all aspects and conditions of remuneration, the Equal Pay Act operates via the mechanism of a statutory implied equality term in the employee's contract of employment.

An equality clause will operate in three sets of circumstances, namely where a woman is employed on like work with a man in the same employment, on work which is rated as equivalent with that of a man in the same employment, or where she is employed on work of equal value with a man in the same employment. In each case it is open to the employer to contend that any variation between the terms on which the man and woman are employed is due to a genuine material factor other than a difference of sex, which in the case of women employed on like work or work rated as equivalent must be a difference between her case and his. Following the decision of the House of Lords in *Rainey v. Greater Glasgow Health Board*,[9] there is no longer any effective difference between the section 1(3) defence in equal value cases, where the material factor need not be a difference between her case and his, and like work and work rated as equivalent cases, where the statute calls for the genuine material factor to be a difference between her case and his.

---

[6] By contrast under the "*China Centre* guidelines" the requirement that the employer furnish an explanation for any primae facie discrimination is "almost common sense" rather than a matter of law, in which any notion of the shifting of the burden of proof or even the "evidentiary burden" is seen as "uneccesary and unhelpful" *King v. Great Britain China Centre* [1991] I.R.L.R. 513 at 518.

[7] Sandra Fredman characterises this aspect of the decision in *Enderby* as one which "prioritizes gender equality" in rejecting the need for any search for "requirements or conditions" which tend to exclude women in order to establish indirect discrimination. In *Industrial Law Journal*, (1994) 23,1, p.37–41 at 39 Evelyn Ellis makes the point, however, that up to *Enderby* the Court had had to deal only with the question of part-timers as regards indirect discrimination and had not had the occasion to consider more complex fact situations. E. Ellis, "Discrimination in European Community Sex Law", (1994) 19 *ELR* 563.

[8] See *Danfoss (n.1)* paras. 19–20.

[9] See paragraphs 6–82 *et seq.* for a discussion of s.1(3).

The chosen comparator

The woman may choose as her comparator any male worker in the same **6-50** employment whom she believes is performing like work, or whose work has been rated as equal under a job evaluation scheme or whom she contends is performing work of equal value.[10] *In British Coal v. Smith* and *North Yorkshire County Council v. Ratcliffe*[11] Balcombe L.J, relying on the opinion of the Advocate General in the *Danfoss* case,[12] held that the male comparator must be representative of the group or class to which he belongs. Indeed, a "rogue male" comparator, or the making of a comparison by a "rogue female", would be likely to provide a basis for the employer to argue that some "material factor" other than sex was at work, under section 1(3).

By contrast with the Sex Discrimination or Race Relations Acts, the Equal **6-51** Pay Act does not provide for hypothetical comparisons to be made.[13] Under Article 119, however, comparison may be made on the basis of concrete appraisals of the work actually performed by non-contemporaneous employees of different sex within the same establishment or service, although the ECJ recognised in *McCarthys Ltd v. Smith*[14] that any disparity between the pay received by a non-contemporaneous male and female may be explained by the operation of factors unconnected with any discrimination on grounds of sex. *Albion Shipping Agency v. Arnold*[15] is a case where economic factors supervened to account for the difference in pay.[16] However, whilst recognising the evidential difficulties which might occur in such cases, the EAT upheld a comparison with a male successor in *Diocese of Hallam v. Connaughton*.[16a]

The same employment

A woman may only make comparison with a man who is engaged in the **6-52** same employment as her chosen comparator, whichever basis of comparison she chooses. Section 1(6) provides that:

> "(M)en shall be treated as in the same employment with a woman if they are men employed by her employer or any associated employer at the same establishment or at establishments in Great Britain which

---

[10] See *Ainsworth v. Glass Tubes Ltd* [197] I.R.L.R. 74, EAT.
[11] [1994] I.R.L.R. 342, C.A.
[12] Case C-109/88, [1989] E.C.R. 3199, [1989] I.R.L.R. 532.
[13] There must be a comparator . In *Meeke v. U.U.A.A.W.* [1976] I.R.L.R. 198, a part-time secretary was found to have been subject to indirect discrimination compared with the rate at which full-timers were paid, but as the claim fell within the Equal Pay Act and there were no male comparators, the Tribunal was compelled to dismiss the claim. See also the decision of the ECJ with respect to Article 119 in *McCarthys v. Smith*, n. 74, ground 15.
[14] Case 129/79, *McCarthys Ltd v. Smith* [1980] E.C.R. 1275; [1980] 2 C.M.L.R. 205.
[15] [1981] I.R.L.R. 525, EAT.
[16] In *Wallis v. Prudential Portfolio Managers Ltd*, Case No. 35372/91 EOR DCLD 15, 1993, the Liverpool Industrial Tribunal took the view that no precise comparator was necessary in a claim brought under Article 119 with respect to the occupational pension entitlement of part-timers, observing that in *Barber* and other such cases, no reliance was placed on a person performing equal work.
[16a] [1996] I.R.L.R. 505.

include that one and at which common terms and conditions of employment are observed generally or for employees of the relevant class.''

6-53   In *Lawson v. Britfish*,[17] the EAT held that where employees are working at
the same establishment they need not be working under common terms and
conditions. Where there are no suitable men working at the establishment
where she is employed, a woman may therefore choose to make a comparison
with a man employed by her employer or any associated employer at some
other establishment at which common terms and conditions are employed.

As regards employees working in different establishments, in *Leverton v.
Clwyd County Council*,[18] the majority of the Court of Appeal held that the
existence of common terms and conditions implied that the terms and conditions of the woman and her chosen comparator must be broadly similar. On
this view, any gross disparity in the terms and conditions of the woman and
the comparators would mean that like was not being compared with like,
whilst if the terms and conditions were identical there could be no ground
for a claim. Thus in the instant case a nursery nurse who enjoyed school
holidays and who worked only school hours, was defeated in her claim with
other workers employed by the authority, who were at different grade points
on the same set of salary scales, because of the disparity between them in
the hours worked. The House of Lords, preferring the dissenting view of
May L.J. in the Court of Appeal, held that:

> "The concept of common terms and conditions of employment observed
> generally at different establishments necessarily contemplates terms and
> conditions applicable to a wide range of employees whose individual
> terms will vary greatly *inter se*. On the construction of the sub-section
> adopted by the majority below the phrase "observed either generally or
> for employees of the relevant classes" is given no content. Terms and
> conditions of employment governed by the same collective agreement
> seem to me to represent the paradigm, though not necessarily the only
> example, of the common terms and conditions of employment contem-
> plated by the sub-section."[19]

6-54   In the complex combined appeal in *British Coal v. Smith* and *North Yorkshire
County Council v. Ratcliffe*[20] the Court of Appeal held that the requirement in
section 1(6) that "common terms and conditions of employment are observed
generally or for employees of the relevant class" allows a comparison to be
made with a male comparator only where the terms and conditions are the
same as those which would be available for male employees doing the same
work at the establishment in which the woman works. It is not necessary
that the terms and conditions for women are the same at the establishments
in question, but evidence as to whether or not this is the case would be
relevant and admissible in relation to the claim that section 1(6) applies.[21]

[17] (1988) I.R.L.R. 53, EAT.
[18] [1988] I.R.L.R. 239.
[19] [1988] I.R.L.R. 239. cf. *British Coal Corporation v. Smith* EAT/29/91.
[20] See paragraph 6–50.
[21] On the facts of the *British Coal* case the Court of Appeal held that the terms of ancillary
and clerical workers were not the same as those of surface mine workers, where the latter
enjoyed the additional benefit of concessionary coal negotiated under local agreements at pit
level. In the *North Yorks. C.C.* case, whilst dinner ladies working for a DSO, who had suffered
a pay reduction, were no longer working under the same terms and conditions as other com-

The Court of Appeal was of the view that this interpretation of the domestic statutes is consonant with the decisions of the ECJ in *McCarthys v. Smith*[22] ("comparisons are confined to parallels which may be drawn on the basis of concrete appraisals of the work actually performed by employees of different sex within the same establishment or service.") and *Jenkins v. Kingsgate Clothing (Productions) Ltd.*[23] ("Amongst the forms of discrimination which may be judicially identified, the Court mentioned in particular cases where men and women receive unequal pay for work carried out in the same establishment or service, public or private.")[24] In the House of Lords,[24a] Lord Slynn, giving the leading judgment, held that the relevant terms and conditions at different establishments "do not have to be identical, but on a broad basis to be substantially comparable." The Lords upheld the tribunal decision that local variations on the entitlement of mineworkers to concessionary coal were not such as to destroy the centralised, industry-wide nature of the entitlement and the existence of, on a broad comparison, common terms amongst the male comparators. The contention that the terms and conditions of comparators had to be identical at the different establishments of the employer, subject only to the *de minimis* differences, was rejected.

Definitions of "associated" employer

Two employers are defined as being associated employers in section 1(6)   **6-55**
(c) if:

> "one is a company of which the other (directly or indirectly) has control or if both are companies of which a third person (directly or indirectly) has control."

Two companies are associated if one has voting control over the other. In *Gardiner v. London Borough of Merton*,[25] it was held that the word "company" is not apt to cover all bodies corporate, so that two local authorities would not be considered as being associated employers. Consequently in *Hasley v. Fair Employment Agency*,[26] when an employee of the Fair Employment Agency sought equal pay with an official of the Northern Ireland Equal Opportunity Commission, her claim failed on the ground, firstly, that neither body was a company but a public corporation, and secondly, that being the case, it was immaterial that both were under the *de facto* control of the Department of Economic Affairs for purposes of establishment. However, in *Scullard v. Knowles and the Southern Regional Council for Education and Training*[26a] the EAT held that Article 119 is of wider impact than s.1(b), the ECJ in *Defrenne (No. 2)* and *McCarthys v. Smith* applying it to employment "in the same establishment or service, whether private or public." The lim-

---

parable women, this was held not to be relevant, as the male comparators continued to enjoy common terms and conditions.
[22] Case 129/79, [1980] I.C.R. 679.
[23] Case 96/80 [1981] I.C.R. 592, [1981] I.R.L.R. 228.
[24] *Umar v. Pliastar Ltd* [1981] I.R.L.R. 727.
[24a] [1996] I.R.L.R. 404, H.L.
[25] [1980] I.R.L.R. 472.
[26] [1989] I.R.L.R. 106, N.I.C.A.
[26a] [1996] I.R.L.R. 344.

itation of s.1(6) to "associated employers" is therefore displaced by the broader terms of Article 119, according to Mummery J. The decision, though overcoming an injustice between employees in the private and public sectors, leaves the definition of the "same service" wide open and invites litigation.

The methods of comparison

6-56   Section 1(4) provides that:

> "A woman is to be regarded as employed on like work with men if, but only if, her work and theirs is of the same or a broadly similar nature, and the difference (if any) between the things she does and the things they do are not of practical importance in relation to terms and conditions of employment; and accordingly in comparing her work with theirs regard shall be had to the frequency or otherwise with which any such differences occur in practice as well as to the nature and extent of the differences."[27]

Like work

6-57   Thus like work must be the same as, or broadly similar to, the work of the chosen comparator, and whatever differences occur must not be such as would reasonably be thought capable of giving rise to differentials in pay or of putting the two jobs into different categories or grades in an evaluation study.[28] In approaching this question, tribunals must first ask whether there is like work or work of a broadly similar nature. In considering whether work is of a broadly similar nature, the tribunals have been enjoined to take a broad approach and not to make too minute an examination, nor to place emphasis upon trivial distinctions which in the real world are not likely to be reflected in the terms and conditions of employment.[29] It follows that where there are differences in responsibility which justify differences in grading, there can be no like work.[30] Greater responsibilities when performing a similar task can lead to the conclusion that like work does not exist, as in *Eaton Ltd v. Nuttal*[31] (a male stock control clerk was responsible for items of greater value than his female colleague).

6-58   The second issue is whether there are any differences of practical importance, and how frequently these differences occur. It is not sufficient merely to compare the contractual obligations of the persons concerned but to examine the actual work performed. Thus in *Dance v. Dorothy Perkins Ltd*,[32] the obligation to move heavier material around the warehouse when deliveries

---

[27] EqPA 1970, s.1(4).
[28] *British Leyland v. Powell* [1978] I.R.L.R. 57, EAT.
[29] *Capper Pass Ltd v. Lawton* [1977] I.C.R. 83, EAT (male assistant chef in directors' dining room found comparable with cook in canteen).
[30] *Capper Pass Ltd v. Allen* [1980] I.C.R. 194, EAT.
[31] [1977] I.C.R. 272, EAT and see *Coley v. Hinckley & Bosworth Borough Council* (unreported) 1983, summarised in "Towards Equality." (EOC, 1989), p. 62., and *Fletcher v. Greenbank Terotech Ltd* EOR, DCLD 12, (Summer 1992).
[32] [1978] I.C.R. 760, EAT and see *McCabe v. I.C.L. Ltd* (unreported) IT 292 Case No. 59/79.

were received resulted not only in a difference in the contractual obligations but also in the performance of the duties. By contrast, the contract of the male employee in *Shields v. Coomes Holdings Ltd*[33] had a special responsibility for assisting with security, but the Court of Appeal found that this responsibility was not frequently exercised in practice and neither did the male employee possess any special skills; nor had he undergone any special training in dealing with security matters. The contractual difference was, therefore, held not to be one of practical importance for terms and conditions. A mere preparedness to work shifts or undertake night duty does not constitute such a difference.[34] It is also necessary to show that such additional duties are performed to a significant extent if they are to be of practical importance.[35] Where the work performed is not sufficiently similar to constitute like work, it is not relevant that those differences are of a much smaller order and in no way commensurate with the difference in pay.[36]

Work rated as equivalent

Where a job evaluation study has been completed it can be relied upon under section 1(2)(b) even if it has not been implemented,[37] although the parties must have accepted its validity.[38] The claimant must base her case upon the study as it is,[39] and can only challenge the results under section 1(2)(b) if there is a plain error on the face of the record. To fall within section 1(2)(b), a job evaluation scheme must satisfy the requirements of section 1(5) in that the scheme must analyse the demands made upon the worker under various headings such as effort, skill, decision.

6-59

Methods of job evaluation

The main distinction in job evaluation methods is between the whole job, or felt fair, methods and the analytical methods. The EAT, in an appendix to the decision in *Eaton Ltd v. Nuttal*[40] set out a note of the principal methods of job evaluation:

6-60

> ''Job ranking
>
> This is commonly thought to be the simplest method. Each job is considered as a whole and is then given a ranking in relation to all other jobs. A ranking table is then drawn up and the ranked jobs grouped into grades. Pay levels can then be fixed for each grade.

---

[33] [1978] I.R.L.R. 263, C.A. and *Waddington v. Leicester Council for Voluntary Service* [1977] I.R.L.R. 32, EAT, *Doncaster Education Authority v. Gill EOR DCLD 14.*
[34] *Dugdale v. Kraft Foods* [1976] I.R.L.R. 369, *N.C.B. v. Sherwin* [1978] I.R.L.R. 122, EAT.
[35] *Electrolux Ltd v. Hutchinson* [1976] I.R.L.R. 410, EAT (the frequency with which additional duties, such as preparedness to transfer to other physically more demanding work or to work at nights, occurred was relevant in considering whether these differences were of practical importance).
[36] *Maidment & Hardacre v. Cooper & Co Ltd* [1978] I.R.L.R. 462, EAT.
[37] *O'Brien v. Sim Chem Ltd* [1980] I.C.R. 573, H.L.
[38] *Arnold v. Beecham Group Ltd* [1982] I.C.R. 744, EAT.
[39] *England v. Bromley Borough Council* [1978] I.C.R. 1, EAT.
[40] See above at n. 4 and see EOR 24, March/April 1987 for a report of an EOC sponsored survey of the practices adopted by independent experts.

Paired comparisons

This is also a simple method. Each job is compared as a whole with each other job in turn and points (0, 1, or 2) awarded according to whether its overall importance is judged to be less than, equal to or more than the other. Points awarded for each job are then totalled and a ranking order produced.

Points assessment

This is the most common system in use. It is an analytical method, which, instead of comparing whole jobs, breaks each job down into a number of factors — for example skills, responsibility, physical or mental requirements and working conditions. Each of these factors may be analysed further. Points are awarded for each factor according to a predetermined scale and the total points decide a job's place in the rank order. Usually the factors are weighted, so that, for example, more or less weight may be given to hard physical conditions or to a high degree of skill.

Factor comparison

This is also an analytical method, employing the same principles as points assessment but using only a limited number of factors, such as skill, responsibility and working conditions. A number of key jobs are selected because their wage rates are generally agreed to be 'fair'. The proportion of the total wage attributed to each factor is then decided and a scale produced showing the rate for each factor for each key job. The other jobs are then compared with this scale, factor by factor, so that a rate is finally obtained for each factor for each job. The total pay for each job is reached by adding together the rates for its individual factors.''

6-61   Job evaluation schemes based only upon the use of paired comparisons or other felt fair methods in which there is no analysis of the job under a number of headings, as required under section 1(5), fall outside the definition. In *Bromley v. H. J. Quick Ltd*,[41] the employer had commissioned consultants to carry out what is often termed a hybrid job evaluation study. The consultants first used a panel of management and employees, including women, to perform a paired comparison of a selection of representative jobs, which were then placed in rank order. These comparisons were based upon job descriptions but the tasks were not broken down or analysed in any way. The jobs were then analysed by factors such as skill and the contribution of each of these factors to the total rank order of the jobs was obtained by multiple regression analysis. The factors were assigned weightings on the basis of the regression analysis. The panels then adjusted the rank order of the benchmark jobs to remove any anomalies they perceived and the remaining jobs were slotted in by management on a felt fair basis. Only in the case of an appeal against the grade given were the remaining jobs analysed according to the

---

[41] [1987] I.R.L.R. 456, EAT; [1988] I.R.L.R. 249, C.A.

factor plan. The jobs of the appellants were therefore analysed, but not those of their chosen comparators, who had not appealed against their grading.

By a majority, the EAT rejected the argument raised on behalf of two appellant female clerical workers that this method of job evaluation fell outside the definition given in section 1(5) and considered that a concentration upon the form and nature of a job evaluation could lead to a failure to identify the real mischief which the Act was designed to meet. The EAT upheld the finding of fact by the Tribunal that the scheme was not discriminatory at any stage and that those responsible for the operation of the scheme had constantly reminded the panels of the dangers of discrimination in their deliberations.[42]

6-62

The Court of Appeal held that the majority of the EAT had erred in the decision that the study fell within section 1(5). It was held that section 1(5) requires that the work of the woman and her comparators has been analysed under the required heading using "analytical" techniques, a usage specifically approved in this context by Dillon L. J. It is not sufficient that the benchmark jobs have been so analysed if the jobs in question have not.[43] A job evaluation scheme includes not only the determination of points for each job, but the allocation of jobs to pay bands on the basis of those points, according to the EAT in *Springboard Sunderland Trust v. Robson*.[44]

6-63

Equal value claims

The equal value claims provided for under section 1(2)(c) arose out of the need to harmonise United Kingdom domestic law with British obligations under the Treaty of Rome. Article 119 provided for equal pay for equal work. This was a narrower concept than the requirement laid down in the I.L.O. Convention 100 of "equal pay for work of equal value." Nonetheless, when the Equal Pay Directive 75/117 was adopted in 1975 as part of the Social Action Programme, Article 1 provided that:

6-64

> "The principle of equal pay for men and women outlined in Article 119, hereinafter called the 'the principle of equal pay,' means, for the same work or for work to which equal value is attributed, the elimination

---

[42] It was considered that the "blemishes" on the scheme in having slotted in the remaining jobs without full evaluation and in management members having altered a couple of the rank orderings were not sufficiently serious to invalidate the scheme as a whole. In the view of the dissenting member these defects were sufficiently serious to bring the scheme outside section 1(5).

[43] Whilst Woolf L.J. held that the scheme as a whole would have satisfied section 1(5) had the jobs of the appellants been analysed, Dillon L.J. specifically declined to go this far. It is surely a moot point as to whether a scheme which operated in such a way that the factors are weighted so as to provide a rationalisation for the results of the initial felt fair approach, which incorporates existing workplace values, does meet the requirements of section 1(5). See also EOR 23, p. 48 and EOR 24, p. 22 for a further discussion of the necessity for weighting the factors in analytical job evaluation and the likelihood that in this process, accepted social mores which incorporate traditional notions of what are more valued and less valued skills, will be built into the results. Some method of factor weighting is inevitable and unavoidable.

[44] [1992] I.R.L.R. 261, EAT.

of all discrimination on grounds of sex with regard to all aspects and conditions of remuneration.''

It was held in the second *Defrenne* case[45] that Article 119 was directly applicable in Member States where there is ''direct and overt discrimination which may be identified solely with the aid of criteria based on equal work and equal pay.''[46] In *Jenkins v. Kingsgate (Clothing Productions) Ltd*[47] the ECJ held that Article 1 of the Directive restates the principle of equal pay set out in Article 119 of the EEC treaty so as to facilitate its practical application and ''in no way alters the content or scope of that principle as defined in the Treaty.''[48] Thus, the right to equal pay for work of equal value was viewed by the Commission as integral to the application of Article 119, in spite of the caveat entered at the time of the adoption of the Equal Pay Directive by the United Kingdom Government that ''work to which equal value is attributed'' applied only where such equal value had in fact been attributed by an existing job evaluation scheme. This argument did not prevail when the Commission brought enforcement proceedings against the United Kingdom Government (and seven other Member States) in 1982.[49] The ECJ held that the United Kingdom was in breach of its obligations under the Treaty in not providing a remedy in its national courts for equal value claims where no system of job classification exists. Subsequently, the United Kingdom Government introduced a discussion document proposing changes in the Equal Pay Act to provide a right for women to bring equal value claims, which eventually resulted in the Equal Pay (Amendment) Regulations 1983.[50]

The Equal Pay (Amendment) Regulations 1983

6-65   The Equal Pay (Amendment) Regulations were introduced under the European Communities Act 1972, under which an Order can only be accepted or rejected by Parliament and cannot be amended. The Parliamentary procedures established under the European Communities Act allow only minimal time for debate, so that even though the language (and the substance) of the Regulations were severely criticised, it was not possible to amend them. In order to implement the regulations, amendments had to be made to the procedural regulations of the industrial tribunals, changes which again generated fierce controversy. The procedural regulations are now incorporated within the Industrial Tribunal (Rules of Procedure) Regulations 1993.[51] Both the Amending Regulations and the procedures established for equal value claims are of considerable complexity and have given rise to some problems of interpretation in the tribunals.

6-66   The essence of the procedure established under section 1(2)(c) is that an

[45] *Defrenne v. Sabena* [1976] C.M.L.R. 98.
[46] At 123. See chapter 1 for a discussion of the concept of direct and indirect discrimination in Community law.
[47] [1981] I.C.R. 692, ECJ; [1981] I.R.L.R. 388, C.A.
[48] At 614. See also *Murphy v. Bord Telecom Eirann* [1988] E.C.R. 673, ECJ; *McCarthy v. Smith* [1981] 1 Q.B. 180, ECJ.
[49] *Commission of the European Communities v. U.K.* [1982] I.R.L.R. 333.
[50] S.I. 1983 No. 1794.
[51] S.I. 1993 No. 2687 and No. 2688 (Scotland).

independent expert is appointed by the tribunal to prepare a report on whether or not the claimant is performing work of equal value to her chosen comparator. The tribunal will then decide, on the basis of the independent expert's report and other evidence, whether the woman is performing work of equal value to the man. This is clearly a slow, cumbersome and expensive process and in consequence a screening test has been provided under which the tribunal can first weed out "hopeless cases." There has been considerable criticism of the role of the independent expert, particularly as regards the time taken, which can average 18 months. Consequently, since 1994 independent experts have been required to estimate how long they are likely to take to produce their reports under regulation 8(5) as amended by S.I. 1994 No. 536.

At the time of writing an employee who wishes to bring an equal value claim must still first pass the screening test designed to sift out the "hopeless cases." The statutory language in which this test is laid down was criticised as incomprehensible when the Order was laid before Parliament[52] and indeed the EAT sought guidance on its interpretation from the Court of Appeal in the first reported case under the section.[53]

6-67

Section 2A (1) provides that the tribunal shall not determine the question of whether the applicant and her male comparator are performing work of equal value unless:

6-68

"(a) it is satisfied there are no reasonable grounds for determining that the work is of equal value; or
(b) it has required a member of the panel of independent experts to prepare a report with respect to that question and has received that report."

Section 2A(1) requires that the tribunal may not determine whether the work is of equal value unless there are no reasonable grounds for so determining, or it has sought the opinion of an independent expert. The effect of this obscure phraseology is that the tribunal has the power to stop the case without commissioning an expert report, only if there are no reasonable grounds for thinking that the case could succeed. The converse would appear to be that unless there are no reasonable grounds for considering that the case could succeed, a report must be commissioned. The claimant therefore needs only to establish an arguable case at this juncture for the tribunal to have to seek the opinion of the independent expert.

In the Green Paper, *Resolving Employment Rights Disputes — Options for Reform* the Government proposed to modify section 2A(1)(b) so as to leave to the discretion of the industrial tribunal (to be renamed employment tribunals) the question as to whether to commission a report from an independent expert. Regulations[53a] have amended s.2a of the Equal Pay Act 1970 from the end of July 1996 to give industrial tribunals discretion as to whether to commission an independent expert or to determine the question of equal

---

[52] Described as "eleven unfathomable lines . . . virtually incapable of comprehension" by Mr Barry Jones M.P. (H.C. Deb., 6th ser., Vol. 489).
[53] *Forex Neptune (Overseas) Ltd v. Miller* [1987] I.C.R. 170.
[53a] The Sex Discrimination and Equal Pay (Miscellaneous Amendments) Regulations (S.I. 1996 No. 438).

value directly. Tribunals would in any event retain their power under Rule 6 to conduct a pre-hearing assessment, and to issue a costs warning where the applicant persists with a case in which there is no reasonable hope of success.

6-69   An employee may be frustrated in her desire to pursue an equal value claim by the existence of a job evaluation scheme which she believes does not adequately reflect the value of the job on which she is engaged. She may believe that she is doing work of equal value with a male worker, but the results of the existing job evaluation may say otherwise. She may challenge the validity of an existing job evaluation scheme by bringing an equal value action under section 1(2)(c), provided she has an arguable case under section 2A(1) and can satisfy the requirements of section 2A(2).[54]

6-70   Under that subsection, a tribunal may not hear an equal value claim if there is a job evaluation scheme in existence as defined in section 1(5)[55] if there are no reasonable grounds for determining that "the study was made on a system which discriminates on grounds of sex." An evaluation scheme discriminates on grounds of sex under section 2A(3) where:

> "the difference, or coincidence, of values set by that system on different demands under the same or different headings is not justifiable irrespective of the sex of the person on whom those demands are made."

6-71   It should be noted that on the statutory language, an applicant who seeks to challenge the results of an existing job evaluation scheme by securing the report of an independent expert on the value of her work would have to establish only an arguable case that the allotment of different points for the two jobs was made under a system which discriminates on grounds of sex, *i.e.* if she has anything more than a "hopeless case," the tribunal must proceed to appoint an independent expert and receive his report before deciding whether the woman and her male comparator are performing work of equal value.

6-72   What of a job evaluation which is on its face neutral, but which is thought to have an adverse impact upon the valuation of the jobs done by women, a far more common and realistic case than a scheme corrupted by elements of direct discrimination? The EOC, in its pamphlet *Job Evaluation Schemes Free of Sex Bias*,[56] argues that a scheme which tends systematically to attribute a lower value to the jobs done by women than to those done by men,

---

[54] Where there is an existing job evaluation scheme section 2A(2) provides that there shall "be no reasonable grounds for determining that the work of a woman is of equal value as mentioned in s.1(2)(c) above if: "(a) that work and the work of the man in question have been given different values in a study such as is mentioned in s.1(5) above; and (b) there are no reasonable grounds for determining that the evaluation contained in the study was (within the meaning of subs. 3, below) made on a system which discriminates on grounds of sex." Subsection 3 provides that: "An evaluation contained in a study such as is mentioned in s.1(5) above is made on a system which discriminates on a grounds of sex where a difference, or coincidence, between values set by that system on different demands under the same or different headings is not justifiable irrespective of the sex of the person on whom those demands are made."

[55] See above para. 6–60.

[56] "*Job Evaluation Schemes Free of Sex Bias,*" (EOC, Manchester 1984) and see the comments in n. 16.

must be tainted by indirect discrimination in the choice of factors to be ranked and/or in the weighting of those factors. This is clearly a circular argument for it presumes that the jobs done by men and women in the particular situation are necessarily of equal value and that an unbiased scheme would merely reflect that state of affairs. There is no Olympian height from which one can look down to decide whether or not a given job evaluation incorporates a correct weighting of the skills and attributes possessed or demanded of men and women. All job evaluation is ultimately subjective; it is merely more systematic than non-evaluated pay structures. This accounts for the fact that almost all schemes incorporate an element of negotiation between management and employees to ensure the acceptability of the results. A job evaluation scheme which produces unacceptable results, results which do not create a framework in which the workforce can assent to the resulting structure of differentials is not achieving the purposes for which it was undertaken.

All job evaluation will therefore incorporate the values of the surrounding culture to a greater or lesser extent, and it can only be as that culture becomes more sensitive to issues of discrimination and places greater weight upon what are seen as typically female skills or qualities, that there will be an opportunity to upgrade the values attributed to "women's work." Thus, it would not be surprising to find that a study might undervalue skills learnt in the home, such as cooking, sewing or child care, with the result that jobs which incorporate those skills (and such jobs are typically undertaken by women), would receive a lower ranking under a job evaluation scheme when compared with typically male jobs of similar skill levels. This would be even more likely where the study used a rank order or paired comparison method, which relies upon an intuitive sense of the relative values of a series of benchmark jobs, to determine the weighting to be given to the different job factors. Such a study would be simply reproducing and rationalising existing perceptions of the value of different skills. It is just because such schemes reproduce the values of the surrounding culture that there is unlikely to be any discriminatory intent in such a situation, although this does preclude the bringing of an equal value claim.[57]   **6-73**

These problems were demonstrated in the German case of *Rummler v. Dato-Druck GmbH*.[58] In this case, which was brought under the provisions of Article 1(2) of the Equal Pay Directive, a female employee challenged the use of absolute muscular effort as a criteria in the construction of the firm's job evaluation scheme. Article 1(2) stipulates that a job classification scheme "must be based on the same criteria for men and women and so drawn up as to exclude any discrimination on the grounds of sex." The employee contended that the scheme contravened Article 1(2) because it did not measure the heaviness of the work relative to the strength of the person performing the task, *i.e.* women's lower levels of strength should have been taken into account. This argument was rejected on the grounds that it would be discriminatory to rely on criteria which were not impartial between the sexes. The ECJ, however, held that although a job classification scheme may utilise a   **6-74**

---

[57] See *R. v. Birmingham City Council, ex p. EOC.* [1988] I.R.L.R. 430, C.A.
[58] [1987] I.R.L.R. 32, cited by Dillon L.J. in *Bromley v. H.J. Quick Ltd* see above, in rehearsing the need for an objective approach to job evaluation, whilst admitting that a subjective element was inevitable.

criterion more commonly found amongst men than women, the Directive requires that job classification schemes be designed so as to take into account the particular characteristics of both men and women and that it is for national courts to assess whether the scheme allows fair account to be taken of all the criteria. Thus, a job evaluation scheme may be held to be discriminatory if it fails to take into account manual dexterity (often seen as characteristic of the work done by women) whilst giving recognition to gross physical effort, which is usually thought to be more characteristic of manual work undertaken by men. For a detailed discussion of the components of a gender neutral comparison system see the Ontario case of *Haldimand Norfolk (No. 6)*.[59]

6-75   A study is said to be discriminatory where the values set under that study are not justifiable irrespective of the sex of the person on whom the demands are made. Seemingly, any objection that the values set by the system are not justifiable would suffice; the requirement that the system is not justifiable because it incorporates an element of either direct or indirect discrimination is implicit.

6-76   The requirement that job evaluation schemes be justifiable irrespective of the sex of the person concerned is clearly a matter of fact. The test for justifiability in the Equal Pay Act[60] is that enunciated by the ECJ in *Bilka-Kaufhaus GmbH v. Weber von Hartz*[61] that a policy or practice which has a discriminatory effect is only justifiable if "the means chosen for achieving that objective correspond to a real need on the part of the undertaking, are appropriate with a view to achieving the objective in question and are necessary to that end."[62] Thus the objectives enshrined in the job evaluation scheme in question must be objectively necessary to the undertaking and appropriate to that end, if the net effect of the procedures adopted is to create a requirement with which a considerably smaller proportion of women than men can comply if they are to achieve a favourable evaluation. The objective of creating a rational and acceptable pay structure via job evaluation would normally be justifiable according to this test if the scheme produced results which were within the band of outcomes which a reasonable employer might accept.[63] In sum, gross and obvious distortions which clearly undervalued the contribution of women workers to the enterprise might not be justifiable. Where the results fall within that area in which reasonable and informed persons might legitimately disagree, the results are likely to be seen as justifiable.

6-77   The blocking effect of a job evaluation scheme may lead to hurried attempts to institute one, as in *Dibro Ltd v. Hore*[64] where the EAT held that even if the study was commenced after the initiation of proceedings, section 2A(2) still provides that there shall be no reasonable grounds for determining that

---

[59] (1991) *Pay Equity Reports* 105.
[60] See chapter 2 for a full discussion of the concept of justifiability in the SDA, s.1(b)(ii).
[61] [1986] I.R.L.R. 317.
[62] At p. 320.
[63] Cf. "Pay Equity—Surprising Answers to Hard Questions" in *Challenge*, (May/June 1987), pp. 45–51, in which Barbara F. Bergman argues as a result of studies of the American concept of "comparable worth", that salary structures do routinely undervalue those jobs in which women predominate.
[64] [1990] I.R.L.R. 129 and see *Henderson v. Jaguar Cars* EOR, DCLD 11, I.T.

the work of a man and woman are of equal value. The EAT held that such evidence is admissible even after the independent expert's report has been received, right up to the point of decision on the equal value claim. It follows that if employers do not like the independent expert's report, they could commence their own job evaluation before the tribunal makes its decision. The existence of an analytical job evaluation scheme which was untainted by discrimination would be a complete defence under section 2(A)2. The EOC has recommended that job evaluation schemes should no longer be a bar to equal value claims, but simply be admissible as evidence, on a par with the report of a specially commissioned expert. The evidence may provide a complete defence, but the present law that it automatically does so must be wrong.

Like work and work of equal value

The other obstacle which has been seen as preventing an equal value claim **6-78** is the requirement in section 1(2) that an equal value claim can only be brought under that subsection where a woman is employed on work to which neither section 1(2)(a) or (b) applies, in other words, which is neither like work nor work which has been rated equivalent to that of a man in the same employment. Although the Court of Appeal in *Pickstone v. Freemans plc*[65] held that the words of section 1(2)(c) are plain, and unambiguously preclude an equal value claim where there is a man engaged upon like work with the applicant, the House of Lords[66] construed this provision as applying only where the woman sought to make comparison with a man who was himself engaged in like work. The House of Lords held that s.1(2)(c) must be read as if it provided "where a woman is employed on work which, not being work to which paragraph (a) or (b) above applies *as between the woman and the man with whom she claims equality.*" (Words in italics implied by the House of Lords). This construction achieves the result required if the 1983 Regulations[67] are to give effect to the decision of the ECJ in *Commission of the European Communities v. United Kingdom*,[68] that the United Kingdom was obliged under the EEC Treaty and the Equal Pay Directive to provide an unqualified right to claim equal pay for work of equal value. Lord Templeman stated the procedure to be followed in cases brought under section 1(2)(c) as follows[69]:

> "To prevent exploitation of para. (c) the Tribunal must decide in the first instance whether the complainant and the man with whom she seeks

---

[65] [1987] I.R.L.R. 218, C.A. The Court of Appeal took the view that the words of Section 1(2)(c) were unambiguous and precluded such a claim, in spite of the fact that the result would be that the U.K. would thereby have failed fully to implement its obligations under the Equal Pay Directive. Consequently the Court of Appeal held that as the Equal Pay Directive had been held in *Jenkins v. Kingsgate* (see above at n. 67) to clarify but not in any way to alter or amend the principle of equal pay expressed in Article 119, and that the inequality in pay between the claimant and her comparator could be identified without recourse to further national measures, as required by the ECJ in *Worringham v. Lloyds Bank* (No. 69/80) [1981] I.C.R. 558 ECJ, there was therefore a directly enforceable Community right to pursue an equal value claim in such circumstances, notwithstanding the wording of section 1(2)(c).
[66] [1988] I.R.L.R. 357, H.L.
[67] S.I. 1983 No. 1794.
[68] Case 61/81, (1982) I.C.R. 578.
[69] *Per* Templeman L.J., at p. 362.

parity are engaged on 'like Work' under para. (a). If para. (a) applies
no ACAS report is required. If para. (a) does not apply, then the Tribunal
considers whether para. (b) applies to the complainant and the man with
whom she seeks parity; if so, the Tribunal can only proceed under para.
(c) if the job evaluation study obtained for the purposes of para. (b) is
itself discriminatory. If para. (b) applies then, again, no ACAS report
is necessary. If paras. (a) and (b) do not apply, the Tribunal must next
consider whether there are reasonable grounds for determining that the
work of the complainant and the work of the man with whom she seeks
parity is of equal value. If the Tribunal are not so satisfied, then no
ACAS report is required . . . Para. (c) enables a claim to equal pay as
against a specific man to be made without injustice to an employer.
When a woman claims equal pay for work of equal value, she specifies
the man with whom she claims equal value. If the work of the woman
is work to which para. (a) or (b) applies in relation to that man, then
the woman cannot proceed under para. (c) and cannot obtain a report
from an ACAS expert. In my opinion there must be applied in para. (c)
after the word 'applies' the words 'as between the woman and the man
with whom she claims equality.' This construction is consistent with
Community law. The employers' construction is inconsistent with Community law and creates a form of permitted discrimination without
rhyme or reason.''

The equal value claim

6-79   The requirement under section 1(2)(c) is for the Tribunal to decide:

> "whether the woman is employed on work which . . . is, in terms of
> the demands made on her (for instance under such headings as effort,
> skill and decision) of equal value to that of a man employed in the same
> employment.''

To accomplish this comparison the procedure calls for the Tribunal to commission a report from an independent expert, unless, as explained above,
there are no reasonable grounds for determining that the work is of equal
value. This section has been widely interpreted by commentators as calling
for the use of ''analytical'' methods of job evaluation,[70] a view confirmed
by the Court of Appeal in *Bromley v. H & J Quick Ltd.*[71]

6-80   An employee who is found to be doing work of a higher value than her
comparators is not to be frustrated in her attempt to achieve equal pay, following the decision of the ECJ in *Murphy v. Bord Telecom Eirann.*[72]

Genuine material differences

6-81   In equal value cases it is open to applicant and her chosen comparator are
due to a genuine material difference other than a difference of sex, under

---

[70] See above para. 6–60.
[71] [1988] I.R.L.R. 249.
[72] [1988] I.R.L.R. 267 and see *Wells v. F. Smales & Sons Ltd* (unreported), Case No. 10701/
84, I.T.

section 1(3)(b), prior to the commissioning of a report from an independent expert.[73] Prior to the amendment of the 1993 Rules of Procedure in 1994, the employer could argue for a material difference prior to the commissioning of the independent experts' report, without prejudice to further consideration of the issue after the tribunal reviews the report, but this is no longer the case.

The employer is provided with a defence in equal pay cases under section 1(2)(a) or (b), or in equal value cases under section 1(2)(c), that the variation in pay "is genuinely due to a material factor which is not the difference of sex." The statute further provides that in cases occurring under section 1(2)(a) or (b), *i.e.* in like work cases or where the work has been rated as equivalent, that the factor must be "a material difference between the woman's case and the man's."   **6-82**

The difference between the wording in equal value and other equal pay cases is related to the dictum established by Lord Denning in *Clay Cross (Quarry Services) Ltd v. Fletcher*[74] that "a difference between her case and his" referred to a difference in the personal equation of the woman as compared to the man, to what appertained to her in her job and to him in his. That case was concerned with the situation where a man had been taken on to perform the same function as an existing woman employee, but because the man, who was the only suitable applicant, would not come for any less than he was already earning, he was paid more than the woman. The Court of Appeal rejected the appeal to extrinsic forces and stated that: **6-83**

> "An employer cannot avoid his obligations under the Act by saying: 'I paid him more because he asked for more.' or 'I paid her less because she was willing to come for less.' If any such excuse were permitted, the Act would become a dead letter. Those are the very reasons why there was unequal pay before the statute. They are the very circumstances in which the statute was intended to operate."[75]

This distinction has, however, been overruled in *Rainey v. Greater Glasgow Health Board*,[76] in which the House of Lords applied the conclusions reached by the European Court of Justice in *Bilka Kaufhaus v. Weber von Hartz*.[77] In *Rainey* the House of Lords did not follow *Clay Cross*, with its restriction of material factors to those which are rooted in the personal equation between the employees. Lord Keith held[78]:   **6-84**

> "The difference must be 'material,' which I would construe as meaning 'significant and relevant,' and it must be between 'her case and his.' Consideration of a person's case must necessarily involve consideration of the circumstances of that case. These may well go beyond what is not very happily described as 'the personal equation' . . . In particular,

---

[73] See Industrial Tribunals (Rules of Procedure) Regulations (S.I. 1993 No. 2687) reg. 8(2E) as amended.
[74] [1979] I.C.R. 1; [1978] I.R.L.R. 361, C.A.
[75] *per* Denning M.R., at 4.
[76] [1987] I.R.L.R. 26, H.L.
[77] [1986] I.R.L.R. 317, ECJ.
[78] At p. 29.

where there is no question of intentional sex discrimination whether direct or indirect, a difference which is connected with economic factors affecting the efficient carrying on of the employer's business or other activity may be relevant.''

Lord Keith drew support for this view of section 1(3) from the decision of the European Court in *Bilka Kaufhaus* in that a policy which has the effect of creating a pay differential between men and women undertaking like work (here by giving pensions only to full-time workers) may only be justified:

"if the national court finds that the means chosen by *Bilka* meet a genuine need of the enterprise, that they are suitable for attaining the objective pursued by the enterprise and are necessary for that purpose.''

This objective standard, though enunciated in the equal pay context of Article 119, has also been applied by the ECJ in the context of equal treatment. The test in *Bilka* of objective justification untainted by sex discrimination can be seen as comprising the need to identify a genuine need on the part of the discriminator, which can be met by suitable and necessary means.

Lord Keith concluded that the true meaning and effect of Article 119 in this context is the same as that attributed to section 1(3), and furthermore argued that there was no difference between the need to demonstrate objectively justified grounds of difference for purposes of section 1(3) and the requirement for justification in cases of indirect discrimination under section 1(1)(b)(i) of the Sex Discrimination Act 1975.

The first requirement of the test of justification in *Bilka* is that the practice in question shall "correspond to a real need on the part of the undertaking". The second requirement is that the practice adopted shall be a suitable method of attaining the objective in question. According to the ECJ this is a matter for the national court to decide, although in some instances this does not have appeared to have precluded the ECJ from going on to consider the appropriateness of the policies in question.

Justification at enterprise level

Discriminatory pay practices may occur at job, enterprise, or government policy level. At job level such matters as differences in working conditions, the level of mechanisation, the requirements for physical strength or manual dexterity, or the capacity to organise and plan one's work were recognised as potential justifications in *Royal Copenhagen*.[79] At the enterprise level, the ECJ in *Kowalska*[80] held that collective agreements fall within the potential ambit of Article 119 and it is for the national court to judge whether a provision in a collective agreement which is in practice discriminatory is objectively justified. Where it is not justified the disadvantaged employees must be treated in the same way and have the same system applied to them as other workers, in proportion to their hours. In *Enderby v. Frenchay Health Authority*[81] the question was referred to the ECJ as to whether, if a discrep-

---

[79] Case C-400/93, [1995] I.R.L.R. 648, ECJ.
[80] Case 33/89, *Kowalska v. Hamburg*: [1990] E.C.R. 1–2591
[81] Case 127/92, [1993] I.R.L.R. 591. Noted by Fredman, II/J, 23, 1, pp. 37–41 who remarks on the focus on results, rather than processes, and the priority given to gender equality over the autonomy of wage setting mechanisms.

ancy in pay exists between a predominantly male and female group of workers who are presumed to be engaged in work of equal value, such a difference in pay can be justified by reference to the fact that the pay scales concerned were negotiated in separate collective bargaining fora, each of which was not discriminatory in itself. Essentially the question was raised as to whether the historical structure and results of collective bargaining can justify unequal pay, or simply explain the existing structure of differentials. The Advocate General concluded that

> "Since justification of the discriminatory result is called for, it cannot be sufficient to explain the causes leading to the discrimination. In particular, references to historical and social reasons cannot . . . be recognised as factors which are objectively justified and unconnected with discrimination on grounds of sex. The historical and social context of a 'purely female profession' is most probably sex related. If an explanatory approach were accepted as sufficient justification, that would lead to the perpetuation of sex roles in working life. Instead of the equality of treatment which is sought, there would be afforded a legal argument for maintaining the status quo,"[82]

The Court concluded that such an explanation of the differences was not a sufficient objective justification.[83] In *British Coal Corporation v. Smith*[83a] the House of Lords held that the mere existence of different pay structures and negotiating machinery did not constitute a justification in itself.

The Court also concluded in *Enderby* that pay inequalities may be justified in whole or in part by the impact of market forces. Where the national court can identify the proportion of a pay differential which can be attributed to market forces, it must accept that the pay differential in question is objectively justified to the extent of that proportion. Thus although national courts are bound to apply the principle of proportionality, it will often be easier for the employer than the employee to muster the relevant labour market data and to offer a favourable interpretation. As this process is a limitation upon the fundamental principle of equal pay in Community law, courts are bound to examine such justifications critically.

There is a distinction between finding that the cause of the difference in pay is not tainted by sex discrimination and concluding that the variation was due to a material factor other than sex, as section 1(3) requires. In *Barber v. NCR Manufacturing*[84] clerical workers whose tasks were directly related to the activities of the shop floor worked a 39 hour week, whilst other clerical staff worked only 35. The two groups were paid the same hourly rate, until in separate pay and hours negotiations the hours of the direct clerical workers were reduced to 38, without loss of gross pay. Basing themselves on the reasoning of the EAT in *Enderby* the majority in the Industrial Tribunal had held that the difference in hourly rate was justified, but Lord Coulsefield, upholding the appeal, held that although the difference in hourly rates was thereby explained, it was not justified by objective factors unrelated to sex,

---

[82] At point 48.
[83] The decision in *Reed Packaging v. Boozer and Everhurst* [1988] I.R.L.R. 322, EAT must therefore be doubted.
[83a] [1996] I.R.L.R. 404.
[84] [1993] I.R.L.R. 95, EAT.

i.e. there was no rational ground for the difference in hourly rates. The reasoning in *Barber v. NCR* could pose a considerable threat to agreements made through the process of collective bargaining which, whilst acceptable to the parties, nonetheless result in discrimination as between men and women which cannot be objectively justified as constituting necessary and appropriate means of achieving the needs of the business.

It is, however, important for the respondent to ensure that any justification is not tainted by discrimination. This is especially true where the justification relied upon is that of the pressure of market forces, which may themselves result from the different position of the sexes in the labour market. In *Ratcliffe v. North Yorkshire County Council*[85] the respondent Council's Direct Service Organisation (DSO) was engaged in a compulsory competitive tendering (CCT) exercise, in relation to the provision of school dinners. The Council's activities were divided into nine areas and the contract for the first of these areas was lost to a private contractor, who paid less than accepted local government rates. In anticipation of the fact that the other eight contracts might also be lost, the DSO dismissed the applicant school dinner ladies and re-engaged them at rates competitive with those paid by the competitor catering contractor. The result was that the dinner ladies employed by the DSO received less pay than male workers on the same grade in other areas of the Council's work. As these grades were set by job evaluation techniques, there was no question as to the ladies receiving lower pay for work of equivalent value. The DSO attempted to justify this discrepancy under section 1(3) by the argument that it was necessary in order to compete and that the female workforce would accept the reduction for lack of any effective alternative in a predominantly rural area. The Industrial Tribunal found, however, that the proffered justification was tainted with sex discrimination arising from the general perception, certainly current in North Yorkshire, that a woman's place is primarily in the home and that work must fit around this fact of life. The Court of Appeal held that the pay discrepancy was genuinely due to market forces, as applied by the DSO, whatever the reasons why the private contractor had been able to pay lower wages. Lord Slynn, giving the judgement of the House of Lords, held that the industrial tribunal was entitled to come to the conclusion that the difference in pay was due to the difference of sex, even though there were two men working in the section. Lord Slynn was convinced that this was the very kind of discrimination which the Act sought to remove. The EOC has shown in its 1995 report on *The Gender Impact of CCT in Local Government* that CCT commonly has an adverse impact on women's wages, so that the reasoning in the *North Yorks.* case has wide potential application.

Although the *North Yorks.* case was decided under the British Equal Pay Act, it is consonant with decisions of the ECJ under Article 119. In *Arbeiterwohlfahrt der Stadt Berlin eV v. Botel* part-time workers received less by way of compensation under a statutorily regulated scheme of compensation for attending staff committee training sessions than did full-timers. This discrepancy arose because part-timers received no compensation in respect of hours for which they would not normally have been at work, although they gave up some of their free time to attend. As there were far more female part-timers on the committee than male, this practice was found to be indirectly discriminatory. The employer argued that as the purpose of the payment

85 [1995] I.R.L.R. 439, H.L., [1994] I.R.L.R. 342, C.A.

was to compensate for wages lost in respect of hours not worked whilst attending the training sessions, the difference in compensation levels was objectively justifiable. The ECJ held[86] that:

> "(S)uch a situation is by its nature very likely to dissuade the category of part-time employees, of whom an undoubtedly larger proportion are women, from acting as a member of the staff committee or from acquiring the knowledge and skills required by that office, making the representation of this category of employees by qualified members of the staff committees all the more difficult. To that extent, the difference in treatment in question cannot be considered as justified by objective factors unrelated to any discrimination on grounds of sex, unless the Member state in question can establish the contrary before the national court."

Under section 1(3) the respondent is required to prove not only that the variation is genuinely due to a material factor, but also that the material factor is not due to the difference in sex, according to the EAT in *The Financial Times Ltd v. Byrne (No. 2)*.[87] Although this involves the respondent in proving a negative, it is for the employer to satisfy the tribunal on the balance of probabilities that each part of the section is established. As Wood J. makes clear in the *Financial Times* case, this may result in a trial within a trial where the applicant alleges that the material factor put forward is tainted by sex discrimination. Should the applicant choose to call evidence to establish that the respondent's alleged material factor is infected with discrimination, that evidence will need to be tested by the normal principles as to the burden of proof in discrimination cases under section 1 of the SDA.[88] **6-85**

Whilst the EAT in *Davies v. McCartneys*[89] held that there was no limit to the factors upon which a respondent may rely under section 1(3) provided they are genuine and not attributable to sex, it is submitted not only that such factors must be capable of objective justification, but also that they cannot encompass the actual constitution of the jobs in issue. Matters such as the demands of the job are properly part of the enquiry as to whether there is like work or work of equal value which it is inappropriate to consider at the stage of the section 1(3) defence, especially if that point is taken before equal work or equal value is established. **6-86**

In *Hayward v. Cammell Laird*[90] the House of Lords considered the question as to whether a difference in pension rights or sick pay might constitute a genuine material difference between men and women engaged upon work of **6-87**

---

[86] Case 360/90, [1992] I.R.L.R. 423 at 426.

[87] [1992] I.R.L.R. 163, EAT.

[88] In a number of tribunal cases the material factor defence put forward by the employer has been rejected as being trainted by sex discrimination, as in *Todd v. Lloyds Bank*, EOR, DCLD 2, *Smith v. British Coal*, EOR, DCLD 7 (separate bargaining structures); *Grieg and Grieg v. Hazell, Watson and Viney*, EOR, DCLD 6 (employer feebleness in resisting all male printing chapel): *Lucas v. West Sussex County Council* EOR, DCLD 7 (market forces): *Fleming v. Short Bros* EOR, DCLD 9 (negotiated bonus scheme).

[89] [1989] I.R.L.R. 439, EAT and see also *Maher v. Vauxhall Motors*, EOR, DCLD 10 in which the Industrial Tribunal found that the operation of the company's grading scheme and the question of equal value were so intimately related that it was impossible meaningfully to deal with the former before the latter.

[90] [1988] I.R.L.R. 257.

equal value, where the men enjoyed a higher hourly rate of pay. In an interesting *obiter dicta* (the argument, not having been raised in the Tribunal, was not open to the employers on appeal) the Lord Chancellor held that for section 1(3) to operate, the unfavourable term in the woman's contract would have to be due to the existence of the more favourable term, *i.e.* in the words of the section it has to be "genuinely due to a material factor which is not a difference of sex."[91]

Goff L.J. observed that it may be possible to argue that the difference was due to the existence of two separate pay structures wholly devoid of sex discrimination, but where discrimination is embedded in a pay structure, then that pay structure will not constitute a material factor which is not a difference of sex.

6-88 An employer may argue that a grading scheme which results in pay differences between men and women, so long as it operates irrespective of sex, may constitute a material difference, even though the scheme is not based upon job evaluation.[92] Such schemes are likely to be examined critically, however. The burden of proving that such a scheme is not tainted by discrimination lies upon the employer, who will be subject to the normal standard of proof in civil cases.[93] Likewise, an employer who protects the pay of an employee on a job transfer or reorganisation, *i.e.* the employee's pay is protected by a "red circle," may argue that such a practice constitutes a genuine material difference, so long as the "red circle" does not perpetuate previous discrimination.[94] Likewise, where under Article 119 a comparison is made over time between successive employments, changed circumstances may constitute a genuine material difference.[95]

6-89 A genuine material factor must be current at the time of the claim. If it is rooted in circumstances which no longer obtain, it will cease to be material as a ground on which unequal pay can be resisted by the employer. In *Benveniste v. University of Southampton*,[96] the plaintiff had been appointed in 1981 at a time of great financial stringency in British universities. For this reason, Ms Benveniste was appointed six points below the point on the salary scale at which a person of her age would normally have been appointed. It was argued that this financial stringency was a genuine material factor within the terms of section 1(3), but Neil L. J. held that "the material difference between the appellant's case and the case of the comparators evaporated when the financial constraints were removed"[97] in 1982. An analogy with

---

[91] At 261.
[92] See the dissenting opinion of May L.J. in *Leverton v. Clwyd County Council* [1968] I.R.L.R. 239 at 244.
[93] *National Vulcan Engineering Insurance Group Ltd v. Wade* [1977] I.C.R. 800, [1976] I.R.L.R. 406, EAT.
[94] *Methven & Musolik v. Cow Industrial Polymers Ltd* [1980] I.C.R. 463, I.R.L.R. 289, C.A. *Charles Early and Marriot (Whitney) Ltd v. Smith* [1977] I.C.R. 700: *Snoxell v. Vauxhall Motors Ltd* [1977] I.R.L.R. 121, EAT.
[95] *Albion Shipping Agency Ltd v. Arnold* [1981] I.R.L.R. 525, EAT. But where a "red circle" has persisted over time it may not still constitute a s.1(3) defence. See *Outlook Supplies v. Parry* [1978] I.R.L.R. 12, EAT.
[96] [1989] I.R.L.R. 122, C.A; and see *The Post Office v. Page*, unreported, EAT No. 554/87.
[97] At 131. And see *Swift v. William Freeman*, EOR, DCLD 1 on the rejection of anachronistic attendance bonus which had been in fact assimilated into normal pay, and also *Fleming v. Short Bros* EOR, DCLD 9 in which a different and separately negotiated bonus paid only to a largely male group was held to have been tainted by discrimination.

"red circle" cases was rejected and although no direct criticism of this practice was offered, it must follow from the reasoning of *Benveniste* that all differences ground in historical circumstances should be examined critically to see if those reasons remain material at the present time. A difference in pay which results from a genuine grading error is not a material factor defence[98] because such a mistake cannot constitute objectively justified grounds.

Justification of direct discrimination in equal pay cases

Neither Article 119 nor the Equal Pay Act distinguish in terms between direct and indirect discrimination. In *Enderby* the ECJ was asked by the Court of Appeal to address itself to the question whether, in the absence of an indirectly discriminatory requirement or condition precluding speech therapists from enjoying the higher rewards enjoyed by the comparator groups, there was an obligation on the respondent to justify any differences in pay. According to the ECJ it is sufficient for a *prima facie* case of discrimination if there is a valid difference between the pay of predominantly male and female groups where the two jobs are of equal value, casting the burden on the employer to show that there are objective reasons for the difference in pay. This results oriented approach does not explicitly distinguish between direct and indirect discrimination with regard to pay. Where the respondent is able to adduce objective non-gender related reasons for the difference in pay, it is therefore more helpful to conceive this as a situation in which direct discrimination based on gender or a gender related criterion is not present. If the difference in pay arises from a non-discriminatory reason then no direct discrimination has occurred, and no question of justification arises. If the employer cannot bring his reasons within *Bilka*, he will have failed to discharge the burden of proof in *Enderby* and discrimination will have been established. On this view *Bilka* provides the standard by which it is possible to judge whether the reasons adduced by the respondent are sufficient to take the facts of the case outside the field of application of the principle of equal pay, *i.e.* did the state of affairs result from measures which are an appropriate and necessary response to a genuine business need. If the reasons put forward are themselves tainted with discrimination, they cannot meet this test.

Where there is like work or work of equal value an employer must show that there is a genuine material difference under the Equal Pay Act. In *Ratcliffe v. North Yorks. C.C.* Lord Slynn held that the Equal Pay Act must be interpreted without bringing in the distinction between direct and indirect discrimination, the Act requiring only that unequal pay be demonstrated for like work or work of equal value. Lord Slynn rested his approach on the words of the statute and did not consider Article 119, but the above analysis developed in the context of Community law could equally be applied to the Equal Pay Act. The reason for the difference in pay in the *North Yorks.* case was found by the industrial tribunal to be the labour market situation of women, transmitted to the DSO via the mechanism of competitive tendering. As the supposed readiness of the dinner ladies to accept lower pay was a

6-90

---

[98] *McPherson v. Rathgael Centre for Children and Young People* [1991] I.R.L.R. 216, N.I.C.A. See also *Duffy v. Barclays Bank* EOR, DCLD 10 in which a grading scheme, though bona fide, was not properly applied.

reflection of the labour market situation of women, the decision was ultimately founded on gender and therefore discriminatory. If the reasons put
forward by the employer had not been tainted with sex there would have
been no direct discrimination, because the ground of the employer's decision
would not have been gender related. In *Tyldesley v. TML Plastics*[99] the EAT
attempts to confine the identity between the test in s.1(3) and the *Bilka* standard of justification to cases of indirect discrimination but this is contrary to
the eschewal of this distinction by Lord Slynn in equal pay cases.

Justification of social policy

6-91   In *Rinner Kühn*,[1] the German Government had argued that the exclusion of
part-timers from entitlement to German statutory sick pay was justified
because such workers "are not integrated in and connected with the undertaking in a way comparable to that of other workers."

These arguments were dismissed by the Court of Justice as "generalised
statements", not meeting the objective standards of justification enunciated
in *Bilka*. A legislative provision, which in practice gives rise to discriminatory
effects, may only be justified where the Member State is "in a position to
establish that the means selected correspond to an objective necessary for its
social policy and are appropriate and necessary to the attainment of that
objective", as in the social security case of *Commission v. Belgium*[2] in which
the ECJ concluded that supplements paid to those with responsibility to support a family fulfilled a legitimate objective of social policy.

In the U.K. there have been several recent high profile judicial review
cases in which plaintiffs have sought to establish that British statutory provisions were incompatible with E.C. law. Amongst these has been *R. v. Secretary of State for Employment, ex p. EOC*, which concerned the service qualification for part-timers as regards redundancy "pay" and unfair dismissal
and *R. v. Secretary of State for Employment, ex p. Seymour-Smith and Perez*
(see chapter 2 for the facts and further discussion of the issues raised in
both of these cases) which concerned the two year qualification period for
redundancy "pay" and unfair dismissal. The arguments advanced by H.M.
Government in both cases to justify the existing legislative arrangements,
that they stimulated the growth of employment opportunities for women,
whilst accepted as a legitimate aim of public policy, were held not to have
been substantiated on the facts. This led Neil L.J. in *Seymour-Smith* to
observe that "any proposed legislation, particularly in the social field, which
may have a disparate impact between the sexes, will have to be examined
before it is introduced to see whether any consequential disparity can be
objectively justified."

The observation by Neil L.J. may prove to be overstated in view of the
subsequent decision by the European Court of Justice in *Nolte v. Hanover*,[3]
in which the German government sought to justify the discriminatory impact
of the exclusion of "minor employment" (fewer than 16 hours a week and
with earnings less than one seventh of average earnings) from statutory old

---

[99] [1996] I.R.L.R. 395.
[1] Case 171/88, *Rinner Kühn v. FwwGmbH* [1989] E.C.R. 2743.
[2] [1991] I.R.L.R. 393, ECJ; [1993] I.R.L.R. 10.
[3] Case C–317/93 [1996] I.R.L.R. 225; [1996] All E.R. (EC) 212.

age and invalidity insurance. The ECJ held that "in the current state of Community law, social policy is a matter for the Member States to choose the measures capable of achieving the aim of their social and employment policy. In exercising their competence, the Member States have a broad margin of discretion."

The Court accepted the justification put forward by the German government that there is a social demand for "minor employment" to which it should respond appropriately. To do otherwise would, in the German government's view, be to drive such work into the black economy and stimulate circumventing devices, such as false self-employment. This policy was held to fall within the margin of discretion of the Member States and to be objectively unrelated to any discrimination based on sex. In *Nolte*, the ECJ seems to be accepting the type of generalised arguments it rejected in *Rinner Kühn* and which the Lords rejected in the *EOC* case. The Court of Justice would appear to have struck a different balance between the defence of the fundamental principle of equality between men and women and the susceptibilities of the Member States which are enshrined in the notion of subsidiarity. Thus *Nolte* may spell the end of the review of national social policies for their conformity with Community discrimination law.

7 INDUSTRIAL TRIBUNAL PROCEEDINGS AND REMEDIES

7-01 In this chapter we shall cover various matters, concerned with the bringing of tribunal proceedings relating specifically to discrimination, which are not otherwise dealt with; and with remedies in the industrial tribunals. Thus we shall not attempt to deal with matters of a procedural nature which might affect industrial tribunal cases generally, but only those where discrimination cases throw up specific issues. Moreover, one matter in particular which involves interlocutory applications, namely discovery and inspection of documents, is dealt with not here but in the chapter on proof, as is material on the statutory questionnaires.

Assistance with proceedings

7-02 Legal aid is not available for representation at tribunal proceedings, although the cost of being represented at such proceedings can be considerable. This is particularly true in equal value cases, where the procedure is longer and where employers frequently engage their own expert witness. The cost and complexity of such proceedings are apt to deter applicants who cannot call on the backing of their trade union or the EOC. Both the EOC and the CRE (but not the National Disability Council) have powers to support litigants in tribunal proceedings[1] but have only limited budgets for this purpose. We deal with this function of the Commissions in chapter 9. Neither body supports fully more than a small proportion of the cases where their assistance is sought, although each helps with preliminary steps in many more cases. Both Commissions have published guidance documents to help litigants[2]. Some other organisations such as Women Against Sexual Harassment, unions, and law centres offer some support. Because of the difficulties of bringing discrimination cases, calls for legal aid to be available have been made in many quarters.[3]

7-03 Frequently employers are insured for the costs of defending discrimination

---

[1] SDA, s.75: RRA, s.66.
[2] *How to Prepare a Case for an Industrial Tribunal* (EOC); Race cases in *Tribunals A Guide to Bringing Cases* (CRE).
[3] They are summarised in the CRE's second *Review of the Act* document (CRE, September 1992).

claims. We hope that insurers are insisting on proper employment practices as a condition of granting the insurance. It also sometimes happens that employees find that they are covered to bring discrimination proceedings under legal expenses insurance that they have taken out. Since these policies are sometimes sold as add-on policies to household insurance, their existence may have been forgotten and legal advisers could help by enquiring as to insurance.

In practice moral support from a friend or colleague is also very helpful, as it can be a lonely experience to take a case. There will almost inevitably be times in a long case when morale flags, particularly when so much of the respondents' evidence in the general type of discrimination case will be directed at pointing out the applicant's failings to explain the less favourable treatment. This sort of evidence can come as a terrible shock, no matter that it is presaged by the respondent's written case.   **7-04**

Restriction of reporting and private hearings

Sections 40 and 41 of the Trade Union Reform and Employment Rights Act 1993 introduced restrictions on reporting in cases involving sexual misconduct and led to new rules for tribunals and the EAT in the event of an appeal. Under Rule 14 of the I.T. 1993 rules a restricted reporting order can be made at any time up to the promulgation of the decision either on application of a party on notice or of its own motion.   **7-05**

Section s 62 and 63 of the Disability Discrimination Act 1995 give a power to make regulations to enable restricted reporting orders by industrial tribunals and the EAT in cases where evidence of a personal nature (i.e. of a medical or other intimate nature which might reasonably be assumed to be likely to cause significant embarrassment to the complainant) is likely to be heard. Application will be able to be made by the complainant, or the tribunal or EAT can act of its own motion. A tribunal should not use Rule 9(1) for these purposes.[4]

Rule 8 of the general I.T. rules also permit sitting in private in certain cases. First, where a Minister of the Crown directs where national security is involved. Second, where evidence could not be revealed without breaching an enactment. These instances may prove quite important in view of use of tribunals in armed forces sex and race employment cases (see end of this chapter). Third, where a matter of confidence is involved. Fourth, where substantial injury could be caused to an undertaking. These instances should be borne in mind in view of the rules on disclosure of documents in discrimination cases (see our chapter on proof) which can enable a party to see some very sensitive information. Particularly in the three last cases only the particular parts of the evidence will be so dealt with.

Parties

The typical case will be the employee or prospective or ex-employee against the employer. However, because there is a special defence available to   **7-06**

---

[4] *R. v. Southampton I.T., ex p. INS News Group Ltd* [1995] I.R.L.R. 247.

employers of taking reasonably practicable steps to prevent discrimination from occurring[5] it will often make sense to join as a party the person who is alleged to have done the act of discrimination. If the employer's defence succeeds, that person could still be held liable, whereas failure to join the person actually responsible may mean that discrimination could be proved without anybody being held liable for it. Joining the person alleged to be responsible is possible because the Acts say that such an employee is deemed to aid the doing of the act by the employer even in cases where the employer's defence succeeds, and knowingly aiding another person to do an unlawful act is itself unlawful.[6] This potential personal liability under the Acts may not be widely known. If the Commissions were to focus some publicity upon it, it might serve to make individual employees more interested in ensuring that discrimination does not occur, if only from self-interest.

7-07 Frequently, several applicants will claim discrimination arising out of substantially the same facts and consolidation of the proceedings will be ordered.[7] In equal pay claims in particular there may well be a very large number of originating applications. It will probably be best, if all the applicants can agree, to pick out certain claims as representative and proceed on those, leaving the others adjourned pending the outcome of the ''test cases''. Or the tribunal may order the selection of representative cases. In *Ashmore v. British Coal Corporation*,[8] representative claims (which arose after an interlocutory order was made when some 1,500 claims were presented) were heard and failed. An application to have heard one of the cases which had been stayed failed and it was struck out under the Rules of Procedure as an abuse of process as being vexatious.[9] The Court of Appeal upheld the striking-out, even though when originally stayed the Tribunal Chair had noted that the decision on the representative cases would not be binding on any others.

7-08 It also not uncommonly happens, especially when proceedings are protracted and the applicant remains employed by the respondent, that the applicant complains of victimisation and files a new originating application. The tribunal will normally order consolidation if the first hearing has not progressed too far, or alternatively that the same tribunal should hear the victimisation case later.

Time limits and proceedings

7-09 To hear a case a tribunal needs to have jurisdiction, which it will have if the case falls under the statutory provisions and is in time; or out of time but where it is considered by the tribunal to be just and equitable to hear the

---

[5] RRA, s.32(3) SDA, s.41(3) and s.58(5) DDA.
[6] RRA, s.33(1), (2) and SDA, s.42(1) and (2) and s.57(2) DDA. In *Barker v. Shahrokni* E.O.R. D.C.L.D. 28 p.11 it was held that each respondent is entitled to be told by the tribunal why he specifically is liable.
[7] Industrial Tribunals (Rules of Procedure) Regulations 1993, r.15.
[8] [1990] I.R.L.R. 283; [1990] I.C.R. 485, C.A. See also Rules of Procedure, r.14(3).
[9] Rules of Procedure, r.12(2)(e).

case. A preliminary hearing to deal with any time point is quite usual, either if the tribunal of its own motion sees a difficulty, or if a party raises it.

Time limit for presenting an application

Applications to an industrial tribunal in respect of discrimination cases other than equal pay claims must normally be presented to the tribunal within three months beginning when the act complained of was done.[10] The exceptions are: **7-10**

    (i) where the Commissions can bring proceedings in their own name, see chapter 8, below (*e.g.* in respect of an unlawful advertisement), when the period is six months; and

    (ii) where there is an appeal from a non-discrimination notice, see chapter 9, below, where the period is not later than six weeks after the notice is served; and

    (iii) where there is an armed forces exception which is in the process of being created; (see the end of this chapter).

Beware, statutory provisions as to time using the words "beginning when" something happens count that day as the first day of the time period, so effectively in the normal case the period is three months less one day. So if the act was done on June 25 the last day for commencing proceedings is September 24. It is different where the provision says "after" an event, as in the case of the appeal from a non-discrimination notice.

An application is "presented" when it arrives at the Central Office of Industrial Tribunals and it is not necessary for it to be registered by the office in order to say that proceedings have commenced. Whilst rule 1 requires that an application sets out the names of the parties and the relief sought, these stipulations are discretionary, rather than mandatory, so that where a complaint was made in respect of the rejection of the complainant for a particular post, it was not fatal that the application did not specify whether the complaint was of sex or race discrimination.[11] **7-11**

In *Quarcopoome v. Sock Shop Holdings Ltd*[12] it was held that a claim of race discrimination covers direct and indirect discrimination as well as victimisation, so that the time limit requirements do not apply to adding one or more of those at a later stage, merely the general approach to amendments where prejudice to a party is a primary consideration. Obviously the same applies under SDA, and there is no reason to suppose that a different line will be taken in respect of the three forms of discrimination under DDA (less favourable treatment, failure to make adjustments and victimisation). This approach makes sense because an applicant will often at the early stage not have a clear idea which head is appropriate. On the other hand the Court of Appeal has made clear in *Chapman v. Simon*[13] that a tribunal can only make a finding of discrimination on a claim made in the originating application or an amendment to it allowed by the tribunal, so it is important that, preferably before trial, (but if necessary at trial if something emerges which was not

---

[10] SDA, s.76(1); RRA, s.68(1); DDA, Sched. 3, Pt. 1.
[11] *Dodd v. British Telecom* [1988] I.R.L.R. 16; [1990] I.C.R. 116, EAT.
[12] [1995] I.R.L.R. 353, EAT.
[13] [1994] I.R.L.R. 124, C.A.

anticipated which changes the basis of the claim) an appropriate amendment is sought.

7-12   In relation to a dismissal, the relevant date is the date at which the contract is terminated, not that on which notice is given.[14] Whilst an act which occurred more than three months prior to the commencement of proceedings in an industrial tribunal cannot give rise to a cause of action, providing that the proceedings have been commenced within the time limits, acts prior to the time limit can be taken into account as similar fact type of evidence. In *Clarke v. Hampshire Electro-Plating Co Ltd*,[15] however, the EAT seemed to take the point that, where a black applicant is rejected at one date and a white comparator was appointed at a later date, the cause of action of the black applicant crystallised at the later date so as to set time running. They also held that the coming into existence of a comparator was a ground for exercising discretion, if an applicant reasonably took the view before then either that he had no cause of action or that it was unlikely he would establish a prima facie case without a comparator. This notion of crystallisation of the claim seems to be perceived as useful by tribunals, and the *Clarke* case is, we think, destined to be amongst those regularly referred to in decisions on jurisdiction.

7-13   In the case of a continuing act or an omission, the Race Relations Act, s.68(7), the Sex Discrimination Act, s.76 and the Disability Discrimination Act Schedule 3, Pt. 1 para. 3(3) provide that:

> "(a) where the inclusion of any term in a contract renders the making of the contract an unlawful act, that act shall be treated as extending throughout the duration of the contract, and
> (b) any act extending over a period shall be treated as done at the end of that period, and
> (c) a deliberate omission shall be treated as done when the person in question decided upon it,

and in the absence of evidence establishing the contrary, a person shall be taken for purposes of this section to have decided upon an omission when he does an act inconsistent with doing the omitted act or, if he has done no such inconsistent act, when the period expires within which he might reasonably have been expected to do the omitted act if it was to be done."

7-14   In *Calder v. James Finlay Corporation Ltd*,[16] the respondent was refused a subsidised mortgage because an unwritten rule of the scheme was that it was only open to men. She left the firm eight months after last being refused an application for a subsidised mortgage, but filed a complaint based on the Sex Discrimination Act within three months of the termination of her employment. The EAT found that the Industrial Tribunal had erred in finding her complaint out of time, in that section 76(6)(b) treats a continuing act as having been done at the end of the period in question, here the termination of her employment. As section 6(2)(a) of the 1975 Act renders it unlawful

---

[14] *Lupetti v. Wrens Old House Ltd* (1984) I.C.R. 348, EAT.
[15] [1991] I.R.L.R. 490.
[16] [1989] I.R.L.R. 55, EAT.

to discriminate in the way in which employees are afforded access to benefits, and that way of affording access to the subsidised mortgage scheme was a continuing act, section 76(6)(b) treats it as taking place at the end of the employment and therefore it falls within the time limit.

A similar conclusion was reached in *Barclays Bank plc v. Kapur*[17] in which ethnic minority employees complained that their service in an associated company in East Africa was excluded for pension purposes, whilst that of expatriate employees who had served in East Africa was included. Whilst the initial exclusion took place in 1970 and 1971, the employees complained under the Race Relations Act, s.4(2)(b) that there was discrimination in the way in which they were afforded access to the pension scheme and that by virtue of section 68(7)(b) that act, being a continuing act, fell to be treated as done at the end of the period. The Court of Appeal held there was a continuing discriminatory act alleged here, in that the way the applicants were afforded access to benefits (*i.e.* without benefit of their overseas service) was a continuing discrimination and there was not simply an act of discrimination in the year when the relevant decision was first made. Neill L.J. held that the right to a pension formed part of the overall remuneration of the employee, and that if his pension entitlement could be shown to be less favourable than that of other employees, that disadvantage continued throughout his employment. The House of Lords followed this approach.[18] (Ultimately the case failed in the industrial tribunal.)

7-15

In *Owusu v. London Fire & Civil Defence Authority*[19] the EAT took the view that an applicant who had repeatedly sought regrading and the chance to act up over a period of time without success could claim continuing racial discrimination. It was held that an act extends over a period if it takes the form of some policy, rule or practice governing the outcome of decisions taken from time to time. However "an act does not extend over a period of time simply because the doing of the act has continuing consequences ... What is continuing is alleged in this case to be a practice which results in consistent decisions discriminatory to Mr Owusu."

7-16

By contrast, in *Sougrin v. Haringey Health Authority*[20] the Court of Appeal held that there was no continuing act of discrimination where after a regrading exercise a black nurse was paid less than a comparator. It would have been different, however, if there had been a discriminatory policy of paying black nurses less which continued in operation.

7-17

Discretionary waiver of time limits

There is a discretion vested in the tribunals in effect to waive the time limits. The Sex Discrimination Act, s.76(5), the Race Relations Act, s.68(5) and the

7-18

---

[17] [1991] I.R.L.R. 136, [1991] I.C.R. 208; [1991] 2 A.C. 355, H.L.
[18] In a county court case one of us persuaded the judge that a policy of excluding gypsies from the lounge bar of a public house which was communicated to a plaintiff was a continuing act for as long as the policy existed.
[19] [1995] I.R.L.R. 574.
[20] [1992] I.R.L.R. 416.

Disability Discrimination Act Sched. 3, Pt. 1, para. 3(2) (except that it refers solely to a complaint) provide that:

> "A court or tribunal may nevertheless consider any complaint, claim or application which is out of time if, in all the circumstances of the case, it considers that it is just and equitable to do so."

The discretion vested in courts and tribunals to entertain applications out of time is wide, so limiting the scope for appeal. For an appellant to succeed he must show that the court or tribunal took a demonstrably wrong approach to the matter, or it took into account facts which it ought not to have done, or the decision was so unreasonable that no properly instructed tribunal could have reached it. The court or tribunal may take into account anything which it judges to be relevant, and though it is not required to hear the entire case before making its decision, it may want to hear enough evidence to gauge the strength or weakness of the complaint.[21]

7-19   Beware, the discretion does not apply to appeals from non-discrimination notices under the SDA or RRA where no power exists to extend the time; nor can it be extended by consent, because after the six week period the notice becomes final and has to be entered on the public register kept by the relevant Commission, and there is no power to take it off again. If, however, the Commission has exceeded its jurisdiction, it might be possible to quash a notice and the register entry by judicial review, for which three months is the usual period for bringing proceedings.

Equal pay–claim in time

7-20   Whether there is a time limit for the bringing of a claim under the equal pay legislation is currently the subject of conflicting decisions in the EAT. The best advice for an applicant, if it is feasible to do so, is to present the claim within six months of the termination of the contract of employment to which it relates or face a trip to the Court of Appeal. (There is no problem while an applicant is still employed if lack of equal pay continues.) Whilst section 2(1) provides that claims may be presented to an industrial tribunal in respect of the contravention of an equality clause, and section 2(3) allows such a claim pending in any court which could be more conveniently disposed of in an industrial tribunal to be referred to a tribunal, section 2(4) provides that:

> "No claim in respect of the operation of an equality clause relating to a woman's employment shall be referred to an industrial tribunal other-wise than by virtue of subsection (3) above, if she has not been

---

[21] *Hutchinson v. Westward Television Ltd* [1977] I.C.R. 279; [1977] I.R.L.R. 69, EAT. Both ignorance of legal rights and erroneous legal advice may be relevant: *Keeble v. British Coal Corporation (No. 2)* E.O.R. D.C.L.D. 28 p.3; *Hawkins v. Ball and Barclays Bank plc* [1996] I.R.L.R. 258. Where a complaint is out of time and the Applicant's representative fails to ask for an extension of time on the basis that it would be just and equitable, a Tribunal Chairman is not obliged to raise the matter: *Dimtsu v. Westminster City Council* [1991] I.R.L.R. 450, EAT.

employed in the same employment within six months preceding the date
of the reference.''

In *British Railways Board v. Paul*, the EAT held that the time limit prescribed **7-21**
by the subsection applied only to a reference to a tribunal by the Secretary
of State and not to an original claim. (Damages or arrears of remuneration
may not be awarded, however, in respect of any period earlier than two years
before the date of the claim.) In *Etherson v. Strathclyde Regional Council*,
the EAT held that the word ''reference'' was not to be so narrowly construed
and it applied to all claims presented as well as references by the Secretary
of State.[22]

Community law–claim in time

As there are no procedures prescribed for bringing a claim directly based **7-22**
upon EEC law, the EAT in *Stevens v. Bexley Health Authority* had taken the
view that there was no time limit on bringing a claim.[23] A later EAT in
Livingstone v. Hepworth Refractiories plc,[24] however, followed the subsequent guidance of the ECJ in *Emmot v. Minister for Social Welfare*[25] to
adopt procedures no less favourable than those in domestic law, provided
they make exercise of Community law rights possible.[26] So the procedures
including the time limits of the SDA were held applicable there. The same
would be true of an equal pay claim based directly on EEC law as regards
Equal Pay Act procedures or the Employment Rights Act if the claim is
brought in respect of compensation for unfair dismissal: see *Biggs v. Somerset County Council*.[27] The EAT there took the view that an industrial tribunal's jurisdiction is statute based, so that it could not entertain ''free-
standing'' Community rights as such, contrary to the view of the EAT in
Rankin v. British Coal Corporation.[28] Instead Community law, where it
applied, was seen as displacing national law requirements in that statutory
jurisdiction as necessary but otherwise leaving intact all the procedural
requirements. It was also pointed out that the proviso in *Emmott*, that national
time limits should only be applied if they make exercise of Community rights
possible, was based upon:

> ''. . .the principle that a respondent State is not able, in contending that
> a claim is time barred, to rely on its own failure to implement properly
> the requirements of Community law. It was held that, in such a case
> time does not start to run in favour of the State and against the applicant
> so long as the respondent state is in default.''

---

[22] *British Railways Board v. Paul* [1988] I.R.L.R. 20 EAT; *Etherson v. Strathclyde Regional
Council*, EAT [1992] ICR 579, followed in *Fletcher v. Midland Bank plc*, *The Times*, July
2, 1996, EAT, which also held that this interpretation was not incompatible with Community
law.
[23] [1989] I.R.L.R. 240; [1989] I.C.R. 224, EAT.
[24] [1992] I.R.L.R. 63, EAT.
[25] [1991] I.R.L.R. 387, ECJ.
[26] See *Cannon v. Barnsley Metropolitan Borough Council*, EAT [1992] I.R.L.R. 474; *Rankin
v. British Corporation* [1993] I.R.L.R. 69, EAT.
[27] [1995] I.R.L.R. 452.
[28] See above, n.26.

This is obviously intended from its context as reference to failure to implement a Directive. On the face of it the passage seems capable of application to the situation where a State misleadingly maintains statutory provisions contrary to a directly applicable Community right. Yet in just such a case the EAT in *Biggs* held that the ordinary national time limit should apply, because it would always have been possible for an applicant to rely on the Community law. It seems to us that all such applicants are thereby deemed to be bold, courageous and either highly prescient or in better command of Community law than the U.K. Government! The EAT decision in *Biggs* was upheld by the Court of Appeal.[28a]

Conciliation in employment cases

7-23   Copies of complaints under the Race Relations Act, the Sex Discrimination Act and the Disability Discrimination Act are sent to an ACAS conciliation officer under the Race Relations Act, s.54, the Sex Discrimination Act, s.64 or the Disability Discrimination Act Sched. 3, Pt. 1, para 1. It is the duty of the conciliation officer to facilitate a settlement in individual cases. He neither possesses investigatory powers nor is he under a duty to promote equality. He must act if he is requested to do so by either party, or he may act in the absence of such requests if he considers that there is a reasonable chance of success. Nothing communicated to a conciliation officer in the course of his duties under the Acts is admissible without the consent of the party who made the communication.

7-24   It is generally recognised that conciliation in a discrimination case is often more difficult than in other types of employment cases, because there is principle at stake. Applicants will often perceive themselves as bringing the case to save others from discrimination. Respondents will often refuse to accept the possibility that discrimination has occurred, even though it may have happened unintentionally. Where employers are prepared to make concessions, however, they may agree to action in respect of equal opportunities generally, even though a tribunal could not order widespread change in the event of a finding of discrimination. It is not uncommon for applicants in discrimination cases to have second thoughts about settlements after the event, particularly when they get home and see their children and wonder whether they have made enough noise to ensure they will not have to go through something similar. It is a wise precaution for a representative to ask the applicant to initial any settlement personally.

7-25   It is not uncommon for employers to try and buy silence about the issues in the case by paying over the odds in a settlement but insisting on a confidentiality clause. Sometimes for one reason or another this suits the applicant's purpose as well, but more often than not the applicant will go away feeling unhappy about the position. Such settlements are often less effective for the employers than they hoped because aspects of the settlement leak out in other ways and the settlement begins to look like a cover-up. Thus, in a local authority context, such a settlement will not achieve its purpose if a councillor thereafter starts asking awkward questions.

[28a] [1996] I.R.L.R. 203.

A settlement of a tribunal claim, which is made with the assistance of an **7-26**
ACAS conciliation officer, constitutes an exception to the provisions of the
Race Relations Act, s.73(3), the Sex Discrimination Act, s.77(3) and the
Disability Discrimination Act, s.9 which render void any term in a contract
which purports to limit or exclude any provision of the two Acts. It followed
that agreements without ACAS assistance, other than actually in front of the
tribunal and recorded in the decision, were not binding. The ACAS officer
will use a form known as COT 3. A COT 3 agreement drawn up under the
Employment Rights Act 1996 will not be regarded as covering claims under
the RRA, SDA, DDA or equal pay legislation unless expressed to do so. The
same rules will be applied to a claim relying on Community law following
the *Livingstone* case referred to in the section on time limits above.

In 1990 ACAS declined involvement in settlements reached without their
involvement, and the law was thereafter changed to permit another exception
to the ban on contracting out of statutory rights. The provisions were inserted
by TURERA[29] as SDA s.77(4A) to (4C) and RRA s.72(4A) to (4C). A settlement agreement has to be in writing and to relate to a particular complaint
which has arisen; the complainant must have received independent legal
advice from a qualified lawyer (carrying relevant insurance) as to the terms
and effect of the proposed agreement and its effect on his or her rights in a
tribunal; the adviser must be identified in the agreement; and the agreement
must state that the statutory conditions have been met. The same is true for
the DDA under the provisions of section 9(2) to (5).

Procedure in equal value claims

Both equal pay claims and claims for equal value under section 1(2)(c) oper-   **7-27**
ate under the Industrial Tribunal (Constitution, etc.) Regulations 1993.[30] The
detailed Rules of Procedure for Industrial Tribunals are contained in Schedule
1 of the Regulations.

A special and more complex procedure is provided in respect of equal value   **7-28**
claims. The average time taken to conclude an equal value case was 17
months, long enough to provoke the President of the EAT in *Aldridge v.
British Telecommunications plc*[31] to observe that the delays are "scandalous
and amount to a denial of justice to women seeking a remedy through the
judicial process." This procedure has to provide a means whereby a comparison can be made of the value of the applicant's work and that of her selected
male comparators. This comparison is undertaken by an independent expert
appointed by the tribunal. The procedures in respect of equal value claims
have been incorporated into the 1993 regulations as Schedule 2, the regulations being numbered in such a way that in so far as possible a matter is
dealt with in the same numbered section in Schedule 2 as it in the main body
of the regulations contained in Schedule 1.

Before proceeding to hear an equal value claim, the tribunal shall invite the   **7-29**
parties to adjourn the proceedings for the purpose of seeking a settlement

---

[29] Trade Union Reform and Employment Rights Act 1993, s.39 and Sched. 6.
[30] S.I. 1985 No. 16.
[31] [1990] I.R.L.R. 10, and see *British Coal v. Smith*, EAT/29/91.

and shall, if both or all of the parties agree, grant such an adjournment under regulation 12(2A).

In this respect it should be noted that the under the Sex Discrimination Act 1975, s.64(1), ACAS conciliation officers are empowered to act in cases brought under section 2(1) of the Equal Pay Act and copies of the Originating Application will have been forwarded to ACAS from the COIT. Whilst possibilities of conciliation are not therefore exhausted and may nonetheless occur at the commencement of proceedings, the likelihood of reaching a settlement at this stage is thereby reduced.

7-30   The tribunal must consider whether it is satisfied that there are no reasonable grounds for determining that the work is of equal value under section 2A(1). If there are no such reasonable grounds, the tribunal must dismiss the application at this stage, before a report is commissioned from an independent expert. The intention behind this provision was that only ''hopeless cases'' should be excluded at this stage, so that all that is required on behalf of an applicant at this stage is an arguable case.

7-31   Under regulation 9(2E) the tribunal may, on the application of a party, if it considers it appropriate to do so, hear evidence and permit the parties to address it on the question of whether there is a genuine material difference other than a difference of sex under the Equal Pay Act 1970, s.1(3), before it requires an expert to prepare a report. The EAT in *McGregor v. GMBATU*.[32] held that the interpretation and application of the material factor defence should be the same whether it fails to be considered at the first or a subsequent hearing. Should the defence succeed at the preliminary stage, the application may be dismissed without calling for a report from an independent expert. Consideration of a material factor defence at this stage is without prejudice to further consideration of this issue after the tribunal has received the expert's report,[33] even though this could be characterised as giving two bites at the same cherry and unnecessarily adding to costs.

7-32   A material factor defence cannot be taken as a preliminary point but, save in wholly exceptional circumstances, requires evidence. In *R. v. Secretary of State for Social Services, ex p. Clarke*[34] in response to claims by female speech therapists that their work was of equal value with male clinical psychologists and pharmacists, the employer health authorities sought to establish as a preliminary point that they were bound to pay only those salaries approved by the Secretary of State under the relevant NHS Regulations following upon agreement in the Whitley Councils. The Divisional Court, on an application for judicial review as to whether the Secretary of State's approval of the Whitley Council rates was contrary to Community law in so far as it failed to incorporate the principle of equal pay for work of equal value and was therefore held that section 1(3) requires evidence to be called as to whether the variation is genuinely due to a material factor other than a difference of sex, and that this requires evidence as to the reasons for the variation. Only if the variation in pay were genuinely shown to be due to the Regulations could they constitute the material factor under section 1(3).

[32] [1987] I.C.R. 505.
[33] Reg. 8(2E).
[34] [1988] I.R.L.R. 22.

A tribunal is not bound to embark upon an enquiry under regulation 9(2E),   **7-33**
but if it hears evidence that the employers have a genuine material factor
defence prior to the commissioning of a report from an independent expert,
the tribunal must decide the point if there is sufficient evidence and only
adjourn the case for preparation of a report from an independent expert where
there is insufficient evidence.[35] If the tribunal decides that the employer has
made out a defence under section 1(3), the tribunal must dismiss the claim
without commissioning a report.

If the material factor defence is heard prior to the commissioning of a report   **7-34**
from an independent expert, the point must be considered on the presumption
that the work is of equal value and it is for the employer to show that the
difference is due to a genuine material factor and that this is a factor other
than sex.[36] The onus of establishing a defence under section 1(3) lies on the
employer whenever it is heard, but in the absence of a finding of equal value
at this early stage, clarity about the burden of proof is particularly necessary.
The EOC, in their document *Equal Pay: Strengthening the Acts*[37] argues that
there should be an obligation to plead particulars of any section 1(3) defence
at the initial stage, so that all the issues are identified at an early stage. The
EOC took the view that the section 2A(1) hearing is neither necessary nor
desirable, in that it facilitates delaying tactics and is redundant in view of
the general power of tribunals[38] to hold pre-hearing assessments and to issue
a costs warning, where there are no reasonable prospects of success.

Until recently a tribunal, after consideration of the above matters, had to   **7-35**
require an expert to prepare a report with respect to the question according
to the provisions of regulation 8A(2) and (3). However the Sex Discrimination and Equal Pay (Miscellaneous Amendments) Regulations 1996 amended
section 2A so that a tribunal will not always have to commission an expert's
report.

Such a requirement for a report shall be made in writing and shall specify   **7-36**
the name and address of the parties, the address where the applicant is or was
employed, the question at issue and the name of the person with reference to
whose work the question arises. A copy of the requirement shall be sent to
each of the parties.

Regulation 8A(3) provides that the requirement shall stipulate that the expert   **7-37**
shall:

   (a) take account of all such information supplied and all such repres-
       entations made to him as have a bearing on the question;
   (b) before drawing up his report, produce and send to the parties a writ-

---

[35] *Reed Packaging Ltd v. Boozer* [1988] I.R.L.R. 333, EAT.

[36] *Financial Times v. Byrne (No. 2)* [1991] I.R.L.R. 163, EAT. *In Byrne v. Financial Times*
[1991] I.R.L.R. 417, the EAT had refused an application for further and better particulars of
the employer's defence under s.1(3) which would have required the employer to have allocated a specific sum to any particular pleaded. This was dismissed as being impossible to
quantify accurately.

[37] *Equal Pay: Strengthening the Acts*, (EOC, 1990).

[38] Industrial Tribunal (Rules of Procedure) Regulations 1985 (S.I. 1985 No. 16) Sched. 1, r.6.
Pre-hearing reviews replaced pre-hearing assessments. See paragraph 7–87 below.

ten summary of the said information and representations and invite
the representations of the parties upon the material contained therein;
  (c) make his report to the tribunal in a document which shall reproduce
      the summary and contain a brief account of any representations
      received from the parties upon it, any conclusions he may have
      reached upon the question and the reasons for that conclusion or,
      as the case may be, for his failure to reach such a conclusion;
  (d) take no account of the difference of sex and at all times act fairly.

7-38 The tribunal shall adjourn the hearing under regulation 4 when it requires an
independent expert to prepare a report. The parties may complain to the tribunal under regulation 5 not less than 42 days after the expert has been required
to prepare the report, that there is likely to be undue delay in the preparation
of the report. The tribunal may, on consideration of any explanation or
information as to the progress of the report, revoke the requirement upon the
expert and commission a fresh report. Although the powers provided under
regulation 5 have not hitherto been exercised, where an applicant fails to
furnish the necessary information, a tribunal may consider dismissing the
claim for want of prosecution.

"A copy of the report shall be sent to the parties upon its receipt by
the tribunal and a date fixed for the resumed hearing, such date to be
not less than 14 days after the Report has been sent to the parties"
(reg. 6).

7-39 Under regulation 8A(12), the report shall be admitted in evidence at the
resumed hearing, unless it is excluded under the powers contained in regulation 8A(13). Under that regulation the tribunal may, if it thinks fit, determine
not to admit the report where, on the application of one or more of the parties
or otherwise, it forms the view:

  (a) that the expert has not complied with the stipulations set out in
      regulation 8A(3) (above); or
  (b) that the conclusion contained in the report is one which, taking due
      account of the information supplied and representations made to the
      expert, could not reasonably have been reached; or
  (c) that for some other material reason (other than disagreement with
      the conclusion that the applicant's work is or is not of equal value
      or with the reasoning leading to that conclusion) the report is
      unsatisfactory.

7-40 Regulation 8A(14) provides that the tribunal shall take account of the representations of the parties and may, subject to regulation 9(2A) and (2B), permit
any party to give evidence, call witnesses and question witnesses upon the
question of admitting the expert's report. Where a party wishes to contest
the factual basis of the independent expert's report, this is best done before
the report is admitted under regulation 8A(12). A party who objects to the
admission of the report may make representations under regulation 8A(14),
give evidence and call witnesses upon any matter relevant to the criteria set
out in regulation 8A(13)(a), (b) and (c) above. This is subject to the proviso
in regulation 9(2A) that the independent expert may be called and cross-
examined on his report. It is, however, only possible for a tribunal to refuse

to admit the report if the conclusion is one which could not reasonably have been reached in the light of the information supplied and the representations made or the report is in some other way unsatisfactory, *i.e.* it can only be rejected where the expert has gone badly wrong and mere disagreement with his conclusions or his reasoning is not sufficient.[39] In *Aldridge v. BT* the EAT held that the tribunal was entitled to take the expert's oral testimony into account in deciding to admit the report. They went on to hold that in view of the inevitable delay which would ensue if a fresh report were required, tribunals should hear all the necessary evidence at the admission stage, which could include evidence from the experts commissioned by the parties. After hearing the experts for the parties the tribunal should give such weight as it sees fit to the independent expert's report and to those of the experts for the parties, along with any other evidence. It is for the tribunal to reach the factual conclusions on equal value, particularly in the light of the requirement laid down in Article 2 of the Equal Pay Directive of a right "to pursue their claims by judicial process after possible recourse to other competent authorities."

This rule must be understood in the context of regulation 9(2C) which provides that the parties may not give evidence upon any matters of fact upon which a conclusion in the report of the expert is based, except as provided by regulations 8A(14) or 9(2D). The purpose of this provision is to prevent continual attack upon the factual basis of the report. Regulation 9(2D) (discussed below) provides that evidence may be admitted and witnesses questioned where the matter is relevant to a genuine material factor defence under section 1(3), or the expert failed to reach a conclusion due to the failure of the parties to supply the necessary information.

7-41

In *Tennant Textile Colours Ltd v. Todd*,[40] the report of the expert had been admitted, after which the employer sought an adjournment, to procure a report from their own expert witness. The tribunal allowed the adjournment but ruled that the findings of fact in the report of the independent expert would be binding on both parties "in circumstances where the report had already been admitted in evidence." The employers appealed by way of a case stated to the Northern Ireland Court of Appeal, which held that whilst regulation 9(2C) provides that new evidence may not be admitted at this stage, parties may make submissions about the findings of fact and may refer back to facts adduced at some prior stage in the hearing, as when considering whether the report should have been admitted under regulation 8A(14), or whether there was a section 1(3) defence under regulation 9(2D). Although the primary fact finding role of the tribunal is thus placed within the remit of the expert, it remains the function of the tribunal to decide whether equal value has been established. Lord Lowry in the N.I.C.A. also held that:

7-42

"Reports obtained in the circumstances created by the present Act and Rules must obviously carry considerable weight, as was clearly intended, but there is no provision or principle that the party challenging an inde-

[39] *e.g.* the independent expert's report was not admitted in *Allsop v. Derbyshire Police Authority*, EOR Case Law Digest No. 4, because the expert refused to answer questions under cross examination as to the basis of the reports commissioned by the parties.
[40] [1989] I.R.L.R. 3, N.I.C.A.

pendent expert's report has to 'persuade the Tribunal that the independent expert's report should be rejected' or that the Tribunal 'could only reject the independent expert's report if the evidence were such as to show that it was so plainly wrong that it could not be accepted,' as stated in paragraph 23 of the Tribunal's decision. The burden of proving a claim under the Act of 1970 is on the applicant. The burden does not in point of law become heavier if the independent expert's report is against the applicant. Nor, if that report is in favour of the applicant, is the burden of proof transferred to the employer.''

7-43   Whilst it is clearly right that there is no change in the burden of proof, an applicant may be driven towards commissioning a report from her own expert witness to overcome this problem, with all the attendant burdens of cost and complexity.

It is now commonplace for one or both of the parties to commission a report from their own expert. The EAT ruled in *Lloyds Bank v. Fox*[41] that whilst a party that had appointed its own expert could require the other side to furnish further and better particulars or discovery of documents under rule 4(1)(b), tribunals have no power to require that the other party consent to be interviewed by the opposing expert in the course of preparing his report.

7-44   The tribunal may require the expert to explain any matter in his report or give further consideration to the question under regulation 8A(15), and the expert shall make his reply in writing, setting down any conclusions which may result from further consideration and his reasons for that conclusion. Copies of the expert's reply shall be sent to the parties, which shall be given such weight as the tribunal thinks fit.

7-45   In those instances where an expert's report is not admitted, regulation 8A(18) requires that it shall be treated as if it has not been received and no further account shall be taken of it. The result will be the appointment of a new expert. In *Davies v. Francis Shaw*[42] the expert's report was not admitted on the grounds that he had failed to take account of the representations of the parties and had failed to give any reasons for his conclusions. The applicant in that case tried to persuade the industrial tribunal to accept her expert's report, but did not succeed in this submission.

Procedure at the hearing

7-46   1. Proceedings on equal value claims are to be conducted in an informal manner, as applies to other industrial tribunal proceedings and likewise the tribunal is not bound by any rule of law as to the admissibility of evidence in courts of law (reg. 9(1)).

2. On the application of a party the tribunal may compel the attendance of the expert under regulation 9(2A), who may be cross examined

[41] [1987] I.R.L.R. 103, EAT in which each side had commissioned an independent report. The Bank appointed a new expert, after the Tribunal had criticised the report of the expert originally appointed. The Bank sought an order to require the complainant to be interviewed by the new expert, but Wood J. held that the Tribunal only had powers to order written interrogations and not to require that a party consent to be interviewed.
[42] Case No. 27668/85A, I.T. Manchester, July 15, 1988.

on his report and any other matters pertaining to the question on which the expert was required to report.

3. A party may, on giving reasonable notice of his intention to do so, call his own expert witness on the question on which the expert was asked to report under regulation 9(2B); any other party may cross examine such a witness. A party who is unhappy about the conclusions of an expert's report, although unable to ensure that the report is not admitted under regulation 8A(13) above, may present an alternative opinion about the conclusions to be drawn from the facts of the case in this way, even though regulation 9(2C) precludes the giving of evidence or calling or questioning of witnesses upon any matter of fact upon which the expert's report is based.

4. Notwithstanding regulation 9(2C), under regulation 9(2D)(b) a party may give evidence, call or question witnesses upon matters of fact upon which the conclusions of the expert's report is based, where the expert reached no conclusions on the question of equal value because of a refusal by a person to furnish information or documents to the expert.

5. The matter may be disposed of or dismissed in the absence of either party subject to the consideration of any written representations made under regulation 8(5).

6. Costs may be awarded in respect of frivolous, abusive, disruptive, vexatious or otherwise unreasonable actions.

7. The costs of the independent expert are born by the Secretary of State. The main burden falling on parties to equal value cases is the expense of the initial preparation and the emerging trend to commission an expert, whose report can be contrasted with that of the independent expert. Once one party has commissioned its own expert, it becomes a practical necessity for the other side to match this expertise. Further substantial costs may be incurred in questioning any material factor defence put forward by the employer, as was the case, for example, in *Lloyds Bank v. Fox*. The result is that without financial support from a trade union or the EOC a complainant needs a high level of commitment effectively to pursue an equal value claim.

Reform of the equal value provisions

Proposals have been made for simplifying and speeding-up this procedure, in particular by the EOC.[43] These proposals include ways of speeding up the initial steps of the proceedings by the introduction of a preliminary review to clarify and record each party's case, at which the respondents would be under an obligation to set out the nature of any genuine material factor defence on which they propose to rely. Correspondingly it is proposed that the "no reasonable grounds" requirement would be removed and that the genuine material factor defence should only be available after equal value has been established.

7-47

Another proposal to speed up and standardise the procedure is the appoint-

---

[43] *Equal Pay: Strengthening the Acts*, (EOC, 1990). The law was altered by the Sex Discrimination and Equal Pay Regulations 1996 to give discretion to the tribunal whether to appoint an expert.

ment of a "chief independent expert", and a cadre of other full-time independent experts. A chief independent expert might be able to ensure greater uniformity of procedures and impose a more brisk timetable on the production of reports.

7-48 The President of the EAT questioned the place of the independent expert in *Aldridge v. British Telecommunications* and advocated that his role become that of an assessor to the Tribunal itself, emphasising that it is for the Tribunal to make the decision as to equal value. Justice has previously mooted that equal value claims should be referred to arbitration before the Central Arbitration Council (CAC), but attractive as this might be from the point of view of trade unions and, perhaps, employers, Community law calls for a judicial remedy to be available.[44] In Ireland an Equality Officer hears such cases, with appeal to the Labour Court. The argument against that approach is that once such an officer is required to produce a reasoned report and safeguards are built in to the system to ensure that the process is operated in a fair and objective manner, it may be no quicker than a reformed industrial tribunal procedure.

7-49 Many of the benefits of referring equal value cases to the CAC may be derived from other recommendations of the EOC, *e.g.* that not only should the terms of the award in any successful case be extended to all other employees engaged on the same or broadly similar work to the applicant also but, that where the discrimination was rooted in the terms of a collective agreement, the tribunal should have the power to require that the offending term be modified or abandoned within a stipulated period, rather than deeming the term void, as now.[45]

7-50 Whilst Article 4 of the Equal Pay Directive provides that collective agreements, wage scales, were agreements or individual contracts of employment which are contrary to the principle of equal pay may be declared null and void or may be amended, in *Nimz v. Freie und Hansestadt Hamburg* the ECJ ruled that:

> "where there is indirect discrimination in a provision in a collective agreement, the national court is required to disapply that provision, without requesting or awaiting its prior removal by collective negotiation or any other procedure, and to apply to members of the group which is disadvantaged by that discrimination the same arrangements which are applied to other employees, arrangements which, failing the correct application of article 119 of the EEC Treaty in national law, remain the only valid system of reference."

7-51 This decision suggests that it is not sufficient simply to render void any discriminatory provisions in a collective agreement, without providing an alternative remedy for those affected. The EAT held in *McKechnie v. UBM*

---

[44] Council Directive 75/117 on the application of equal pay for men and women calls in Article 2 for claimants to be able to pursue their claims "by judicial process".

[45] The Sex Discrimination Act 1975, s.77(5) provides that such a term may be modified by application to a county court.

Building Supplies (Southern) Ltd[46] that industrial tribunals may rely on directly enforceable Community rights, so that tribunals may be able to rely on *Nimz* in applying the same arrangements to those disadvantaged by the discrimination as are applied to other employees. In Britain this means that those disadvantaged by an indirectly discriminatory provision in a collective agreement can look to the application of an equality clause where the term in question has been incorporated into their contracts of employment[47] or at least to a declaration that they are to enjoy comparable rights with their comparator group, as was done in *Secretary of State for Scotland and Greater Glasgow Health Board v. Wright and Hannah.*[48]

Hearings of discrimination claims

In proceedings under the RRA, DDA and SDA, the applicant presents his or her case first because the burden of proof lies on the applicant. Sometimes the cases will be linked with unfair dismissal claims under the Employment Rights Act 1996. If the unfair dismissal case stood alone, in a case where the dismissal is admitted the respondent goes first, but where it is joined with a discrimination claim then it is usual for the applicant to start unless the parties agree otherwise and the tribunal agrees, which they sometimes do.

7-52

Except in Scotland, the applicant is usually allowed an opening speech. If the case is fairly simply, sometimes tribunals in England and Wales do not allow opening speeches. It is quite usual in England and Wales to deal with liability alone in the main hearing and leave the question of compensation, if it arises, to agreement or a further hearing. Tribunals do differ in approach, however, and it is well worth asking the tribunal during opening which approach they will take. In Scotland the question of compensation is dealt with in the main hearing. Whenever compensation is dealt with, it is as well to deal with injury to feelings when the applicant first gives evidence, because such evidence seems very contrived when the only issue is the amount of compensation and much more natural at the end of a description of what has happened.

7-53

In England and Wales, but not in Scotland, witnesses other than the parties themselves are permitted to sit in the tribunal room and hear the rest of the case. It is possible to apply to the tribunal for them to be excluded. It is actually very difficult to cross-examine effectively each of a number of people on an interviewing panel when they are all present in the tribunal. However imaginative the questions, there is bound to be some repetition and witnesses can square their evidence if they hear what each other says. Sometimes, though, if the respondents are spinning a ludicrous line it helps the applicant for them to be seen to be consistently ludicrous! It has happened that a respondent has had so many witnesses in the tribunal that the atmo-

7-54

---

[46] [1991] I.R.L.R. 222.
[47] *e.g.* in *Alexander v. Standard Telephones and Cables Ltd (No. 2)* [1991], the terms of a redundancy procedure which could well have been discriminatory (had the issue been in point), in that it relied upon service as a criteria for selection, was held not to be capable of incorporation into the individual workers contracts of employment.
[48] [1991] I.R.L.R. 187.

sphere has become intimidating for the applicant and a tribunal may see that as a reason for excluding witnesses.

7-55   The course of a trial is no different in a discrimination case from other tribunal cases. The strict rules of evidence do not apply, so hearsay is admissible, but otherwise normal conventions are followed. Thus examination-in-chief, cross-examination and re-examination of witnesses are as usual and representatives of parties are expected to put their case to the opposing witnesses. The state of mind of the witnesses on the respondent's side who made the relevant decision about the applicant is crucial in a direct discrimination case and therefore cross-examination of those witnesses is extremely important. As a Manchester industrial tribunal in the case of *Freeman v. Salford Health Authority* said, "So much of an applicant's case depends upon in-depth cross-examination of the respondents' witnesses."[49] The importance for the tribunal of hearing what the respondent has to say about his or her reasons for the decisions in question has been recognised in the rule that unless the circumstances are exceptional the tribunal should not dismiss the case at the end of the evidence for the applicant.[50] Indeed, quite often the applicant's own oral evidence does not carry the matter very far at all on the issue of liability if, for example, he or she is complaining about a decision not to short-list after a written application from outside.

7-56   The most difficult problem for representatives in making speeches when unfamiliar with the particular tribunal is to judge how far the tribunal understands the nature of discrimination, and how much to take for granted on this topic. It is better to be safe than sorry and err on the side of full explanation since the tribunal is likely to indicate what it is already aware of, but in the nature of things cannot indicate much about what it does not know. Most of the jurisdiction of the tribunals concerns unfair dismissal, and these days Wages Act claims, and they may not have much familiarity with discrimination cases. The notion of reasonableness serves them well in the unfair dismissal jurisdiction, but in the discrimination area it is often doing things in ways which have traditionally been regarded as reasonable, such as appointing people who "fit in", that is the cause of the problem.[51] If the applicant has had an opening speech, then at the end the respondent has the first closing speech followed by the applicant. In Scotland, of course, there are no opening speeches so at the end the applicant's speech is first.

Remedies in discrimination claims

7-57   Industrial tribunals have three remedies at hand on a well-founded complaint of discrimination: a declaratory order; an order for compensation; and a recommendation. The limits pertaining to each are set out below. But there is an overall qualification, however, that the tribunal shall make such of those

---

[49] The Tribunal was arguing for Legal Aid to extend to discrimination cases: cited in the CRE's consultative document for Second Review of the RRA, 1991.
[50] *Oxford v. DHSS* [1977] I.R.L.R. 225; [1977] I.C.R. 884. Except in the rarest case an employer should not make a "no case to answer" submission where an applicant is unrepresented: *Austin v. British Telecommunications plc*, EAT 238/94, 1995.
[51] See *Baker v. Cornwall County Council* [1990] I.R.L.R. 194; [1990] I.C.R. 452, C.A.

orders "as it considers just and equitable".[52] It has been held that these words refer to the issue whether or not to make an order not to the contents of the order: *Hurley v. Mustoe (No. 2)*.[53] Thus a declaration has to deal with the legal rights, compensation be based on usual principles of assessment in tort, and a recommendation made according to what is practicable not in any of those cases according to what is just and equitable.

In certain circumstances the Equal Opportunities and Racial Equality Commissions have the power to bring proceedings in their own names in the industrial tribunals before commencing proceeding in the county court to obtain injunctions for persistent discrimination, or to restrain the doing of further acts concerning unlawful advertisements or pressure or instructions to discriminate. If such a case is well founded and it is just and equitable, the tribunal may make either a declaratory order, or a recommendation, or both.

7-58

Declaratory order

1. A Declaratory Order The duty is to make where just and equitable "an order declaring the rights of the complainant and the respondent in relation to the act to which the complaint relates".[54] This calls for no comment, save that it would seem to be a rare situation in a well-founded complaint where a tribunal not making an order of compensation, or a recommendation, did not find it appropriate to make a declaratory order.

Compensation

2. An Order for Compensation The tribunal's duty, where it is considered just and equitable, is to make "an order requiring the respondent to pay to the complainant compensation of an amount corresponding to any damages he could have been ordered by a county court or by a sheriff court to pay to the complainant if the complaint had fallen to be dealt with" there.[55]

The exception for indirect discrimination

In an indirect discrimination case (which cannot apply in the case of disability discrimination) the Race Relations Act 1976, s.57(3) and Sex Discrimination Act 1975, s.66(3) provided that[56] "no award of damages shall be made if the respondent proves that the requirement or condition was not applied with the intention of treating the claimant unfavourably on racial grounds [on the ground of his sex or marital status as the case may be]". However the SDA

7-59

[52] SDA 1975, s.65; RRA 1976, s.56; DDA 1995, s.8(2).
[53] *Hurley v. Mustoe (No. 2)* [1983] I.C.R. 422, EAT.
[54] SDA 1975, s.65(1)(a); RRA 1976, s.51(1)(a); DDA 1995, s.8(2)(a).
[55] SDA 1975, s.65(1)(b); RRA 1976, s.56(1)(b); DDA 1995, s.8(2)(b).
[56] See *Oprhanos v. Queen Mary College* [1985] I.R.L.R. 349; [1985] A.C. 761, H.L.

has been recently amended (see below). What follows therefore is now only of relevance in the race relations context.

7-60   In *London Underground Ltd v. Edwards*[57] the EAT held that what is relevant under these provisions is the intention with which the requirement or condition was applied rather than the general intention underlying the formulation of the requirement or condition. Thus if the employer fails to prove that the requirement was applied without a discriminatory intent a tribunal can infer that it was applied with knowledge of the discriminatory consequence and an intention to produce that result. It seemed to follow from this that if the discriminatory consequence of applying the requirement to the particular individuals had been drawn to the employer's attention and without holding a different view of the effect he applies the requirement anyway a liability to pay compensation would arise where the requirement is subsequently found to be unlawful.

And indeed this is what was held in *J.H. Walker v. Hussain.*[58] A company had changed its holiday requirements so that holidays could not be taken in certain busy months which in 1992 included Eid, a major Muslim occasion which the company had forgotten about. About half the workforce were Muslims originating from the Indian subcontinent and in previous years had taken off Eid. There was a willingness to work other hours at different times to make up the difference. The requirement was found to be indirectly discriminatory against those from the subcontinent and not justifiable. The company had been given several days warning of the impact of their requirement on Muslims and of the importance of Eid. Nevertheless they insisted on their requirement being met and warned of the disciplinary consequences of not doing so. Several Muslim employees had taken Eid off anyway and were given a final written warning. This crass piece of management in race relations terms ultimately led to the industrial tribunal awarding £1,000 each for injury to feelings which the EAT upheld. Its reasoning is as follows and merits citation at length as it stands at the threshold of a major opening up of the scope of the remedial provisions of the RRA:

> "In our view, as a matter of ordinary English, 'intention' in this context signifies the state of mind of a person who, at the time when he does the relevant act (i.e., the application of the requirement or condition resulting in indirect discrimination),
>
> a) *wants* to bring about the state of affairs which constitutes the prohibited result of unfavourable treatment on racial grounds; and b) *knows* that that prohibited result will follow from his acts ... Depending on the circumstances, a tribunal may infer that a person wants to produce certain consequences from the fact that he acted knowing what those consequences would be ...
>
> The tribunal took account of the company's knowledge of the consequences of its acts and made an inference that it wanted to produce those consequences. The company knew that Eid was important to the Muslim employees, that they were the only employees affected by the application of the condition or requirement, and that they were required to work on that day. As part of the process of applying that condition

---

[57] [1995] I.R.L.R. 355.
[58] [1996] I.R.L.R. 11.

or requirement, the company inflicted upon them a disproportionate punishment. The fact that the company's reason or motive in adopting and applying the holiday policy was to promote its business efficiency does not, in our view, either displace the company's knowledge of the consequences, which follow from applying that condition or requirement, or prevent the industrial tribunal from inferring that the company wanted to produce a state of affairs in which the applicants were in fact treated unfavourably on racial grounds. The tribunal were entitled to find that the company did not have the benefit of s.57(3).''[59]

Following *Marshall (No.2)* before the ECJ as to the adequacy of remedies[60] some tribunals, in our view rightly, accepted the argument that compensation is payable under the Equal Treatment Directive Article 6 in respect of unintentional indirect sex discrimination where the applicant is a public employee who can rely on the provisions of the Directive against the employer.[61]

But where the respondent is not an emanation of the state such that an applicant cannot rely directly on the Directive, what then? This question arose before the EAT in *MacMillan v. Edinburgh Voluntary Organisations Council*[62] where it was held that as section 66(3) of the SDA was clear in its terms it could not be construed so as to accord with the provisions of the Directive. Nothing, however, was said to cast any doubt on the contention that section 66(3) *is* in breach of Community law: so the possibility of a *Francovich* claim against the state was there. (After the EAT's decision in *Secretary of State for Employment v. Mann and others*[63] a *Francovich* claim cannot be made as an add-on to the industrial tribunal proceedings or by new tribunal proceedings but has to be dealt with by writ against the Attorney General in the High Court or equivalent in Scotland.) In order to comply with the Equal Treatment Directive the Sex Discrimination and Equal Pay (Miscellaneous Amendments) Regulations 1996 amended SDA 1975, s.65 so that a tribunal can award compensation in a case of indirect sex discrimination where the discrimination is unintentional. This applies where it is satisfied that the power to make a declaration and a recommendation is not sufficient, and it is just and equitable to award compensation as well. For the moment, therefore, the position under the SDA differs from that under the RRA.

Types of damages

Compensation for financial loss

Although the usual tort principles apply, the subject of financial loss merits specific attention here. Particularly in the area of discrimination in relation to applicants for jobs, or promotion, the situation may not be straightforward. The simple case is where it is clear that the applicant would have got the post but for the discrimination; yet it may be the case that there was discrim-

7-61

---

[59] At page 15.
[60] [1993] I.R.L.R. 445, ECJ.
[61] *Mulligan v. Eastern Health & Social Services Board* (Belfast I.T.), EOR, DCLD No. 20, p. 2; *Tickle v. Governors of Riverview CE School & Surrey County Council*, (London South I.T.) EOR, DCLD, No. 21, p. 1.
[62] [1995] I.R.L.R. 536.
[63] [1996] I.R.L.R. 4.

ination in relation to the appointment and it is unclear whether or not the applicant would have got the job but for the discrimination; and finally, it may be the case that discrimination is proved, but it is clear that the applicant definitely would not have got the post even if there had been no discrimination. The fact that it is possible for there to be discrimination in the "arrangements made"[64] for determining who should get a post as well as in the final selection makes the two latter possibilities all the more likely to occur.

7-62 Is compensation for actual loss payable if they do? If it is unclear whether the applicant would have got the job but for the discrimination, what the applicant has lost is the chance of getting the post. There has been a tendency for tribunals simply to award a sum for injury to feelings in these circumstances, and indeed it may be that advocates have not thought to ask for more. But it is well-established[65] that a sum can be awarded for loss of a chance, to be assessed according to the circumstances. So generally there can be awarded a proportion of the compensation for pecuniary loss which would have been awarded had it been clear that the applicant would have got the job but for the discrimination.

7-63 Obviously compensation based upon loss of a chance cannot be awarded in the situation where it is clear that the applicant would not have got the post even if there had been no discrimination. Even here, however, limiting the compensation to damages for injury to feelings may not always be appropriate. There is also the head of compensation based upon expenditure rendered futile by the unlawful acts. If the effect of the discrimination is such that the applicant was never really considered seriously at all for the post, as (s)he was entitled to be, it is arguable that the applicant should be entitled to compensation in respect of expenditure incurred in putting him or herself forward (for example postage, costs of interview attendance if these were not otherwise met) because (s)he would not have incurred that expenditure had (s)he known that (s)he would not be seriously considered at all. Everyone of course takes the chance in applying that someone else better may apply.

There are other situations where a "loss of a chance" approach is appropriate in assessing damages. The EAT in *Ministry of Defence v. Cannock*[66] have so held in relation to what might have happened in relation to dismissed pregnant servicewomen had they not been dismissed, including the possibility of promotion. Where what might have happened if the discrimination had not occurred is essentially speculative the tribunal should assess the chances of a particular outcome occurring and use the percentage level of probability as a basis of calculation, and not find that it would or would not have happened on the balance of probabilities and award all or nothing accordingly.

The EAT in *Cannock* evidently had in mind that some of the awards in the MOD cases had been very large. Nevertheless, it can be seen that using the "loss of a chance" approach would work to an applicant's advantage if the chances of an advantageous outcome are assessed at less than 50 per cent, say 30 per cent. On the "loss of a chance" approach the applicant would receive something, whilst on an all or nothing approach the applicant would receive nothing.

---

[64] See *ante* chapter 5.
[65] See *Chaplin v. Hicks* [1911] 2 K.B. 786.
[66] [1994] I.R.L.R. 509.

Damages for financial or other loss can relate to loss which has been incurred   **7-64**
at the time of the hearing, and any prospective future loss. Obviously where
the result of the discrimination is that a person is without a job and that
situation continues, an estimate of the likely time which will elapse before
a job is found has to be made, based upon the state of the job-market.

It is very often the case that an industrial tribunal will hear the case on the   **7-65**
issue of liability without hearing evidence on the issue of compensation, and
in the event of finding the case proved, express the hope that the parties will
reach a settlement on the issue of compensation and not need to reinstate the
case for a hearing on this issue. (In Scotland, however, evidence relating to
compensation should normally be led along with the other evidence.) If a
tribunal which has not heard any evidence or submissions on the subject of
compensation were to find on liability and purport to make an award of
compensation, the way for the dissatisfied party to deal with that situation is
to ask the tribunal for a review of its decision.
  Even if the issue of compensation is to be adjourned by the tribunal, it is
as well for the applicant to give evidence at the original hearing as to the
effect of the alleged discrimination on his or her feelings, because it will
probably be more convincing as part of the whole picture than later when
the amount of compensation is the sole issue.

Damages for injury to feelings

The Sex Discrimination Act, the Race Relations Act and the Disability Dis-   **7-66**
crimination Act all make it clear that compensation may include damages
for injury to feelings.[66a] Save for a run of Scottish cases concerning sexual
harassment, the level of damages awarded by courts and tribunals under this
head once tended to be very low. For example, an industrial tribunal is
reported by the CRE in their 1985 Review of the Act to have awarded £30
to a young man who lost a YTS placement as a result of discrimination and
was said by the tribunal to be "shattered". This was perhaps a particularly
low award, but the typical award did not rise above a few hundred pounds.
However, two decisions of the Court of Appeal in 1988 gave the green light
for considerably higher awards under this head, as well as making clear that
an award may include aggravated damages.

Principles for compensation for injury to feelings

Alexander v. The Home Office[67] sets out the basic principles for the assess-   **7-67**
ment of compensation for injury to feelings. In the county court Mr Alexander had been awarded compensation of £50 when he proved racial discrimination by the prison service in not permitting him to work in the prison
kitchens. His induction report, which was considered by those dealing with
allocation of work, said that "he shows the anti-authoritarian arrogance that
seems to be common in most coloured inmates". So he was not treated as

---

[66a] *Ministry of Defence v. Lowe, The Times*, June 27, 1996, EAT deals with servicewomen who
  had abortions rather than leave the service.
[67] [1988] I.R.L.R. 190, [1988] I.C.R. 685, C.A.

an individual, but by reference to a damaging racial stereotype. In making the award the county court took into account that he had been vindicated by the court in his assertion of his rights. His appeal to the Court of Appeal as to the level of compensation was allowed and an award of £500 substituted. It is clear from the Court's reasoning that £500 now represents a figure at the lower end of the scale of damages for injury to feelings. May L.J. said[67]:

> "As with any other awards of damages the objective of an award for unlawful racial discrimination is restitution. Where the discrimination has caused actual pecuniary loss, such as the refusal of a job, then the damages referable to this can be readily calculated. For the injury to feelings, however, for the humiliation, for the insult, it is impossible to say what is restitution and the answer must depend on the experience and good sense of the judge and his assessors. Awards should not be minimal, because this would tend to trivialise or diminish respect for the public policy to which the Act gives effect. On the other hand, just because it is impossible to assess the monetary value of injured feelings, awards should be restrained. To award sums which are generally felt to be excessive does almost as much harm to the policy and the results which it seeks as do nominal awards. Further, injury to feelings, which is likely to be of a relatively short duration, is less serious than physical injury to the body or the mind which may persist for months, in many cases for life.
> Nevertheless damages for this relatively new tort of unlawful racial discrimination are at large, that is to say that they are not limited to the pecuniary loss that can be specifically proved ... [C]ompensatory damages may and in some instances should, include an element of aggravated damages where, for example, the defendant may have behaved in a high-handed, malicious, insulting or aggressive manner in committing the act of discrimination".[68]

7-68   It was held that the judge was wrong to take into account that Mr Alexander had been vindicated in court in mitigation of the damages to which he was entitled. The Court of Appeal thought it appropriate to take into account, in aggravation of damages, that an unjustified, prejudiced and damaging appraisal of Mr Alexander had been disseminated within the prison system.

7-69   The subsequent case of *Noone v. North West Thames Regional Health Authority*[69] concerned a Sri Lankan microbiologist who was not appointed to a consultancy post on grounds which the Court of Appeal held to be racial. She had superior qualifications, greater experience and more publications than the successful candidate. The industrial tribunal found her interview "little more than a sham". They had awarded £5,000 compensation for injury to feelings. The EAT in fact allowed an appeal against liability but indicated that £1,000 would have been an appropriate figure. When the Court of Appeal restored the industrial tribunal's finding of racial discrimination it substituted an award of £3,000. The Court took into account the fact that section 56 of the Race Relations Act 1976 imposed an upper limit on compensation

[67] [1988] I.R.L.R. 190, [1988] I.C.R. 685, C.A.
[68] At p. 193 in the I.R.L.R. version.
[69] [1988] I.R.L.R. 195, C.A.

awarded by industrial tribunals (fixed by the Secretary of State), and that such a figure should make allowance, not only for a sum for injury to feelings, but also any actual loss, and any sum payable for failure to comply with a recommendation. The limit at the relevant time was £7,500. The Court were of the view that the appellant's injury to feelings was severe and that the award should be at the top end of the bracket, but that £5,000 was too high.

The upper limit (after being progressively raised to £11,000 which was followed to some extent by a corresponding rise in the level of compensation for injury to feelings) has now been abolished. So the basis on which the Court of Appeal reduced the industrial tribunal's award in *Noone* seems to have no application today. Some tribunals have recently seen this as a green light to award much higher sums by way of injury to feelings, (*e.g.* £20,000 by a London tribunal, but where there was an exacerbation of an existing illness[70]) and it is inevitable that the right level will eventually be determined on appeal, probably in relation to appeals against awards alleged to be too high. It would be surprising if the upper level is not a good deal higher than that fastened on in *Noone*. But an early EAT reaction to a case at the other end of the scale in *Orlando v. Didcot Power Station Sports & Social Club*[71] has been to hold that an award of £750 is not so low as to be perverse despite the removal of the cap. The case concerned dismissal of a part-time barmaid because of pregnancy. The EAT looked at statistics relating to awards in the months following the removal and found that tribunals had not thought it right to increase awards because of that factor.

In the case of *Sharifi v. Strathclyde Regional Council*[72] a tribunal award of £750 compensation for race discrimination in respect of intangible loss, covering loss of opportunity, disadvantage in the job market and injury to his feelings was set aside by the EAT and an award of £1,500 substituted. Dr Sharifi applied for a post as a Divisional Scientist in the respondent's Water Department and had not been short-listed, whilst many white applicants without equivalent or indeed any appropriate qualifications were selected. The Appeal Tribunal said that an award of £500 for injured feelings is at or near the minimum appropriate level of award. They added, however, that there was no need to make separate assessments in respect of the various elements of the award.   7-70

Can exemplary damages be awarded?

After dicta in the Court of Appeal in *Alexander v. Home Office* and the decision of that Court in *Bradford Council v. Arora*[73] it seemed that exemplary damages could be sought in an appropriate discrimination case.[74] However, the Court of Appeal in a public nuisance case *AB v. South West Water Services Ltd*[75] held that the question whether it was right to apply the prin-   7-71

---

[70] *Obasa v. London Borough of Islington and Langan*, EOR, DCLD No. 26, p. 10.
[71] EOR, DCLD No. 26, p. 9.
[72] [1992] I.R.L.R. 259. And see the *Deane* case n. 77 below. See also *Murray v. Powertech (Scotland) Ltd* [1992] I.R.L.R. 257 where the EAT suggest that claims for injury to feelings in a discrimination case are "almost inevitable".
[73] *City of Bradford v. Arora* [1991] I.R.L.R. 165, [1991] I.C.R. 226, C.A.
[74] Case No. 36145/86 (Birmingham) was an example: cited in *Arora*.
[75] [1993] 1 All E.R. 609.

ciples in *Rookes v. Barnard*[76] to a tort created since that case was not argued in *Arora* and it was not appropriate to do so. The EAT in *Deane v. Ealing L.B.C.*[77] followed this decision in a race discrimination appeal and ruled that a claim for exemplary damages must therefore fail.

7-72 Unless this point gets before the House of Lords and is reconsidered, therefore, we shall see no more awards for exemplary damages in discrimination cases in Britain. Nevertheless it is probably worth pleading a claim in appropriate cases, because one of the Commissions may well feel it worthwhile to pursue a test case on this issue.

Compensation limit removed in discrimination cases

7-73 As originally passed both the SDA and the RRA contained provisions under which a maximum limit on compensation could be prescribed and indeed limits were prescribed. However the ECJ in *Marshall v. Southampton and South-West Hampshire Area Health Authority (No. 2)* found that Article 6 of the Equal Treatment Directive meant that national law should ensure that compensation for loss resulting from discrimination covered by the Directive should be adequate and should also allow for the payment of interest from the time the loss is sustained.

In consequence the Sex Discrimination and Equal Pay (Remedies) Regulations 1993 were brought forward under the European Communities Act 1972 removing the limit under the SDA (and allowing for the payment of interest on awards). These regulations have been held by the EAT to apply to any award made after they came into operation notwithstanding that the act of discrimination preceded the regulations.

To keep race discrimination law in line the similar limit on awards in the Race Relations Act was removed by section 1 of the Race Relations (Remedies) Act 1994 and section 2 of that Act made provision for regulations to be made with regards to interest.

The Disability Discrimination Act 1995 similarly does not contain a limit on compensation as a whole. (However it does contain a power to prescribe a limit to compensation for injury to feelings in non-employment cases perhaps to prevent the situation where the Government thinks awards have got out of hand as a result of excessive displays of sympathy with the disabled.)

Interest

7-74 There are two basic sets of provisions under which interest is payable: one set covering the period between the discriminatory act and the finding of discrimination; and the other set covering the period after the tribunal makes its award up to the date of payment.

The Sex Discrimination and Equal Pay (Remedies) Regulations 1993, the Race Relations (Interest on Awards) Regulations 1994, and regulations to be

---

[76] [1964] A.C. 1129, H.L.

[77] [1993] I.R.L.R. 209. Also in *Ministry of Defence v. Meredith* [1995] I.R.L.R. 539 the EAT held that there is no right to exemplary damages in a claim based on European Community law. See also *Ministry of Defence v. Mutton* [1996] I.C.R. 590, EAT.

made under s.8(6) and (7) of the Disability Discrimination Act 1995 provide for the payment of interest on awards made after their commencement. Normally for awards for injury to feelings interest is payable for the period from the act of discrimination to the day of the decision. And in relation to other compensation from a date half-way from the date of discrimination to the day interest is calculated. Obviously this is intended to do rough justice where losses are likely to be continuing over a period. Nevertheless in exceptional circumstances where serious injustice would be caused if interest were awarded in the ways provided for a different approach can be used. It seems fairly obvious that interest should not be payable for future losses and indeed the Regulations so provide.

In *Cannock* the EAT made it clear that although inflation and appreciation of the the seriousness of discrimination has led to an increase in the level of awards for injury to feelings these are not such circumstances as to prevent an award of interest. On the other hand the fact that the whole financial loss was suffered at the start of the period could well lead to a departure from the normal rule of taking the period from the mid-point date.

The Industrial Tribunals (Interest) Order 1990 as amended makes interest payable on awards in discrimination cases as from the day after the day of decision, but no interest is payable if the award is paid in full within 14 days.

Recommendations

The Sex Discrimination Act, Race Relations Act and Disability Discrimination Act give an industrial tribunal the power on a well-founded complaint to make a recommendation if it considers it to be just and equitable. The scope of such recommendations is limited, however, by the terms of the provisions and by case law thereon. The power is to make: **7-75**

> "a recommendation that the respondent take within a specified period action appearing to the tribunal to be practicable for the purpose of obviating or reducing the adverse effect on the complainant of any act of discrimination to which the complaint relates."[78]

The most obvious limitation on the recommendation power is that it is limited to the adverse effect "on the complainant". In the nature of things, discrimination rarely happens on a one-off basis. If a person has been treated in a particular way because of perceptions of, or beliefs about, the group to which that person belongs rather than the individual's merits, then obviously the same thing is likely to happen to other persons from that group. Tribunals are not empowered, however, on a complaint brought by an individual to make even a recommendation with statutory effect to deal with that possibility.   **7-76**

This may be seen as a major flaw in the legislation. It is farcical that a tribunal might listen for days to similar fact evidence and evidence relating to measures which could have been taken to avoid discrimination, yet be powerless even to make a recommendation themselves. It seems to be the case that the legislators contemplated the sex and race Commissions follow-   **7-77**

[78] SDA 1975, s.65(1)(c), RRA 1976, s.56(1)(c), DDA 1995, s.8(2)(c).

ing up individual cases to deal with the wider implications, either by promotional work (employers are often amenable to an approach after having been caught out) or by use of the formal investigation power which the Commissions possess. (We are not aware of the formal investigation power being used in this way.) This can be asserted with some confidence, because the power to issue non-discrimination notices in formal investigations lists the unlawful acts to which it applies and then says ''and so applies whether or not proceedings have been brought in respect of the act''.

7-78   The statutory effect of a recommendation is that:

> ''If without reasonable justification the respondent to a complaint fails to comply with a recommendation made by an industrial tribunal . . . then if it thinks it just and equitable to do so . . . the tribunal may . . . increase the amount of compensation required to be paid to the complainant in respect of the complaint . . . or if [an order for compensation had not been made but could have been] the tribunal may make such an order.''[79]

7-79   Recommendations for an apology are sometimes made, but if the respondent has denied the discrimination and had it proved against him, unless there has been some change in attitude during the hearing, the absence of an apology up to that point would also need to be reflected in the compensation awarded.

Power to make a recommendation

7-80   Case law has imposed limitations on the power to make a recommendation. First, it cannot be used to give the applicant priority in respect of future similar jobs over other applicants, so the Court of Appeal in *Noone v. N. W. Thames Regional Health Authority (No. 2)*[80] held, because other possible contenders for such a post might be better qualified for that post. However, the *Noone* post was a highly specialised consultancy post. It is open to question whether, when an employer has many similar vacancies of a less specialised kind, it is not being unduly sensitive not to allow a recommendation that the next such vacancy should be offered to the applicant. This is particularly the case where the applicant is demonstrably better than the person who got the post to which the complaint relates. The *Noone* case does make clear that a recommendation that a person be notified of the vacancy which next occurs is lawful. Second, questions of monetary compensation are to be dealt with under the power to award compensation and not under the power to make a recommendation. A tribunal may not, therefore, make a recommendation that an employer should increase a person's wages.[81]

Reasoned decisions

7-81   A tribunal is required to furnish a reasoned decision in race relations, sex discrimination and equal pay cases under regulation 10(4) of the Industrial

---

[79] SDA, s.65(4), RRA, s.56(4), DDA 1995, s.8(5).
[80] [1988] I.R.L.R. 530, C.A.
[81] See *Irvine v. Prestcold Ltd* [1981] I.R.L.R. 281, C.A.

Tribunal (Rules of Procedure) Regulations 1993. No doubt this rule will apply to disability discrimination cases. In equal value cases, a copy of the report supplied by the independent expert is appended to the decision.

In *Meek v. City of Birmingham District Council*, Bingham L.J. set out the approach to be adopted by tribunals when reasons are required:

    7-82

> "It has on a number of occasions been made plain that the decision of an Industrial Tribunal is not required to be an elaborate formalistic product of refined legal draftsmanship, but it must contain an outline of the story which has given rise to the complaint and a summary of the Tribunal's basic factual conclusions and a statement of the reasons which have led them to the conclusions which they do on those basic facts. The parties are entitled to be told why they have won or lost. There should be sufficient account of the facts and of the reasoning to enable the EAT or, on further appeal, this court to see whether a question of law arises."[82]

In *Hampson v. DES*[83] Balcombe L.J. relied upon the decision in *Meek* arguing that, in the absence of authority on the meaning of "full reasons," no less standard is required than was formerly the case when only "reasons" were prescribed. He was critical of the findings of justifiability by the tribunal in *Hampson* because the standards used to test the Department's justification of the requirements placed upon the applicant were not identified, nor was it clear what precise findings of fact had been relied upon in coming to the conclusion that the requirement was justifiable.

    7-83

Costs

Costs are not normally awarded in the industrial tribunals. An industrial tribunal has the power to award costs under regulation 12 of the Industrial Tribunal (Rules of Procedure) Regulations if, in the view of the tribunal, the proceedings were brought or conducted frivolously, vexatiously, abusively, disruptively or otherwise unreasonably. The restrictions do not apply in respect of a party who applies for an adjournment.

    7-84

Cost awards are uncommon and lie within the discretion of the tribunal, both as to whether they are awarded and as to their sum. In making such an award, the tribunal may take into account the means of the party in question. The costs of the EOC or CRE in assisting applicants constitute a first charge upon any costs or expenses recovered by the assisted person.[84]

    7-85

Under the old rules a costs warning could be issued against either party at a pre-hearing assessment if the tribunal was of the opinion that there is no reasonable prospect of success. The introduction of the pre-hearing assessment did not result in a costs award being made in a substantial number of cases, and in a fair number of the cases in which a costs warning was given

    7-86

---

[82] [1987] I.R.L.R. 250, C.A.
[83] [1989] I.R.L.R. 69 (the case subsequently went to H.L.)
[84] SDA, s.75 (3)(a), RRA, s.66(5)(a).

the applicant was ultimately successful at the full hearing in discrimination cases.

7-87 Nonetheless, the Employment Act 1989 introduced a provision under which regulation 7 of the 1993 rules provide for a pre-hearing review. At that review the tribunal is empowered to require a deposit of up to £150 from a party as a condition of proceeding further if there is no reasonable prospect of success, or the proceedings are judged to be being brought frivolously, vexatiously or otherwise unreasonably. It will be interesting to see whether the Commissions will ever pay deposits as part of their assistance. The review will take place without the benefit of any evidence being heard and must entail the prospect that a deposit will be required in a certain proportion of cases which will ultimately be successful. Discrimination cases are not normally thrown out without hearing the respondent's side and giving the applicant the chance to cross-examine, and knowing this should make tribunals wary of taking deposits on the strength of the papers alone.

Tribunal procedure and the armed forces

7-88 At the time of writing there is a Bill before Parliament which would amend the Sex Discrimination Act 1975, the Equal Pay Act 1970 (and the equivalent Northern Ireland Orders) as well as the Race Relations Act 1976. Members of the armed forces will be able to bring claims in the industrial tribunals relating to their service (for the first time in race cases), but only after first making use of the internal redress procedures. The usual time limit for commencing proceedings is extended from three to six months. (There is in the Bill a service requirement in respect of bringing an Equal Pay claim.)

By virtue of section 64(6) of the Disability Discrimination Act 1995 Part 2 of that Act does not apply at all to "service in any of the naval, military or air forces of the Crown".

Appeals to the EAT

7-89 Appeal may be made to the EAT on a point of law only, within 42 days beginning with the notification of the written decision. Appeals in discrimination and equal pay cases are governed by the normal Employment Appeals Tribunal Rules 1980 and are the subject of a Practice Direction dated March 29, 1996. The Practice Direction contains the observation that it is not usually a good excuse for delay in appealing that legal aid has been applied for or support is being sought from the EOC or CRE. Employee appellants have had a very poor success rate in discrimination cases in front of the EAT in recent years, such that by 1992 it had become a matter of comment by the editor of the Industrial Relations Law Reports.[85]

---

[85] See [1992] I.R.L.R. 333.

8 DISCRIMINATION OUTSIDE EMPLOYMENT

This chapter deals with race and sex discrimination outside the employment area. We have put the statement of the provisions of the Disability Discrimination Act 1995 (DDA) in the chapter on disability discrimination, so that the reader can gain an overview of the disability legislation. Nevertheless much from the existing statute law has been borrowed by the Disability Discrimination Act in relation to the provision of goods, facilities and services and the disposal and management of premises. Accordingly much relevant case law on the wording is to be found in parts of this chapter. Rather than repeat all the case law what we have done is to indicate in the chapter on disability discrimination where there are similarities with the Sex Discrimination Act 1975 (SDA) and the Race Relations Act 1976 (RRA), so that the reader can then follow up on specific points here in this chapter.

Education

Part III of each of the Sex Discrimination Act 1975 and the Race Relations Act 1976 deals with discrimination in other fields than employment. Each opens with the subject of Education. The disability discrimination provisions are completely different and the reader is referred to the chapter on that subject. **8-01**

In the context of education, it is perhaps worth repeating the general point that, if less favourable treatment occurs on the prohibited grounds, *direct* discrimination occurs even though the person acting on those grounds was paternalistic or well-intentioned. Much discrimination as a result of sterotyping falls into this category. A teacher stops a girl doing science-based subjects, because of a belief that girls in general are better at arts subjects, despite the fact that the particular girl has the right aptitude for science-based subjects. A teacher stops an Afro-Caribbean boy doing academic subjects, because of a belief that Afro-Caribbeans are good at sport but not academic subjects, despite the fact that the particular boy is academically bright. In both cases, the teacher is doing as much harm as one who malevolently sets out to do down girls and blacks, and this is the way that the law looks at it.

In *Debell, Sevket and Teh v. London Borough of Bromley*,[1] there was sex discrimination where a headmistress departed from a written policy for the **8-02**

[1] See *Sex Discrimination Paper No. 7* (EOC).

allocation of pupils by age to different classes and made decisions on the basis of sex. She tried to even up the number of each sex in each class for socialisation and curriculum opportunity reasons. The complainant girls were kept in a class of predominantly third year pupils with a female teacher, instead of being moved to a class of predominantly fourth year pupils as had happened to some younger boys. The headmistress also claimed that a class with a female teacher was best for the girls concerned.

8-03   The law of *indirect* discrimination says in effect that a practice which has a discriminatory result will be unlawful unless justifiable.[2] In the context of education, one will be looking for an educational justification for the practice. Educational thinking on various subjects, however, tends to develop and change as understanding increases. This means that not only do practices have to be examined to assess whether they have discriminatory impact, but also that the justification should be re-examined from time to time to see whether it still holds good. A good example is the CRE's Formal Investigation of Calderdale Local Education Authority. The LEA operated an English Language testing system. Before admission to main-stream schooling, children either had to be exempt or pass the test. Those who did not were predominantly of Asian origin and were placed either into special language centres or special language classes within schools. The effect was that they were separated from other children and there were other disadvantages including a narrower curriculum. No doubt when the system was set up it had been thought the best way of teaching English as a second language, but in the meantime, educational research and thinking had reached the conclusion that teaching English as a second language was actually best done in the ordinary classroom with special help on tap. The LEA conceded in the light of this development that their procedures were not justifiable, and the CRE concluded that they amounted to indirect discrimination. The Secretary of State accepted these findings.

The provisions dealing with education

8-04   Section 17 of the Race Relations Act 1976 and section 22 of the Sex Discrimination Act 1975 are phrased in similar terms and make unlawful the following types of discrimination by certain bodies in charge of educational establishments:

> (a) in the terms on which it offers to admit him or her to the establishment as a pupil; or
>
> (b) refusing or deliberately omitting to accept an application for his or her admission to the establishment as a pupil; or
>
> (c) where he or she is a pupil of the establishment —
>
> > (i) in the way it affords him or her access to any benefits, facilities or services, or by refusing or deliberately omitting to afford him or her access to them;

---

[2] See chapter 2.

(ii) by excluding him or her from the establishment or subjecting him/
her to any other detriment.''

The establishments to which this applies with the responsible body are set **8-05**
out in the relevant section together with orders made from time to time under
section 24(1) of the Sex Discrimination Act 1975. As the educational system
changes, so the sections and orders alter. Reference should be made to the
current provisions.

It should be noted that under section 17 of the Race Relations Act and section **8-06**
22 of the Sex Discrimination Act, unlawful discrimination occurs only in
respect of a particular establishment. Under these provisions it is not possible
to compare the treatment of say girls or black pupils in one school with that
of boys or white pupils, as the case may be, in another school. But section
18 of the Race Relations Act and section 23[3] of the Sex Discrimination Act
impose a wider duty on local education authorities.[4]

Possibly the worst case of direct discrimination under both Acts to come to **8-07**
light was in the admission process of St George's Hospital Medical School.
A computer programme used to sift UCCA admission application forms and
grade them for a decision to be made as to whether the applicant would be
interviewed had a built-in bias against women and ''non-caucasians'', which
deliberately mimicked the decision-making of the academics who read the
forms before the computer took over the task. The real question for every-
body in education is how typical this bias in decision-making is of other
educational institutions, (although of course the manifestation of the bias in
a computer programme may be very rare).[5]

An indirect racial discrimination case which went to the House of Lords was **8-08**
Mandla v. Dowell-Lee[6] in which it was held to be indirectly discriminatory
to require agreement to the wearing of a school uniform cap because turban-
wearing orthodox Sikh boys could not comply consistently with their cultural
norms and could not therefore enter the school, and the requirement was not
justifiable.

More complex was the (Commission for Racial Equality's) (CRE's) investi- **8-09**
gation into access to the Watford Grammar Schools (in fact all-ability
schools) where the selection process seemed to involve a need for a minimum
number of reasons to be specified by parents in choosing the schools. This
had an indirectly discriminatory impact on those Asian children whose parents' first language was not English and who encountered difficulty in
expressing themselves in writing. The Commission found indirect racial discrimination (but the passage in the report dealing with justifiability is barely
more than an assertion by the Commission, and would hardly have satisfied

---

[3] See below.
[4] See *R. v. Secretary of State for Education and Science, ex p. Keating* [1985] L.G.R. 469.
[5] See *Medical School Admissions*: A CRE formal investigation.
[6] [1983] 2 A.C. 548.

an appeal court if a tribunal had been so skimpy with its reasons on justifiability: see Balcombe L.J. (in *Hampson v. DES*).[7]

The single-sex exemption

8-10 Where the single-sex exemption under the Sex Discrimination Act 1975 applies, a single-sex establishment is exempt from the Sex Discrimination Act duty not to discriminate in admissions. There are transitional arrangements for establishments becoming co-educational in section 27 and Schedule 2.

A single-sex establishment is defined by section 26 of the Sex Discrimination Act 1975 as an establishment which admits pupils of one sex only, or where the admission of pupils of the opposite sex is exceptional, or comparatively few in number and confined to particular courses of instruction or teaching classes. A school which is not a single-sex school may nevertheless discriminate in its admission of boarders and in relation to boarding facilities if it takes both boarders and non-boarders, but the boarders are wholly or mostly of one sex only. Section 27 of the Sex Discrimination Act enables schools to gain sanction for transitional arrangements in becoming co-educational, by application for a "transitional exemption order" under Schedule 2 of the Act.

8-11 It should be noted that, unlike the Race Relations Act 1976, the Sex Discrimination Act 1975 has no provision equating segregation with less favourable treatment.[8] In this way, the Act does not prohibit the continuation of separate facilities for boys and girls within a co-educational school, provided that the facilities afforded to each sex can justifiably be regarded as providing equal opportunities. Any facility or course provided must be available to both sexes. By contrast, segregation of black pupils from white pupils on racial grounds amounts in law to less favourable treatment of both groups.

8-12 Since the cultural practices of particular racial groups may be such as to require single-sex education for their children, lack of sufficient places provided by a local authority to meet this need might be indirectly racially discriminatory in that it would have the effect of denying them access to schools of their choice. This would, however, fall to be dealt with not under section 17 of the Race Relations Act 1976 which relates to *particular establishments*, but under section 18 which sets out a wider duty of local education authorities (education authorities in Scotland).

Duties on Education Authorities

8-13 Section 18 of the Race Relations Act 1976 and section 23 of the Sex Discrimination Act 1975 are in similar terms and impose a duty on those education authorities in carrying out their functions under the Education Acts not to do any act which constitutes discrimination (excepting functions already

---

[7] See [1989] I.R.L.R. 69.
[8] See RRA 1976, s.1(2), and see the Cleveland case on the meaning of segregation, see n. 11 below.

covered by sections 17 of the RRA and 22 of the SDA). (Later additions to sections 18 of the RRA and 23 of the SDA have applied similar duties not to discriminate to the Further Education and the Higher Education Funding Councils, the Funding Agency for Schools, the Schools Funding Council for Wales, and to the Teacher Training Agency.) An example usually referred to in this context is the award of discretionary educational grants, but the provision can also cover wider educational functions. For example, a local education authority could fall foul of the Sex Discrimination Act provisions by treating girls less favourably in, say, the provision of places for advanced physics, even though the underlying reason for this is that the extra facilities exist for boys in exempt single-sex schools. This is a necessary implication from the fact that the single-sex establishment exception does not apply in relation to section 23.

In *R v. Secretary of State for Education and Science, ex p. Keating*,[9] it was   **8-14**
held that a local education authority was obliged to have regard to the Sex Discrimination Act 1975 in carrying out its duty under section 8 of the Educa-
tion Act 1944 to provide secondary schools in its area "sufficient in number, character, and equipment". Thus, if the policy of the authority was to provide single-sex education for both boys and girls, the treatment of one sex less favourably than the other was contrary to section 23 of the 1975 Act. The local education authority's publication of a proposal to close the only boys' comprehensive school in its area would therefore, being an act done pursuant to section 8 of the Act of 1944, constitute discrimination on the grounds of sex.

The *Keating* case was an example of the use of judicial review procedures   **8-15**
to obtain relief. In that case it was the parents who took proceedings. In *R. v. Birmingham City Council*,[10] (a case which went to the House of Lords) it was the EOC who took judicial review proceedings. This method of proceeding is an ideal way of avoiding the cumbersome procedure of a formal investigation where the facts are not in dispute, and what is in issue is the lawfulness of what has occurred. The decision was similar to that in the *Keating* case, though here the council was discriminating unlawfully in providing more grammar school places for boys than for girls.

The parental choice provisions were held by the Court of Appeal to override   **8-16**
the Race Relations Act insofar as there was a conflict in the case of *R. v. Cleveland County Council, ex p. CRE*. A local education authority had taken the view that a parental choice of school had been expressly made on racial grounds,[11] yet felt obliged to comply with it because of the wording of the Education legislation. The Court upheld the view of the authority against a contrary finding by the CRE in a formal investigation that the Race Relations Act provision in section 18 prevailed. It held that discrimination in carrying out duties in relation to parental choice was protected by section 41 which protects acts done in pursuance of any enactment.

Section 19 of the Race Relations Act 1976 and section 25 of the Sex Discrim-   **8-17**

---

[9] [1985] 84 L.G.R. 469.
[10] [1989] I.R.L.R. 173.
[11] *Times Law Report*, August 25, 1992. The parent was held not to have acted on racial grounds.

ination Act 1975 further impose a general duty in the public sectors of education to secure that facilities for education and any ancillary benefits or services are provided without discrimination. These provisions are really
concerned with *planning* in education to ensure freedom from discrimination.
As the Equal Opportunities Commission point out, as far as the Sex Discrimination Act 1975 is concerned, the purpose of the planning is not to ensure
that there is a balance between the sexes, but that pupils and applicants for
admission have access to education provision irrespective of sex. With appropriate modification, the same could be said of race. In the course of planning,
questions may have to be asked why existing imbalances exist, and whether
the cause is discrimination.

Enforcement

8-18 The Secretary of State has the exclusive power to enforce this general duty
using Education Act powers.[12] Those same powers also apply to breaches of
the other provisions, creating liability for discrimination in addition to an
individual's right to enforce them in the county court. In this sector of education there are also two modifications to the normal enforcement procedure.
First, an individual has to give notice to the Secretary of State before commencing legal proceedings and this has an effect on the time limit for their
commencement.[13] Second, neither the EOC nor the CRE can issue a non-
discrimination notice in a formal investigation, but instead give notice of
findings of discrimination to the Secretary of State, who can use his Education Act powers if appropriate.

LEAs and the promotion of good race relations

8-19 The education provisions in the Sex Discrimination Act and the Race Relations Act are concerned with the elimination of discrimination. But LEAs,
being local authorities, are also subject to the wider duty under section 71
of the Race Relations Act 1976,[14] requiring them in addition:

> "to make appropriate arrangements with a view to securing that their
> various functions are carried out with due regard to the need—
>
> (a) to eliminate unlawful racial discrimination; and
> (b) to promote equality of opportunity, and good relations, between per-
> sons of different racial groups."

Clearly (a) above covers much the same ground as section 19 of the Race
Relations Act 1976, but (b) goes beyond, particularly insofar as it relates to
the promotion of good race relations. This adds a whole new dimension to
the educational function of LEAs. However, the opting out arrangements
for schools obviously mean that the influence of LEAs will diminish in the
future.

---

[12] RRA 1975, s.19 and SDA 1975, s. 25.
[13] See at the end of this chapter.
[14] See also chapter 10.

Goods, facilities and services

(For the provisions relating to disability discrimination please see chapter 3 on that subject, followed by this section).

Both the 1975 and 1976 Acts contain similar sections prohibiting discrimina-   **8-20**
tion in the provision of goods, facilities and services to the public or a section of the public. It is generally unlawful for any person concerned with the provision (for payment or not) of goods, facilities or services to the public, or a section of the public, to discriminate either by refusing or deliberately omitting to provide them, or to provide them of like quality, in the like manner, and on the like terms as he normally provides them (section 20, RRA, section 29, SDA). (The DDA provisions have considerable similarities but the reader is referred to chapter 3 first on that subject.)

However, certain differences have arisen between the SDA and RRA. First,   **8-21**
the reference to "the public or a section of a public" has meant that the activities of private clubs *vis-à-vis* membership matters are outside of the prohibition. Under the Race Relations Act 1976, this has led to a separate provision dealing with such associations (see section 25), but not, despite, it seems, a need, under the Sex Discrimination Act 1975.[15] Second, a restrictive interpretation of the application of the provision to the functions of public authorities by the House of Lords in *R. v. Entry Clearance Officer, Bombay, ex p. Amin*[16] has led to a new section 19A in the Race Relations Act 1976 to ban racial discrimination in the exercise of planning functions, but there is no similar ban on sex discrimination.

Use of the word "normally" in section 20 of the RRA and section 29 of   **8-22**
the SDA indicates that they do not extend to cover *provision* on a one-off occasion.[17] They do, of course, cover even a one-off case of *discrimination* where the provision is sufficiently frequent for the word "normally" to be appropriate.

Public or section thereof
The words "to the public or a section of the public" limit the application   **8-23**
of the sections. The leading cases on the meaning of those words all arose in the context of the Race Relations Act 1968. The House of Lords held that a Conservative Club was not offering the facility of membership to a section of the public,[18] and similarly nor was a working men's club, in refusing to admit a member of another club, offering facilities or services to a section of the public, even though the clubs were all affiliated in a union.[19] The consideration which weighed with their Lordships was whether there was genuine selection on personal grounds in electing candidates for membership.

---

[15] See *Legislating for Change*, (EOC).
[16] [1983] 2 A.C. 818.
[17] On the similar provision on the RRA 1968 see *Dockers Labour Club and Institute Ltd v. Race Relations Board* [1976] A.C. 285, at 297 *per* Lord Diplock, and on the 1976 Act *Hector v. Smethwick Labour Club Institute* (1988) (unreported).
[18] *Charter v. Race Relations Board* [1973] A.C. 885.
[19] *Dockers Labour Club and Institute Ltd v. Race Relations Board* see above, p. 00.

Even the fact that there were more than a million members of the union normally entitled to avail themselves of affiliated membership rights did not make them a section of the public. By contrast, the House held that children in the care of a local authority were a section of the public to whom foster-parents provided services or facilities.[20] The cases remain authoritative on the meaning of the words "to the public or a section of the public". Nevertheless, the sequel to these cases was that the Race Relations Act 1976 legislated specifically to bring private clubs within that Act, whilst foster-parents were themselves taken outside the Act.[21]

8-24   The latter was achieved by section 23(2) of the Race Relations Act 1976 which says that:

> "section 20(1) does not apply to anything done by a person as a participant in arrangements under which he (for reward or not) takes into his home, and treats as if they were members of his family, children, elderly persons, or persons requiring a special degree of care and attention".

Since the reference is to the person who "takes into his home," the exception would cover the foster-parent who discriminates on racial grounds, but not discrimination by local authorities or private agencies in providing their services to children or others in need of such provision, except insofar as they were satisfying racial preferences expressed by the homeowners. (However, if the authorities or agencies were by written circular to invite the expression of racial preferences, it would seem that they would fall foul of the ban on discriminatory advertisements since "advertisement" is defined very widely. There is no exception relating to section 23(2), and the ban applies whether the act of discrimination would be lawful or not, and where the advertisement might reasonably be understood as indicating an intention to discriminate.)

The meaning of "goods, facilities and services"

8-25   There is no attempt to provide a close definition of "goods, facilities and services" in the legislation. Instead, the phrase is exemplified. The Acts do, however, state that references:

> "to affording by any person of access to benefits, facilities or services are not limited to benefits, facilities or services provided by that person himself, but include any means by which it is in that person's power to facilitate access to benefits, facilities or services provided by any other person."[22]

This is a general provision, but its main application is likely to be in relation to section 29 of the Sex Discrimination Act 1975 and section 20 of the Race Relations Act 1976.

---

[20] *Applin v. Race Relations Board* [1975] A.C. 259.
[21] See RRA 1976, ss. 23(2), 25.
[22] RRA 1976, s.40(1) and SDA 1975, s.50(1).

The examples given of the provision of facilities and services by the legisla-   **8-26**
tion are not intended to be exhaustive[23]:

> "(a) access to and use of any place which members of the public are
> permitted to enter;
> (b) accommodation in a hotel, boarding house or other similar
> establishment;
> (c) facilities by way of banking or insurance or for grants, loans, credits
> or finance;
> (d) facilities for education;
> (e) facilities for entertainment, recreation or refreshment;
> (f) facilities for transport or travel;
> (g) the services of any profession or trade, or any local or other public
> authority."

A few points need to be made here. There is an exception relating to insurance under the Sex Discrimination Act 1975[24]; "education" is defined as
including any form of training or instruction, "profession" as including any
vocation of occupation, and "trade" as including any business.[25]

What is being provided

What if the goods, facilities or services are of such a nature that they cater   **8-27**
in practice for members of one sex only, or one particular race only — would
the provider have to modify the service accordingly? The example of a sari
shop raises the same problem under both pieces of legislation. There is no
doubt that a white man is entitled to buy a sari on the same terms as an
Asian woman, but does the shop also have to sell clothes that specifically
cater for persons of other ethnic origins or for men? The Sex Discrimination
Act 1975, s.29(3) attempts to solve a similar problem "for the avoidance of
doubt" in the context of sex discrimination. Where the provision of a skill
is normally for one sex only, and it is commonly exercised in a different
manner for different sexes, it can either be provided in the like manner to a
person of the other sex, or if it is considered reasonably impracticable to do
so, it can be refused. Presumably since the provision is only for the avoidance
of doubt, it follows that a sari shop need not also stock clothes which cater
for persons of non-Asian ethnic origin or men.

There is a distinction, it seems, between what is there to be provided and   **8-28**
the circumstances of the provision itself. The legislation is aimed at discrimination relating to the latter, not the former. In some circumstances drawing
the line may not be altogether easy, and may become most acute in the
context of indirect discrimination when what constitutes goods, facilities or
services will need to be distinguished from conditions or requirements
applied to persons seeking those goods, facilities or services. Thus, in the
case of building societies who made loans only on houses with front gardens,
the CRE took the view that the facility or service was that of making loans
upon mortgage in respect of houses, and a requirement or condition was

---

[23] *R. v. Entry Clearance Officer, Bombay, ex p. Amin* [1983] 2 A.C. 818 *per* Lord Fraser, at
834 and Lord Scarman at 842.
[24] See SDA 1975, s.45.
[25] SDA 1975, s.82(1); RRA 1976, s.78(1).

applied to persons that they could only make use of the facility or service if they came forward with houses with front gardens. Since disproportionately few Asians could comply with this in the circumstances prevailing in Rochdale, this amounted to unlawful indirect discrimination, with the building societies admitting that they could not justify the practice.[26]

Facilities, services and the public sector

8-29　Among the examples of the application of section 20 of the Race Relations Act and section 29 of the Sex Discrimination Act is reference to the services "of any local or other public authority". It is, however, misleading to suppose that when applied to the public sector the provision is comprehensive. Judicial interpretation has meant that this is not the case. The leading case on this point is the House of Lords decision *R. v. Entry Clearance Officer, Bombay ex p. Amin.*[27] Mrs Amin was a British Overseas Citizen. Pursuant to legislation introduced in 1968, her right to entry to the United Kingdom depended on a special voucher scheme. Vouchers were only available to heads of household and generally a woman was assumed not to be the head of a household. For this reason, Mrs Amin was refused a voucher. The House of Lords were clear that this amounted to sex discrimination, but a majority held that it was outside section 29 of the 1975 Act because the supply of vouchers was the provision of neither a facility nor a service.

8-30　Two reasons were relied upon. First, section 29 was held to apply "to the direct provision of facilities or services and not to the mere grant of permission to use facilities".[28] If this is right, it is difficult to see why issuing somebody a ticket to enter a swimming bath should not equally be regarded as the mere grant of permission to use a facility, yet nobody could really doubt that it was intended that the Acts cover discrimination by refusing somebody such a ticket. Second, the section was held to apply only to acts which "are at least similar to acts that could be done by private persons". There was said to be a "necessity" for construing the Act in that way, although the House entirely failed to explain this assertion. Had the House of Lords not said otherwise, one could have been forgiven for thinking that the necessity was to construe the "goods, facilities and services" as widely as possible so as to provide a remedy in the county courts for as much racial and sex discrimination as possible. Privatisation may undermine the impact of their reasoning.

8-31　Prior to the *Amin* case in *CRE v. Riley*,[29] a county court judge held that the granting of planning permission fell within section 20 of the 1976 Act, and issued an injunction to restrain the bringing of pressure on a planning authority to commit racial discrimination. In the light of *Amin*, the CRE found itself unable to embark on an accusatory investigation relating to an allegation of discrimination in the making of a planning decision by a local authority. In

[26] Mortgage Allocation in Rochdale: CRE Formal Investigation Report (1985).
[27] [1983] 2 A.C. 818 approving *R. v. Immigration Appeal Tribunal, ex p. Kassam* [1980] 2 All E.R. 330.
[28] *Ibid. per* Lord Fraser at 834.
[29] CRE, *Annual Report 1982* p. 18.

consequence, a provision in the Housing and Planning Act 1986 brought planning functions specifically within the 1976 Act in a new section, section 19A.

To be fair to their Lordships in *Amin*, the case did not stand alone. Two earlier Court of Appeal cases were approved in *Amin*. In the first, *R. v. Immigration Appeal Tribunal, ex p. Kassam*,[30] it was held that the Home Secretary when exercising powers under the Immigration Act 1971 to control entry to the United Kingdom was not providing a "facility". In the second case, *Savjani v. IRC*[31] it was held, distinguishing *Kassam*, that insofar as it operated the tax relief system the Inland Revenue was providing a "service" within section 20 of the 1976 Act. The case concerned a requirement that a taxpayer born in the Indian subcontinent should produce a full birth certificate to substantiate a first-time claim for tax relief for a child born in the United Kingdom. Such a birth certificate cost £2.50. For other taxpayers claiming the same relief, a short birth certificate costing nothing sufficed. In *Amin* Lord Fraser referred to this decision as follows: "In *Savjani* Templeman L.J. took the view that the Inland Revenue performed two separate functions — first a duty of collecting revenue and secondly a service of providing taxpayers with information." He went on, "In the present case the entry clearance officer in Bombay was in my opinion not providing a service for would-be immigrants; rather he was performing his duty of controlling them".[32]

The notion of a "duty of controlling" contrasted with the provision of a facility or service is particularly important when it comes to sorting out the functions of, say, the prison service into those not covered by the law enforcement provision of the Acts and those which are. Southampton County Court held in *Alexander v. Home Office (Prison Department)*[33] that allocation of work to prisoners in the prison (including highly desirable kitchen work) was within section 20. Presumably, access to education facilities for prisoners would also be within the provision. Matters such as allocation of security classifications, however, may be seen as an exercise of the duty of controlling prisoners.   **8-32**

The CRE, in criticising the *Amin* decision, make the point that the lack of a financial remedy under the 1976 Act: **8-33**

> "occurs precisely where the individual is most vulnerable. In the private sector, if there is discrimination at one source the individual generally has both the opportunity of going elsewhere to another provider of services and also has his or her remedy under the Act. The individual appears to have neither when facing an immigration officer, prison officer or police officer prepared to discriminate improperly."[34]

Some of their activities will of course be inside section 20 of the Race Relations Act 1976 and section 29 of the Sex Discrimination Act 1975, but they will tend to be those ancillary to the main functions of the officials concerned.   **8-34**

---

[30] [1980] 2 All E.R. 330.
[31] [1981] Q.B. 458.
[32] *Amin* Case, *supra*, p. 835.
[33] CRE, *Annual Report 1987*. The case went on to the Court of Appeal on question of damages. Liability was not an issue there.
[34] CRE *Review of the RRA 1976* (1985) p. 8.

8-35　Public authorities are of course amenable to judicial review. Even where there is no duty under the legislation not to discriminate, a public body will generally be acting wholly unreasonably if it does so and open itself up to judicial review.

8-36　When section 95 of the Criminal Justice Act 1991 was passed, it adopted the position that all those engaged in the administration of criminal justice were under a duty not to discriminate against any person "on the ground of race or sex or any other improper ground" and imposed on the Secretary of State a duty to publish information to facilitate "the performance by such persons of their duty".

8-37　The case of *James v. Eastleigh Borough Council*[35] highlighted a new problem. Concessions have often been offered to people of state pension age. In this case, a 61 year old man complained that concessionary entry to a swimming pool was not available to him in circumstances where it would be available to a woman because the state pension ages were different. The House of Lords held that this amounted to direct sex discrimination (A sim ilar problem can occur in the race field if a service provider makes use of the voting register as a basis for eligibility for a facility because this register is based on nationality which itself is a prohibited ground under the 1976 Act).

A very similar point occurred in *R. v. Secretary of State, ex p. Richardson*[36] with the added complication that the discrimination was backed up by regulations. Charges for NHS prescriptions depended on pensionable age and this was different for men and women. The ECJ, on a reference in judicial review proceedings, held that there was an infringement of Council Directive 79/7 (progressive implementation of the principle of equal treatment for men and women in matters of social security). On the other hand the ECJ held in *Secretary of State for Social Security v. Graham*[37] that where invalidity benefit was necessarily linked to pensionable age as part of a coherent benefit scheme this fell within the derogation permitted under Article 7(1)(a) permitting the setting of different pensionable ages.

Section 20 of the RRA 1976, section 29 of the SDA 1975 and the private sector

8-38　The application of section 20 of the Race Relations Act and section 29 of the Sex Discrimination Act in the private sector is subject to few problems. Thus, retailers who refuse a woman hire-purchase facilities unless her husband enters into a guarantee when they would not have done the same for a man in similar circumstances, commit sex discrimination.[38] Similarly, refusal to serve women at the bar in a wine club where they were served only at tables when men could be served at the bar fell foul of section 29.[39]

---

[35] [1990] I.R.L.R. 288.
[36] [1995] All E.R. (E.C.) 865.
[37] [1995] All E.R. (E.C.) 736. See also Atkins v. Wrekin D.C. C228/94 [1996] All E.R. (E.C.) 719, ECJ where statutorily protected concessionary bus fares available to women aged 60 and to men at 65 were held to be outside the scope of Directive 79/7.
[38] *Quinn v. Williams Furniture Ltd* [1981] I.C.R. 328, C.A.
[39] *Gill v. El Vino Co. Ltd* [1983] Q.B. 425.

The absence of a provision under the Sex Discrimination Act 1975 dealing **8-39**
with discrimination by associations, equivalent to section 25 of the Race
Relations Act 1976, was rejected as a reason for construing section 29 of
the Sex Discrimination Act differently from section 20 of the Race Relations
act 1976 by the Court of Appeal in *Jones v. Royal Liver Friendly Society.*[40]
The Society offered its policies to anyone prepared to apply and pay the
premium and was therefore providing facilities to the public or a section
thereof. Accordingly, it amounted to unlawful discrimination to refuse to
allow female members to participate in the elections for the governing body
of the friendly society. The point to be gleaned from this case is that the
activities of clubs and associations are not *per se* outside of section 20 of
the Race Relations Act 1976 and section 29 of the Sex Discrimination Act
1975, but only if they provide their facilities or services in such a way that
they cannot be said to be provided to the public or a section thereof.

Exceptions

The Sex Discrimination Act has a special exception in section 45 permitting **8-40**
differential treatment in insurance where it:

1. "was effected by reference to actuarial or other data from a source
   on which it was reasonable to rely and
2. was reasonable having regard to the data and any other relevant
   factors."

There is no equivalent provision in the Race Relations Act 1976, and indeed **8-41**
racial discrimination relating to the granting of insurance policies is not
uncommon. The EOC refer to the "near-universality of the present practice"
of differential treatment on the grounds of sex in insurance, and to the only
test case on the scope of section 45, *Pinder v. Friends Provident,*[41] in which
the County Court found it reasonable for a company to justify its practice
of charging women 50 per cent more than men for Permanent Health Insurance, which it had done since 1953, largely by reference to social security
statistics at the time. The court took the view that once the case for differential treatment was made out it was largely a matter of commercial judgment
how large it should be. Leaving county court judges to make judgments under
the rubric of words like "reasonable" in the context of how far sex discrimination should be permitted is apt to produce such a result.

Both section 20 of the Race Relations Act and section 29 of the Sex Discrim- **8-42**
ination Act have a small premises exception, but since this is an exception
which also applies to the sections dealing with discrimination in the disposal
or management of premises it is dealt with below under that heading.

Territorial extent
Section 20 of the Race Relations Act and section 29 of the Sex Discrimina- **8-43**
tion Act only apply to the provision of goods, facilities and services outside
Great Britain in limited circumstances. They apply in relation to facilities for

---

[40] *The Times*, December 2, 1982, C.A.
[41] *The Times*, December 16, 1985.

travel outside Great Britain where the refusal or omission occurs in Great Britain, and apply generally in relation to any ship registered at a port of registry in Great Britain, or in relation to any aircraft or hovercraft registered in the United Kingdom and operated by a person with a principal place of business or ordinary residence in Great Britain. The Sex Discrimination Act, but not the Race Relations Act, also applies in relation to any ship, aircraft or hovercraft which is the Queen's in right of the Government of the United Kingdom. Neither Act applies to various financial facilities for a purpose to be carried out, or in connection with risks wholly or mainly arising outside Great Britain. There is a general caveat, however, that nothing done within another country or its territorial waters to comply with that country's laws is rendered unlawful by these provisions.

Political parties

8-44   Section 33 of the Sex Discrimination Act 1975 contains an exception for political parties to the effect that section 29 is not to be construed as affecting any special provision for persons of one sex only in the constitution, organisation or administration of the political party and nothing in section 29 renders unlawful an act done to give effect to such special provision. The Secretary of State can amend this section by Order. This is perhaps rather odd, in that it could permit a Secretary of State to render unlawful the arrangements of an opposing political party. Special women's groups are of course permitted under this provision. Political parties are those having as a main object promotion of parliamentary candidates for the Parliament of the United Kingdom, or having formal links with such a party.

8-45   There is no similar exemption in the Race Relations Act 1976, which raises the question of the lawfulness of special black groups within parties. Political parties will, *vis-à-vis* their members either be within section 20 as providing facilities or services to a section of the public, or, if more exclusive, but having 25 or more members, within section 25 of the Act. Giving special extra facilities for meetings, etc. to black members will therefore constitute unlawful discrimination unless a general exemption can be prayed in aid. If, as is likely, the purpose of the black group is to meet the special needs of that racial group in regard to their education, training or welfare, or any ancillary benefits, then section 35 can be relied upon to legitimize the group.

Premises and housing

(For the provision relating to disability discrimination readers are referred initially, to chapter 3 on that subject.)

8-46   The law under the Sex Discrimination Act and the Race Relations Act is identical in the provisions relating to the creation of liability in the disposal or management of premises[42] and in relation to consent for assignment or sub-letting,[43] and the principal exception for small dwellings.[44] The law

---

[42] SDA 1976, s.30 and RRA 1976, s.21.
[43] SDA 1975, s.31 and RRA 1976, s.24.
[44] SDA 1975, s.32 and RRA 1976, s.22.

applies only to premises in Great Britain. The term "premises" includes land of any description. There is a difference between the two Acts inasmuch as the CRE can issue codes in the field of housing and has done so, whereas the EOC cannot. Except that discrimination is defined differently the DDA provisions are very similar.

It is unlawful for a person, having the power to dispose of premises, to discriminate in the terms on which he offers them, or by refusing an application for them or in the treatment of a person in relation to any list of persons in need of premises of that description. The term "dispose" includes granting a right to occupy premises, so the provision covers discrimination against both the prospective purchaser and the prospective tenant. Except insofar as they may knowingly aid an unlawful act, persons such as estate agents, accommodation bureaux and building societies who may be involved in a housing transaction will not *normally* be covered by this provision, lacking as they do the power to dispose of the property. Their facilities or services will, however, be covered by section 29 of the Sex Discrimination Act 1975, section 20 of the Race Relations Act 1976 of section 19 of the Disability Discrimination Act 1995. There is a "private transaction" exception: there is no liability where a person, who owns an estate or interest in property which he wholly occupies, discriminates unless he uses the services of an estate agent or advertises in any way.

8-47

The reference to a list of persons is apt to cover those on a local authority housing list. Perhaps the most notable finding of racial discrimination under this head was by the CRE in its Formal Investigation of the London Borough of Hackney. There may be an overlap between section 20 and 21 of the Race Relations Act 1976 in that one example given of facilities or services under section 20 is "the services of . . . any local . . . authority". The finding in the Hackney investigation was, in summary, that the Council had practised:

8-48

> "unlawful direct discrimination against black applicants and tenants who had been allocated housing from the waiting list, or who had been homeless or decant cases, in that whites had received better-quality allocations of properties than blacks."

This finding was expressed in legal terms as amounting to the following contraventions:

8-49

> "of section 20(1)(b) read together with section 1(1)(a) of the Act by refusing or deliberately omitting to provide them with housing accommodation (provision of such accommodation being a service of the local authority) of the like quality to that afforded to white persons in similar need of housing accommodation and/or in contravention of section 21(1)(c) read together with 1(1)(a) of the Act in its treatment of them in relation to lists of persons in need of council accommodation."

This formal investigation is referred to above under the heading of "proof of discrimination" and is significant for the reason set out in the preface to the Report. "It is worth noting that an important precedent was set in issuing this non-discrimination notice against Hackney Council, in that it is the first time such a notice has been issued solely on the basis of statistical evidence."

8-50

8-51   It is also unlawful for a person who manages premises to discriminate against a person occupying them in the way he affords access to any benefits or facilities, or by refusing or deliberately omitting to afford access to them; or by evicting or subjecting the person to any other detriment. An example is the 1994 unreported county court case *Rani and Khan v. Birmingham City Council* concerning complaints made by local authority tenants to a housing officer. Various white tenants were complaining of noise and other problems from Asian neighbours who were themselves complaining of racial harassment from the white tenants. The housing officer provided white tenants with forms on which they could log their complaints, but no such facility was provided to the Asian couple. In the absence of any explanation for this less favourable treatment the court drew the inference of racial discrimination and awarded damages.

The term "manages" is clearly far wider than the notion of having power to dispose, and therefore is capable of covering actions by housekeepers and estate agents, for instance, who may manage property by collecting rents and/or arranging particular facilities or benefits for occupants. If it seems inherently unlikely that a landlord would, for example, take a black person as a tenant and then proceed to harass that person on racial grounds so as to fall foul of this provision, it should be borne in mind that personalities do change in estate agents' offices and so forth, and so do the personalities of the principals for whom they act, or persons in neighbouring properties, who may bring pressure to bear on them to discriminate. Being given a tenancy is therefore no guarantee of freedom of discrimination. It is also conceivable that sexual harassment of a woman tenant could occur and put the person concerned in breach of this provision.

8-52   Both the Sex Discrimination Act 1975, s.35(3) and the Race Relations Act 1976, s.23(1) deal with the problem of overlap between various parts of the legislation, so that the sections dealing with discrimination in the provision of goods, facilities and services and of accommodation do not render unlawful discrimination in the provision of accommodation for the purposes of residential employment or education where it is permitted elsewhere in the legislation.

8-53   Section 24 of the Race Relations Act 1976, section 31 of the Sex Discrimination Act 1975 and section 22(4) of the Disability Discrimination Act 1995 deal with the situation where the tenant of a property requires the consent or licence of a landlord in order to assign the tenancy or sublet part of the accommodation. They render unlawful discrimination by a landlord by refusing the consent.

The small premises exception

8-54   Section 22 of the Race Relations Act, section 32 of the Sex Discrimination Act and section 23 of the Disability Discrimination Act permit discrimination by a person in letting accommodation (and an equivalent provision applies to discrimination in granting consent to assign or sublet) if that person, or a near relative (as defined) resides and continues to reside on the premises, and shares a significant part of the accommodation with other persons living on the premises, and the premises are small. Where there is residential accommodation for one or more households (under separate letting or similar agreements), in addition to that of the landlord or his near relative, the premises are small if there is not normally residential accommodation for two such households, and only members of his household live within the accommodation occupied by the landlord or his near relative. In other cases, the premises are small if there is not normally residential accommodation on the premises for more than six persons in addition to the landlord or his near relative and any members of that household.

Planning: the Race Relations Act 1976

For reasons which are set out under the heading concerned with the provision of goods, facilities and services, discrimination by a planning authority in carrying out its planning functions was thought, in the light of the *Amin* case, to be outside the scope of the Race Relations Act 1976. In the context of racial discrimination this was a significant loophole in the Act, because although judicial review was available to deal with discrimination by a planning authority itself, there was no remedy for the racist pressure to discriminate that was put upon authorities in respect of some developments.

8-55

It seems that sex discrimination in carrying out a planning function is also outside the Sex Discrimination Act, but is not thought to be a problem in that area. In any event, the position has been altered by legislation only in the context of the Race Relations Act 1976, to which a new section, section 19A, has been added by the Housing and Planning Act 1986, which makes it unlawful for a planning authority to discriminate. A planning authority is defined in England and Wales as a county, district or London borough council, a joint planning board, a special planning board or a National Public Committee, and in Scotland as a planning authority or regional planning authority, and includes an urban development corporation and a body having functions under Schedule 32 of the Local Government, Planning and Land Act 1980. Planning functions are defined in the legislation.

8-56

Inasmuch as this is an example of a decision to which a right of appeal attaches being subject to the discrimination legislation, the provision is an interesting development. If one of the arguments against extension of the legislation to other areas is that there are statutory rights of appeal, or complaints bodies in existence, an explanation is needed as to why the same argument was not applied to planning authorities.

8-57

RRA 1976, s. 25

Discrimination by Associations other than trade unions or similar organisations

Section 25 of the Race Relations Act covers discrimination by any association of persons whether incorporated or not, and whether a profit-making organisation or not, where it has 25 or more members and admission to membership is regulated by its constitution and is so conducted that the membership do

8-58

not constitute a section of the public.[45] But organisation to which section 11 applies (organisation of workers, employees, etc.) are exempted.

8-59   It is made unlawful for such an association to discriminate against a non-member in the terms on which it is prepared to admit him to membership, or by refusing or deliberately, omitting to accept his application for membership. In practice, one major problem with clubs is that they will normally require applicants for membership to be sponsored by existing members. This will often be a problem for black potential applicants trying to get into an all-white club, and represented a challenge for the courts to use the indirect discrimination law to break down barriers in relation to a matter which goes to the heart of the membership system. Birmingham County Court, hearing an appeal from a non-discrimination notice, showed that it was willing to conclude that the traditional rule needed modifying in a case where the membership of a club was all white in the middle of multi-racial Handsworth.

8-60   In relation to members or associates (persons having some or all membership rights without actually being members) it is made unlawful to discriminate by depriving the person of those rights or varying them, in the way access to benefits, facilities or services are afforded, or by refusing or deliberately omitting to afford access to them; or by subjecting the person to any other detriment.

8-61   Section 26 provides for an exception to section 25 for certain associations providing the discrimination is not on the ground of colour. Those are associations where the main object is to enable the benefit of membership to be enjoyed by a particular racial group defined otherwise than by reference to colour. So, for example, a Polish cultural society, an Irish dance group or a Welsh choral society can discriminate *vis-à-vis* membership applications and in its relation with members or associates, but not on the ground of colour.

Barristers and advocates

8-62   Section 64 of the Courts and Legal Services Act 1990 deals with discrimination by, or in relation to, barristers, and section 65 does the same for advocates in Scotland. They do so by inserting provisions in Part 3 of the SDA and RRA, and thus proceedings lie in the county courts (designated in the case of a race claim) or sheriff courts. Otherwise the provisions are akin to those dealing with employment, and so we have decided to deal with them in chapter 5.

Exceptions under the Sex Discrimination Act 1975

Voluntary bodies
8-63   Section 34 of the Sex Discrimination Act 1975 contains a wide exception relating to voluntary bodies, *i.e.* a body carrying on its activities other than for profit and not set up under any enactment. It is not unlawful for such a body to restrict either its membership or the benefits, facilities or services it

---

[45] See *supra*, para. 7.23.

provides to its members to one sex (disregarding any minor exception), even though membership of the body is open to the public, or to a section of the public. In addition, where any such body has as its main object to confer benefits on one sex (disregarding any exceptional or relatively insignificant provision to persons of the other sex), it is not unlawful to have a provision to that effect or to do anything to give effect to such a provision.

SDA 1975, s. 35, special cases

It is lawful to provide facilities or services to one sex only at, or as part of, an establishment for persons requiring special care, supervision or attention, *e.g.* a hospital or reception centre provided by the Supplementary Benefits Commission.   **8-64**

Likewise, it is lawful to provide facilities or services restricted to one sex at a place occupied or used (permanently or for the time being) for the purposes of an organised religion if the restriction is to comply with the directives of that religion or to avoid offending the religious susceptibilities of a significant member of its followers. An exception for religious susceptibilities, even where not stemming from religious doctrine, seems to be an open invitation to members of a religion to masquerade their prejudices as "religious susceptibilities." No doubt they would answer to God rather than the law in such matters.   **8-65**

It is also lawful to provide facilities or services restricted to one sex where they are provided for, or likely to be used by, two or more persons at the same time, and the facilities or services are such, or the persons are such, that users of one sex are likely to suffer serious embarrassment at the presence of a member of the other sex. The same applies where the facilities or services are such that a user is likely to be "in a state of undress" and a user might reasonably object to the presence of a member of the opposite sex. A single-sex facility or exercise can also be provided, if it is such that physical contact between the user and any other person is likely and that other person might reasonably object if that user were of the opposite sex.   **8-66**

Charities

Section 43 of the Sex Discrimination Act 1975 provides a general exception for provisions in charitable instruments conferring benefits on persons of one sex only (disregarding exceptional or insignificant benefits to the other sex),[46] but sections 78 and 79 provide a means to alter to charitable instruments or endowments of an education character.   **8-67**

Sports activities

Section 44 of the Sex Discrimination Act 1975 provides that nothing: **8-68**

"shall, in relation to any sport, game or other activity of a competitive nature where the physical strength, stamina or physique of the average woman puts her at a disadvantage to the average man, render unlawful

---

[46] See *Hugh-Jones v. St John's College, Cambridge* [1979] I.C.R. 848. Special arrangements were made in the Employment Act 1989.

any act related to the participation of a person as a competitor in events involving that activity which are confined to competitors of one sex.''[47]

Communal accommodation

8-69   Section 46 of the Sex Discrimination Act 1975 permits sex discrimination in admission to communal accommodation and associated benefits, but the section nevertheless demands "fair and equitable" treatment of men and women.

Special Race Relations Act provisions

8-70   Parts 5 and 6 of the Race Relations Act contain certain provisions which have no exact counterpart in the Sex Discrimination Act.

Charities

8-71   Discriminatory provisions in charitable instruments are rendered lawful by section 34 of the 1976 Act. The exception is where there is provision for conferring benefits on persons of class defined by reference to colour. In this case, the offending reference is effectively disregarded, leaving either a wider class, or persons generally, as the case may be, as persons who may benefit.

8-72   Although the 1976 Act does not deal with the point, both the Charity Commissioners and the Board of Inland Revenue have indicated that they regard working towards the elimination of racial discrimination, and promoting equal opportunity and good relations between persons of different racial groups as being charitable objects. Case law to the contrary should therefore be regarded as outmoded, on the basis that the law of charity develops with the social climate.[48] This means that the way is open for a civil rights movement to take advantage of charitable status in fund-raising activities.

RRA 1976, s.35

Special needs in relation to education, welfare and training

8-73   The Race Relations Act 1976, s.35 renders lawful any act done in affording persons of a particular racial group access to facilities or services to meet the special needs of persons of that group in relation to their education, training or welfare, or any ancillary benefits.

8-74   It is probable that "special" in this context means that the need does not have to be exclusive to the racial group to be benefited; it could also be a need that is experienced by all, but experienced to a much greater degree by members of a particular racial group.

8-75   Typically, special language training facilities have been regarded as covered

---

[47] See *Bennett v. Football Association Ltd* Court of Appeal July 28, 1988 (unreported) *GLC v. Farrar* [1980] I.C.R. 266; *British Judo Association v. Petty* [1981] I.C.R. 660, [1981] I.R.L.R. 484.

[48] See *Re Strakosch* [1949] Ch. 29 and the annual report of the Charity Commission 1983, para. 20.

by this provision. In addition, matters such as special housing need, or special need for counselling on starting businesses have been addressed under this rubric. The needs must relate to education, training or welfare, or any ancillary benefits, however. Accordingly, whilst advice for new Afro-Caribbean businesses may be covered, for example, as by and large there is a specially felt need for such education or training in that community, the provision of actual business funds would be outside the provision. Likewise, whilst training courses may be laid on, and financial support provided to those on the courses, under the rubric of "ancillary benefits", the financial support should not go beyond what is truly ancillary.

Section 35 ought to be perceived as providing exemption for essentially tem-   **8-76**
porary schemes in the sense that once the need is met, the statutory protection will fall away. Of course this may take years to achieve.

RRA 1976, s.36

Such schemes are protected where it appears to the person concerned that   **8-77**
the persons in question do not intend to remain in Great Britain after their period of education or training here.

RRA 1976, s.39

Sports and competitions
This provision renders lawful discrimination on the basis of nationality, place   **8-78**
of birth, or length of residence in selecting persons to represent a country, place or area in any sport or game, or in the rules of a competition relating to eligibility to compete in a sport or game.

Procedure and remedies in the county court

Generally, proceedings relating to discrimination in non-employment matters   **8-79**
whether under the SDA, RRA or DDA, have to be brought in the county courts in England and Wales, and the sheriff court in Scotland.[49] Appeals lie to the Court of Appeal in England and Wales and to the Court of Session in Scotland. In the case of proceedings relating to racial discrimination, only designated county courts have jurisdiction. The reason for this is that arrangements exist for the county court judges to sit with the help of Assessors.[50]

As in the case of employment discrimination, individuals may apply to the   **8-80**
EOC or CRE as the case may be (but not to the National Disability Council (NDC)) to ask for assistance with litigation. Cases are, however, brought in the names of the individuals concerned and whether or not a Commission assists is discretionary. Legal aid may be available.

---

[49] RRA, s.57 and SDA, s.67.
[50] RRA, s.67.

8-81   As in the case of alleged employment discrimination the questionnaire procedure is available prior to the commencement of proceedings relating to sex
or race discrimination (but not to disability discrimination); but thereafter it
is available only with leave of the court.[51] Moreover, it is possible to apply
for an order as to the admissibility of the questionnaire and the answers.[52]

8-82   The time limit for commencing proceedings is different in a non-employment
case, although the discretionary power of the court to consider a claim out
of time is the same as that possessed by an industrial tribunal. The limitation
period is six months beginning with the date of the act complained of.[53] The
exception is the case of those sex or race education complaints where the
Secretary of State for Education has general responsibilities and has to be
informed before a claim is commenced. In those cases, the period is eight
months. Within that period the proceedings cannot be commenced until either
the Secretary of State has said he does not require further time to consider
the matter, or two months have elapsed. The period is, however, modified
under the Race Relations Act 1976 in all those cases where an individual
has applied to the CRE for assistance with the proceedings within the time
limit. In effect, two further months are automatically added. The same is true
if there has been an approach to a person appointed under section 28 of the
DDA to assist with promoting a settlement. If the CRE has served notice
extending the time by which it has to respond to the application, one further
month is added. Thus, in an education case under the Race Relations Act
1976 where notification has to be given to the Secretary of State, and where
an application for assistance is made to the CRE who extend the time for
responding, the limitation period is 11 months (and even then is subject to
the county court's discretion).[54] For more detail and interpretation of the time
provisions, see chapter 7 on the tribunal position.

8-83   The principles which apply to the questions of discovery and proof in the
county court are the same as those applying to the Industrial Tribunal jurisdiction and are dealt with there.[55] Discovery by lists is the usual way in the
county court. The strict rules of evidence apply in the county court, whereas
they do not in the industrial tribunals. Where the two jurisdictions differ is
in the field of remedies available. Whereas in the Industrial Tribunal
injunctive relief is not available, in the county court or sheriff court the position is different. The two statutes say that cases "may be made the subject
of civil proceedings in like manner as any other claim in tort, or in Scotland
for reparation of breach of statutory duty" and add "all such remedies shall
be obtainable in such proceedings as ... would be obtainable in the High
Court or the Court of Session, as the case may be."[56] It is reasonably clear
that this means that the normal limit on damages in the county court does
not apply. Full injunctive relief is also available.

8-84   As to heads of damages, the same rules apply as in the Industrial Tribunal

[51] RRA, s. 65(4), SDA, s. 74(4).
[52] County Court Rules, Ord. 49, r.17(6).
[53] RRA, s. 68, SDA, s. 76, DDA Sched. 3.
[54] See generally RRA, s. 68. Oddly the exceptional cases were forgotten when the time limit
for serving questionnaires was set.
[55] See chapter 4.
[56] RRA, s. 57 and SDA, s. 66.

to awards of damages in indirect discrimination cases (save that in employment sex discrimination cases s.65 SDA has now been amended), and as to damages for injury to feelings. But the secretary of state has power to impose a limit to awards for injury to feelings under the Disability Discrimination Act.

Judicial statistics reveal that non-employment discrimination litigation initiated by individuals is sparse, which raises the question whether those courts can build up much expertise.[57]   **8-85**

Sometimes formal consequences flow from a finding of discrimination in the county courts. For example, these are matters to be taken into account by the Director General of Fair Trading under the Estate Agents Act and the Consumer Credit Act. Also, licensing magistrates are specifically enjoined to take into account findings of sex discrimination. Presumably they may, without being required to do so, take into account findings of racial or disability discrimination.   **8-86**

Much of the county court litigation where racial discrimination is proved does concern discrimination on licensed premises. (Proof is generally fairly easy, since the defences available for failure to serve are few, and resort is often had to evidence of "testing" the public house using comparable black and white testers to back up the original complainant. The testing is arranged either by local racial equality councils or by the CRE exercising its powers to assist individuals.)   **8-87**

---

[57] See the *Annual Judicial Statistics*.

9 STRATEGIC ENFORCEMENT POWERS

9-01   The Equal Opportunities Commission (EOC) and the Commission for Racial Equality (CRE) have largely equivalent duties and functions in their respective fields of operations. The CRE's are somewhat wider. When it came into being, it replaced both the Race Relations Board and the Community Relations Commission. The latter body's functions have been generally subsumed in the CRE's duty to "promote good relations between persons of different racial groups generally."[1] No equivalent duty exists for the EOC.

The National Disability Council (NDC) established under the Disability Discrimination Act 1995 is a radically different body from either the EOC or CRE. It has no law enforcement function of its own, and has no power to assist individuals with litigation, or to investigate complaints of discrimination. The main duty of the NDC is an advisory one towards the Secretary of State. Because it is so different it is dealt with separately at the end of this chapter.

What follows immediately therefore relates to the EOC and CRE.

General duties of the EOC and CRE

General duties in common

9-02   The general duties in common are:

1. to work towards the elimination of discrimination;
2. to promote equality of opportunity; and
3. to keep under review the working of the constituent legislation and, when required, by the Secretary of State or otherwise think it necessary, draw up and submit proposals for amending that legislation.[2]

The first two general duties are amplified by a list of more specific duties and powers which enable the tasks to be carried out, on which more below. Under the power to review the legislation, the EOC produced documents in 1988, *Legislating for Change* and *Equal Treatment for Men and Women: Strengthening the Act* and in 1990 a set of proposals called *Equal Pay for Men and Women: Strengthening the Acts*. In mid-1985, in a document entitled

---

[1] RRA 1976, s.43(1)(b).
[2] SDA 1975, s.53, RRA 1976, s.43.

Review of the Race Relations Act 1976: Proposals for Change,[3] and in 1992 in a further document entitled *Second Review of the Race Relations Act 1976* the CRE has sent proposed changes to the Secretary of State.

Status and manner of operation of the Commissions

The two Commissions are independent of Government (though funded out of Departmental Votes: the EOC now comes under the Department of Education and Employment and the CRE the Home Office). Thus, in the exercise of its law enforcement functions, the CRE has on more than one occasion been involved in litigation against the Home Office.[4] In addition, both Commissions now use judicial review as a method of resolving legal issues involving public bodies, failing other methods; and this will inevitably lead to more confrontations between the Commissions and the Government which sponsors them.[5]   **9-03**

It is doubtful how far real independence from Government can in fact be maintained when Government holds the purse strings, appoints the Commissioners, approves Additional Commissioners for formal investigations, approves the decision-making arrangements internally, frequently sends in review teams, provides observers to sit in on chief executive appointments, and receives the papers for Commission meetings.   **9-04**

The Commissions each consist of up to 15 Commissioners. Much of their work is delegated to committees under arrangements approved from time to time by the Secretary of State.[6] The Commissions are served by staff who, although paid at civil service rates, are by statute specifically not civil servants. As from the summer of 1987, the Commissions came under the jurisdiction of the Parliamentary Commissioner (Ombudsman).[7]   **9-05**

Publications, and the Codes Funding of research and educational activities

Each Commission is obliged to produce an Annual Report and Accounts.[8] The Report is to the Secretary of State who lays the same before Parliament. Each Commission also publishes much material each year under various other powers. Both Commissions have the power to undertake or assist (financially or otherwise) the undertaking by other persons of any necessary or expedient research and educational activities.[9]   **9-06**

Each Commission may issue codes of practice in the employment field,[10]   **9-07**

---

[3] See Jeanne Gregory *Sex, Race and The Law, Legislating for Equality* (EOC, 1987) chapter 8.
[4] *Home Office v. CRE* [1982] Q.B. 385; *Alexander v. Home Office* [1988] I.R.L.R. 190.
[5] See chap. 10 on Judicial Review.
[6] For the law relating to the functioning of the Commissions see the SDA 1975, Sched.3. Evelyn Ellis in *Sex Discrimination Law* (1989), p. 238 suggests abolishing the EOC Commissioners altogether leaving just the chair.
[7] See Parliamentary and Health Services Commissioners Act 1987.
[8] SDA 1975, ss.53, 56, Sched.3, RRA 1976, ss.43, 46, Sched.1.
[9] SDA 1975, s.54, RRA 1976, s.45.
[10] RRA 1976, Sched.4 inserting s.56A in SDA 1975, and RRA 1976, s.47. See *Codes in a Cold Climate: Administrative Rule-Making by the CRE* C. McCrudden, 1988 M.L.R. 409.

following consultation. A draft code needs the approval of the Secretary of State and to be laid before Parliament. A tribunal must take it into account if it appears relevant to a question in the proceedings. One of the purposes of such codes is to inform the reader as to what steps are reasonably practicable to avoid the occurrence of discrimination. Taking such steps gives the employer a defence in employment cases. The CRE was recently given power to produce codes in the field of housing and has done so.[11]

9-08   When the Commissions conduct formal investigations, they are obliged to produce reports which are either published or made available for inspection.[12] Non-discrimination notices issued in the course of investigations are to be made available for inspection.[13] Each Commission has a general power to make charges for educational or other facilities, or services made available by them.[14]

The CRE's power to fund organisations

9-09   The CRE has a power for which there is no EOC equivalent: to give financial or other assistance to any organisation appearing to the Commission to be concerned with the promotion of equality of opportunity, and good relations between persons of different racial groups.[15] The giving of such financial assistance is subject to the Home Secretary's approval, which in practice takes the form of financial limits above which items need to be referred specifically to the Home Office for approval and below which they do not. This function of the CRE is by statute given specifically to a committee of at least three, and not more than five, Commissioners of whom one is a deputy chairman of the Commission. Under current arrangements it is the Public Affairs Committee which exercises this function.

9-10   The power is used, for example, to fund many racial equality officer posts throughout the country, and the funding is subject to arrangements for the approval by the Committee of annual work plans of racial equality councils. In practice, funding of such posts attracts considerably more funding to racial equality councils from local authorities. It is often mistakenly assumed that racial equality councils are emanations of the CRE. They are not. The councils are autonomous bodies with their own constitutions, which employ the racial equality officers, albeit in some cases entirely with CRE funded monies. At the time of writing, several million pounds are spent on RECs. Examples of the use of the CRE's funding power are set out in the Annual Reports. In practice, it is the financial commitment to RECs which means that only a small proportion of the CRE's budget is spent on law enforcement. If the RECs were to be brought fully into law enforcement at a local level, a better balance might be achieved in the CRE's expenditure.

---

[11]   s.47, RRA was amended by s.137(2) and (5) of the Housing Act 1988 and s.180 of the Local Government and Housing Act 1989.
[12]   SDA 1975, s.60; RRA 1976, s.51.
[13]   SDA 1975, s.70; RRA 1976, s.61.
[14]   SDA 1975, s.54(2); RRA 1976, s.45(2).
[15]   RRA 1976 s.44, Sched.1, para.13.

The EOC's duty to review health and safety legislation

The EOC has one duty for which there is no CRE parallel. It is obliged to
keep under review discriminatory provisions in the health and safety legislation and submit proposals for amending it to the Secretary of State, who also
has power to call for a report.[16] The Employment Act 1989 made a number
of legislative changes in this area.

9-11

Law enforcement by the Commissions

Each Commission has a major law enforcement function. Essentially this
function is exercised in one of three ways:

9-12

1. Assisting individuals to bring discrimination cases, in the case of the
   EOC including equal pay and equal value cases.
2. Bringing proceedings in the name of the Commission. The power
   here is, surprisingly, given that the Commissions are both law
   enforcement agencies, limited in the statutes to a small range of matters, see below. However, the Commissions will often have *locus
   standi* to bring judicial review proceedings and, given the burgeoning
   of such proceedings generally in recent years, it is not surprising to
   find both Commissions participating in this growth area.[17]
3. Carrying out formal investigations. These are under case law[18] of
   two types, which can conveniently be called general investigations,
   and accusatory investigations. Whether it is right to call a general
   investigation part of the law enforcement function must be in some
   doubt since probably in this type of investigation no remedy is available, save the power to make recommendations. The power to conduct general investigations is perhaps closer to the power to conduct
   research. There are two important advantages to the Commissions of
   doing general investigations as opposed to research: powers to
   compel provision of information can be sought from the Secretary
   of State and the research convention of anonymity of subjects need
   not be followed in the reports.

The power to assist individuals to bring cases

This power is, in most respects, similar for both organisations. The CRE has
imposed upon it a time limit of two months (which it can extend by notice
to three months), within which it has to respond to a request for assistance.[19]
The EOC has no such obligation.[20] The CRE often finds it difficult to give
a final decision whether or not to provide actual representation in court or
tribunal as the case may be, even within the extended period of three months,

9-13

---

[16] SDA 1975, s.55.
[17] See chapter 10.
[18] See in particular *R. v. CRE, ex p. Hillingdon* LBC [1982] A.C. 779 and *CRE v. Prestige
Group plc* [1984] I.C.R. 473.
[19] RRA 1976, s.66(3), (4).
[20] See SDA 1975, s.75.

because enquiries will not be complete. It therefore adopts the practice of deciding to provide continued advice and assistance until those enquiries are complete and it can make a fully informed decision. This is generally the result of delays by respondents in returning answers to the statutory questionnaire.[21]

9-14 The Commissions *must* consider applications in respect of proceedings or prospective proceedings under the relevant legislation. In practice this is done by Legal Committees. They have a *discretion* whether to grant assistance and as to the form it will take. The decision in practice will be taken on the basis of a report and assessment of the application prepared by staff in the light of enquiries made. The criteria upon which the Commissions can grant assistance are set out in the statutes and are similar in both cases:

> "the Commission shall consider the application and may grant it if they think fit to do so on the ground that —
>
> (a) the case raises a question of principle, or
> (b) it is unreasonable, having regard to the complexity of the case of the applicant's position in relation to the respondent or another person involved or any other matter, to expect the applicant to deal with the case unaided, or
> (c) by reason of any other special consideration."[22]

Factors to be taken into account by the Commissions

9-15 Both Commissions now give applicants for assistance a written explanation of the factors which the Commissions take into account and their priorities in making decisions on applications. The EOC takes the following matters into consideration:

> "i) whether the case is likely to clarify important points of law or principle
> ii) whether the case is likely to affect large numbers of people
> iii) whether the case is likely to bring about change
> iv) whether the case has a strong likelihood of success
> v) whether the case has a likely potential for Commission follow-up work.

The Commissioners also consider whether the case falls within one of the Commission's current priorities."[23]

9-16 The CRE's criteria are similar. The CRE were criticised in *Racial Justice at Work* for not taking a strategic stance in relation to assisting individuals, other than in relation to cases testing important points of law. There may come a point, however, at which complainants cease to bring their complaints to an agency if it is perceived as selecting cases on the basis of its own

---

[21] See RRA 1976, s.65.
[22] SDA 1975, s.75(1); RRA 1976, s.66 (1)(1).
[23] EOC's document sent to applicants for assistance 1992.

strategic concerns with little regard to individual injustice. The statutory criterion pertaining to whether it is unreasonable to expect the applicant to proceed unaided means that the Commissions could not anyway lose sight of that factor without falling foul of the law. It also not infrequently happens that cases selected for support for one reason turn out later to be significant for quite different reasons, and, given this serendipity factor, strategic omniscience at the outset is not possible. Nevertheless clearly a strategy is important in bringing about wider change.

Whilst both Commissions will discuss informally with the applicant a refusal **9-17** of assistance, it has not been their practice to give written reasons. But this may be changing.

It is important for both applicants for assistance and respondents to proceed- **9-18** ings to realise that a refusal of assistance by the Commission may, having regard to the statutory criteria, say nothing in itself as to the merits of the applicant's case against the respondent. Cases for which the Commissions have refused assistance have succeeded in tribunals. Indeed if, for example, the Commissions are to carry out a policy of encouraging, say, unions to support discrimination cases, refusals of assistance for cases with merit *vis-à-vis* respondents are inevitable. For county court cases (non-employment) legal aid may be available, but this is not the case for the conduct of industrial tribunal proceedings (employment).

The forms of assistance which the Commission may grant may include: **9-19**

"(a) giving advice;
(b) procuring or attempting to procure the settlement of any matter in dispute;
(c) arranging for the giving of advice or assistance by a solicitor or counsel;
(d) arranging for representation by any person including all such assistance as is usually given by a solicitor or counsel in the steps preliminary or incidental to any proceedings, or in arriving at or giving effect to a compromise to avoid or bring to an end any proceedings."[24]

The Commissions seem to differ on the question whether the power to assist **9-20** covers assistance with enforcement in the county court of awards made by industrial tribunals. The CRE takes the view that it does; the EOC seemingly not. It appears to be the sort of "assistance as is usually given by a solicitor . . . incidental to any proceedings." The CRE's view is to be preferred, unless applicants are to be left ultimately to their own devices at the mercy of unscrupulous respondents who ignore tribunal awards.

Legal Aid

Expenses incurred by a Commission under the power to assist constitute a **9-21** first charge on any costs or expenses recovered, but subject to any charge

---

[24] SDA 1975, s.75(2); RRA 1976, s.66(2).

under legal aid legislation[25]. Whether the individual himself can recover costs which the Commission can then recover depends on the rules of the particular tribunal or court. For the EAT it was held in *Walsall MBC v. Sidhu*[26] that if assistance is given by the Commission on the terms that the individual would not personally incur any costs, then the Commission, not being a party, could not through that individual recover any costs. However, the position is probably different if the Commission retains a discretion to ask the individual to pay the costs which it exercises upon costs being awarded to the individual.

Proceedings in the name of the Commission

9-22   The power to bring proceedings under the Act in the name of a Commission for law enforcement purposes is very limited in scope. Where it applies, the Commission has exclusive jurisdiction. The following are the areas covered: discriminatory advertisements; instructions to discriminate; pressure to discriminate; persistent discrimination and preliminary proceedings in industrial tribunals relating thereto.

Discriminatory advertisements

9-23   Proceedings in respect of an unlawful advertisement can be brought only by a Commission.[27] Of course an unlawful advertisement may itself be some *evidence* that an act unlawful under the provisions of the Act under which an *individual* can bring proceedings has been committed. If, for example, it is alleged that a discriminatory appointment to a job has been made, it will be material evidence that it followed an advertisement for the job indicating an intention to do an act of discrimination of just that sort.

Definition of advertisement
9-24   An advertisement is very widely defined as including:

> "every form of advertisement or notice, whether to the public or not, and whether in a newspaper or other publication, by television or radio, by display of notices, signs, labels, showcards or goods, by distribution of samples, circulars, catalogues, price lists or other material, by exhibition of pictures, models or films, or in any other way."[28]

It is unlawful to publish or cause to be published an advertisement which indicates, or might reasonably be understood as indicating, an intention to do an act of discrimination.[29] At this point the two pieces of legislation take a different line.

9-25   The Sex Discrimination Act ban applies only to advertisements indicating an intention to do any act unlawful under Parts 2 or 3 of that Act. It does not

---

[25] SDA 1975, s.75(4); RRA 1976, s.66(6).
[26] [1980] I.C.R. 519.
[27] SDA 1975, s.72; RRA 1976, s.63.
[28] SDA 1975, s.82; RRA 1976, s.78.
[29] SDA 1975, s.38; RRA 1976, s.29(1).

apply to an advertisement if the intended act would not in fact be unlawful. There is also a clarifying provision to the effect that the "use of a job description with a sexual connotation (such as 'waiter', 'salesgirl', 'postman' or 'stewardess') indicates an intention to discriminate unless the contrary is indicated." The Race Relations Act ban is wider, applying to advertisements indicating an intention to discriminate, whether or not the discrimination would be unlawful by virtue of Parts II or III of that Act. Because of this approach it becomes necessary to spell out a list of exceptions in detail. The ban does not apply if the intended act would be lawful by virtue of any of the Race Relations Act 1976, ss. 5, 6, 7(3) and (4), 10(3), 26, 34(2), 35 to 39 and 41. Two other specific examples relate to the services of an employment agency if the intended act concerns employment which the employer could by virtue of section 5, 6 or 7(3) or (4) lawfully refuse to offer to persons against whom the advertisement indicates an intention to discriminate; and to advertisements relating to employment outside Great Britain requiring persons by reference to their nationality. Since there is no reference to section 4(3), for example, in this list, it follows that although it is lawful to discriminate on racial grounds in relation to employment for the purposes of a private household, it is nevertheless unlawful to advertise such a discriminatory intention.

The two pieces of legislation are similar in providing a time limit of six months for proceedings, and a defence to a publisher if he proves that he reasonably relies on a statement made by the person who caused it to be published that the advertisement would be lawful under the exempting provisions. It is a criminal offence knowingly or recklessly to make such a statement which is false or misleading.   **9-26**

In practice, proceedings in relation to unlawful advertisements have been rare. Signs put up by landlords such as "no blacks" have now largely disappeared. There has been litigation in relation to "no travellers" signs in public houses. The Court of Appeal in *CRE v. Dutton*[30] held that such a sign is potentially discriminatory and needs to be justified. The case is authority for the hitherto unresolved point that the advertisement provisions cover indirect discrimination.   **9-27**

Many of the problems for the Commission relate to keeping "positive action" advertisements within the bounds of what is permitted by law. Since the various exceptions are vaguely worded, this is not an easy task, and the Commissions have normally preferred to act by way of guidance and conciliation. As a result, cases are relatively few. For an example see *Lambeth L.B.C. v. CRE*.[31]   **9-28**

Instructions and pressure to discriminate

It is convenient to deal together with these two instances where the Commissions can bring proceedings, since it is common for both to be alleged in the same proceedings. The provisions in the two pieces of legislation are   **9-29**

---

[30] [1989] I.R.L.R. 8, C.A.
[31] [1990] I.R.L.R. 231, [1990] I.C.R. 768, C.A.

approximately the same.[32] The Sex Discrimination Act is clearer on what actually constitutes pressure, and it took litigation to clarify the same point in relation to the Race Relations Act. These particular breaches of the law do not entail the same problems of proof as beset discrimination proceedings generally. There is normally available the direct evidence of the person given instructions or subjected to pressure. Both Commissions have brought proceedings under these heads, and are usually successful because this type of case does not depend on inference.

9-30   It is unlawful for a person who has authority over another person, or in accordance with whose wishes that other person is accustomed to act, to instruct him to do any act unlawful under Parts 2 or 3 of the two pieces of legislation, or procure or attempt to procure the doing by him of such an act. It matters not that no unlawful act occurs in consequence. (If it does, of course, an individual may be able to bring proceedings himself, and it is not unusual in such a case for the Commission's proceedings to be joined with those of the individual. It is convenient in those cases for the Commission to provide representation to the individual under its power to assist, and facilitate the conduct of the proceedings.) In *CRE v. Imperial Society of Teachers of Dancing*,[33] it was said that for a person to be accustomed to act in accordance with the instructions of someone:

> "requires that there should be some relationship (between them). It does not seem to us to be possible to construe the section as meaning that it is sufficient to show that the other person is accustomed to act in accordance with the wishes of persons in the same position as the person giving the instructions."[34]

This seems to be an extremely literal interpretation.

9-31   It is unlawful to induce or attempt to induce a person to do any act which contravenes Part 2 or 3 of either legislation. The Sex Discrimination Act 1975, s.40 spells out the fact that either a carrot or a stick, as it were, suffices:

> "(1) It is unlawful to induce, or attempt to induce, a person to do any act which contravenes Part II or III by —
>
> (a) providing or offering to provide him with any benefit, or
> (b) subjecting or threatening to subject him to any detriment."

9-32   In the case of the Race Relations Act there is no similar provision, but the same is true. In *CRE v. Imperial Society of Teachers of Dancing*,[35] it was held that a request to someone to act in contravention of the Act can amount to an attempt to induce a contravention.

9-33   Whether a question such as "Is he black?" in answer to, say, a job centre trying to place that person with the employer amounts to instructions or pres-

---

[32] 1989 EOC 23.
[33] SDA 1975, ss.39, 40; RRA 1976, ss.30, 31.
[34] At 447, *per* Neill J.
[35] See n. 33.

sure to discriminate will depend on whether in all the circumstances it is clear that the employer is instructing or requesting the job centre not to send the person because of his colour. It does not necessarily follow that that is so, though it may very well be. A person's colour may, for example, being an obvious feature, be a handy way of identifying him when he arrives. So a mere request for information needs to be distinguished from discriminatory instructions or pressure; and some cases have turned on this point.[36]

Persistent discrimination: preliminary proceedings relating thereto

A Commission has power to bring special proceedings within five years of a non-discrimination notice or a court or tribunal finding of unlawful discrimination if it appears to the Commission that, unless restrained, that person is likely to commit an unlawful act or apply a discriminatory practice.[37] The proceedings would be in a designated county court or sheriff court for a restraining order. The court may grant the order in the terms applied for, or in more limited terms. In so doing, the Commission cannot allege discrimination within the jurisdiction of an industrial tribunal unless a finding by a industrial tribunal on that matter has become final.

9-34

With a view to making an application for a restraining order to the county court, a Commission may present to an industrial tribunal a complaint that the respondent has done an act within the jurisdiction of an industrial tribunal. The tribunal can make a finding to that effect and if it thinks it just and equitable to do so in a case concerning the employment provision of the Act it can make an order declaring the rights of a person discriminated against, and/or a recommendation as though the complaint had in fact been presented by the person discriminated against.[38]

9-35

Formal investigations[39]

One may be forgiven for thinking, as both Commissions once did, that a provision with the side-note "power to conduct formal investigation" which reads:

9-36

> "the Commission may if they think fit, and shall if required by the Secretary, conduct a formal investigation for any purpose connected with the carrying out of those duties",[40]

sets out a very wide power; and that the following provisions which have the side-notes "terms of reference" and "power to obtain information" apply where there is the power to conduct an investigation.[41] However, the

---

[36] e.g. CRE v. Powell and City of Birmingham (1986), unreported, EAT (37).
[37] SDA 1975, s.71; RRA 1976, s.62.
[38] SDA 1975, s.73; RRA 1976, s.64.
[39] G. Appleby and E. Ellis "Formal Investigations: The CRE and EOC as Law Enforcement Agencies." (1984) Public Law 236, and chapter 11 C. McCrudden, "The Commission for Racial Equality: Formal Investigations in the Shadow of Judicial Review" in Regulation and Public Law (McCrudden ed. and others), and passim in Racial Justice at Work (PSI 1991).
[40] SDA 1975, s.57; RRA 1976, s.48.
[41] SDA 1975, ss.58, 59 as amended by RRA 1976, Sched.4; RRA 1976, ss.49, 50.

House of Lords in *Re Prestige Group plc*[42] construed those following provisions as actually limiting the power to conduct investigations. Neither Commission can now conduct an investigation into a *named respondent's* activities unless it has a suspicion that an unlawful act may have been committed. This is almost certainly not what Parliament intended,[43] and the powers of the two Commissions are more limited than those of the Fair Employment Agency and its successor the Fair Employment Commission in Northern Ireland, who have been able to investigate a named respondent without suspecting an unlawful act.[44] The CRE had to abandon a number of invalid investigations in the light of the *Prestige* decision.

Types of investigations

9-37   The investigations which can be conducted by the Commission now fall into just two categories: *accusatory*, where an unlawful act is suspected to have been committed by a named respondent, or *general* which does not name a respondent as such, but looks at an area of activity. In the category of general investigations, for example, the CRE has investigated the provision of equal opportunities at a particular new shopping centre in Leicester, where there were many businesses situated; the provision of equal opportunities in entry to training contracts in the chartered accountancy profession; and the provision of equal opportunities in certain parts of the hotel trade in named towns. Since the CRE's general duties include the promotion of good race relations, general investigations are also possible under this rubric.[45]

9-38   The CRE has conducted many more formal investigations than has the EOC. However, in recent years the CRE has been sharper in the non-employment areas than in the field of employment, and the majority of the EOC's work concerns employment. Yet it would seem that there is plenty of scope for investigations concerning non-promotion by employers as this is an area where the vast majority of tribunal cases brought by individuals fail.

Accusatory investigations
9-39   The level of suspicion required for a named person accusatory investigation is, however, low. In relation to the CRE, the House of Lords has pronounced twice on the level required:

> "To entitle the Commission to embark upon the full investigation it is enough that there should be material before the Commission sufficient to raise in the minds of reasonable men, possessed of the experience of covert racial discrimination that has been acquired by the Commission, a suspicion that there may have been acts by the person named of racial discrimination of the kind that it is proposed to investigate."[46]

---

[42] [1984] I.C.R. 473.
[43] See CRE's "Review of the Race Relations Act 1976: Proposals for Change" (1985), Appendix C setting out parts of the Parliamentary debates. No doubt in a post *Pepper v. Hart* era a different court result would have been reached.
[44] See now Fair Employment (Northern Ireland) Act 1989.
[45] *Home Office v. CRE* [1982] Q.B. 385.
[46] *R. v. CRE, ex p. Hillingdon* LBC [1982] A.C. 779, *per* Lord Diplock at 791.

In the *Prestige* case the Lords affirmed and quoted the foregoing passage   **9-40**
and added (their emphasis):

> "... and had at any rate *some* grounds for so suspecting albeit that the
> grounds upon which any such suspicion was based might, at that stage,
> be no more than tenuous because they had not yet been tested."[47]

The question arises whether purely statistical material showing a huge dispar-   **9-41**
ity between say the actual black, or female, employment rate, and what might
have been expected to be the case without discrimination, gives rise to the
necessary suspicion. If those figures cry out for an explanation, the Commission relying on its experience may take the view that the figures alone are
sufficiently suspicious to warrant investigation. Certainly it is the practice of
the CRE to rely on statistical material in appropriate cases, and it has not yet
been challenged in court. In the light of *West Midlands Passenger Transport
Executive v. Singh*,[48] such a challenge would seem doomed to failure. In an
accusatory investigation, the terms of reference must not go beyond the belief
held by the Commissioners as to the unlawful acts which may have been
committed.[49] Investigating without a suspicion is not allowed. However, a
Commission may in an appropriate case draw the inference that if one discriminatory act appears to have occurred, there may well have been others
of a similar kind.[50] The important point is that if that is the Commission's
belief it should say so, because the right to make representations:

> "cannot be exercised effectively unless that person is informed with
> reasonable specificity what are the kinds of acts to which the proposed
> investigation is to be directed and confined. The Commission cannot
> 'throw the book at him'."[51]

The obligation on the Commission to set out its belief in the terms of refer-   **9-42**
ence and the supporting grounds for its belief is best seen as a duty to produce
a document more akin to the pleadings in a civil case than the bundle of
statements which might be received by the defence in a trial on indictment.
There is no requirement on a Commission to set out all the *evidence* which
is to hand, but, on the other hand, it would necessarily have to set out the
general effect of that evidence in reaching its belief.

Conduct of investigations

A Commission may delegate the functions in a formal investigation to one   **9-43**
or more Commissioners, who may include additional Commissioners
appointed with the approval of the Secretary of State specially for the purpose
of the formal investigation.[52] Certain functions in the conduct of investigations, such as the hearing of representations by respondents, would be very
difficult to organise without exercising the power to delegate. The power to

---

[47] [1984] I.C.R. 473 *per* Lord Diplock at 481.
[48] [1988] I.R.L.R. 186.
[49] *Hillingdon* case, see above.
[50] *Prestige* case, see above.
[51] *Hillingdon* case, see above.
[52] SDA 1975, s.57(2), (3); RRA 1976, s.48(2), (3).

appoint additional Commissioners is a useful way of bringing special expertise and familiarity with the subject-matter to bear on a particular investigation, and the choice of an appropriate person can lend considerable weight
to the findings of the Commissioners. Inevitably the Commissioners will rely
on Commission staff to collect evidence upon the basis of which the Commissioners make their decisions.[53]

Terms of reference and representations

9-44   Terms of reference have to be drawn up by the Commission or, if the Secretary of State has ordered the investigation, by him after consulting the Commission. For a general investigation, general notice of the terms of reference
suffices. But in the case of a named-person accusatory investigation, a special
procedure applies. The legislation says:

> "Where the terms of reference of the investigation confine it to activities
> of persons named in them and the Commission in the course of it pro-
> pose to investigate any act made unlawful by this Act which they believe
> that a person so named may have done, the Commission shall —
>
> (a) inform that person of their belief and of their proposal to investigate
> the act in question; and
> (b) offer him an opportunity of naming oral or written representations
> with regard to it (or both oral and written representations if he thinks
> fit);
>
> and a person so named who avails himself of an opportunity under this
> subsection of making oral representations may be represented —
>
> (i) by counsel or a solicitor; or
> (ii) by some other person of his choice, not being a person to whom
> the Commission object on the ground that he is unsuitable."[54]

9-45   This procedure provides an opportunity to raise various matters. Particularly
relevant arguments are likely to be: that the grounds of the Commission's
belief when properly explained do not warrant an investigation; or that the
unlawful acts did take place, but have ceased and adequate steps to ensure
no repetition have been taken; or that the terms of reference are too wide.
There is no entitlement to call witnesses or adduce evidence during the course
of representations, or to cross-examine the witnesses on whose statements
the Commission relies.[55] However, if, for example, a legal representative
wished to ask a local authority housing manager to talk about the housing
management system, the Commission may well in its discretion permit that
course of action. It is an occasion for the Commissioners to hear argument
as to whether such an investigation is appropriate. There is power in the
Commission to vary the terms of reference.[56]

---

[53] *R. v. Commission for Racial Equality, ex p. Cottrell and Rothon* [1980] 1 W.L.R. 1580.
[54] SDA 1975, s.58(3A) inserted by RRA 1976, Sched. 4; RRA 1976, s. 49(4).
[55] *R. v. CRE, ex p. Cottrell and Rothon* [1980] 1 W.L.R. 1580; [1980] I.R.L.R. 279.
[56] SDA 1975, s.58(4); RRA 1976, s.49(5).

Powers to compel production of information

Whether or not the Commission has any power to compel the production of   **9-46**
information in the course of an investigation differs according to whether it
is a general or an accusatory investigation.[57] In the former case, the Commission only has the power to serve the requisite notice requiring information
where it is authorised by the Secretary of State. In the case of an accusatory
investigation, the power to serve a notice is an automatic adjunct of that type
of investigation.

The notice must be in prescribed form and served in the prescribed manner   **9-47**
and:

> "(a) may require any person to furnish such written information as may
>   be described in the notice, and may specify the time at which, and
>   the manner and form in which, the information is to be furnished;
> (b) may require any person to attend at such time and place as is speci-
>   fied in the notice and give oral information about, and produce all
>   documents in his possession or control relating to, any matter speci-
>   fied in the notice."

A notice: **9-48**

> "shall not require a person —
>
> (a) to give information, or produce any documents, which he could not
>   be compelled to give in evidence, or produce, in civil proceedings
>   before the High Court of the Court of Session; or
> (b) to attend at any place unless the necessary expenses of his journey
>   to and from that place are paid or tendered to him."

If a person fails to comply with a notice served on him or the Commission   **9-49**
have reasonable cause to believe that he intends not to comply with it, the
Commission may apply to a county court, or, in Scotland, a sheriff court,
for an order requiring him to comply with it or with such directions for the
like purpose as may be contained in the order. The penalty for failure to
comply is the same as that for neglecting a witness summons, or diligence
in Scotland.

A person commits an offence if he: **9-50**

> 1. wilfully alters, suppresses, conceals or destroys a document which
>   he has been required by a notice order to produce; or
> 2. in complying with such a notice or order, knowingly or recklessly
>   makes any statement which is false in a material particular.

In practice, in a large general investigation the Commission may prefer not   **9-51**
to delay the investigation while it asks the Secretary of State for authorisation
for service of a notice requiring information. It may instead, in its report of
the investigation, simply praise the co-operation of those who did provide

---

[57] See generally, SDA 1975, s.59; RRA 1976, s.50.

information, and condemn the lack of co-operation of those who did not and list them. The Commission could, it seems, make a finding that a person failed to co-operate. Persons may well prefer to co-operate rather than risk such adverse publicity. Whether the Commission adopts this course of action is likely to depend on how far the purpose of the investigation will be frustrated by lack of co-operation.[58] That may be something which one person from whom information is sought is not in a position to judge. It is also possible that in combination with other known facts, failure to co-operate with a general investigation could lead the Commission to suspect that unlawful acts may have taken place so as to justify an accusatory investigation.

Recommendations

9-52 It is the duty of the Commissions to make recommendations which appear necessary or expedient in the light of any of their findings in a formal investigation.[59] These recommendations may be directed at any person with a view to promoting equality of opportunity and may relate to changes in policies or procedures or as to any other matters; or at the Secretary of State relating to changes in the law or otherwise. They may be made during an investigation.

Reports of investigations

9-53 The Commissions are obliged to prepare a report of their findings in a formal investigation. If it is a formal investigation required by the Secretary of State, it is his obligation to publish it. (Neither Commission has been required to carry out such an investigation.) In other investigations, the Commission concerned has the choice whether to publish the report or just make it available for inspection and copying. Although the statutes refer to a requirement to prepare a report of "findings,"[60] it would be nonsensical if the Commissions did not in their report make reference to those recommendations of general significance which merit publication and without which the findings would be pointless. There is nothing in the statutes to prohibit the inclusion of such recommendations, or indeed other material such as a non-discrimination notice, in a report. There are, however, certain specific prohibitions on disclosure of information by the Commissions.[61] In preparing any report for publication or inspection a Commission has to:

> "exclude, so far as is consistent with their duties and the object of the report, any matter which relates to the private affairs of any individual or the business interests of any person where the publication of that matter might in the opinion of the Commission prejudicially affect that individual or persons."

---

[58] The authors of *Racial Justice at Work* (PSI 1991) took the view that the CRE had perhaps avoided going to the Secretary of State too often, p.102: "the concept of an allowable drop-out rate has . . . grown and grown".

[59] SDA 1975, s.60; RRA 1976, s.51.

[60] See n. 59.

[61] SDA 1975, s.61; R.A.A. 1976, s.52.

It is standard practice for the Commissions to allow persons referred to in   **9-54**
the report the opportunity to comment on a draft or draft of the relevant part
before publication. It is a step which natural justice would probably in any
event require. At the end of the day, however, it is the Commission's report,
and respondents have no entitlement to insist on any particular form of words,
although they may be able to prevent publication if it would be maliciously
defamatory, or where no reasonable Commission could have made the findings in question, or formed the particular view on whether an individual or
person is being unnecessarily prejudiced by the report.

Disclosure of information

There are restrictions on disclosure of information given by an informant to   **9-55**
the Commission in connection with a formal investigation which apply to
Commissioners, Additional Commissioners and staff, past and present alike.
Disclosure outside the Commission is a criminal offence except on the order
of a court, or with the informant's consent, or in the form of a summary or
other general statement published by the Commission which does not identify
the informant or any other person to whom it relates, in the formal report of
the investigation, or so far as necessary for the proper performance of the
functions of the Commission, or for the purpose of certain legal proceedings.
(The informant's position is also protected against certain forms of retaliation
by employers and the like by the somewhat imperfect and incomplete victimisation provisions of the Act.)

Non-discrimination notice

If in the course of a formal investigation a Commission becomes satisfied   **9-56**
that an unlawful act or practice has taken place, it has the power (except in
certain education matters where the Secretary of State has a responsibility)
to issue a non-discrimination notice in respect of the person concerned.[62]
However before so doing, the statutory procedure again requires that the
Commission gives the person notice, specifying the grounds, and provides
an opportunity to make oral or written representations at not less than 28
days' notice. There is no entitlement to cross-examine witnesses at these
representations.[63] In principle there seems to be no reason why the Commission should not send the draft report of its investigation as the grounds for
the proposed notice if it is specific about which points it is relying on. This
would conveniently shorten the procedure.

The non-discrimination notice must be in the prescribed form or as near as   **9-57**
possible.[64] It will require the person not to commit any such unlawful acts.
Although it cannot require any particular changes in practice, it can, where
changes in practice or arrangements are necessary, require that the person

---

[62] SDA 1975, s.67; RRA 1976, s.58
[63] See n. 55
[64] Sex Discrimination (Formal Investigations) Regulations 1975 (S.I. 1975 No. 1993, as
amended by S.I. 1977 No. 843); Race Relations (Formal Investigations) Regulations 1977
(S.I. 1977 No. 841).

inform the Commission of changes and notify other persons of them within specified periods. The Commission has a monitoring function, and to this end the notice can require that information be provided to the Commission for up to five years to enable them to check that the notice has been complied with. It would seem to be good practice for the notice to set out the areas where changes in practice are necessary.

Appeals against non-discrimination notices

9-58 When the non-discrimination notice is served, it should be accompanied by a statement of the facts upon which it is based either fully or by reference to the grounds upon which the "minded letter" was based if those have not changed. An appeal against any requirement in a notice may be made within six weeks to an industrial tribunal in an employment matter, or to a designated county court or sheriff court in other matters. The time limit is strict and there is no discretion to extend it. A requirement found to be "unreasonable because it is based on an incorrect finding of fact or for any other reason" may be quashed. There is power to substitute another requirement.

9-59 On such an appeal, the findings of fact upon which the notice was based may be reopened. The procedure is for the person served with the notice to respond to the Commission's statement of the facts upon which it relies by a notice stating which of the findings are disputed. The burden is on the person appealing to demonstrate that the true facts are different from those relied upon by the Commission.[65] A recent example of an appeal against a non-discrimination notice was *Handsworth Horticultural Institute v. CRE* where an appeal to the county court failed in relation to admission requirements in a private club.[66]

9-60 If there is no real dispute on the relevant facts the High Court can entertain judicial review proceedings in relation to a non-discrimination notice. It is possible that the High Court will reconsider whether it is sensible to add in this way to an already cumbersome procedure. In *R. v. CRE, ex p. Westminster City Council*,[67] the judicial review failed, there was a subsequent appeal to the Court of Appeal which failed, and the appeal in the industrial tribunal was therefore pursued. Nothing seems to have been gained by the High Court exercising jurisdiction, since the tribunal has powers to quash a requirement in a notice at least as wide as the High Court ("*Wednesbury* unreasonableness" appears, if anything, to be less exacting than the "unreasonableness" test in the statutes); and the industrial tribunal has the merit of being the specialised tribunal envisaged by the statute.

9-61 The obligation on the Commission to produce a report of an investigation is not without difficulty of application where there is an appeal against a non-discrimination notice. The statutes say that the report is to be of the

---

[65] For appeals see SDA 1975, s.68; RRA 1976, s.59. For procedure see: *CRE v. Amari Plastics Ltd* [1982] I.C.R. 304, C.A.; affirming [1981] I.C.R. 776, EAT.
[66] See the CRE's investigation report. For the CRE an investigating Commissioner, an investigating Officer and the former Legal Director gave evidence. The Commission attached particular importance to the case as a test case on private clubs.
[67] [1984] I.C.R. 827 C.A. affirming [1984] I.C.R. 770.

findings of the Commission. The Commission would be entitled to publish a report even though the findings are under challenge on appeal. However, it may take the view that it would be unfair to do so in view of the fact that the appeal is the first opportunity that the person concerned will have had to challenge the evidence by cross-examination. Either course is apparently lawful.[68] The disadvantage of delaying the report until after the appeal is decided is that the whole matter will be stale.

Enforcing a non-discrimination notice

There are several methods of enforcing a non-discrimination notice which has become final. A county court order may be obtained in respect of breach of a requirement. A further formal investigation may be carried out to determine whether the requirements of a notice are being carried out. A county court injunction may be sought if, within five years of the notice becoming final, it appears likely that the person will commit further unlawful acts.[69] Finally, if a local authority is involved, much the same effect or enforcing a non-discrimination notice in the race field could be achieved with judicial review relying on the section 71 duty under the Race Relations Act.

9-62

Opportunities for delay

It will be observed that in relation to an employment investigation it is possible for there to be a whole variety of proceedings in different *fora*; the industrial tribunal for appeal against a non-discrimination notice; the High Court for judicial review; a (designated in a race case) county court for enforcement of a non-discrimination notice. A resourceful respondent to an investigation, exploiting these and other opportunities in a cumbersome system, therefore has enormous scope for delaying tactics. A note of caution, however: both Commissions have in the past demonstrated a tenacity in sticking with some investigations, for many years if need be, to the bitter end.

9-63

The National Disability Council

The National Disability Council (NDC) established under the Disability Discrimination Act 1995 is a radically different body from either the EOC or CRE. It has no law enforcement function of its own, and has no power to assist individuals with litigation, or to investigate complaints of discrimination.

9-64

The main duty of the NDC is an advisory one towards the Secretary of State either on the Council's own initiative or at his or her request. The advice will relate to matters relevant to the elimination of discrimination against disabled persons and those who have had a disability, to measures likely to reduce or eliminate such discrimination, and to the operation of the law. (Those functions may be added to by order of the Secretary of State, but not so as to enable the Council to investigate complaints which may be

---

[68] *CRE v. Amari Plastics*, see above.
[69] See SDA 1975, ss.67(7), 69, 71; RRA 1976, ss.58(7), 60, 62.

the subject of proceedings under the Act.) The NDC is to have particular regard to costs/benefits of its recommendations and where reasonably practicable actually has to make a cost/benefit analysis. In coming to its recommendations the NDC has a duty to consult as set out in the Act.

The make-up of the Council is set out in a schedule. It is to consist of at least 10 and not more than 20 members appointed by the Secretary of State from those having knowledge or experience of the needs of disabled persons or particular groups of disabled persons, or of those who have been disabled, or who are members of, or otherwise represent, professional bodies or bodies which represent industry or other business interests. The Secretary of State must try to ensure that at all times at least half of the Council consists of disabled persons, persons who have had a disability, or the parents or guardians of disabled persons. The Council is to be provided with a staff. There is power to make regulations as to the commissioning by the Secretary of State of research to be undertaken by the Council. As one might expect the NDC is to produce an annual report.

Codes envisaged under the DDA are of two forms: those *prepared or reviewed by* the NDC on the request of the Secretary of State and those *prepared or revised by* the Secretary of State. In either case there are requirements for consultation and for publishing a draft and taking into account representations made. Where a code is prepared by the NDC the Secretary of State does not have to approve it and and can make modifications. He or she has power, subject to a negative resolution of either House of Parliament, to issue codes of practice containing practical guidance: with a view to eliminating discrimination in the field of employment against, or encouraging good practice in relation to the employment of, disabled persons or those who have had a disability. And a code may include practical guidance on what steps it is reasonably practical for employers to take for the purpose of preventing their employees from doing, in the course of their employment, anything which is made unlawful by the Act. Codes may also include practical guidance as to the circumstances in which it would be reasonable, having regard in particular to the costs involved, for a person to be expected to make adjustments in favour of those persons.

Codes, when issued, have the same effect as codes under the other discrimination legislation: they are admissible in evidence and must be taken into account in determining any question to which they appear relevant.[70]

---

[70] Provisions relating to NDC and its relationship to the Secretary of State, to the Code-making powers, and to the constitution of NDC are to be found in Parts VI and VII and Schedule 5 of the 1995 Act.

10 PUBLIC ASPECTS OF DISCRIMINATION LAW

Public bodies

Whether an organisation is a public body and, sometimes, what sort of public   **10-01**
body is increasingly of importance in equality law.

First, public bodies are amenable to judicial review proceedings in England
and Wales. (In Scotland however the Court of Session's supervisory jurisdiction does not depend on the nature of the body whose decision it is sought
to review.) This offers the Commissions and an aggrieved person a useful
way of getting a determination where the facts are reasonably clear and point
to a possible breach of discrimination law and (i) the law itself needs clarification, and/or (ii) a discriminatory decision needs to be quashed, and/or (iii)
a discriminatory system needs to be ended. This is dealt with below.

Secondly, in instances where Community law is relied upon which is not
directly applicable but should have been implemented by the state, then
whether the respondent body is a manifestation of the state will determine
the issue of whether the tribunal or court can apply the Community law. This
is dealt with in Chapter 1 above.

Thirdly, local authorities and some housing bodies are subject to a special
duty under section 71 of the Race Relations Act 1976 (RRA). This is dealt
with below.

Fourthly, there are statutory rules which apply to the contracting processes
of many public bodies which either prohibit them from concerning themselves with the question whether prospective contractors are providing equal
opportunities, or limit the extent to which they can do so. This is dealt with
below.

Judicial review

The Sex Discrimination Act 1975 (SDA), the Race Relations Act 1976   **10-02**
(RRA) and the Disability Discrimination Act 1995 (DDA) allow for proceedings to be brought for judicial review relying on unlawfulness by virtue of
provisions of those Acts.[1] This means that judicial review under R.S.C., Ord.
53 may be an alternative way of proceeding to either industrial tribunal proceedings in employment matters or county court proceedings in non-
employment matters, provided the body accused of unlawfulness is a public

---

[1] s.62, SDA, s.53, RRA and Sched. 3, DDA.

body amenable to such review. (In Scotland, judicial review proceedings may be brought without regard to whether it is a public body.) Where the body concerned is alleged to have adopted a discriminatory policy, judicial review would seem to be appropriate. Where a number of individual discriminatory acts are alleged, however, proceedings under the enforcement provisions in the tribunals or county courts are preferable. See the *Hammersmith* case referred to below.[2]

10-03   In addition judicial review provides an alternative way of proceeding for the Commissions instead of formal investigations where there is no real dispute as to the facts. (Evidence on judicial review is by way of affidavit.) In *R. v. Birmingham City Council, ex p. Equal Opportunities Commission*, judicial review was used to establish that the provision by the Council of more Grammar school places for boys than girls was unlawfully discriminatory and a declaration was granted.[3]

10-04   Some areas of activity of public bodies are outside the enforcement provisions of the Acts. For example, the House of Lords case of *Amin v. Entry Clearance Officer Bombay*[4] is to the effect that the control functions of government do not fall within the provisions making discrimination unlawful in the provision to the public of facilities or services. This puts many of the activities of the police, customs and immigration authorities outside of the scope of the Acts. Nevertheless, it is not to be supposed that they are entitled to act on discriminatory grounds unless there is specific statutory or ministerial authorisation to do so (obviously, if the concept of citizenship is to mean anything, some discrimination on grounds of nationality is bound to be lawful). Thus even where the equality statutes do not specifically apply, decisions may be challenged relying on the proposition that the public body acts wholly unreasonably (in the *Wednesbury* sense) in taking into account irrelevant considerations. Since allegations of discriminatory treatment by officials at ports of entry are not infrequent, it is inevitable that the CRE will be drawn into challenges in this area.

Locus standi

10-05   Even where the public body is apparently protected by some statutory provision, judicial review can provide the way of testing the validity of the provision against European Community law. There is a substantial amount of Community law on sex discrimination. Thus both the British and the Northern Ireland EOCs began judicial review proceedings against the Government to challenge the lawfulness under E.C. law of the minimum hours requirement for statutory protection rights on the basis that most part-time workers are women.[5] In *R.v. Secretary of State for Employment, ex p. EOC*[6] the House of Lords not only explicitly held that EOC had *locus standi* to bring the judicial review proceedings (overruling a majority decision of the Court of

---

[2] *R. v. London Borough of Hammersmith and Fulham, ex p. NALGO* [1991] I.R.L.R. 249.
[3] [1989] I.R.L.R. 173; [1989] A.C. 115, H.L.
[4] See chapter 8 for a discussion of this case.
[5] See *R. v. Secretary of State for Employment, ex p. EOC* [1991] I.R.L.R. 493.
[6] [1994] I.R.L.R. 176.

Appeal to the contrary), but also held the minimum working hours exclusion to be unlawful because of the Equal Treatment Directive. Their Lordships further rendered unnecessary in such a case the need to show a particular decision that needed to be reviewed by the court which would be amenable to the prerogative orders under R.S.C., Ord.53 since the court was able to make a declaratory judgement.

The CRE has also challenged Government action (by way of a national security certificate issued under the Race Relations Act), relying on the Community law relating to the freedom of movement of Community nationals.[7] In the particular circumstances the case did not succeed but the door was not closed to a case with greater merit.

10-06 The applicant needs leave of the court to pursue the review, and this will only be granted where the court considers that he or she has a sufficient interest in the matter. The two Commissions, which have the statutory function to work towards the elimination of unlawful discrimination will often have a sufficient interest to maintain proceedings.[8] They may also be able to support proceedings brought by an individual where they are brought to clarify procedures under which the individual is pursuing a claim under the Act concerned. Thus, in *R. v. Army Board of the Defence Council, ex p. Anderson*, a soldier was subjected to racial harassment in the Army. His complaints had not been properly dealt with under the Army procedures (a serving soldier's complaint against his employers was not, but the position will change, subject to the industrial tribunal jurisdiction in race matters). He was aided in judicial review proceedings by the CRE, who were supporting him in pursuing his case before the Army authorities. The outcome was a clarification of the procedures to be followed by the Army to ensure proper standards of fairness and the Army Board's decision was quashed.[9] In a case against the Ministry of Defence, two military nurses were supported by the EOC who themselves also brought proceedings. The Government conceded that a policy of dismissing military nurses who became pregnant breached the Equal Treatment Directive, and also that Service personnel could bring proceedings in the industrial tribunals as the Directive had displaced the exemption under the SDA.

10-07 In education matters, parents of children affected by decisions or policies will generally have sufficient interest to maintain judicial review proceedings. *R. v. Secretary of State for Education and Science, ex p. Keating*,[10] was such a case where it was held that a Local Education Authority was obliged to have regard to the SDA in providing secondary schools. Thus if the policy of the Authority was to provide single sex education, the treatment of one sex less favourably than the other was contrary to section 23 of the SDA, and the parents were able to challenge a proposal to close the only boys' comprehensive school.

10-08 In *R. v. London Borough of Hammersmith and Fulham, ex p. NALGO*, the court was content to assume in accordance with counsel's submissions:

---

[7] An unreported case.
[8] [1993] I.R.L.R. 10, C.A.
[9] [1991] I.R.L.R. 425; see also *R. v. Department of Health, ex p. Gandhi*. [1991] I.R.L.R. 431.
These two cases were heard consecutively by the High Court.
[10] [1985] L.G.R. 469.

"that if a public authority proposes to embark upon an employment or redeployment policy which is in breach of the Sex Discrimination Act or the Race Relations Act, or is otherwise unlawful, the public law remedies should be available to the unions and employees affected."

In fact, however, certiorari was refused on the basis that unlawfulness had not been made out in the council's policy of redeployment and redundancy.

"The most that can be said on the available evidence is that the implementation of the policy might offend the law in individual cases, depending on how the implementation is carried out ... I have referred to the wealth of conflicting evidence which the parties have brought to bear upon these issues. In my judgement their opposing contentions can only properly be tested on a case-by-case basis in pursuance of the applicants' private law remedies. The numerous factual issues involved are eminently suitable for consideration by an Industrial Tribunal, and are wholly unsuitable for resolution by the single drastic remedy of certiorari."[11]

10-09   We set out below a general statutory duty on local authorities in race matters under section 71, RRA. At the present time, this has only been relied on by local authorities as a shield in judicial review proceedings[12] except in a case brought by the CRE against Tower Hamlets L.B.C. which was eventually settled. However, no doubt it will be relied on in future to take local authorities to task and it is a good question how widely the court will construe the "sufficient interest" criterion in respect of local inhabitants.

10-10   Legal aid is available for judicial review proceedings.

10-11   The time limits for judicial review are short and an application has to be made promptly and in any event within three months from the date when grounds for the application first arose, unless the court considers that there is good reason for extending the period.[13]

10-12   The Commissions are themselves both amenable to judicial review, and at one time the CRE tended to be on the receiving end rather than taking the initiative.[14] Various points concerning formal investigations were established in judicial review proceedings. The EOC carried out far fewer formal investigations and therefore never invited the same attention.

Local authorities and section 71 of the Race Relations Act 1976

10-13   The 1976 Act contains a general duty imposed upon local authorities for which there is no equivalent in the Sex Discrimination legislation, though the EOC evidently think such a duty would be desirable. Section 71 reads:

---

[11] [1991] I.R.L.R. 249.
[12] See later in this chapter where the cases are dealt with.
[13] R.S.C., Ord. 53, r. 4.
[14] As Legal Director, CRE one of the authors can recall five sets of judicial review proceedings against CRE when or shortly after he took up the job in 1982.

"Without prejudice to their obligation to comply with any other provision of this Act, it shall be the duty of every local authority to make appropriate arrangements with a view to securing that their various functions are carried out with due regard to the need—

(a) to eliminate unlawful racial discrimination; and
(b) to promote equality of opportunity, and good relations, between persons of different racial groups."

The Housing Act 1988 extended the duties to the Housing Corporation and to housing action trusts and equivalent provision has been made in Scotland.

The scope of this provision was considered by the House of Lords in *Wheeler*   **10-14**
v. Leicester City Council.[15] Although the way in which the Council tried to carry out its duty under the section was held to be invalid, the case is important in the main for establishing that section 71 is justiciable and not just a pious aspiration. However since the litigation took the form of a challenge to a council's action, the reasoning of their Lordships is couched in terms of what a council is *empowered* to do under the provisions, rather than in terms of what it is *required* to do. The section is phrased in terms of a *duty*. As, in principle, section 71 is justiciable, it seems that a party with appropriate *locus standi* could bring proceedings to enforce the duty against a local authority (although, given the vague terms of the duty, establishing a failure to carry it out may well prove difficult in practice).

In *Wheeler*, the Council had licensed a rugby club to use its recreation   **10-15**
ground. Three members of the club were invited to join the English rugby team to tour South Africa. The Council supported the Commonwealth Gleneagles Agreement to withhold support for and discourage sporting links with South Africa. It asked the club to endorse these views, condemn the tour, and put pressure on its members not to take part in the tour. The club agreed with the Council in condemning apartheid in South Africa, but said it could only advise its members of the arguments for not going on the tour since to do so was not unlawful, nor was it contrary to the club rules or those of the Rugby Football Union. After the members went on the tour, the Council resolved to ban the club from using the recreation ground for twelve months. The club members applied for an order of certiorari to quash the council decision, and the Council's attempt to rely on section 71 of the 1976 Act succeeded at first instance and in the Court of Appeal, but failed in the House of Lords.

The club argued that section 71 should be given a narrow construction. It   **10-16**
was suggested that the section was only concerned with the actions of the council as regards its own internal behaviour and was what was described as "inward looking". It was said that it had no relevance to the general exercise by the council of its statutory functions as, for example, in relation to the control of open spaces or in determining who should be entitled to use a recreation ground and on what terms. The House of Lords, as had the courts below, rejected this argument. *Per* Lord Roskill:

---

[15] [1985] 2 All E.R. 1105, H.L.

"I think that the whole purpose of this section is to see that in relation to matters other than specifically dealt with, for example, [in Parts II and III of the 1976 Act] local authorities must in relation to 'their various functions' make 'appropriate arrangements' to ensure that those functions are carried out 'with due regard to the need' mentioned in the section. It follows that I do not doubt that the Council were fully entitled in exercising their statutory discretion under, for example, the Open Spaces Act 1906 and the various Public Health Acts . . . to pay regard to what they thought was in the best interests of race relations."[16]

And later he goes on:

"I do not doubt for one moment the great importance which the Council attach to the presence in their midst of a 25 per cent population of persons who are either Asian or of Afro-Caribbean origin."[17]

10-17   Ultimately, however, the House of Lords held that the decision of the council was invalid. In Lord Templeman's words, with which three other members of the House expressed agreement: "The club could not be punished because the club had done nothing wrong." He goes on:

"Of course this does not mean that the Council is bound to allow its property to be used by a racist organisation or by any organisation which, by its actions or its words, infringes the letter or the spirit of the 1976 Act."[18]

Lord Roskill, who gave the only other reasoned speech with which three members of the House agreed was perhaps less forthright in his reasoning, but his approach may best be summed up in his words:

"Persuasion, even powerful persuasion, is always a permissible way of seeking to obtain an objective. But in a field where other views can equally legitimately be held, persuasion, however powerful, must not be allowed to cross that line where it moves into the field of illegitimate pressure coupled with the threat of sanctions."[19]

He adds:

"If the club had adopted a different and hostile attitude different considerations might well have arisen. But the club did not adopt any such attitude . . . In my view . . . this is a case in which the court should interfere because of the unfair manner in which the Council set about obtaining its objective."[20]

10-18   There appears to be some wavering in the reasoning. If the true ratio is that the club had done nothing wrong, suppose a club were to have said it

---

[16] At 1110.
[17] At 1111.
[18] At 1113.
[19] At 1111.
[20] At 1112.

approved of the system of apartheid as suitable for the special conditions of South Africa? Quite possibly such a view could have been advanced in circumstances where it would not amount to incitement to racial hatred for the purposes of the Public Order Act. Could a Council have taken action to punish a club in these circumstances? The statements in the speeches that a council would not be bound to allow its property to be used by a racist organisation, and that different considerations might well have arisen had the club been hostile, seem to indicate that a Council would have been justified in taking action here.

It should be borne in mind that the case concerned the termination of a **10-19** facility once granted. It is possible that a council, which at the outset sets out a policy of granting facilities only where it is satisfied on certain points, may be on stronger ground than a council taking away a facility on a basis which was not apparent when it was granted. A court may grant more leeway to a council which has carefully weighed up a policy and set it out at some length, provided that in accordance with ordinary administrative law principles the council is prepared to consider the facts of the particular case before it in deciding whether to apply the policy. To take the example of contract compliance before the provisions of the Local Government Act 1988, it is improbable that a court would have struck down as wholly unreasonable conditions for entry on to an approved list for tendering which required compliance with the Code of Practice under the 1976 legislation as well as the legislation itself. Strictly speaking, it is not unlawful to fail to comply with the Code, although the failure could have certain consequences in litigation under the Act (see chapter 4). If this is correct, then it follows that ancillary conditions, such as requirements to provide monitoring information, there to ensure compliance with the Code, would necessarily have had to be upheld. In the light of the *Wheeler* decision, however, a condition which prohibited trading links with South Africa was obviously legally more doubtful, since that fell into the areas where opinions could legitimately differ as to what constituted the right approach.

R. v. Lewisham London Borough Council, ex p. Shell U.K. Ltd[21] was another **10-20** decision predating the Local Government Act 1988. The applicant was a United Kingdom company which was part of a multinational group of companies which had subsidiaries operating in South Africa. The Council — 18 per cent black population — decided, pursuant to section 71, to promote good race relations within the borough by adopting a policy of boycotting the applicant's products subject to alternative products being available on reasonable terms. The Council also sought to persuade other local authorities to follow suit and so maximise pressure on the parent companies of the group to withdraw their interests from South Africa.

It was held that the purpose of the council's decision was not simply to **10-21** satisfy public opinion or promote good race relations in the borough, but to exert pressure on the company and the group to sever all trading links with South Africa. Since that purpose had exerted a very substantial influence on the Council's decision and was inextricably mixed up with any wish to improve race relations in the borough, and since the group's policy towards

[21] 1 All E.R. 938.

South Africa was not unlawful, it followed that the Council's decision had been influenced by an extraneous and impermissible purpose which vitiated the decision as a whole. A declaration was granted.

Contract compliance

The U.S. experience[22]

10-22   The term "contract compliance", of U.S. provenance, is now commonly used to describe those procedures used by governmental agencies (whether central or local) to ensure that companies to which they give contracts to supply goods or services are pursuing equal opportunities policies as employers. Many black people and women in the USA point to the operation of contract compliance being an effective instrument of policy for bringing about improvements towards equality. Amongst the most vociferous supporters of contract compliance in the USA can be found the National Association of Manufacturers, which is the U.S. equivalent of the CBI. Because contract compliance is fairly new in Britain, a brief survey of the position in the USA may serve the purpose of indicating possible trends here in this developing area.

Presidential executive orders
10-23   During the Second World War, Presidential Executive Orders were used to bar discrimination on the grounds of race, creed, colour or national origin by defence contractors. The rationale was that "the prosecution of the war demands that we utilise fully all available manpower, and that discrimination by war industries is detrimental to the prosecution of the war". The Fair Employment Practice Committee reported that the Orders had had a positive effect, noting that the percentage of black workers employed in the war industries had risen from 3 per cent in March 1942 to 8 per cent by the end of the war. However, they also pointed out that the Orders had been repeatedly and consistently breached, and that sometimes had not been applied: "the wartime gains of Negro, Mexico-American and Jewish workers are being lost through an unchecked revival of discriminatory practices."

10-24   In 1953, an Executive Order extended the ban on discrimination to all government procurement contractors and suppliers, not just those involved in the defence industry. The rationale was stated to be that persons of different races or religions were entitled to fair and equitable treatment. A Government Contract Committee was set up with powers to receive violation complaints, and to further and encourage equal opportunity programmes. By 1954 it had established precontractual discussions, field checks, investigations and conciliation services, and a central reporting system. In 1961 President Kennedy signed his first Executive Order, in which he expanded the justification for the Orders to include efficiency as well as entitlement:

---

[22] The material collected under this heading owes much to work done by Brian O'Neill when on student placement with the CRE.

"It is in the general interest and welfare of the United States to promote its economy, security, and national defence through the most effective and efficient utilisation of all available manpower."

A new obligation was placed on contractors

"The contractor will take affirmative action to ensure that applicants are employed, and that employees are treated during employment, without regard to their race, creed, colour, or national origin . . ."

Power was given to the President's Committee on Equal Employment Opportunity to recommend specific sanctions, including termination for non-compliance.

When in 1964 Title VII of the Civil Rights Act was passed outlawing employment discrimination, attempts to make this the exclusive remedy for employment discrimination failed. The President's power to deal with discrimination by federal contractors remained intact. The main Executive Order was No. 11246 signed by President Johnson. Supervision of contracting agencies was transferred to the Department of Labor and led later to the creation of the Office of Federal Contract Compliance (OFCC). The scope of the contractual provision was expanded to cover not only the performance of work under the contract in hand, but also the contractor's other operations. In 1967, discrimination on the grounds of sex was added to the list of prohibited discrimination. Current requirements are for the setting of goals and time-tables by companies subject to the programme for the employment of qualified members of minority groups where they are under-utilised.   **10-25**

Research on the operation of contract compliance is worthy of note. A study by Leonard of the operations of the Order between 1974 and 1980 found that "the employment goals that firms agree to are not vacuous; neither are they adhered to as strictly as quotas". He says that the higher the goal is set, the better the company performs, but that on average firms achieve only about 10 per cent of their goals.[23] In 1981, OFCC commissioned research to assess the impact of affirmative action, which reviewed 77,000 companies employing 20 million employees during the period 1974 to 1980. The study was published in 1983. In the period under survey, federal contractors employed 20 per cent more racial minorities and 15 per cent more women, whilst the comparable increases for the non-contractors were 13 per cent and 2 per cent.[24] A 1984 survey by Organisation Resources Counselors, Inc, a firm of management consultants, of chief executives of companies showed 95 per cent indicating that they would use numbers as a management tool to measure progress, whether or not the government required them to.[25]   **10-26**

[23] Jonathan S. Leonard, *The Impact of Affirmative Action on Minority and Female Employment* (1983).

[24] OFCCP, U.S. Department of Labor *A Review of the Effects of Executive Order 11246 and Federal Contract Compliance Programs on Employment Opportunities of Minorities and Women* (1983).

[25] Organisation Resources Counselors Inc., *Managing Diversity: the challenge of EEO to 1990* (1984).

Local government and contract compliance

10-27   A number of local authorities set up contract compliance units following the lead given by the Greater London Council in April 1983 (when the GLC was abolished its unit passed to the Inner London Education Authority until that too was abolished).[26] The legal position is that, prior to the Local Government Act 1988, there was no statute law which specifically dealt with the subject of contract compliance. It was therefore neither required nor forbidden, but in principle permissible. In the case of eliminating racial discrimination and promoting equal opportunities and good relations between different racial groups, section 71 of the Race Relations Act 1976, imposing a duty on local authorities, provided a statutory framework within which contract compliance, though not specifically referred to, found a general authority. There is no equivalent provision in the sex discrimination legislation, and this was to prove an important distinction under the Local Government Act 1988.

Towards consistency and fairness in contract compliance

10-28   Before the 1988 Act, there were developments aimed at consistency and fairness in the operation of contract compliance.[27] First, the Association of Metropolitan Authorities proposed a model questionnaire. The point of a model questionnaire is that, if widely used, the burden upon companies in providing information is much reduced, since the answers given to one local authority will suffice for others also. Secondly, the CRE produced a set of Principles of Practice relating to contract compliance with the aims of maximising the effectiveness of such schemes; minimising any burden schemes may impose; ensuring consistency between schemes; and ensuring fairness in the application of schemes. The Principles did not have the status of a Code under section 47 of the 1976 Act.[28] The views of the CRE following consultation may well have carried weight with a court in the event, say, of judicial review of a council's actions.[29]

The Local Government Act 1988

10-29   Contract compliance concerning race relations and sex equality matters carried out by the public authorities listed in Schedule 2 to the Local Government Act 1988 (see below) is banned by that Act, save for local authorities where it is permitted in certain circumstances which relate to section 71 of the 1976 Act. However, any body not listed in Schedule 2 can carry out contract compliance on the general principle of our law that what is not forbidden is permitted. For such bodies, the CRE's document *Principles of Practice for Contract Compliance* may still be useful. Lawyers acting for

---

[26] See ILEA Contract Compliance EO Unit, 1985–1986 *Contracting for Equality: First Annual Report of the G.L.C.* (1986).

[27] See Institute of Personnel Management, *Contract Compliance — The UK Experience* (1987).

[28] See now CRE, *Local Authority Contracts and Racial Equality-Implications of the Local Government Act 1988* (CRE 1989); *Racial Equality and Council Contractors* (CRE 1985).

[29] See *R. v. London Borough of Lewisham, ex p. Shell U.K. Ltd* [1988] 1 All E.R. 938.

such bodies, however, will need to ensure that their own governing constitution or statute does permit such action.

The Local Government Act 1988 requires the scheduled public authorities **10-30**
to exercise their public supply or works contract functions without reference
to the non-commercial matters specified in section 17(5).

Public supply or works contracts are contracts for the supply of goods and
materials, the supply of services or the execution of works.

Contractual functions covered by s.17
The contractual functions covered by section 17 are: **10-31**

1. The inclusion or exclusion of anybody from a list of approved contractors or lists of persons from whom tenders are invited.
2. The acceptance or non-acceptance of tenders.
3. The selection of the successful contractor.
4. The approval, non-approval, selection and nomination of subcontractors for proposed or existing contracts.
5. The termination of a contract.

Two of the matters listed under section 17(5) as "non-commercial matters" **10-32**
are of particular concern here:

"(a) the terms and conditions of employment by contractors of their
workers or the composition of, the arrangements for the promotion,
transfer or training of or the other opportunities afforded to, their workforces ..."

These are known as "workforce matters", and

"(e) the country or territory of origin of supplier to, or the location
in any country or territory of the businesses activities or interests of,
contractors."

As drafted, it was arguable that the definition of "workforce matters" at **10-33**
section 17(5)(a) did not include the policy and practice relating to recruitment
and dismissal of members of the workforce. The only way in which they
would fall within that provision is if they are caught by the words "composition ... of their workforce". This clearly comprises the make-up of the
existing workforce. Recruitment and dismissal policy and practice will inevitably affect the future composition of the workforce, but it is at least odd that
the definition of workforce matters did not include those matters explicitly
if it was intended to cover them. This is particularly true in the light of
section 18(6), which makes it clear that the phrase "composition of the workforce" also includes a reference to "matters which occurred in the past as
well as matters which subsist when the function in question falls to be exercised". However, a judicial review case brought by an organisation representing potential contractors has ruled out this line of argument.[30] A scheduled
public authority cannot therefore have regard to equal opportunity as con-

---

[30] *R. v. London Borough of Islington, ex p. Building Employers' Confederation* [1989] I.R.L.R.
382.

cerns recruitment and dismissal in relation to sex or disability in exercising its contractual functions.

Race relations matters

10-34 The one area where local authorities, but not the other scheduled public authorities, are allowed under the Act to take account of non-commercial matters during the contractual process is in the field of race relations. This is in view of the fact that section 71 of the Race Relations Act 1976 places a duty on local authorities to ensure that their various functions are carried out with due regard to the need to eliminate unlawful racial discrimination and to promote equality of opportunity, and good relations, between persons of different racial groups.

10-35 Section 18 of the Act therefore allows local authorities to ask approved written questions and include terms in a draft contract which relate to the workforce matters in section 17(5)(a) if it is reasonably necessary to do so to secure compliance with section 71.

It should be noted that the provision relating to approved questions is quite separate from the provision entitling the inclusion in a draft contract or draft tender of terms or provisions relating to workforce matters. In both cases the local authority has to consider whether its actions are reasonably necessary to secure compliance with section 71. The implication seems to be that it may not in some cases be reasonably necessary to ask all the approved questions. On the other hand, the further implication is that, as regards the *terms or provisions in a draft contract or tender*, it may be reasonably necessary, depending on the circumstances, to stipulate terms or provisions which go beyond the matters referred to in the approved questions. It also follows that it is section 71, and not the Local Government Act or any approved questions under it, which the courts must look to in considering a local authority's view as to what is "reasonably necessary" in the particular circumstances. Terms or provisions might therefore cover such matters as compliance with particular recommendations in the Commission for Racial Equality's Code of Practice pursuant to section 47 of that Act. (The current Code came into operation in April 1984.)

10-36 It should be noted that the impact of the E.C. Directives relating to public procurement is yet to be resolved in litigation. The real problem is that criteria relating to the pre-contract stage under the directives do not include equal opportunities matters. How far the approved questions under the local government legislation can stand in the light of the directives remain to be seen. On the other hand it is far more likely that the inclusion of contractual terms will be unaffected.

Questions specified under section 18(5), LGA 1988

10-37 The following questions and description of evidence are specified under section 18(5) of the Local Government Act 1988 as approved:

"1. Is it your policy as an employer to comply with your statutory obligations under the Race Relations Act 1976 and, accordingly, your practice not to treat one group of people less favourably than others because of their colour, race, nationality or ethnic origin in relation to decisions to recruit, train or promote employees?

2. In the last three years, has any finding of unlawful racial discrimination been made against your organisation by any court or industrial tribunal?

3. In the last three years, has your organisation been the subject of formal investigation by the Commission for Racial Equality on grounds of alleged unlawful discrimination? If the answer to question 2 is in the affirmative or, in relation to question 3, the Commission made a finding adverse to your organisation,

4. What steps did you take in consequence of that finding?

5. Is your policy on race relations set out —

(a) in instructions to those concerned with recruitment, training and promotion,

(b) in documents available to employees, recognised trade unions or other representative groups or employees,

(c) in recruitment advertisements or other literature,

6. Do you observe as far as possible the Commission for Racial Equality's Code of Practice for Employment, as approved by Parliament in 1983, which gives practical guidance to employers and others on the elimination of racial discrimination and the promotion of equality of opportunity in employment, including the steps that can be taken to encourage members of the ethnic minorities to apply for jobs or take up training opportunities? Description of evidence —

In relation to question 5: examples of the instructions, documents, recruitment advertisements or other literature.''

The major omission from the list of approved questions and description of evidence is a question relating to the actual results of ethnic monitoring (*i.e.* a numerical question). The CRE's suggested questionnaire would have provided such a question. There is a case for the CRE to carry out a general investigation into the working of the approved questions, and if necessary to make recommendations for change to the Secretary of State.

Section 20 of the Act requires the authorities to notify forthwith any person   **10-38** in relation to whom certain contractual decisions are taken. Those decisions are:

1. To exclude him from an approved list;
2. Not to invite him to tender when he had asked to be invited;
3. Not to accept the submission of his tender;
4. Not to enter into a contract with him when he has submitted a tender;
5. Not to approve, or to select or nominate, persons to be subcontractors for a proposed or subsisting contract; and
6. To terminate a contract.

Section 20 also provides that where the person so requests in writing within

15 days of the date of notification, the authority must provide him, within 15 days of the date of the request, with written reasons for the decision.

10-39   Prior to any decision being taken on the basis of responses to approved questions, or responses to draft terms or provisions, the legislation envisages their consideration in the light of what is reasonably necessary to secure compliance with section 71. This is briefly adverted to in section 18. In practice, this may be a considerable over-simplification of the problem which may face the local authority at that stage. Prior to the Local Government Act 1988, the general approach of local authorities to contract compliance was to proceed by way of advisory and counselling methods, rather than immediate use of sanctions. Answers to approved questions which are inadequate may now lead to a decision not to include on an approved list, whereas previously they could have led to a further approach to the company and satisfaction all round. This could prove to be an unintended consequence of the legislation. There seems to be nothing to prevent the local authority sending a letter saying that they are intending to make a decision against the company on specified grounds, however, unless they are persuaded otherwise. This is not asking unapproved questions, and would be a reasonable administrative step to take which mitigates the otherwise potentially harsh consequences of the Act. If a potential contractor provides further information in consequence of such a letter, that is his decision. However, the whole procedure should not be designed by the local authority to procure further information other than from the questions approved by the Secretary of State, because the courts will probably strike down use of the procedure in that way. It is a different matter, however, for the local authority to say in effect "Well, we have your response to our approved questions. This is the interpretation we place upon it. As a result, the following consequences will ensue, unless you persuade us otherwise."

10-40   Some further points arise in respect of terms or provisions relating to equal opportunities for persons of different racial groups in draft contracts or draft tenders. First, it is essential that negative responses to those terms or provisions are considered fully on the question whether it is reasonably necessary to include them in the contract or tender to secure compliance with section 71. Secondly, where they do become incorporated into a contract, what is the position if they are broken? The Local Government Act does not regulate the contractual effects of breach except in the important respect that a scheduled public authority cannot terminate a subsisting contract by reference to a non-commercial matter. (Section 18(3) expressly applied this position to a local authority acting under the section 18 exemption to section 17 in respect of section 71 of the 1976 Act.) There are, however, two other possibilities. One is a claim in damages, but in practice proof of loss will be virtually impossible. The second is to provide that payment under the contract, or at least some part of the payment, should only fall due upon all the equal opportunity terms of the contract having been met, as well as all other essential terms. The assistance of a skilled contract lawyer would be essential to draft such a term to avoid falling foul of the law relating to penalty clauses.

No charge may be made by a public authority as a condition of inclusion on an approved list.

10-41   The various provisions referred to above do not create any criminal liability but, for the purpose of proceedings for judicial review, those having an interest in a matter are clarified by section 17 and include any body representing contractors (see the *Islington* case). Failure to comply with the section 17(1) duty is actionable by any person who in consequence suffers loss and damage, but a tenderer is limited to damages in respect of expenditure reasonably incurred in submitting the tender.

Effect of section 71, Race Relations Act 1976

The effect of the Local Government Act 1988 is to make the race relations **10-42** and sex discrimination position markedly different in this area. The supposed justification for this distinction lay in section 71 of the Race Relations Act 1976, for which there is no equivalent in the Sex Discrimination Act 1975. Contract compliance by all scheduled public authorities in respect of matters covered by the 1975 Act is therefore prohibited. The CRE had called for the section 71 type of duty to extend to all public authorities (*Review of the Act 1985*), and the EOC have now called for a similar provision in relation to sex (*Strengthening the Acts*, 1988). If there were provisions extending a section 71-type duty in respect of both race and sex to all public authorities presumably the contract compliance provisions would have to be widened accordingly. As the CRE pointed out in comments on the Local Government Bill, it is odd that an urban development corporation, for example, is prohibited from carrying out contract compliance in relation to race relations matters when it is likely to take over local authority functions in just those inner-city areas where the ethnic minority concentration is higher, and urban renewal most urgently needed.

Schedule 2, Local Government Act 1988: public authorities

The scheduled public authorities are as follows: **10-43**

"A local authority.

An urban development corporation established by an order under section 135 of the Local Government, Planning and Land Act 1980.

A development corporation established for the purposes of a new town.

The Commission for the New Towns.

A police authority constituted under section 2 of the Police Act 1964 or as mentioned in section 3(1) of that Act, or established by section 24 or 25 of the Local Government Act 1985.

A fire authority constituted by a combination scheme and a metropolitan county fire and civil defence authority.

The London Fire and Civil Defence Authority.

A metropolitan county passenger transport authority.

An authority established by an order under section 10(1) of the Local Government Act 1985 (waste disposal).

A joint education committee established by an order under paragraph 3 of part II of Schedule 1 to the Education Act 1944.

A water development board in Scotland.

The Scottish Special Housing Association.

The Boards Authority.

The Lake District Special Planning Board.

The Peak Park Joint Planning Board.

A Passenger Transport Executive, that is to say, any body constituted as such an Executive for a passenger transport area for the purposes of Part II of the Transport Act 1988.

A probation and after-care committee, that is to say, any body constituted as such a committee for a probation and after-care area by paragraph 2(1) of Schedule 3 to the Powers of Criminal Courts Act 1973.

A joint committee discharging under section 101 of the Local Government Act 1972 functions of local authorities (within the meaning of that section).''

Central government and contract compliance

10-44   From 1969, there was a clause in all government contracts requiring contractors to conform to the employment provisions of the Race Relations Act as follows:

> ''Racial discrimination —
> (1) The Contractor shall not unlawfully discriminate within the meaning and scope of the provisions of the Race Relations Act 1968 or any statutory modifications or re-enactment thereof relating to discrimination in employment.
> (2) The Contractor shall take all reasonable steps to secure the observance of all the provisions of clause (1) hereof by all servants, employees or agents of the contractor and all subcontractors employed in the execution of the Contract.''

10-45   No attempt has been made to monitor compliance with this clause, notwithstanding the fact that The White Paper on Racial Discrimination preceding the 1976 Act recognised this as unsatisfactory. This differs from the approach to religious discrimination in Northern Ireland, where the Government has introduced compulsory monitoring of the religious composition of workforces and tied this in with contract compliance relating to Government contracts.[31] Now that the Government has set out a scheme of contract compliance for local authorities in Great Britain, it remains to be seen whether they will follow a similar scheme for their own supply and works contracts. It would ill behove central Government to pray in aid of the absence of a section 71 duty on themselves, particularly given the developments in Northern Ireland.

---

[31] Fair Employment (Northern Ireland) Act 1989.

Privatisation

The increasing tendency to privatise entities that were previously part of the **10-46** public service creates new needs to ensure that equal opportunities are being provided, and contract compliance would seem to be the best way of doing this. For example, it is all very well the prison service claiming exemplary equal opportunity policies, but what system other than contract compliance will ensure that they are followed in a privatised prison? And if it is right to have contract compliance here, it is difficult to see why the same should not apply wherever the State buys in service provision regardless of whether the function has or has not been in the public sector at any stage.

Indeed, privatisation presents problems for public bodies other than central **10-47** government. One of the authors has experience of a case concerning a privatised company where the relevant managers had no idea what policies concerning equal opportunities had existed previously under local authority control, and had been too busy making people redundant to develop their own policies. It seems probable that the effect of much privatisation will be a weakening of existing equal opportunity initiatives. No doubt the policy of the present Government is to loosen bureaucracy, but was it also to make the position of women and ethnic minorities more difficult, or was this an unintended consequence?

Some public aspects of discrimination law

Application to the Crown of discrimination law

Section 75(1) of the Race Relations Act applies to an act done by, or for the **10-48** purposes of, a Minister of the Crown or a government department, or to an act done on behalf of the Crown by a statutory body or by a person holding a statutory office, as it applies to employment by a private person. Identical provisions occur in the Sex Discrimination Act, s.85(1) and the Disability Discrimination Act, s.64(1). Both the SDA and RRA, but not DDA, apply to service in the armed forces.
   The Race Relations Act does not apply to rules restricting employment in the service of the Crown or certain public bodies to persons of any particular birth, nationality, descent or residence (RRA, s.75(5)). The Crown Proceedings Act 1947 applies to proceedings under the discrimination Acts as they apply to civil proceedings by or against the Crown. (RRA, s.75(6–7), SDA, s.85(8–9), DDA, s.64(3–4)).

Acts to safeguard national security

Under the Sex Discrimination Act, s.52(1) the Race Relations Act, s.42(1) **10-49** and the Disability Discrimination Act, s.59(3) nothing in the Acts shall render unlawful an act done for the purpose of safeguarding national security. The Sex Discrimination Act, s.52(2) provides that a certificate issued by a Minister certifying that an act was done for the purpose of national security shall be conclusive proof that it was done for that purpose. In *Johnston v. Chief Constable of the Royal Ulster Constabulary*[32] the Chief Constable decided that the exigencies of policing the Province meant that all police on active duty needed to be armed, so that in his view there was no longer any place for women in the full-time reserve force and the complainant's contract was not renewed. The complainant brought an action under the 1976 Northern Ireland Sex Discrimination Order, which is in the same terms as the Sex Discrimination Act 1975, but her claim under domestic legislation was impeded by a certificate issued by the Secretary of State for Northern Ireland under Article 53 of the Northern Ireland Order, (which is in the same terms as s.52 of the 1975 Act) and which was conclusive proof under the Order that the act was done for the purpose of safeguarding national security or protecting public safety or public order. The industrial tribunal referred a series of questions to the ECJ under Article 177, as to whether the facts of the case fell within the derogations from the principle of equal treatment which are contained in Articles 2(2) and 2(3) of the Equal Treatment Directive. The principle of equal treatment itself, as set down in Article 2(1), had been held to be directly applicable in the *Marshall* case, as had its application to dismissal in Article 5(1), if and in so far as, these had not been implemented properly.[33] Article 6 requires that Member States take such measures as are necessary to enable all persons who consider themselves wronged by failure to apply to them the principle of equal treatment within the terms of the Directive, to pursue their claims by judicial process. Article 2(2) of the Equal Treatment Directive provides that a Member State may exclude from the field of application of the Directive those occupational activities where sex is a determining factor.

10-50   The ECJ approached the application of the Directive to the facts of the case along two routes. It relied firstly on the concept of indirect effect as stated in the *Von Colson* case,[34] but the Court had no difficulty in holding that the application of the principle of equal treatment to access to employment in Article 3(1) and vocational training in Article 4(1) were directly applicable as against the Chief Constable, who, in spite of his constitutionally independent status, was considered to be an emanation of the State. Therefore, the applicant could rely upon the terms of the Directive "to have a derogation from that principle under national legislation set aside in so far as it exceeds the limits of the exceptions permitted by Article 2(2)." The ECJ also held that Article 6 was sufficiently precise and unconditional to be relied upon by persons who consider themselves wronged by sex discrimination, in so far as it stipulates that all such persons must have an effective judicial remedy.[35]

10-51   The ECJ first concluded that the issuing of a certificate precluding the application of claims within the ground occupied by the Directive constituted a failure to ensure effective judicial control of compliance with the terms of the Directive, as required by Article 6. The ECJ based its conclusion on the

---

[32] Case 222/84, [1986] 3 C.M.L.R. 240, [1987] I.C.R. 83; ECJ.
[33] Where the requirements of a directive have been correctly implemented, it is to the the national provisions that complainants must look. See ground 51 of *Johnston*.
[34] See chapter 1.
[35] The Court held, however, that Article 6 did not contain any unconditional and sufficiently precise obligations as to sanctions for discrimination for these to be directly effective. See the discussion of the *Marshall (No. 2)* case in chapter 1 for further consideration of this issue.

view that the requirement of effective judicial control reflects a general principle of law underlying the constitutional traditions of the Member States, which is also laid down in the European Convention of Human Rights.[36] As the Directive contains no specific reservations or qualifications to do with public safety or security, and the ECJ was of the opinion that there is no general proviso in the scheme of the Treaty to do with public safety, the next logical question was whether the facts of the case fell within the ambit of Article 2(2) or 2(3).

Acts done under statutory authority

The position under the Race Relations Act

The Race Relations Act provides in section 41(1) that: **10-52**

"Nothing in Parts II to IV shall render unlawful any act of discrimination done—

(a) in pursuance of any enactment or Order in Council; or

(b) in pursuance of any instrument made under any enactment by a Minister of the Crown; or

(c) in order to comply with any condition or requirement imposed by a Minister of the Crown (whether before or after the passing of this Act) by virtue of any enactment.

References in this subsection to an enactment, Order in Council or instrument include an enactment, Order in Council or instrument passed or made after the passing of this Act."

(S.59(1) of the Disability Discrimination Act is very similar in terms.) The   **10-53**
RRA section was considered by the House of Lords in *Hampson v. Department of Education and Science*,[37] in which a teacher from Hong Kong was seeking approval of her teaching qualification to enable her to teach in a State school in Britain. Her initial course of teacher training was of only two years, although she had eight years later taken a further one year course. Mrs Hampson was refused approval under the relevant regulations which were made pursuant to the Education Act 1980, as it was the practice of the Secretary of State for Education to refuse approval for any course of less than three years length. The Department conceded that the action constituted indirect discrimination in that a requirement (a three year course) was imposed with which a smaller proportion of persons of the applicant's racial group (Hong Kong Chinese) could comply. The Department contended, however, that the action of the Secretary of State was an act of discrimination in pursuance of an instrument (the regulations) made under an enactment (the Education Act 1980) by a Minister of the Crown. It was argued on behalf of the complainant that the section does not protect administratively chosen requirements or conditions which represent one of a variety of possible modes of doing those

[36] Grounds 18–21.
[37] [1990] I.R.L.R. 302, H.L., [1989] I.R.L.R. 69, C.A.

acts. The majority of the Court of Appeal held, however, that the section was apt to cover this act, albeit based upon the exercise of a discretion by the Secretary of State as to the actual choice made. Nourse L.J. held that the Secretary of State was under a duty to make a decision under the regulations, a duty to either approve or not to approve the particular qualification. On this view, a power to give or withhold approval is not a power to give or withhold a decision. The House of Lords preferred the dissenting judgement of Balcombe L.J. in the Court of Appeal, in which he argued that a wide interpretation of section 41 could frustrate the purposes of the Act, because the actions of most public bodies must necessarily be derived from the exercise of statutory powers. For this reason Lord Lowry, giving the judgement of the Court, held that the words "in pursuance of any instrument" are confined to acts done in the necessary performance of an express obligation contained in the instrument and do not also include acts done in the exercise of a power or discretion conferred by the instrument. Lord Lowry went on to hold that the allegedly discriminatory act was not protected because the Secretary of State had to set up and rely upon an administrative criterion not found in the regulations, namely that of three consecutive years of training. Thus the decision was based on administrative practice and not upon a requirement laid down by the regulations. He was fortified in that view by the observation that a wide approach to the exceptions to the Act laid down in section 41 would be capable of nullifying and defeating the purposes of the Act as regards not simply central but local government and many other public bodies.

10-54 The House of Lords in *Hampson* cited with approval the decision of Wood J. in the EAT in *General Medical Council v. Goba*.[38] In that case the GMC had argued as a preliminary point that section 41(a) provided an "umbrella" protection for all actions taken in pursuance of any statute or Order in Council. The EAT held that such a blanket protection would render nugatory those sections of the Act which deal with public bodies such as the Training Agency and that section 41 "does not provide a defence whatever the act complained of and however heinous it may be in terms of discrimination."[39] The EAT also held that only those actions reasonably necessary to comply with any requirement or condition of the statute or order were protected by section 41.

10-55 The saving in relation to acts done under statutory authority goes further in relation to nationality or place of ordinary residence or the length of time a person has been present or resident in or outside the United Kingdom, and includes not merely actions undertaken pursuant to prior legislation or statutory instruments, but also includes arrangements made with the approval of, or for the time being approved by, a Minister of the Crown (RRA, s.41(2)(a)) or in order to comply with any condition imposed by a Minister of the Crown. (RRA, s.41(2)(b)). The effect of these provisions is to exclude from the ambit of the Race Relations Act Departmental circulars and Ministerial pronouncements. In this way the structure of immigration control is removed from the ambit of the Race Relations Act's enforcement provision.

---

[38] [1988] I.R.L.R. 425, EAT.
[39] At 426, and see also *Savjani v. IRC* (1981) 1 Q.B. 458, in which a narrow construction of section 41 was implicitly favoured.

The position under the Sex Discrimination Act

Acts undertaken which are necessary to comply with the requirements of a   **10-56**
statute passed before the Sex Discrimination Act and instruments issued
under the authority of such Acts were saved by the Sex Discrimination Act
1975, s.51.[40] These provisions were considered by the EAT in *Page v. Freighthire (Tank Haulage) Ltd*[41] in which it was held that acting in the interests
of safety is not in itself a justification for discrimination on the grounds of
sex, unless the action complained of was undertaken to comply with prior
legislation, such as the Health and Safety at Work Act 1974. The EAT went
on to hold, however, that the action in question, in this case the exclusion
of a woman from driving a tanker loaded with a chemical thought potentially
harmful to women of reproductive age, need not be the only possible method
of complying with requirements of the Health and Safety at Work Act 1974.
It was said to be important to consider all the circumstances, the risks
involved and the measures which are reasonably necessary to eliminate the
risks in question, but if the employer was in reality using such a restriction
as a device to prevent the employment of women that would be a different
situation.

The extent of this saving was brought into question, however, by the decision   **10-57**
of the ECJ in *Johnston v. The Chief Constable of the Royal Ulster Constabulary*, which cast doubt upon the scope of any restrictions as the scope of
work which could be undertaken by women, in so far as these did not arise
from a specific reproductive concern. The result was the removal of restrictions on the conditions under which women may undertake certain types of
work and consequently section 51 of the Sex Discrimination Act 1975 was
amended by the Employment Act 1989.

The Employment Act 1989

The Employment Act 1989, s.1 requires that any provision of any Act passed   **10-58**
before the Act of 1975, or any instrument made or approved under such an
Act, shall be of no effect in so far as it imposes a requirement to do an act
which would be rendered unlawful by any provision in Parts 2 (employment),
3 (in so far as it applies to vocational training) or 4 (in so far as it relates
to employment or vocational training) of the Act.[42] In any legal proceedings
concerning indirect discrimination, a party may argue that the Act does not
operate in so far as the requirement or condition in question is justifiable
within subsection (b)(ii) of sections 1 or 3 of the Act of 1975. Thus an
employer, who imposed a minimum height or weight requirement for a job

---

[40] In *Greater London Council v. Farrar* [1980] I.C.R. 266, the EAT held that a licence to
allow wrestling to be performed in public which imposed discriminatory conditions, was an
instrument issued under an Act of a date prior to the date of the SDA and it was immaterial
that the licence itself was issued after the date of the SDA. This proviso extends to the
re-enactment of a statute originally enacted prior to the date of the SDA or RRA.

[41] [1981] I.R.L.R. 13, EAT (see above). Also by a reasoned opinion of the European Commission in 1986.

[42] s.6(2) also provides that any re-enacted legislation will be treated as if contained in an Act
prior to 1975. S.6 (1) enables the Secretary of State to make an order as appropriate to
disapply the provision of s.1 in any case where he considers that provision would otherwise
apply.

involving heavy lifting, would be able to argue that such a requirement was justifiable and therefore he could rely on his statutory duty not to require employees to lift weights so heavy as to be likely to cause themselves injury. This is complemented by section 2 which provides that the Secretary of State may by order amend any provision of any Act which would require the doing of an act of discrimination within the terms of section 1 above.

10-59   Section 3 amended section 51 of the Sex Discrimination Act 1975 to restrict the exceptions to Parts 2, 3 or 4, in so far as these relate to employment or vocational training matters, to those which are necessary to comply with a requirement of an existing statutory provision concerning the protection of women, whether within the ambit of the Health and Safety at Work Act 1974 or otherwise. For this purpose, a statutory provision which has as its object the protection of women, is one which protects women as regards pregnancy or maternity, other risks specifically affecting women. An existing statutory provision means an Act passed before the Sex Discrimination Act or an instrument made under such an Act, whether passed before or after the Act of 1975.

10-60   The effect of the new section 51 is to render lawful discriminatory actions based upon previous enactments only where the purpose of those enactments is to protect women or to comply with a relevant statutory provision as regards the Health and Safety at Work Act 1974, in so far as that provision has effect for the purpose of protecting women as regards pregnancy or maternity, or in other circumstances giving rise to risks specifically affecting women, such as ionising radiation, working with lead, etc. This much tighter definition of the scope of protective legislation is intended to preserve only those derogations from the principle of equal treatment which are permitted under Article 2(3) of the Equal Treatment Directive. The amended provisions will ensure that women are excluded only from those forms of employment which are deleterious to them as regards pregnancy, maternity or reproductive matters more generally. It can be observed that the construction placed upon "necessary" in *Page v. Freighthire (Tank Haulage) Ltd*[43] did, however, already reflect this concern that health and safety legislation is not used as a pretext to exclude women from employment.

10-61   The 1989 Act, s.9 repeals the restrictions on the employment of women underground, or on heavy work or on the supervision of winding apparatus under the Mines and Quarries Act 1954. Likewise, the restrictions on the employment of women in the cleaning of machinery are repealed, as are a variety of other restrictions on the employment of women listed in Schedule 2 of the Act. Otherwise, the amended section 51 is subject to section 4 of the 1989 Act, which renders lawful an act of discrimination, if it was necessary for a person to do it to comply with a requirement of any of the remaining provisions concerned with the protection of women at work specified in Schedule 1 of the Act.

---

[43] See n. 41 above.

INDEX